in defense of

reading

A READER'S APPROACH
TO LITERARY CRITICISM

edited by REUBEN A. BROWER
and RICHARD POIRIER

E. P. DUTTON & CO., INC., NEW YORK, 1962

Published simultaneously in Canada by Clarke, Irwin & Co., Ltd.,
of Toronto

Library of Congress Catalog Card Number: 62-11512

The Editors are grateful for various services rendered in preparing
the manuscript by the staff of the Center for Advanced Study in
the Behavioral Sciences, Mr. William Abrahams, and Dr. David
Kalstone.

ACKNOWLEDGMENTS AND INDIVIDUAL COPYRIGHT DATES:

Poetry of Robert Frost reprinted from *Complete Poems of
Robert Frost*. Copyright 1916, 1921, 1930, 1939, 1947 by Holt,
Rinehart and Winston, Inc. Copyright 1942 by Robert Frost.
Copyright renewed 1944, 1951 by Robert Frost. Reprinted by
permission of Holt, Rinehart and Winston, Inc.

"Reading in Slow Motion," reprinted from *Reading for Life*
(The University of Michigan Press, 1959), copyright by the
University of Michigan, and is reprinted here with the publisher's
permission.

"Coole Park and Ballylee, 1931" reprinted with permission of
the publisher, from *Collected Poems of W. B. Yeats*, copyright
1933 by The Macmillan Company, copyright 1961 by Bertha
Georgie Yeats.

Poetry of Wallace Stevens reprinted from *The Collected Poems
of Wallace Stevens*, by permission of Alfred A. Knopf, Inc.

Excerpts from Parkman's *Discovery of the Great West: La
Salle*, edited by William R. Taylor, published by Holt, Rinehart
and Winston, Inc., reprinted with permission of the publishers.

CONTENTS

PREFACE In Defense of Reading   vii

I *Introductory*

Reading in Slow Motion—REUBEN A. BROWER   3

II *Lyric and Narrative Poetry*

Symbolic Landscape in Wordsworth and Yeats
—PAUL DE MAN   22

North of Boston: Frost's Poetry of Dialogue
—WILLIAM H. PRITCHARD   38

Poetry in an Age of Prose: Arnold and Gray
—NEIL H. HERTZ   57

The Authority of the Narrative Voice in *Paradise
Lost*—ANNE DAVIDSON FERRY   76

The Poet-Readers of Wallace Stevens
—THOMAS B. WHITBREAD   94

III *Shakespeare*

New Uses of Adversity: Tragic Experience in
The Tempest—STEPHEN KITAY ORGEL   110

King Lear and the Theory of the "Sight Pattern"
—PAUL J. ALPERS   133

Henry VIII: The Conscience of the King
—PAUL BERTRAM   153

IV *Satire*

Swift and the Common Reader
—OSWALD JOHNSTON   174

Heroic Folly: Pope's Satiric Identity
—THOMAS R. EDWARDS, JR.   191

Generality in Augustan Satire
—WILLIAM YOUNGREN   206

V *Fiction and History*

Jane Austen's *Emma:* The Truths and Disguises of
Human Disclosure—G. ARMOUR CRAIG   235

That Way Madness Lies: Nature and Human Nature in Parkman's *La Salle*—WILLIAM R. TAYLOR   256

Mark Twain, Jane Austen, and the Imagination of
Society—RICHARD POIRIER   282

CONTRIBUTORS   310

THE WRITERS of this book have had the good fortune during the past eight years to share a common experience of teaching and talking about literature—a common experience, not a system; an action and an attitude, not a rigid method. During this time we have found ourselves acting on the belief that it is important to know what one is doing when interpreting a work of literature, and that there are some ways of approaching a work or a genre that can be learned by civilized discussion and practice. We have had only one sure principle: the necessity of confronting the work in all its particularity and life. We have therefore tended less to create "methods" than to resist them, knowing that when any way of paying attention to literature becomes fixed it may too easily become a substitute for the freer and more difficult activity of reading and of accurately describing what the activity was like. We have wanted to avoid the most common fault of modern criticism, particularly evident in critical anthologies, of letting method determine in advance—like a sort of gridiron—what we see in the work and what we miss. We have tried simply to be as variously and flexibly intelligent as possible in the face of literary events, to be all things to all kinds of literary experience.

However different our reasons might have been for finding a work interesting, however variously we have considered its historical importance, we have all felt certain that to "confront" a work of literature means responding to particular uses of language—not "to begin with" or "at some point," but continuously and alertly, our final purpose being to interpret the work as a *total* expression. We have relied therefore on the scarcely revolutionary principle that the safest clue to the order and quality of the expression lies in the closest attention to style, and we have been willing to test our hints and guesses about what is going on in the work by turning to words and their arrangement. No critic, of course, ever attends merely to words or to style. He is always—it is hoped—trying to answer some questions about the literary event, about the place of the work here and now in relation to himself and to all he has read. As we have not thought that there were any certainly "right" methods, so we have not thought that there were any certainly "right" questions. But we have felt that it was our first responsibility to be clear about the questions we were asking at the moment, and to share with others a sense that they were important and necessary. Much of our effort in teaching and in communicating with one another has been directed at clarifying questions and testing answers. We have, then, shared three concerns: the necessity of confronting the work, the belief that reading and criticism begin and end with attention to words, the insistence on being clear about the questions we were trying to answer.

But why, it may be asked, should a group of critics who pursue their work in this way ask to be heard now? Hasn't this sort of thing had its day—a day that has lasted for some thirty-five strenuous years? It is true, as we have already suggested, that some of the analytical criticism of this period, particularly when it has taken the form of teaching "methods," has tended to become standardized and mechanical. But the current reactions against "close" criticism, apparent both here and in England, often give evidence that these mechanical versions have been equated with the whole approach. Simplifying critics and their often credulous opponents have encouraged us to think of the situation as a kind of melodramatic allegory, with something called the New Criticism in the role of obnoxious but doomed dragon. It may be true that the critical revolution of a generation ago, initiated by Eliot, Richards, and Empson and continued in this country by Ransom, Blackmur, Tate, and others has in some instances degenerated into a trivial hunt for images or ambiguities or symbols—precisely the manifestations of the movement that in the last few years have found acceptance in academic journals. Such unrewarding forms of critical analysis only confirm the suspicions of those who choose to insist on a sharp distinction between the activity of the critic and the activity of the historian of literature or of ideas. It is our hope that the essays in this volume will show that no such separation can profitably exist, and that, in fact, literary history is the benefactor, not the rival, of intelligent and close critical attention to literary expression. Surely those who now call for a "return to literary history" cannot be thinking that history is a "thing" that we can study without first helping to construct it. Literary history, now as in the past, depends on the exercise of critical discrimination—on personal discoveries by critics and writers of connections and contrasts between the works of one period and another.

It will be apparent that the writers of these essays are constantly going beyond "close reading" and "analysis" in pursuit of their own individual interests, and that these are necessarily to some extent historical. What is demonstrated by those who are now reacting against the critical movement of the twenties and thirties—or what they choose to understand of it—is a refusal to take advantage of the most obvious and least "new" consequences of this movement: a recovery of the respect for the text that has been central in European criticism since Aristotle. Where the reaction does not take the form merely of a placid return to older patterns of biographical and historical criticism, it often involves the creation of new patterns that are in fact more archaic. In Canada and the United States there has developed an interest in doing to all of literature what has often been done by medievalists: the cataloguing in a given book—almost any will do—of themes and motifs and structures that are recurrent in other books of whatever time or place. Thus the nearly spontaneous recognitions of any intelligent reader—that there are elements of the fairy tale in *Great Expectations*, for example—are abstracted and codified as if they formed a new system of knowledge. In the interest of gathering material for the system, the reader is discouraged from making qualitative distinctions between, say, *Lycidas* and *The Waste Land*, from remarking that each poem offers a distinctly different experience, however "archetypically" similar they may be. The English reaction, as might be expected, has been markedly in the other direction, toward a kind of personal, willfully "unscientific" tone in criticism, an earnestness that exists in default of any of the disciplines of verbal analysis. The result is often a caricature of Dr. Leavis's moral seriousness, lacking the bite of his wit, his concern for fineness of response, his attention to dramatic orderings of language. Among English reviewers "complexity" is on the way to becoming a bad word, an evidence that the writer who exhibits it is ironically evasive and insufficiently personal, while to be elegant is even worse, a sign that a writer has sold out to the Establishment. Criticism is confused with a wistful approval of literature that exhibits worthy attitudes and characters, a kind of moral endorsement thus replacing any more complicated concern for literary value.

Many of the reactions we describe represent little more than an evasion of the difficulties of criticism. It is absurd to suppose that a concern for style or for the literary event as experienced in reading is in conflict with a concern for history and literary tradition. Words, literature, the forms of expression in any given age, it need hardly be said, are implicated in a historical context, and in a context of literary tradition. The critic's attention to the condition of language in a work of a given time offers him a unique opportunity: he can re-create the relevant historical and literary contexts in a way that not only makes use of "factual" information but also considerably increases and enriches it. It is equally absurd to suppose that a concern for the work as made of words, as an imaginative order created through various uses of language, is in conflict with moral seriousness or precludes an interest in evaluation. Though it is hard to describe or analyze a work without implying some evaluation of it, the common reader might still want to ask—after he has been led through the maze of analysis—"Well, what of it?" "And where am I?" As both critics and historians of literature, we feel an obligation to the unspecialized reader to whom works of literature are ordinarily addressed, the relatively skeptical reader who cannot be interested in a work merely because, boring though it may be, it reflects what someone decided at some time was the "spirit" of some other time.

We would stress again that we are against any limitation on the kinds of questions that may be put to a literary work. The moral question is no more "right" than the historical question or the linguistic question or the psychological question. The papers that make up this volume illustrate the freedom and variety of the questions we have been asking. The unity of the collection lies in a shared concern for describing what it is "like" to read a particular work, in the common pursuit of ways of talking about this elusive matter within the relevant literary and historical contexts. Each of us had numerous reasons for being interested in the subject of his essay. We have sometimes begun with no initial concern for style, but perhaps for some theme, such as "nature" or the "hero," or for the study of myth or history or literary tradition. But whatever the initial or final interest, we have found ourselves making our richest discoveries at moments when we were closest to qualities of expression.

The introductory essay, "Reading in Slow Motion," should be taken not as a program but as a rendering in general terms of our experience in teaching ourselves and our students. We have all been students of one another and of the undergraduates in Humanities 6 from Harvard and Radcliffe who came to us officially as students but with whom, as each year went on, we often felt the kinship of a common enterprise.

R.A.B.   R.P.

Reading in Slow Motion

BY REUBEN A. BROWER

THE QUESTION put to me at a conference [1] on undergraduate education, "How shall we encourage and influence the lifetime reading habit?" brought to mind the words of Solon that Croesus recalled on the funeral pyre: "I shall not call you fortunate until I learn that the end of your life was happy too." Call no student a lifetime reader until . . . No teacher can be quite sure that he has a lifetime habit of reading, and if asked whether his students have acquired it or formed good reading habits, he will probably feel most uneasy about making an answer. But assuming that we could see each student's life as a whole, *sub specie æternitatis*, we should have to ask the further question: What reading habit are we evaluating? In the age of the New Stupid (a term Aldous Huxley once used for the age of mass literacy), nearly everyone has a reading habit of some sort. Everyone runs through the morning newspaper or *Time* and *Life* strictly as a matter of daily or weekly routine. Each social group has its "great readers," a term of admiration used to cover a wide range of activities that have little more than the printed page in common. There is, for example, reading as anodyne, and reading as extended daydream. There is reading as pursuit of fact or of useful technical know-how, and reading that may or may not be useful, when we are interested solely in understanding a theory or a point of view. Still more

[1] This essay was originally published in *Reading for Life: Developing the College Student's Lifetime Reading Interest*, edited by Jacob M. Price (The University of Michigan Press, Ann Arbor, 1959), Copyright by the University of Michigan, and is reprinted here with the permission of the publisher. The description of an imaginary course later in the text is based on courses given at Amherst College and Harvard University. The particular exercises and devices described are all drawn from these courses, but all were not used in any one course. My colleagues in both institutions will best know how much I owe to their ingenuity and their cheerful support in making many experiments in slow reading.

remote from immediate usefulness comes reading as active amusement, a game demanding the highest alertness and the finest degree
of sensibility, "judgment ever awake and steady self-possession with
enthusiasm and feeling profound or vehement." Reading at this
level—to borrow Coleridgean terms a second time—"brings the
whole soul of man into activity." Coleridge was speaking of the poet
and the power of imagination, but his words describe very well the
way we read when we enter into, or rather engage in, experiences of
imaginative literature. I say "amusement," not "pleasure," to stress
the play of mind, the play of the whole being, that reading of this
sort calls for. I am hardly suggesting that literary experience is not
a "good," that it is not in some indirect and profound way morally
valuable. But if it is to do us any good, it must be fun. The first
line of a poem by D. H. Lawrence offers an appropriate motto for
teachers and students of literature:

If it's never any fun, don't do it!

Active "amusement" is the reading habit I am concerned with
here and more especially with the role played by the teacher of literature in encouraging students to acquire it. I prefer to speak of the
"teacher of literature," not the "humanities," because that noble
term has become so debased in current usage, and because teachers
of texts in humanities courses are or should be teachers of literature.
The teacher of Plato or Hobbes or Hume is not only interpreting a
system but an expression, an expression that uses many resources of
language and uses them in ways that profoundly influence how we
take the writer's radical meaning. We cannot subtract from our interpretations the effect of Platonic comedy or of Hobbesian metaphor
or of Hume's dispassionate irony. But it remains true that the teacher
of literature in the conventional sense has a special interest in encouraging students to respond actively to all the uses of language,
from the barely referential to the rhythmic. He is always more or
less consciously urging his students to make themselves readers of
imagination.

How will the teacher go about reaching this noble aim? By a
method that might be described as "slow motion," by slowing down
the process of reading to observe what is happening, in order to
attend very closely to the words, their uses, and their meanings.
Since poetry is literature in its essential and purest form—the mode
of writing in which we find at the same time the most varied uses of

language and the highest degree of order—the first aim of the teacher of literature will be to make his students better readers of poetry. He will try by every means in his power to bring out the complete and agile response to words that is demanded by a good poem.

But in order not to create a wrong impression, a word needs to be said here about method, a term liable to please some and displease others for equally bad reasons. There is certainly no single sacred technique for teaching reading at the level I have in mind. In teaching literature—unlike science, one may suppose—no holds are barred, providing they work and providing that the injury to the work and to the student does not exceed the limits of humanity. The most distinctive feature of the kind of literature course I am about to describe is that the teacher does have some "holds," some ways of reading that he is willing to demonstrate and that his students can imitate. In this respect "Literature X," as I shall call it, differs from the old-time appreciation course in which the teacher mounted the platform and sang a rhapsody which he alone was capable of understanding and which the student memorized, with the usual inaccuracies, for the coming examination.

But why a course in slow reading? The parent who has a son or daughter in college may well feel confused, since almost certainly he has at least one child with a reading difficulty, the most common complaint being that the child cannot read fast enough. As the parent himself watches the mounting lists of important books, and as he scans the rivers of print in the daily paper, he may well feel that like Alice and the Red Queen, he and his children are going faster and faster but getting nowhere.

The difficulties of parent and child point to conditions that have led to the introduction of how-to-read courses in our colleges and universities. We might note first the sheer mass of printed material to which we are exposed—not to mention the flood of words and images pouring through radio and television. If by temperament or principle we resist the distracting appeals of the press and other media, we must nevertheless read a great deal as we run if we are to perform our tasks as citizens and wage earners. Add to such facts the changes in family life that have altered reading habits of both parents and children. Memorization of Bible texts and poetry is hardly common in school or home, and the family reading circle where books were read aloud and slowly, has all but disappeared even from the idyllic backwaters of academic communities. Yet many

if not all of the writers of the past, from Homer to novelists like
Jane Austen and Dickens, have assumed reading aloud and a relatively slow rate of intellectual digestion. Literature of the first order
calls for lively reading; we must almost act it out as if we were taking parts in a play. As the average high school student reads more
and more with less and less wholeness of attention, he may become
positively incapacitated for reading the classics of his own or any
literature. Incidentally, the parent of the slow reader should take
heart: his child may not be stupid, but more than ordinarily sensitive to words. He may in fact have the makings of a poet.

Another change in precollege education is almost certainly connected with the decline in the ability to read literature of the first
quality, a change that points also to profound changes in the literary
public of the past century and a half. Until thirty or forty years ago
a high proportion of students of literature in our liberal arts colleges
had received a considerable training in Latin or Greek. If we move
back to the much smaller reading publics of the seventeenth and
eighteenth centuries, the audiences for whom much of our greatest
literature was written, the relative number of readers trained in the
classics becomes much higher. The principal method of teaching the
ancient languages, translation into English or from English into
Latin or Greek, may have had disadvantages compared with the
direct method of today, but as a basic preparation for the study of
literature it can hardly be surpassed. It may be doubted whether
learning of a foreign language can take place without some translation, at least into what experts in linguistics call the "meta-lan-
guage" of the learner. To translate from Latin and Greek demanded
close attention to the printed word, and since the ideas being com-
municated and the linguistic and literary forms through which they
were expressed were often quite unlike those in English, translation
compelled the closest scrutiny of meanings and forms of expression
in both the ancient and the modern language. Although the old-time
classicist may not always have been successful as a teacher of literature, he cannot often be accused of lacking rigor. His students had
to spend a good many hours in school and college reading some
pieces of literature very attentively. One purpose of a course in slow
reading is to offer a larger number of present-day undergraduates an
equivalent for the older classical training in interpretation of texts.

It might be noted that Coleridge, who harshly criticized the practice of Latin versemaking in English schools, paid the highest tribute
to that "severe master, the Reverend James Bowyer":

At the same time that we were studying the Greek tragic poets, he made us read Shakespeare and Milton as lessons: and they were the lessons too, which required the most time and trouble to *bring up*, so as to escape his censure. I learned from him, that poetry, even that of the loftiest and, seemingly, that of the wildest odes, had a logic of its own, as severe as that of science; and more difficult, because more subtle, more complex, and dependent on more and more fugitive causes. In the truly great poets, he would say, there is a reason assignable not only for every word, but for the position of every word; and I well remember that, availing himself of the synonymes to the Homer of Didymus, he made us attempt to show, with regard to each, why it would not have answered the same purpose; and wherein consisted the peculiar fitness of the word in the original text.

In our own English compositions (at least for the last three years of our school education) he showed no mercy to phrase, metaphor, or image, unsupported by a sound sense, or where the same sense might have been conveyed with equal force and dignity in plainer words. *Lute, harp,* and *lyre, Muse, Muses,* and *inspirations, Pegasus, Parnassus,* and *Hippocrene* were all an abomination to him. In fancy I can almost hear him now, exclaiming: "Harp? Harp? Lyre? Pen and ink, boy, you mean! Muse, boy, Muse? Your nurse's daughter, you mean! Pierian spring? Oh aye! the cloister-pump, I suppose!"

The Reverend James Bowyer and not Coleridge, it appears, was the original New Critic, which is to say that much New Criticism is old criticism writ large. Bowyer's example suggests another important point to which I shall return: that teaching of reading is necessarily teaching of writing. The student cannot show his teacher or himself that he has had an important and relevant literary experience except in writing or in speaking that is as disciplined as good writing.

To teach reading or any other subject in the style of the Reverend Bowyer demands an attitude toward the job that is obvious but easily overlooked in our larger universities, where increasing numbers of students often impose mass production methods. The most important requirement for teaching an undergraduate course—beyond belief in what one is doing—is to keep this question in mind: What is happening to the student? Other questions soon follow: What do I want him to do and how can I get him to do it? Planning and teaching from this point of view makes the difference between a course that engages the student and one that merely displays the teacher. The perfect model for the teacher of literature as for the teacher of science is Agassiz, who would come into the laboratory, pour out a basket of bones before the student, and leave him alone to sort them out. We learn that after this introduction to the "material" of the course, Agassiz limited his teaching to infrequent visits, when he checked on the learner's progress by an occasional nod or shake of the head to say "That's right!" or "No, not that!" The great thing in teaching is to get the basket of bones before the student and get him to sorting them for himself as soon as possible. What we must avoid at all costs is sorting out all the bones in advance. Agassiz' principle is of great importance in the teaching of literature, where far too often we present the undergraduate with the end products of literary scholarship without being sure he has read or has the capacity of reading the works we are interpreting.

If we are interested in fostering a habit of reading well, we must set up our introductory courses on a principle very different from that underlying the older survey or the now more fashionable history-of-ideas course. We are not handing the student a body of knowledge, so much "material"—the history of the Romantic Movement or an anatomy of the concepts labeled "Romanticism"—however useful such knowledge may be at a later stage in literary education. Our aim rather is to get the student in a position where he can learn for himself. If we succeed, we have reason to believe that he may acquire a lifetime habit of learning independently. The teacher who is working toward this noble end will always be working *with* the student, not *for* him or *over* him. Whitehead used to say that the student should feel he is present while the teacher is thinking, present at an occasion when thought is in process. Those who knew Whitehead in the classroom will know what he meant and why he never seemed to be lecturing, even before a class of a hundred or two hundred students. His listeners never knew exactly where he was coming out. Not knowing where one is coming out is an essential part of the experience of thinking.

To get the student to a point where he can learn for himself requires therefore a redefinition of a "lecture." It asks the teacher to share his ignorance with his students as well as his knowledge. Or if professors shrink from admitting less than omniscience, it calls for at least a Socratic simulation of ignorance. What is wanted is the "nonlecture," to borrow E. E. Cummings's happy term, an action performed by the teacher but clearly directed to the next performance of the student. The ideal nonlecturer is setting a job for the student and showing him how he would go about doing it. If he is not in fact setting a job, he will clearly indicate a relevant kind of job to be done. A proper job means setting a question and offering a way, not a formula, for answering it. Student and teacher must clearly understand that a course in interpretation is a course in "right answering," not a course in "right answers."

Let me now attempt to describe Literature X, a course in slow reading that aims to meet the general requirements I have been outlining and that is designed also to meet the needs of young readers in our colleges and universities. I have said that we want students to increase their power of engaging in imaginative experience, and we assume—this was implied by our earlier reference to Coleridge—that a work of literature offers us an experience through words that is different from average, everyday experience. It is different in its mysterious wholeness, in the number of elements embraced and in the variety and closeness of their relationship. When Othello, just before Desdemona's death, says, "Put out the light, and then put out the light," we feel not only the horror of his intention but also a remarkable concentration of much that has gone on before: the moving history of the relations between the lovers and between them and Iago, the echoed presence of earlier moments of "lightness" and "darkness."

We all agree that such experiences in literature are wonderful, but what can a teacher do to guide a student to discover them? He will of course start from his own excitement, and he will do everything he can to infect his students with it: he will try to express in other words what Othello and the audience are experiencing; he will read the passage aloud or get a student to do it; he will exhort and entreat. But finally he cannot hand over his feelings to his students; he cannot force them to be more sensitive than they are. What can he do that the students may also do and that they can imitate when they read another scene or another play? He can do a great deal if he remembers that while he and his students do not have a common nervous system, they do have the same printed page and they share some knowledge of the English language. He will therefore direct their attention to the words, to what they mean and to their connection with other words and meanings. In considering the "put out the light" speech from *Othello*, the teacher may begin by asking what the words mean in terms of stage business. He may then call for a paraphrase: for "put out the light" someone may offer "bring darkness," or "put an end to." The class can next be asked to connect this expression with others used elsewhere in the play. Someone may recall Othello's earlier line associating Desdemona with darkness and death: ". . . when I love thee not,/ Chaos is come again." The reader can now begin to appreciate the poignancy and the irony of Othello's picturing his action as "putting out the light." So by directing attention to words, their meanings, and relationships, the teacher may put his students in a position where they too will feel the pity and terror of this moment in the play.

We might describe Literature X as a "mutual demonstration society," the work of the course being carried on mainly through student-teacher explorations of the kind I have been attempting to illustrate. For the students the most important and most strenuous demonstrations will be the exercises that they write on their own after being suitably prepared by the teacher. *Othello* may serve as an example once more. After several classes of reading aloud and exploring connections in the earlier acts of the play, an exercise will be set on a speech or scene from the last act. The students now have an opportunity to show whether they can practice independently the sort of interpretation they have been attempting in class. To guide them, they will be given an exercise sheet with a very carefully planned series of questions. Beginning with queries on words and phrases, the exercise goes on to ask about relationships of various kinds, and it concludes with a question demanding a generalization about the work as a whole or about a type of literature or experience. An exercise on *Othello* might finally call for a statement about the nature of Othello's tragedy and for a tentative definition of "tragic" as used in Shakespearean drama. But the words "tragic" or "tragedy" will not necessarily appear in the directions; rather, the students will be impelled to talk about these concepts because they are relevant. In the class on the exercise papers the students and his teacher will be admirably prepared to consider what is meant by tragic literature and experience. These discussions of the exercises should be among the most valuable classes in the course. Here the student can learn by comparing where he succeeded or failed as an interpreter, and frequently he may have the pleasure of finding that he has taught his teacher something, an event that can give satisfaction to both parties and that can take place more often in a course where the student is an active participant, not a passive member of an audience.

Literature X as a whole will consist of a series of these exercise waves, with some more terrifying than others, the seventh and last coming when the students are given two or more weeks without classes in which to read new material—poems, plays, or novels—with no teacher to guide them.

The course will not begin with Shakespeare, although Shakespeare is the necessary measure of imaginative experience and of the capacity to engage in it. We shall begin rather with the smaller model of the short poem, because as I have said it offers literary experience in its purest form. By beginning with poems we can be reasonably sure that the student learns early to distinguish between life and literature and not to be unduly distracted by questions of biography and history or by social and psychological problems of the type raised so often by the novel. Most important, the student will learn at the outset to deal with *wholes,* since within the limits of a class hour or a brief paper he can arrive at an interpretation of a whole literary expression. Poems may come to stand in his mind as Platonic forms of true and complete literary experience.

Beginning with poems has another advantage if students are to learn the value of attending closely to language and if they are to see the satisfactions that come from alert and accurate reading. In the small world of a sonnet, a reader can see how a single word may cause a shift in the equilibrium of feeling in the whole poem. So when Shakespeare says:

> For thy sweet love remember'd such wealth brings
> That then I scorn to change my state with kings.

"state" carries connotations of Elizabethan *state,* and as a result the speaker's voice takes on a tone of grandeur, a somewhat stagey grandeur that reminds us of gestures in a play. But the word "state" would hardly impart that quality without the reference to "kings." This fairly simple example brings home the importance in interpretation of considering the context. A course in interpretation is a course in definition by context, in seeing how words are given rich and precise meaning through their interrelations with other words. The student who acquires this habit of definition will be a better reader of philosophy or law or any other type of specialized discourse, and he may learn something about the art of writing, of how to control context in order to express oneself.

Reading poems also offers one of the best ways of lifting the student from adolescent to adult appreciation of literature. The adult reader realizes that reading a work of literature is at once a solitary and a social act. In reading we are alone, but we are also among the company of readers assumed by the poem or play or novel. The poem is more than a personal message, it invites us to move out of ourselves, to get into an "act," to be another self in a fictive drama. The sonnet of Shakespeare we have just quoted seems to call for a

very simple identification of the actual reader with the imagined
speaker,

> When in disgrace with fortune and men's eyes
> I all alone beweep my outcast state . . .

(Many will recall their own youthful readings of the poem.) Yet
even this simple if not sentimental sonnet asks something more of
us in the end; it asks us to take on the demonstrative air of the
theatrical lover, to protest in language we would never actually use
in our most romantic moments.

In Literature X we shall start by reading poems, and start with no
apparent method or at least with method well concealed. We begin,
as Frost says, with delight, to end in wisdom. "What is it *like*," we
say rather crudely, "to read this poem?" "With what feeling are we
left at its close?" "What sort of person is speaking?" "What is he
like, and where does he reveal himself most clearly?" "In what line
or phrase?" We may then ask if there is a key phrase or word in the
poem, and we can begin to introduce the notion of the poem as a
structure, as an ordered experience built up through various kinds
of meaning controlled in turn by various uses of language.

Remembering our questions about the speaker, we first direct attention to dramatic uses of language, to the ways in which the words
create a character speaking in a certain role. We may ask, for example, who is speaking in Keats's sonnet on Chapman's *Homer*. An
alert student may point out that he is a traveler (many do not see
this), and that he uses idioms with a medieval coloring: "realms,"
"goodly," "bards in fealty," "demesne." But the speaker does not
continue to talk in this vein:

> Till I heard Chapman speak out loud and bold.

He has changed, and the drama moves into a second act. We hear a
voice that is powerful and young, the voice of the New World dis-
coverer and the Renaissance astronomer. We now point out to our
young reader (if he is still listening) that the poem is indeed an
"act." The poet is speaking *as if* he were a traveler-explorer, and the
whole poem is built on a metaphor. So, while reading many poems,
we may introduce a few basic notions of literary design and some useful critical terms. But our emphasis will always be on the term as
a tool, as a device for calling attention to the poem and how it is

made. In time we can turn to study of the poem as an experience of ordered sounds, but not, we hasten to add, of sounds divorced from sense. Our aim in talking about rhythmic pattern, as in considering dramatic and metaphorical design, is to show how the poem "works" and what is expresses. We see, for example, that as Keats's sonnet moves from the medieval to the modern speaker, and as the metaphor also shifts, the rhythm changes from the "broken" couplets and inversions of the octave to the long and steady sweep of the sestet. The whole sonnet in its beautiful interaction of parts gives us the sense of discovery and release into a new world of literary and aesthetic experience.

Following a period of reading poems, the course will move ahead to a play by Shakespeare so that students can see at once that the way in which they have read poems works also for a poetic drama and that there are some basic similarities between the structure of these different types of literature. They may see, for example, that the man speaking in a poem corresponds to the character in a play, that Shakespeare has his large metaphors just as Keats has his smaller ones.

From drama we go to the reading of a novel, often via short stories. The short story like the poem gives us literary experience in microcosm and makes it easier to see analogies between fiction and poetry, to see that a tale by Hawthorne is the unfolding of a single metaphorical vision, or that the narrator in a story by Joyce controls our sense of being within the child's world, exiled from adult society. The novel, especially as we have it in its classic nineteenth century form in Dickens or George Eliot, demands a very different reading from a Shakespearean drama, but by putting the same questions to both genres their likeness and their unlikeness can be defined, and the exact quality of a particular work can be discovered. The student will find, for example, that the "marshes" and "mists" of *Great Expectations* are nearer to the fixed symbols of allegory than to the fluid metaphors of Shakespeare. But he can also see that in a novel as in a poem the narrative voice is of immense importance. Comparison of the opening scene in the film of *Great Expectations* with Dickens's telling shows that when the sanely humorous, entertaining voice of Dickens is removed, we are left with images of pure nightmare. The major themes of *Great Expectations*, guilt and innocence, justice and injustice, are not un-Shakespearean, but we can hardly read the novel without an awareness that unlike *King Lear* and *Macbeth* and like most novels, the imaginative world of *Great Ex-*

pectations has a date. Jaggers is an awesome symbol of the link between criminality and legal justice, but he also embodies a sharp
criticism of the actual court and prison world of mid-nineteenth
century England.

Reading a novel forcibly reminds us that literature is embedded in
history, that the meaning of the work in itself changes when we
view it in relation to other works and to the social situation in which
it first appeared. Literature X will move on in its later phases to some
experiments in historical interpretation, "historical" being used here
to include the relation of a work to its time, especially to more or
less contemporary works, and to literary tradition. If we return to
Othello or *Coriolanus* after reading the *Iliad* and after gaining some
familiarity with the heroic tradition in Renaissance epic and drama,
we find that both plays are clearer and richer in their meaning. We
see in *Coriolanus* what happens when an Achilles enters the Roman
forum: the simple absolutes of the hero, the code that makes Coriolanus prefer a "noble life before a long" one, bring confusion in a
civil society. The teacher of our ideal course will not merely lay a
comparison of this sort before his students, he will try to get them
into a position where they can make the comparison for themselves.
He will use all the ingenuity he can muster to devise assignments in
which the student can practice thinking historically about works of
literature.

In a year in which the class has made some study of the hero in
Homer and in the Renaissance, a project might be focused on Fielding's *Tom Jones*. While the students are reading the novel outside
class (it takes time!), they would study with their teacher readings
useful for interpreting the novel in relation to the heroic tradition
and to the climate of moral opinion in the eighteenth century. They
could observe in Dryden's *Mac Flecknoe* the shift from the Renaissance "heroick" to the mock-heroic, and in *The Rape of the Lock*,
they could see how allusions to the ancient heroic world are used to
satirize eighteenth century high society while giving the world of the
poem splendor and moral seriousness. After comparing the mock-
heroic in Pope and Fielding, they might attempt a definition of the
hero in *Tom Jones*. By skillful prodding (in an exercise) they could
be led to see that Fielding has created a new type of hero, a youth
who is at once ridiculous and charmingly "good-natured," that although he finally gains a modicum of "prudence," he wins his way
largely through "benevolence" and "goodness of heart."

As a final step in this experiment, there might be a series of read-

ings in Chesterfield, Hume, and Dr. Johnson, all concerned with
social "goodness," and more especially with "prudence" and "benevolence." The students would then be asked to define and place the
moral attitudes expressed in *Tom Jones*, through comparing them
with similar attitudes expressed in these eighteenth century moralists.
By projects of this type undergraduates could be given some practice
—at an elementary level—in writing intellectual history. At the same
time their earlier practice in interpretation would protect them from
reducing the experience of the novel to the abstracted idea. But they
would also begin to see that a purely literary judgment is finally impossible, that we are impelled to move back from literature to life.
Dr. Johnson's famous comparison of Fielding and Richardson might
be used to show that "liking" or "disliking" a novel is an act of moral
evaluation. At the end of Literature X, by returning to poetry we
could make the point that a choice between poems is a choice between lives.

You may be asking by now what the connection is between our
ideal course and the lifetime reading habits of undergraduates. I
should reply that Literature X attempts to influence future reading
habits by keeping to the principle of student activity. No test or
exercise or final examination asks the student to "give back" the
"material" of the course. On the contrary, each stage of the work is
planned with a view to how the student reads the *next* work, whether
poem or play or novel. At the end of the first half of the course the
student is sent off to read and interpret on his own another play of
Shakespeare and another novel. He is given leading questions that
impel him to do likewise "differently." An appropriate midyear examination in the course might consist of a sight poem to interpret
and an essay-exercise on a longer work read outside class. The test
for the second half-year (whether an examination or a long essay)
would ordinarily be based on a set of texts to be used in interpreting
a work in the manner of the project on *Tom Jones*.

But the teacher of a course in slow reading will always be haunted
by the question once asked by a colleague of mine: "Our students
learn *how* to read, but *do* they read?" Do they, for example, ever
read an author, read every one of his books they can lay their hands
on, with an urge to know the writer's work as a whole? Can we do
anything in our ideal course to stimulate this most valuable habit?
Some modest experiments can be made, I believe, and with some
assurance of success. A model can be set by reading generously in a
single poet, preferably a contemporary, such as Frost, Yeats, or Eliot.

Or the teacher can give the class a start by reading a few poems in each of a number of writers, and then send the students off to read one of the poets independently. After some weeks they might write an essay "On Reading So-and-So." The essay must have a point (surprisingly few students know what a point is) supported by deft and apt interpretation of particular poems. The novel, the most important form for habitual readers in this generation, presents a problem, since we can hardly read all or even several novels of the same writer within the limits of an introductory course. But two novels and some stories by a single writer may rouse some readers to go ahead on their own, and sometimes the discovery that a difficult writer—James or Joyce—is understandable and rewarding or that an old-fashioned writer—Fielding or Jane Austen—is amusing, will start a student along the right path. The best way to influence later habits is the natural way: recommending without system books we have read with pleasure and without ulterior motives. Students recognize the difference between love and duty, and they will respond to genuine enthusiasm and avoid books that they "ought to" read or—and this is the lowest of all academic appeals—that "fill a gap" in preparing for general examinations or graduate school placement tests.

If we turn our attention from lifetime reading habits to the larger educational influence of courses in slow reading, we can note some possible correlations between classroom and later performances. In this connection we should recall the value for close reading of practice in equally close writing. The student who looks at poems as carefully as we have suggested will understand that poetry begins in grammar and that to express a just appreciation of a poem demands fine control of grammar on the part of the appreciator. But to help the student make such discoveries calls for guidance in small classes or at least careful criticism of written exercises. Good writing is an art not amenable to mass production methods.

Attentive criticism of written work is almost certainly of much more value for teaching good reading and writing than the usual discussions or section meetings. The value of a discussion meeting does not depend primarily on size, as many assume, but on the planning that precedes the meeting and the direction of the conversation to a defined goal. In our course in slow reading the discussion is not an addendum, but the culminating act toward which the teacher's demonstration and the student's exercise have been directed. Under these conditions student and teacher are fully prepared to say something meaningful to each other, since they have before them well-defined questions to pursue and alternative expressed answers to compare and judge.

But discussion of this type need not be vocal. The student can carry it on internally during a lecture, if the lecture is an exercise in how to ask and answer a question of interpretation. The indispensable requirement for an active course in literature is not "sections," but some form of independent performance for an attentive critical audience of one. Here is where large-scale production methods break down, and limitations in size are necessary. Very few readers can handle more than twenty to twenty-five papers of the type I have been describing and maintain the necessary vigilance and the power of viewing them as individual performances. A reader can handle them in the usual fashion—grade them and add a complimentary or devastating comment—but he cannot give them critical attention at a high level. The student who is to rise to the kind of reading and writing called for in our ideal course must feel that he has a responsible reader, one who addresses himself to this essay and to this mind. The most valuable discussion a teacher can give is a comment surely directed to an individual written performance. Here we have the ideal section: two actors engaged in a Socratic dialogue. A teacher who is not bewildered and dulled by reading too many papers on the same topic will be able to judge the student's present achievement in relation to what he has done in the past. He can also help him keep track of his development and show him where he is going, and when he has failed, show him how to build on an earlier successful performance. Again Coleridge's Reverend Bowyer may serve as a guide:

. . . there was one custom of our master's, which I cannot pass over in silence, because I think it imitable and worthy of imitation. He would often permit our exercises, under some pretext of want of time, to accumulate, till each had four or five to be looked over. Then placing the whole number abreast on his desk, he would ask the writer, why this or that sentence might not have found as appropriate a place under this or that other thesis: and if no satisfying answer could be returned, and two faults of the same kind were found in one exercise, the irrevocable verdict followed, the exercise was torn up, and another on the same subject to be produced, in addition to the tasks of the day. The reader will, I trust, excuse this tribute of recollection to a man, whose severities, even now, not seldom furnish the dreams, by which the blind fancy would fain interpret to the mind the painful sensations of distempered sleep; but neither lessen nor dim the sense of my moral and intellectual obligations.

The marker of an English paper, as Coleridge realized though with "painful sensations," is a very important person indeed; he becomes the higher literary conscience, the intellectual guardian angel of his students.

It is evident that education in literature of this kind must be personal, and expensive, though scarcely more expensive than education in the sciences. Let us have at least as generous a supply of readers and conference rooms as we have of laboratory assistants and laboratories. The Humanities cannot flourish without *humanitas*. A protest is in order against the inhumanity of the Humanities when in some of our larger institutions the study of Great Books is reduced to display lectures before audiences of five and six hundred, and when the individual performance is measured by machine-graded examinations.

The teaching of great literary texts in Humanities courses has also had other if less depressing results which the teacher of literature should note if he is to fulfill his proper educational role. Because many works are taught in translation and taught often by staffs including many nonspecialists in language and literature, and because the texts are often presented in some broad historical framework, a work of imaginative literature tends to be treated either as a document for studying the history of ideas or as a text for illustrating and enforcing desirable moral and social attitudes. Though neither of these approaches is in itself harmful or inappropriate to a university, it may involve serious losses, especially in courses in which many students are reading for the first time—or for the first time at an adult level—masterpieces of European literature. There is a danger, which is increased by the large amounts of reading assigned in Great Books courses, that rich and special experiences will be too readily reduced to crude examples of a historic idea or a moral principle. Though the reductions may be necessary and useful for certain purposes, we must not let students make them too soon or too easily, not if we are seriously concerned with lifetime habits of reading. The undergraduate who masters the trick too early and too well may in the process suffer real damage. He may have acquired the dubious art of reading carelessly, of making the reduction *before* reading, and he may have lowered rather than increased his capacity for responding precisely to a particular work and for making fine discriminations between works.

Hence the special function of the teacher of literature, which is not to be confused with that of the historian or the moral philosopher. The teacher of literature in a Humanities course must feel he has betrayed a trust if he has not given the lay reader what he is best qualified to give: training in the literary disciplines of reading and writing. It is pertinent to recall the historic definition of the Humanities as it stands in the *Oxford English Dictionary*: "Learning or literature concerned with human culture, as grammar, rhetoric, poetry, and especially the ancient Latin and Greek classics." I suspect that some of the more enthusiastic general educators may be surprised by the words that follow "human culture": "as grammar, rhetoric, poetry . . ." (The order of items in the list is instructive, too.) The disciplines named are the ones that the teacher of literature has a special responsibility to impart. He is, like Horace's poet, a guardian of the language who shows (as Pope translates it) "no mercy to an empty line." His prime object is to maintain fineness of response to words, and his students rightly assume that he will be adept in discovering and illustrating refinements in writing whether in a great book or a student essay. This guardianship, once performed by teachers of the ancient Latin and Greek classics, now falls to the teachers of English and other modern literatures. Why is this so? Because they are committed to the principle that the study of letters is inseparable from the study of language.

Study of literature based on this principle can hardly be carried on in a course based mainly on texts in translation. Translations have their place in a course in interpretation, but only as ancillary to the main business of close reading in the original. The finer distinctions, the finer relationships which we are training our students to discover and make are almost invariably dulled or lost in the process of translation. We want the student to acquire the habit of recognizing and making such distinctions in his *own* language, and we can hardly teach him to do it if the examples before him are relatively crude. Whitehead once remarked when discussing Plato's cosmology, "After all, the translators of Plato have had B+ philosophic minds." With rare exceptions the translators of literature have had literary minds of similar quality. There are of course the handful of translations that are masterpieces, such as Pope's *Iliad*, North's *Plutarch*, and Dryden's *Aeneis*, texts that can bear the close study necessary for literary education. Ironically enough, these are the very translations avoided in most Great Books courses.

In speaking of the necessity for close attention to language, I am not forgetting that teachers of literature are also teachers of human culture and that they are therefore guardians of important values.

But they do not set out to teach these values, although they inevitably impart them by the way they talk and act in the presence of works of literature. But they are especially concerned with another task, with teaching ways of discovering and experiencing values expressed through literary objects. The most precious thing they can give their students is some increase of power, some help however humble in getting into Shakespeare or Dr. Johnson or Joyce.

We may hope that a student who has learned how to get into these writers will go back for further experiences after he has left the classroom and the university. That he surely will we cannot say. Even if he does not return to Shakespeare or Johnson, the experiences in the classroom almost certainly have their value and their effect in determining the quality of his later reading. One play well read with a good teacher and well digested in a reflective essay may serve as a touchstone of what literary experience can be. But finally, our belief that students' habits of reading are permanently affected is Platonic. The model for most cultural education is to be found in the third book of the *Republic:*

> . . . our young men, dwelling as it were in a healthy region, may receive benefit from all things about them; the influence that emanates from works of beauty may waft itself to eye or ear like a breeze that brings health from wholesome places, and so from earliest childhood insensibly guide them to likeness, to friendship, to harmony with beautiful reason.

In the effort to realize this Platonic vision in a modern university the undergraduate library plays its part by surrounding our youth with fair works of literature through which they may come into "harmony with beautiful reason." No one knows how born readers are produced, but we can put books in their way and in the way of the less happily born in the hope that proximity will have its effect as it does in the formation of more mundane habits. Of one thing I am convinced: that a born reader on a library staff can have a tremendous effect on young readers who come his way. I remember with gratitude two librarians of that description, one in school and one in college, who led us to read books we might never have looked into by sharing their love for what they had read. If I were to found a library dedicated to influencing the reading habit, I should place a half-dozen of these enthusiasts at strategic points to ensnare wandering students. They would not necessarily be trained librarians, and they would surely waste students' time and occasionally disturb their colleagues, but like great authors they would create an ever-widening circle of readers. Mere teachers of literature could hardly hope to compete with them, and might in time quietly disappear from the academic scene.

Symbolic Landscape in Wordsworth and Yeats

BY PAUL DE MAN

WORDSWORTH's narrative poem *The Prelude* opens with an invocation to a "gentle breeze" blowing "From the green fields and from yon azure sky" and shows the poet guided in his work by ". . . nothing better than a wandering cloud." Very early in Book I —by line 60—one moves from general nature to a specific and "known Vale," the first in a series of landscapes that will recur to mark the main articulations of the narrative. Keats's epic *Hyperion* begins by introducing the fallen Titan Saturn with more attention given to the setting than to the figure—a setting that captures beautifully the sheltered quiet of a summer landscape. In both cases, where we would traditionally, in works of epic tonality, have expected an invocation to the muse, we are given a landscape instead. As so often in romantic poetry, the landscape replaces the muse; and just as the relationship between poet and muse can take on a variety of shades, the dramatic interaction between poet and landscape acquires a rich diversity in romantic writing.

In the case of a "natural" romantic like Wordsworth, who urged "at all times, to look steadily at the subject," one might be tempted to think of the poet as a painter, whose language merely records and imitates sense perceptions. It is well known, however, that this urge to keep the eye on the subject is only Wordsworth's starting point and that, perhaps more than any poet, he appreciates the complexity of what happens when eye and object meet. The delicate interplay between perception and imagination could nowhere be more intricate than in the representation of a natural scene, transmuted and recollected in the ordering form of Wordsworth's poetic language. The sonnet I have chosen for illustration is a typical instance: in the short span of its fourteen lines, one can observe the juxtaposition of two very different attitudes toward a landscape, held together by a dramatic progression which constitutes the key to the interpretation. Similar tensions can be shown to underly the entire work.

Wide as the scope of Wordsworth's vision extends, it would never encompass Yeats's occasional claim of rejecting natural reality altogether, to ". . . scorn aloud/ In glory of changeless metal/ Common bird or petal." A considerable distance separates Wordsworth's involved but persistently reverent "look(ing) at the subject" from Yeats's intermittent contempt for "natural thing(s)"; one is not surprised to find Yeats much more reserved in his praise of Wordsworth than in his laudatory references to Blake and Shelley. Before venturing any speculation, historical or other, on the significance of this fundamental discrepancy between two poets both labeled "romantic," the nature of the difference needs to be clarified; one way of attempting this is by comparing a characteristic use of landscape in one of the later Yeats poems with an equally representative example from Wordsworth.

I

Our first example will be the sonnet by Wordsworth, "Composed by the Side of Grasmere Lake":

> Clouds, lingering yet, extend in solid bars
> Through the grey West; and lo! these waters, steeled
> By breezeless air to smoothest polish, yield
> A vivid repetition of the stars;
> Jove, Venus, and the ruddy crest of Mars
> Amid his fellows beauteously revealed
> At happy distance from earth's groaning field,
> Where ruthless mortals wage incessant wars.
> Is it a mirror?—or the nether Sphere
> Opening to view the abyss in which she feeds
> Her own calm fires?—But list! a voice is near;
> Great Pan himself low-whispering through the reeds.
> "Be thankful, thou; for, if unholy deeds
> Ravage the world, tranquillity is here!"

As so often in Wordsworth, the statement, the message of the poem is made explicit in the concluding lines. The poem names "tranquillity," and this alone would be a sufficient reason to single it out from the other words, since it is to convey a feeling that recurs in numberless places throughout the work of this writer, including his most famous definition of poetry as "taking its origin from emotion recollected in tranquillity." Of the three terms of that definition, "tranquillity" is perhaps the most subjective, and any text that conveys Wordsworth's particular feeling of tranquillity deserves full attention.

Although suggestion partly yields to assertion in the last two lines of the sonnet, the term "tranquillity" still appears in a dramatic setting, in the form of an appeasing promise spoken by "great Pan" himself. But the immediate context does not suffice for a full understanding of the feeling; it could even be misleading. That Pan, as the voice of nature echoed in the poet's own voice, should be the speaker here is no doubt important, but Pan can take on many forms, and the traditional connotations of the myth are perhaps more a hindrance than a help in this case. Wordsworth's "tranquillity" is not a pantheistic oneness with nature, not even the subtler adjustment between mind and object referred to in the "Preface" to the *Lyrical Ballads*. One should perhaps forget the traditional Pan for the moment and ask instead what makes this landscape the place in which he would choose to appear.

Another element of indetermination keeps the final lines in a state of suggestive suspense. Pan affirms that ". . . tranquillity is *here*," but such a complex set of spatial ambiguities have preceded this concluding assertion that one may well wonder where this "here" is located. The landscape makes us experience various kinds of quietness in various places, and the full impact of the final "here" depends entirely on the changing relationship between poet and landscape that develops in the main body of the sonnet.

We receive a first and literal impression of tranquillity from the near absence of wind in the "breezeless air," just enough stirred to allow for the slight motion and rustling of the reeds at the end. This absence of movement allows for the reflection, at sundown, of the brighter planets in the still surface of the lake. That this reflection will eventually convey the true meaning of "tranquillity" will become increasingly evident as the poem progresses, but not until we have been first led to believe in another, more obvious kind of peace. For in the lines

> Jove, Venus, and the ruddy crest of Mars
> Amid his fellows beauteously revealed
> At happy distance from earth's groaning field
> Where ruthless mortals wage incessant wars

the poet's eye rests not on the reflection, but on the actual planets in the sky. The world "field," in the singular, transforms the pastoral earth into the one huge battlefield of the Napoleonic wars, and in contrast to this turmoil, the order of the heavens exists in a peaceful serenity, at a safe and "happy distance" from all this strife. But this kind of tranquillity is certainly not to be found *here*, on this earth, but emphatically *there*, away from it and among the stars. It is not from "there," however, that Pan's voice finally reaches the poet's ear. Wordsworth's "tranquillity" does not dwell in the detached serenity of the stars.

In the temporal development of the poem, we first encounter the stars in line 4 as a "vivid repetition," a reflected presence on this earth. They are no random constellation, but three specific planets with obvious and commonly known mythological associations, so obvious that the least esoterically inclined of readers cannot fail to notice them. This simplicity of mythological allusion is important, especially in comparison with what we shall have to say later about Yeats, and also because it serves Wordsworth's overriding desire for simple concreteness, his genuine aversion for an elaborate use of mythology as a rhetorical device. Here Jupiter, Venus, and Mars are first and foremost the actual planets, observed by the poet at a definite time and place and participating in the poem as real, nonsymbolic presences. Yet as he looks, still with his outer eye, at their reflection, the mythological meaning begins to partake more and more in the action. The traditional couple of Love and War (Venus and Mars) plays an important part in the stormy destiny (Jupiter) of human passions and human history, and the relatively strong emphasis on the personified Mars with his ruddy crest "Amid his fellows beauteously revealed" establishes a mirrorlike correspondence between the order of the heavens and the realities of earth, where war also occupies a most untranquil prominence. The "happy distance" between earth and the stars is perhaps not so difficult to bridge as physical observation would tend to suggest. For if the opaque surface of the lake is indeed a mirror of celestial order, then this order is present on earth, albeit in a mediate, reflected form. It follows that the agitation of our loves and our wars mirrors in fact a turbulence that exists on a cosmic scale among heavenly bodies as well as on a human scale on this earth. There is a slight suggestion, perhaps more intuitive than conscious, of a correspondence between macrocosm and microcosm, but the harmony of the spheres is jarred

by "incessant wars" and Mars's persistent presence on earth would
seem to ban tranquillity not only from this earth but from heaven
as well. How then can Pan nevertheless make his final promise that
"tranquillity is here"?

Up to the phrase "Is it a mirror?" in line 9, which marks the
turning point of the poem, we have been using the outward eye of
direct perception. The relationship between landscape and poet has
been that of observer and thing observed, and consequently the language has been mimetically descriptive throughout. After an entirely
objective beginning:

> Clouds, lingering yet, extend in solid bars
> Through the grey West . . .

a slight intensification of tone stresses the joyful surprise of discovery
as the eye catches sight of the reflected stars:

> . . . and lo! these waters, steeled
> By breezeless air to smoothest polish, yield
> A vivid repetition of the stars . . .

The increased liveliness of description, apparent in the somewhat
unexpected verb "yield" and in the willed abstraction of "repetition,"
indicates the more active role played by the imagination in the
visual description. This imaginative activity, however, is not yet
strong enough to break through the surface of things. It could go so
far as to conceive of human order as a reflection of cosmic order, and
to make the connection between the planet Mars, and Mars the God
of War. But it remains firmly rooted in observation. It could never
seriously ask the question in line 9: "Is it a mirror?" To a rational
mind, fed by the observation of outward things, the question could
not make sense; it knows without doubt that the light in the lake
reflects the light of the stars above and that the lake acts like a mirror.
The poem, however, suggests an alternative:

> Is it a mirror?—or the nether Sphere
> Opening to view the abyss in which she feeds
> Her own calm fires?

"Nether Sphere" has an unmistakably Miltonic ring, and the presence of Miltonic diction in Wordsworth generally indicates a rise
in the pitch of imaginative intensity. Up till now, the surface of the

lake ". . . steeled/ By breezeless air to smoothest polish" has been as opaque as a sheet of metal, its depth hidden from the poet's eye. But by suddenly allowing that the light may very well not emanate from the stars at all, but from fires burning in another sphere buried deep under the surface, a radical change of perspective has taken place. We have moved far beyond the borders of empirical observation. The careful observer is now able to reach beyond the surface and to penetrate into a realm that lies hidden from the light of day, well beyond the reach of earthly vision. The lake becomes a kind of gate to the underworld, mysterious and unfathomable enough to be called an "abyss." And it is difficult to escape the implication that the "fires" have some infernal quality, a slight hint of a passing beyond a line which it is unsafe to cross—although one must hasten to add that these fires nowise imply the moral torment and punishment of Hell. Wordsworth's "nether Sphere" seems to be a curious synthesis between a pagan Hades and a Christian Inferno, a world of fire that lies beyond life but which, strangely enough, brings calmness rather than turmoil to the soul. Whereas the poem has first taken us upward into the distant sky, it now discovers a corresponding "nether Sphere" and, paradoxically enough, it is in that realm that the final "tranquillity" seems to originate. As we have seen, the peace of the heavens was a mere illusion to a mind that refuses to separate human destiny from cosmic order. The world "calm" appears for the first time explicitly in association with the "nether Sphere," who feeds her "own *calm* fires" in contrast with the natural fires of earth. The latter are seen as the disquieting fires of love and war, and are not granted the attribute of calmness. There is tranquillity on this earth, the poem seems to be saying, but only for those who are *also* able to see, with the inward eye, beyond the surface, and discover the quiet that inhabits depths where no natural light could reach.

Is this calmness then the tranquillity of death, to which the victims of "incessant wars" are destined? It certainly contains elements of this kind of peace, but only as it also contains elements of the harmonious peace of planetary movements, or the natural peace of a breezeless evening. For the final tranquillity is to be found neither in the "nether Sphere" nor upward "at happy distance from earth's groaning field"—although the particular strategy of the poem stresses the elusive peacefulness of the underworld over the more obvious quiet of the heavens. Still, the dominant movement stems from the return to earth, enriched by discoveries made in far-flung excursions; although the eye covers a very large scope, it finally comes to rest by the reeds at the side of the lake. Tranquillity is in *this* place on *this* earth, and it exists for the poet who can hear its voice, not because he is endowed with supernatural wisdom, or because he can dwell beyond the boundaries of space or of life, but because he possesses the kind of double vision that allows him to see landscapes as objects, as well as entrance gates to a world lying beyond visible nature. "Tranquillity," it seems, is the right balance between the literal and the symbolic vision, a balance reflected in a harmonious proportion between mimetic and symbolic language in the diction of the poem.

Perhaps we can now understand why the landscape should be as it appears in the opening lines:

> Clouds, lingering yet, extend in solid bars
> Through the grey West . . .

The delicate balance between direct and imagined vision demands precisely this degree of twilight grayness—so different from the sunlit noonday landscape of Mediterranean poets—with just enough light to perceive shapes and contours but not so much that the brilliance of the surfaces would prevent the eye from penetrating beyond them. Nor should the sky be cloudless; in that case the eye would be irresistibly drawn upward, whereas the clouds force it to turn inward, from an open to an enclosed space, and thus prepare for the necessary descent into the underworld. And the emphasis on "solid bars" draws, at the beginning of the poem, the strong horizontal line which, in spite of subsequent ascents and descents, becomes the final level on which the resolved poem comes to rest. Finally, the reflected light in the lake reminds us that this rest does not exclude the awareness of a cosmic realm above and a supernatural realm beyond. Both have to be present in the final vision; Wordsworth's Pan—since this is how he chooses to call his god here—is by no means devoid of transcendental dimensions. But even those transcendental elements are first revealed to sight before they can become an audible voice. All the action in the poem stems from visual events and obeys the logic of the eye. Wordsworth's landscape of tranquillity symbolizes in fact the complex act of pure vision.

II

During his later years, Yeats wrote several poems of tribute to the aged or deceased friends and companions of his literary life, in which he officiates somewhat like the Poet Laureate of a small court ruled over by Lady Gregory. In those "official" poems, he frequently bewails the passing of a gracious world of aristocratic refinement, brought to ruin by "this filthy modern tide." Because these poems appeal to a very public and readily comprehensible kind of emotion, and are bound to provoke a very direct response in the reader (favorable or unfavorable, depending on the strength of his own conservative leanings), they have contributed greatly to the picture of Yeats as the courtier of a bygone age—although numerous unsettling poems of the same period create a very different impression.

One of the most successful poems in this manner is "Coole Park and Ballylee, 1931" (a text which has been recorded in part as read by Yeats himself):

1   Under my window-ledge the waters race,
     Otters below and moor-hens on the top,
     Run for a mile undimmed in Heaven's face
     Then darkening through 'dark' Raftery's 'cellar' drop,
5   Run under ground, rise in a rocky place
     In Coole demesne, and there to finish up
     Spread to a lake and drop into a hole.
     What's water but the generated soul?

     Upon the border of that lake's a wood
10 Now all dry sticks under a wintry sun,
     And in a copse of beeches there I stood,
     For Nature's pulled her tragic buskin on
     And all the rant's a mirror of my mood:
     At sudden thunder of the mounting swan
15 I turned about and looked where branches break
     The glittering reaches of the flooded lake.

     Another emblem there! That stormy white
     But seems a concentration of the sky;
     And, like the soul, it sails into the sight
20 And in the morning's gone, no man knows why;
     And is so lovely that it sets to right
     What knowledge or its lack has set awry,
     So arrogantly pure, a child might think
     It can be murdered with a spot of ink.

25 Sound of a stick upon the floor, a sound
     From somebody that toils from chair to chair;
     Beloved books that famous hands have bound,
     Old marble heads, old pictures everywhere;
     Great rooms where travelled men and children found
30 Content or joy; a last inheritor

Where none has reigned that lacked a name and fame
Or out of folly into folly came.

A spot whereon the founders lived and died
Seemed once more dear than life; ancestral trees,
35   Or gardens rich in memory glorified
Marriages, alliances and families,
And every bride's ambition satisfied.
Where fashion or mere fantasy decrees
We shift about—all that great glory spent—
40   Like some poor Arab tribesman and his tent.

We were the last romantics—chose for theme
Traditional sanctity and loveliness;
Whatever's written in what poets name
The book of the people; whatever most can bless
45   The mind of man or elevate a rhyme;
But all is changed, that high horse riderless,
Though mounted in that saddle Homer rode
Where the swan drifts upon a darkening flood.

Several of Yeats's poems, at all periods, contain or sometimes begin
with landscapes, and it has often been observed that, as the style
gains in maturity and control, they become more and more concrete
and specific. The river at the beginning of "Coole Park and Ballylee,
1931," certainly seems as "real" as can be, its course described in
circumstantial and matter-of-fact detail, with almost geographical
precision. And the general unity of the poem is brought about by
equally natural means: the single locale of the lake in Coole Park,
to which Yeats takes us in the first stanza, following the course of the
river that connects his house, at Thoor Ballylee, with Lady Gregory's
estate at Coole.

Beyond this first unifying principle, the question remains as to the
experience conveyed by the juxtaposition of the three scenes: the
stream, the swan in the woods, and finally Lady Gregory, her house
and all they have come to stand for in Yeats's life. At first sight, the
poem seems to be built on a broad system of analogies between a
natural, a semimythical, and a personal event, the last having overtones of a more general historical significance. The pattern is most
concretely shown by the movements of the river in Stanza 1: after
running alternately through phases of light and darkness, it loses
itself in the shapeless anonymity of the lake and "drops into a hole"
(l.7). The presence of realistic detail (the otters and the moor-
hens) and of specific place names helps to make this description as
literal as possible; one is not tempted to read it as still another ver-

sion of the recurrent romantic metaphor likening the course of human existence to that of a river. It merely defines a pattern of motion, from a charted and controlled course to the final "drop" into nothingness. The landscape seems as "natural" as Wordsworth's, and although we may be somewhat taken aback by the sudden leap into total generality in line 8,

> What's water but the generated soul?

we could still interpret this as a transition to the next scene.

Within another analogical setting—the autumnal landscape suggestive of old age and decay—the swan suddenly appears. It is still a natural, real swan; the reader can well imagine such swans inhabiting Coole Park, and he may remember having met them before in an earlier poem "The Wild Swans at Coole." But this time Yeats's language makes it clear that the swan is more than a mere natural bird: it is called an "emblem" in line 17; in line 19 it is explicitly likened to the soul, and although the terms "loveliness" and "purity" fit the physical characteristics of the swan, it is clear from the development in Stanza 4 that they are primarily intended as attributes of the "soul." The reference is without doubt to the passage in the *Phaedo* where Plato likens the human soul to a swan. The general effect of the stanza, however, remains pictorial and concrete rather than speculative—and this is due, in large measure, to the analogy between the movement of the swan and that of the stream in Stanza 1, both departing from this earth irresistibly drawn into another realm, the river "drop(ping) into a hole," the swan disappearing "no man knows why."

In this reading of the poem, the two first episodes are a preparation for the second half: the homage to Lady Gregory's world, in sharp contrast to the homeless, uprooted condition of modern man. The more general considerations in the final stanza lead to the picture of Lady Gregory and Yeats, allied in a vast historical perspective as the last representatives of a tradition about to disappear into chaos—as the swan and the river both disappeared into a void. The swan and the lake recur in the recapitulating last line to mark Coole Park as the place where no lesser poetic spirit than Homer's was for the last time manifest:

> Though mounted in that saddle Homer rode
> Where the swan drifts upon a darkening flood.

It is well known that Yeats compared Lady Gregory's rather pedestrian collection of folk tales to Homer, and called it the "greatest book to come out of Ireland in our times"—a fact that James Joyce was all too eager to record for posterity by making it the object of one of his relatively few open allusions to Yeats in *Ulysses*.

Read in this manner, the poem's main theme becomes the decadence "of a time/ Half dead at the top," treated not "In mockery . . ." (as, for instance, in "Blood and the Moon") but in an elegiac confrontation between the splendors of the past and the uncertainties of a shapeless future. The landscapes in the first two stanzas function as natural images, enriching by their concreteness the abstract analogous movement of history evoked in the concluding part. Although the relationship between landscape and statement is no doubt less intimate and more rhetorical than in Wordsworth's sonnet, it does not seem to be essentially different; the symbolic action springs naturally from a perceived scene, the starting point for the imagination as it grows from natural to historical and mythical vision.

The only weakness of this reading is that it makes "Coole Park and Ballylee, 1931" into a rather recondite and not very tightly organized poem. Perhaps one can attribute to overgenerosity the somewhat embarrassing comparison between Lady Gregory and Homer, and forget, too, Yeats's pomposity in heralding himself, linked to Lady Gregory as the river links Ballylee to Coole Park, as one of the last representatives of heroic grandeur in a decaying world. Such considerations are, after all, extraneous to the poem—as is the rather trite definition of romanticism as a union between nobility and the true "people." But—always assuming that our proposed reading is the correct one—the economy of the poem is open to criticism on purely formal and intrinsic grounds; a great deal of superfluous detail in the descriptive passages rather seems to blur the movement which they are to convey; the development on the "soul" and the reference to the *Phaedo* may appear like a very elaborate windup to deliver a rather weak pitch; the link between the natural stream and the myth of the swan, though outwardly motivated by real incident, is not organically necessary, nor does it enrich the meaning of the poem as much as could be expected from such a striking and authoritative symbol. One could also quarrel with a discrepancy between tone and statement: this would indeed be a poem of rather grim despair, predicting no less than the end of a civilization with which Yeats has entirely identified himself. Yet the poem does not sound desperate, not even elegaic. The river and the swan do not behave as if they were symbols of destruction, although the text leaves no doubt that they have forever departed from this earth. They could easily have been made into poignant death symbols and made to utter the "swan-song" of a vanishing world, but they appear instead as a welcome relief to the eye among the tragically barren trees of the wood. On the whole, the poem renders a decidedly heroic ring, which makes even the final stanza appear altogether plausible. This supposes an assertive assurance which nothing that is being said would seem to warrant.

Before thus censoring Yeats, as poet or as courtier, one should remember that this reading is founded on a literal interpretation of the opening landscape. We assumed the stream to be a description of an actual scene in nature; it gains symbolic significance later in the poem by analogy with other events, but it was a natural fact *prior to* becoming symbolic. This was certainly also the case for Wordsworth's landscape. Everything in "Composed by the Side of Grasmere Lake" grows directly out of the landscape; the sonnet is entirely self-contained, and no need exists to bring other texts, whether by Wordsworth or someone else, to bear on the interpretation (unless, of course, one wanted to show that the poem is typical of Wordsworth in general). Nor does the reader have to possess any special knowledge beyond the most commonplace mythological information. Even this is less essential than the careful attention which Wordsworth demands for his natural setting. Coming from this kind of romantic nature-poetry, one is inclined to expect a similar primacy of the natural landscape in Yeats.

There can be no doubt, however, that a richer reading of a poem like "Coole Park and Ballylee, 1931" can only be obtained by giving up the illusion of natural realism. Yeats's landscapes have a symbolic meaning prior to their natural appearance, and act as predetermined emblems embedded in a more or less fixed symbolic system which is not derived from the observation of nature. One therefore has to go outside the poem to find the "key" to such symbols. The point is, of course, still highly controversial in the interpretation of Yeats, and this is certainly not the place to argue it more extensively. I merely want to give some indication of what happens to this poem if one extends the perspective in this manner.

The concluding line of the first stanza "What's water but the generated soul?" marks the sudden intrusion of expository language into pure description. It acts as a signal to the reader that a more elaborate kind of symbol is being used. The theme of "generation"

is a very frequent one in Yeats, who likes to treat it in Platonic
terms, as a descent of the immortal and divine soul into the finite
world of nature and matter. The recurrent emblem for this process
is described at length in the early volume of prose essays *Ideas of
Good and Evil*—a much richer source of information on Yeats's
symbolism, be it said in passing, than the later and much more
devious *A Vision*. It derives from Porphyry's esoteric interpretation
of the Homeric ode "The Cave of the Nymphs," in which the Cave
is said to represent the descent of the soul into matter by means of
the act of generation. (Other uses of this myth occur in several of
Yeats's major poems, for instance in "Among School Children"—
where it is explicitly referred to in a footnote—in "Meditations in
Time of Civil War" and so on.) Alerted by line 8, we recognize the
description of the river to be a modified and personal version of
Porphyry's Cave: the " 'dark' cellar" corresponds to the "obscurity
of the cavern" (*Ideas of Good and Evil*, p. 119); the underground
course of the water corresponds to the actual Cave, bounded by the
gates of generation and of death. The successive stages of the river
above and below ground mark the different incarnations which according to Yeats's poetic mythology extend the existence of the
individual soul over several lives; the subterranean stretches correspond to life on earth, the others presumably to a partly immaterial,
purgatorial state. In its final return to the divine principle, the ultimate death of the body, the soul drops into the "hole" of the lake.
The "moor-hens on the top" are the divine principle, which Yeats
generally associates with birds, while the "otters below" are the animal principle, indicating the composite nature of the generated
world. The entire construction is not more or less fantastic than,
for instance, Spenser's Garden of Adonis in Book III of *The Faerie
Queene* (with which it shares Platonic sources), except for the fact
that it is presented as a reality and not as a fiction.

   If one grants the identity of the river scene with the Cave of the
Nymphs, a new dimension is introduced into the poem. For it marks
Yeats's allegiance (whether real or apparent cannot concern us at
this point) to a body of doctrine that considers the incarnate state
of the soul as a relative degradation, and looks upon death as a return to its divine origin and, consequently, as a positive act. The
allusion to the *Phaedo*, one of the main sources of esoteric Neo-
platonism, now becomes altogether understandable. In opposition to
the generated "water" of Stanza 1, the swan "But seems a concentration of the *sky*"—air being an element closer to the divine than

water—joyously "mounting" from the decaying wood of matter toward its true abode. Its purity and its loveliness are due to the desire for the eternal that inhabits the swan's breast, and make it impervious to those who think that divine essence can be found on this natural earth.

After this, the second half of the poem takes on a very different significance. The "great glory" (l. 39) of the historical world created by a successful culture is bound to become an ambiguous compliment, since we now must assume that no earthly achievement, no matter how impressive, can have absolute value. The passing of the Irish gentry, Yeats's most closely personal experience of the mortality of civilizations, becomes a much less momentous and definitive event when any death, whether individual or collective, marks in fact a desirable escape from earthly embroilments. Like all earthbound civilizations, the Irish aristocracy made the mistake of imagining that its world of marriages, houses, and "generations" was "more dear than life" (l. 34), whereas the only thing dearer than life can be the immortal and immaterial soul, loosened from earthly fetters. Faced with the tragic decay of history, the man of true wisdom can only cry out, as Yeats proclaims in another poem, "Let all things pass away" ("Vacillation"). Here, in a *poème de circonstance*, written in homage to his benefactor and her class, the reservations are of course expressed in a much more oblique and allusive way. They are tacitly implied by the values established in the first three stanzas. Moreover, in a poet who makes deliberate ironic use of the technique of repetition, it is revealing that the two ear-striking words "stick" and "spot," when they appear in reference to Lady Gregory and her kind (ll. 25 and 33), have previously been given derogatory connotations associated with the decaying and misleading world of matter (ll. 10 and 24).

But it is in the last stanza that the esoteric symbolism makes its greatest contribution to an enriched complexity of statement. On a first level, the passage indeed expresses the extravagant compliment of Yeats to his patron and fellow writer, and his apocalyptic pessimism about the decadence of the Western world. Much is added, however, to complicate Yeats's own attitude toward this assertion. Two verbal echoes from the earlier stanzas help to give access to a difficult section. The "last romantics"—and nothing in the syntax indicates that "we," in line 41, necessarily refers to Yeats and Lady Gregory—are said to have chosen ". . . for theme/ Traditional sanctity and loveliness." The adjective "lovely" has been prominently

used before as an attribute of the liberated soul (l. 21), in opposition
to the earthbound, natural beauty of the woods and the waters.
Those who glorify the beauty of the soul are called "romantics,"
and "traditional sanctity" surely indicates the wisdom of the esoteric
tradition to which Yeats claims allegiance. The "romantics" are
those initiated in that tradition or spontaneously attracted to it, not
the "natural" romantics like Wordsworth or Keats. The true "romantics" know "Whatever's written in what poets name/ The book
of the people . . ." and from Yeats's essays on folklore we know
that what he and other "poets" find there is precisely the esoteric
tradition in a particularly otherworldly form—so otherworldly, in
fact, that it rejects much of Plato himself as too earthbound.

The final line, "Where the swan drifts upon a darkening flood,"
echoes the "darkening" of line 4' (". . . darkening through 'dark'
Raftery's 'cellar' drop") and takes us back, closing the cycle, to
Homer, whose ode "The Cave of the Nymphs" actually began the
poem in a disguised version. The swan drifting on a "darkening
flood" refers to a soul still imprisoned in generated matter (water)
(unlike the "mounting swan" in line 14), and Yeats is suggesting that
ever since men have been willing to found their values upon the
incarnate world and to praise the act of generation, Pegasus has been
riderless—there has been no truly great poetry. This came about with
Homer, a transitional figure who, in his esoteric aspects (as in "The
Cave of the Nymphs") still belongs to an uncorrupted past, but in
his exoteric aspects stands at the dawn of a literature which will get
increasingly enmeshed in the servitudes of original sin. The passage
repeats what Yeats had explicitly been saying about Homer in an
early essay, "The Autumn of the Body" (*Ideas of Good and Evil*,
pp. 301 ff.); it now uses symbolic language to mask a direct statement
on which Yeats has not changed his mind over the years. Homer
is in fact the real "last romantic," the last representative of a tradition that nearly died with him, and Yeats pretends to see himself
in a somewhat similar situation, as one of the few to have kept contact with "traditional sanctity." In a sense, the "we" in "We were
the last romantics . . ." refers to Homer and Yeats, whereas the
statement that follows "But all is changed . . ." (l. 46) points not
so much to the present, the 1931 of the poem, as to the entire time
span of Hellenic and Christian civilization. Tragic as it is, the threatening destruction of the West can be contemplated with the kind
of heroic gaiety for which Yeats is striving—perhaps in vain—in the
Last Poems. For if ever since "all is changed" (that is, ever since

Homer) the "high horse" of poetry has been "riderless," a poetic rebirth can only be expected in an altogether new type of civilization. We have moved a long way beyond Lady Gregory into speculations for which this very practical lady would have had little sympathy but which, for poetic reasons, obsessed Yeats during his entire life.

Two distinct readings thus become apparent. They do not necessarily cancel each other out, but represent very different attitudes toward a common situation. Each of these readings, however, depends on altogether divergent uses of imagery, as epitomized in the role played by the opening landscape; in the first interpretation it acts as a natural analogical image, in the second as an emblematic "key." The descriptive, mimetic use of landscape remains quite similar to Wordsworth's first kind of vision, in which nature is seen as an exterior object. But Yeats's symbolism has nothing in common with Wordsworth's second or symbolic kind of language. The emblematic landscape, in which a familiar river is used to mask an esoteric text, differs entirely from Wordsworth's transcendental vision, as we encountered it in the first poem. Both, it is true, lead from material to spiritual insights, but whereas Wordsworth's imagination remains patterned throughout on the physical process of sight, Yeats's frame of reference, by the very nature of his statement, originates from experiences without earthly equivalence. The texture of his language, in the poetry written after 1900, thus depends on an altogether composite style, held together by almost miraculous skill. On the one hand, the poems seduce by the sensuous "loveliness" of their natural landscapes and images, while gaining their deeper structural unity and most of their intellectual content from nonnatural or even antinatural uses of language. The juxtaposition of two truly incompatible conceptions of style is much more precarious even than Wordsworth's delicate balance between perception and imagination. In Yeats, the imagination in fact scorns the perception, but seems unable to do without it: stripped of its natural attributes the poem would become a lifeless skeleton. The result, in Yeats's masterful hands, can be intensely dramatic, but it could certainly never end, like Wordsworth's sonnet, in a promise of "tranquillity."

North of Boston: Frost's Poetry of Dialogue

BY WILLIAM H. PRITCHARD

I

WITH THE publication of *North of Boston* (1914) Frost's poetic career was marked as a fact to be taken seriously. This second volume of poems, most of them probably written at about the same time as the earlier-published *A Boy's Will* (1913), met with high praise from, among others, Lascelles Abercrombie, Edward Garnett, Edward Thomas, and most loudly—Ezra Pound. Pound used its publication in England as a club to beat American editors with, but he also made a valuable remark about the kind of literary experience offered by the narratives and dialogues that comprise the book. He was struck, as many have been, by Frost's "humor," and was at pains to distinguish it from cracker-barrel sagacity:

> Mr. Frost has humor, but he is not its victim. "The Code" has a pervasive humor, the humor of things as they are, not that of an author trying to be funny, or trying to "bring out" the ludicrous phase of some incident or character because he dares not rely on sheer presentation.

And he remarked of Frost's characters, "I don't want much to meet them, but I know that they exist, and what is more, that they exist as he has portrayed them."

Pound's tribute to Frost's realism seems at first to contradict certain of our notions about the poet, since a great deal of attention has subsequently been paid to exactly that side of Frost's humor which Pound was grateful *not* to find in *North of Boston*. Some frequently quoted lines from a later poem, "New Hampshire," reveal something quite other than "the humor of things as they are":

> I may as well confess myself the author
> Of several books against the world in general.

> To take them as against a special state
> Or even nation's to restrict my meaning.
> I'm what is called a sensibilitist
> Or otherwise an environmentalist.
> I refuse to adapt myself a mite
> To any change from hot to cold, from wet
> To dry, from poor to rich, or back again.

Here we are asked to be interested in a performer who commands an expansive colloquial manner for purposes of reeling off a series of jokes on the world, and there seems little point in separating the speaker of such a poem from what we call "Frost himself." But in most of the poems from *North of Boston* we look in vain for the presence of "Frost himself." Instead we hear voices, speaking to one another or to themselves. The voices make no direct appeal to us; instead we are permitted to overhear them as they talk out their concerns. Nor are we oppressed by the sense that these voices—the characters created in a literary form—are being used for purposes of some philosophical statement about experience. They are not pushed out of the way or put in their proper places so that the poet can make a shrewd comment on the human scene. For Frost's sympathy with his characters is of a very special kind that asks to be distinguished from identification or pity. It consists rather in a reliance on the sufficiency of what Pound called "sheer presentation," or an unwillingness to go *behind* speech and dramatic gesture for some psychological or sociological essence that would "explain" the voices heard.

Frost's procedure may come clearer when placed against instances from two earlier practitioners in what is at least roughly the same mode of poetry—the dramatic monologue or dialogue. In "Bishop Blougram's Apology," for example, Browning lets the bishop develop an ingenious pragmatic defense of his occupation to the point where the skeptical Gigadibs has nothing left to do, it seems, but leave for Australia. Then when Blougram finishes, Browning enters with a flourish, nudging the reader to inform him that the bishop only believed half of what he spoke—that "He said true things, but called them by the wrong names." The reader may justifiably be angry at such a trick, but he has no alternative to this truth about Blougram. Any feelings he may have developed about the bishop's argument must be bound by the limits Browning introduces at the end of the poem. A similar explanation of speech occurs at the end of Edwin Arlington Robinson's "Isaac and Archibald," a poem that has been mostly taken up with the conversations of two old men, each of whom attempts to warn the youthful narrator about the senility and approaching death of the other. Finally the narrator looks back upon the conversation and tells us that

> Isaac and Archibald have gone their way
> To the silence of the loved and well-forgotten.
> I knew them, and I may have laughed at them;
> But there's a laughing that has honor in it,
> And I have no regret for light words now.
> Rather I think sometimes they may have made
> Their sport of me;—but they would not do that,
> They were too old for that. They were old men,
> And I may laugh at them because I knew them.

On this comfortable note the case is closed. If we were at all undecided in our attitudes toward the old pair, Robinson solves our problem by telling us the right way to feel. Like Browning, he reassures us by providing a general category of behavior under which the specific instance can be placed: the bishop was talking for victory and so didn't believe all he said; the old men might have been making sport of the youth but they really weren't, since they were so old.

Frost sacrifices such narrative reassurance in favor of a dramatic integrity, gained as we realize that there is no essential truth underlying the appearances, no real explanation behind his characters' talk. In these dialogues "character" *is* talk, so that when we praise Frost's "realism" we are in fact praising his style. One would hesitate to argue that his characters are more "real" than Browning's or Robinson's because of the poet's mysterious ability to seize and express the psychological essence of human beings. "Realism" can make sense as a label only if it refers to the uncompromising way Frost's characters have their say, and say it without benefit of narrative omniscience and intrusion. The interesting risk Frost takes in these poems is that the sheer presentation of the characters' speech will sufficiently engage the reader; even if we share Pound's sense of the characters' existence we ask that this existence be of concern to us. Although there are poems in *North of Boston* to which we do not return with much interest, the book also contains what Edward Thomas was unashamed to speak of as "masterpieces of deep and mysterious tenderness." I assume that Thomas was not merely throwing off rich sentiment here, but speaking truly about the power of certain poems, and furthermore that the tenderness is felt only because of Frost's firm and unsentimental respect for his own imagined persons.

II

> Sudden and swift and light as that
> The ties gave,
> And he learned of finalities
> Besides the grave.

These lines conclude "The Impulse," the last section of "The Hill Wife," a five-part poem about the fears and oppressive solitude of a childless young wife who lives with her husband in a lonely and wild place. She has little to do but sing to herself, and one day out of idleness, caprice, madness—an impulse—she disappears forever. Although the earlier sections of the poem give adequate preparation for her disappearance, Frost's concern is not with motivation, but with the moment—"Sudden and swift and light as that"—the moment when all the ties of human relatedness, the bonds of love, obligation, and habit that hold people together are broken by an impulse, a spontaneous movement "light as that." In this poem the impulse is equally a finality; acted upon it becomes irrevocable, and so the husband learns.

This stanza from "The Impulse" will serve as a gloss for the most interesting dialogues in *North of Boston*: "Home Burial," "The Death of the Hired Man," "A Servant to Servants," "The Black Cottage," "The Housekeeper," and "The Fear." In all these poems, the "ties" have given or are close to giving. A character, seemingly immune to disruptive impulse, sustained by the endless repetition of daily experience and its proper vocabulary, suddenly confronts an event, a person, or a memory which calls into question the validity of that experience and its vocabulary—which threatens to dissolve the ties. In a later dialogue the Witch of Coös tells her visitor a story of how one night a pile of bones marched up her cellar stairs, continuing on up and up until she resourcefully trapped them in the attic. Her son assures the visitor that "We never could find out whose bones they were," but unexpectedly the mother contradicts him:

> Yes, we could too, son. Tell the truth for once.
> They were a man's his father killed for me.

> I mean a man he killed instead of me. . . .
> Son looks surprised to see me end a lie
> We'd kept all these years between ourselves
> So as to have it ready for outsiders.
> But tonight I don't care enough to lie—
> I don't remember why I ever cared.

What happens in "The Witch of Coös" is an almost literal enactment of what occurs in all the dialogues we are considering: the skeleton in the family closet (or attic) can no longer be contained by those defenses which have hitherto proved successful against it. Letting the skeleton out involves a risk since it is a "finality" against which all previous experience must be reappraised; yet the release is necessary and liberating. As the Witch tells her story to the end, the past ceases to be horrible. Conversation *can* deprive the skeleton of its power to haunt, and it is the only possible alternative to the private madness of the Hill Wife.

Furthermore the moment of sudden truth is often revealed by the character in a style notably different from that which is usual in the dialogues. In the poems I shall consider—"Home Burial," "The Black Cottage," and "The Death of the Hired Man"—Frost makes the revelation significant by certain strong variations from the colloquial mode which his characters share. At these moments the verse takes on a heightened "poetic" quality that is overlooked by those who would praise the poems simply for their faithful renditions of actual speech. And the importance of this change in stress lies in its signaling a world that is not the ordinary one in which the characters live and talk but rather a world of "finalities besides the grave."

"Home Burial," the most strikingly concentrated of the dialogues, shows Frost's art at its full objectivity. The conversation takes place between husband and wife, with the narrator intervening only to fill in certain gestures and movements. The poem begins at an impasse, with questions that aren't replied to:

> He saw her from the bottom of the stairs
> Before she saw him. She was starting down,
> Looking back over her shoulder at some fear.
> She took a doubtful step and then undid it
> To raise herself and look again. He spoke
> Advancing toward her: 'What is it you see
> From up there always—for I want to know.'

> She turned and sank upon her skirts at that,
> And her face changed from terrified to dull.
> He said to gain time: 'What is it you see,'
> Mounting until she cowered under him.
> 'I will find out now—you must tell me, dear.'
> She, in her place, refused him any help
> With the least stiffening of her neck and silence.
> She let him look, sure that he wouldn't see,
> Blind creature; and awhile he didn't see.
> But at last he murmured, 'Oh,' and again, 'Oh.'

What she looks at is the little graveyard where their dead child is buried; what she sees is an image of her husband's behavior that at this point in the poem he doesn't understand. Nor does the reader, but we know that something has happened. The wife has been caught in an act of private uncertainty—"starting down" yet "looking back"—by a husband who demands to be let into this privacy. Their uneasy situation is conveyed by precise alternation between speech and physical gesture. As the husband mounts the stairs so he can look down on the wife, her own expression changes from "terrified to dull"—the terror of private grief momentarily replaced by that insensibility to any grief at all of which she is to accuse him. At the same time the husband's demand to be advised of her grief is seen as a painful and loving solicitude; his "you must tell me, dear" bears perfectly the awkward care with which he approaches her. The narrator briefly assumes the woman's point of view by using the phrase "Blind creature" to describe him, but we are not asked to adopt her view as precisely right; his blindness is paralleled by as serious a defect in her own way of seeing. ·

He mounts the stairs, literally attempting to enter her vision as at last he sees the graveyard:

> 'The wonder is I didn't see at once.
> I never noticed it from here before.
> I must be wonted to it—that's the reason.
> The little graveyard where my people are!
> So small the window frames the whole of it. . . .
> But I understand: it is not the stones,
> But the child's mound—'
>
> 'Don't, don't, don't, don't,' she cried.

She is reduced to a repeated cry by the untroubled deliberateness of his recitation. His reference to "the child's mound" works as a gross violation of all the proprieties of her grief, for she sees him as "wonted to it"—to death as well as to life—in a way that precludes him from responding correctly to finalities like the child's death. She knows that he cannot respond correctly because he does not know "how to speak." When she reaches the bottom of the stairway and prepares to leave the house, the narrator ceases to fill in details and builds their estrangement to full pitch as the husband makes a last attempt at communication:

> 'Tell me about it if it's something human.
> Let me into your grief. I'm not so much
> Unlike other folks as your standing there
> Apart would make me out. Give me my chance.'

But he cannot let it rest here. "Wonted to it" as he is, he suggests that perhaps she does "overdo it a little," since "To take your mother-loss of a first child/ So inconsolably—in the face of love" is an extreme response beyond his comprehension. She can only interpret his criticism as "sneering"—as willful mockery of her private, incommunicable grief. Angrily he comes down to her with 'God, what a woman! And it's come to this,/ A man can't speak of his own child that's dead.' This manly exasperation with the ways of woman, combined with his asserted rights as a father, serves as the key which unlocks the secret. For the first time in the poem she lets him in on her grief with a vengeance; and we see exactly what it is she has been looking at over her shoulder—an image from the past, all too fully present to her. She denies him the right to speak of the child:

> 'You can't because you don't know how to speak.
> If you had any feelings, you that dug
> With your own hand—how could you?—his little grave;
> I saw you from that very window there,
> Making the gravel leap and leap in air,
> Leap up, like that, like that, and land so lightly
> And roll back down the mound beside the hole.
> I thought, Who is that man? I didn't know you.
> And I crept down the stairs and up the stairs
> To look again, and still your spade kept lifting.'

The power of this extraordinary passage is not simply a matter of an event successfully evoked through particular details and conveyed by the rhythms of colloquial speech. Although the first three lines are representative of the colloquial norm for most of the dialogues

—the use of contractions, the interpolated, questioning aside "how could you?" the ever-present sense that someone is speaking to someone else—these are only part of the story. The image of the digging itself is commanding precisely because of the way its presentation varies from, in a sense denies, the norm that has been established. Admittedly there is no reason to praise a poet because he makes use of alliteration. All too often such use simply calls attention to itself, and the critic is left with some "f" sounds or "s" sounds with which he can do little. But in these lines from "Home Burial"— "Making the gravel leap and leap in air,/ Leap up, like that, like that, and land so lightly"—we are not embarrassed by the resources of sound. Here alliteration, the repetition of "like that" and "leap," the unstressed syllable of "lightly" imitating the return to earth of gravel thrust upward in previous leaps, and the deadly assonant regularity of the final line, all serve to violate the colloquial decorum to which we have been accustomed. This stylized artificial speech brings home to us the specially heightened presence of a dream or vision from the past that has been the wife's private possession until this moment. The speech is also rhetorically appropriate in the way it confronts the husband with the shocking energy of his own performance at the grave; the vigorous repetition and alliteration of her style both imitate and rebuke his energy by setting it in implicit contrast with the dead child and her own motionless grief.

If the poem ended with this revelation of the wife's secret, a cruelly neat resolution would occur: the husband's pathetic insensitivity shown forth for our pity; the wife's silent heroism to be applauded. But Frost has spoken of tragedy as a situation in which "something terrible happens and nobody's to blame." This makeshift and admirable definition is borne out by what happens in the remainder of "Home Burial," as the woman goes on to criticize her husband. His speech had appalled her even more than his actions, for after digging the grave he sat in the kitchen and talked of everyday concerns—the ruinous effects of bad weather on a good birch fence:

> 'Think of it, talk like that at such a time!
> What had how long it takes a birch to rot
> To do with what was in the darkened parlor.
> You *couldn't* care! The nearest friends can go
> With anyone to death, comes so far short
> They might as well not try to go at all.
> No, from the time when one is sick to death,

> One is alone, and he dies more alone.
> Friends make pretense of following to the grave,
> But before one is in it, their minds are turned
> And making the best of their way back to life
> And living people, and things they understand.
> But the world's evil. I won't have grief so
> If I can change it. Oh I won't, I won't!'

What begins as a horrified reprimand of a particular person turns rapidly into something quite different. His specific failure to grieve properly has been generalized into a human defect, as the impersonal "one" is substituted for "you." Even more important than the generalization is the thoroughness with which she develops a case for what "one" does in response to death. "Making the best of their way back to life/ And living people . . ." necessarily involves a variety of methods, different ways of talking—one of which is to rattle on about bad weather and birch fences. Ironically, she has answered the question that began her speech: of course birch fences have nothing to do with the finality of death, and because of this irrelevance they provide the materials for refurnishing one's life, for reestablishing the ties that have broken.

A denunciation of one particular husband's manner of grieving has ended up as a protest against the world's evil. Since there *is* no decorum for grief, since everyone fails to summon up a proper response, the wife can no longer single out his action as a violation but can only rail at grief and the world in general. Her talk has taken her almost further than she meant to go; near the end of the poem he refers to her grief by saying "The heart's gone out of it," and in a sense this is true. Her secret has been revealed, and although she has not yet accepted a world in which people respond to death in odd and unseemly ways, she has, nevertheless, articulated it. But the conclusion of the poem emphasizes that this articulation does not automatically mean reunion with her husband—the final lines show her "opening the door wider," and carry his threat to follow and bring her back by force. It would be misguided for us to infer either a future reconciliation or a continued estrangement. The wife's last angry outcry—"*You*—oh, you think the talk is all"—might almost be addressed to the reader, for we are interested in the threatened pursuit only insofar as it is made out of words. Any summation or explanation of action by the narrator would be out of place; the reality of Frost's characters has been attested to by their speech, and the poem ends when there is no more to say.

III

In his review of *North of Boston* mentioned earlier, Edward Thomas spoke of the volume as an "experiment," comparing it to Wordsworth's attempt at purification of language in the *Lyrical Ballads*. Thomas was pleased that Frost had "got free from the habit of personal lyric" and moved beyond the often self-regarding concerns of *A Boy's Will*, his first book of verse. The justness of Thomas's comparison may be felt if we recall some of the language from Wordsworth's preface:

> The principal object, then, proposed in these poems was to choose incidents and situations from common life, and to relate or describe them, throughout, as far as was possible in a selection of language really used by man, and, at the same time, to throw over them a certain colouring of imagination.

Rustic life is chosen because "the essential passions of the heart" are free to speak a "plainer and more emphatic language"; because "the manners of rural life germinate from these elementary feelings"; and because these passions are "incorporated with the beautiful and permanent forms of nature." Further on, Wordsworth insists that in each poem "the feeling therein developed gives importance to the action and situation," not vice versa, and that since he is determined to keep the reader "in the company of flesh and blood" he rejects personifications and other "mechanical devices of style" which "do not make any natural or regular part of the language." Finally, he insists that "a large portion of the language of every good poem can in no respect differ from that of good prose."

Surely Frost's procedure in the dialogues shows much that is in accord with Wordsworth's aim, yet it would not be of much use to set up a tally sheet and triumphantly check off the Wordsworthian principles which are borne out in Frost's practice. Any poet who is attempting to purify the language will go about it in at least some of the ways Wordsworth did. For example, personification is only one mechanical device of style among many; in Frost's case he ceases to write poems which begin with an automatic reach to dreamy introspection—the opening lines of "Waiting" ("What things for dream there are . . .") or "Ghost House" ("I dwell in a lonely house I know/ That vanished many a summer ago") or "A Dream Pang" ("I had withdrawn in forest . . .")—and which often depend upon a self-conscious "literary" diction ("the antiphony of afterglow" is perhaps the most notable example). Nor do the wistfully ironic epigraphs, which adorned nearly every poem in the early editions of A Boy's Will, persist. With North of Boston specifically designated as "a book of people," Frost no longer needed to write explanatory accompaniments about the grandeur of the boy's ambitions. Instead, as in "Home Burial," the qualifying and correcting voice is placed within the drama of the poem. We are not allowed to accept the wife's castigation of her husband as the whole truth because his voice is there as well; the narrator has become absorbed in his created dialogue.

My argument is not, of course, that Frost simply rejected artifice so he could record the language really used by men. In Wordsworth's own case readers from Coleridge on down have been at pains to point out how this or that passage does not conform to his own prescription, and it would be trivial to use this discovery for purposes of exulting in the separation between poetic theory and practice. Indeed Wordsworth himself made it clear that he was "attempting in so far as possible" to make a "selection of language really used by men" (my italics), and he went on to invoke that "certain colouring of imagination" which would be thrown over this selection. The vagueness of the last phrase is entirely appropriate. Since Words-worth was not a recording machine taking down the language as it "really" came, but a poet who admired Milton, Spenser, and Shake-speare, the "certain colouring of imagination" is a convenient and necessary way to assert the difference between mechanism and art. By the same token, as we read Frost's dialogues between rural folk we need not be shocked or annoyed when we meet local effects in the language that cannot adequately be described by labels such as "colloquial speech rhythm" or "the way New England farmers really talk." Again, with reference to "Home Burial" we located the peculiar power of those lines about the gravedigging in their variation and remoteness from the usual decorum of ordinary speech.

Undoubtedly when Thomas reviewed North of Boston he did not quite foresee that Frost would eventually come to be thought of by his public as the "poet of nature" to an extent hardly less than the Wordsworth he was compared with. I attempt no large account of either poet's sense of nature and its relationship to the writing of poetry, but it is evident from the dialogues, and indeed from Frost's poetry taken together, that his "nature" is as much the product of selection, as much informed by "a certain colouring of imagination" as any rendering to be found in Romantic poetry. It is not useful to think of "nature" in the dialogues as either a brooding presence, existing behind the characters and forcing itself on their attention, or even as the ordinary physical landscape of rocks, stones, and trees in which rural affairs take place. For if we insist that "character" in these poems should not be viewed as a substance which lies behind and determines conversation but rather as the way a voice sounds, the way it "takes things," so "nature" can more justly be equated with our sense, vague enough when it is stated abstractly, of the way things are. Against this stock reality made up of ordinary routine, gesture, and response, all carried by the expected rhythm of a voice, are placed those moments when particular dreams assert themselves in an attempt to transform nature.

These moral and stylistic qualities—the momentary vision of a world other than the way things are and a corresponding change in the speech used to express that vision—are present most notably in "The Black Cottage," a rather ordinary poem which turns suddenly into something else. Here the dialogue is actually an inner one as "we," the narrator-tourist and a minister, visit an abandoned cottage which has been caught "in a sort of special picture." The minister does the talking by giving us a history of the house's owner, an old lady whose husband died in the Civil War and whose sons forsook the place, leaving her alone. The minister rambles on about her life and beliefs, admires her innocence (she hadn't seen the other races but *knew* that all men were created equal), and recalls his own decision to leave the Apostles' Creed unchanged—even though the young people objected to certain lines—for the sake of her peace of mind:

> 'It was the words "descended into Hades"
> That seemed too pagan to our liberal youth.
> You know they suffered from a general onslaught.
> And well, if they weren't true why keep right on
> Saying them like the heathen? We could drop them.
> Only—there was the bonnet in the pew.'

If we are reminded of Bishop Blougram it is not merely because both clergy adopt pragmatic arguments for keeping the faith as it is. Frost is drawing, like Browning, on a conversational manner that combines worldliness and sentimentality, as in Blougram's demonstration of the vulnerability of unbelief:

> Just when we are safest, there's a sunset-touch,
> A fancy from a flower-bell, some one's death,
> A chorus ending from Euripides,—
> And that's enough for fifty hopes and fears . . .
> To rap and knock and enter in our soul.

It is a matter of course that any argument falls into insignificance when seen in the light of homely heart-warming images like the sunset or the bonnet in the pew. Frost's minister protests somewhat archly, "For dear me, why abandon a belief/ Merely because it ceases to be true/" and the archness only suggests that this bit of homely wisdom is somewhat embarrassed at itself. Fortunately the poem does not end with this moral. It is picked up by the final twenty lines and turned into perhaps the most compelling vision of permanence in Frost's poetry, anticipating the close of "Directive" thirty years hence. The minister moves off from worldly wisdom into a new world, shaped to the demands of imagination:

> 'As I sit here, and oftentimes, I wish
> I could be monarch of a desert land
> I could devote and dedicate forever
> To the truths we keep coming back and back to.
> So desert it would have to be, so walled
> By mountain ranges half in summer snow,
> No one would covet it or think it worth
> The pains of conquering to force change on.
> Scattered oases where men dwelt, but mostly
> Sand dunes held loosely in tamarisk
> Blown over and over themselves in idleness.
> Sand grains should sugar in the natal dew
> The babe born to the desert, the sand storm
> Retard mid-waste my cowering caravans—
> There are bees in this wall.' He struck the clapboards,
> Fierce heads looked out; small bodies pivoted.
> We rose to go. Sunset blazed on the windows.

No longer does it occur to us to invoke Browning as an antecedent of this poetry. From the fifth line on, the verse moves with a precision of reference and a rhythmic propulsion that add up to the most sustained writing of Frost's early career. The homely minister is suddenly transformed into a seer through whom the poet speaks to summon up a world without change or death. With the picture of sand dunes moving about idly yet protecting themselves as they protect "the babe born to the desert" and impede the monarch's caravan, a strange pastoral cooperation is imagined, reminiscent of Gonzalo's ideal kingdom in *The Tempest*. This pastoral nature takes the babe to itself and preserves it from change somewhat as Wordsworth's Lucy was preserved, and while earlier the minister had speculated on the power of the old lady's innocence, he now imagines a nature in which such innocence would be forever protected. This protection is not only seen in the sand dunes but heard through the thickened and deliberate texture of the verses which present them: the repeated "over" and the stressed alliterated consonants of those lines slow up the movement and act out in their way the "retard" that is described. Then when this dream nature has been fully developed as a kingdom of invulnerable truths—a social completion of isolated innocence—we are brought back to the way things are, to an actual cottage in a real nature of angry bees. The minister's secret has been fully expressed in a poetry as far from colloquial speech as one could imagine, and the narrator is left tersely to name the changes that replace visionary permanence. With five brief assertions the quiet room is animated, alive with the hostility of bees and the violence of sunset. The two men make their departure—leaving the house to be reassumed by nature.

If these remarks about the focus of our interest in the dialogues are sound, then the most popular of them, "The Death of the Hired Man," needs some relocation of its center. Its acceptance into the mainstream of classic American poems meant, for at least this reader, that it was taught in the grade schools along with "The Vision of Sir Launfal" and "The Chambered Nautilus" as a species of noble poetry. This popularity can partly be explained as a matter of subject; the poem contains just enough familiar material to verify a simple notion of what Frost's poetry is like: a rural couple, the figure of old Silas, the famous lines about "home," and a certain number of references to haying. But more significant for our purposes are the misleading assumptions about character which permit the hired man himself to be blown up into a tragic figure, symbolic of New England, old age, or whatever the reader's imagination chooses to invest in him, and which turn Silas into a pathetic oddity like Peter Bell or Eben Flood.

This approach forgets that we do not observe the hired man in either speech or action. Throughout the poem he is a presence whom we learn about only by listening to the moderate, thoughtful opposition and agreement of Mary and Warren as they talk of him. Often their interpretations are so incompatible that we question any notion of the "real" Silas, symbol of New England or otherwise. What we concern ourselves with instead is the drama that develops through the modulations and corrections of voices speaking to one another, and our final impression of Silas is a balance between rival claims of understanding. The drama reveals itself in the movement of Warren's responses to the hired man from an original refusal of sympathy to a growing involvement in Silas' fate. Early in the poem he replies to Mary's pleas for kindness with

> 'When was I ever anything but kind to him?
> But I'll not have the fellow back,' he said.
> 'I told him so last haying, didn't I?
> If he left then, I said, that ended it.
> What good is he? Who else will harbor him
> At his age for the little he can do?'

Warren's righteous insistence on what he did and said shows him on the defensive, and the pointed implications of his last question—"Who else will harbor him"—suggest that a sense of justice rendered is not quite enough to guarantee peace of mind. His early refusal to become involved—"I'm done"—quickly gives place to a mood which denies the assertion. As Mary describes the "miserable sight" of the hired man's return, Warren interrupts her narrative with questions like "Where did you say he'd been?" or "What did he say? Did he say anything?" finally completing the movement of her thought with "Anything? Mary, confess/ He said he'd come to ditch the meadow for me." By this time Warren is caught up in the narrative as he watches the pattern repeat itself. Although he separates himself from Mary's recital of the old conflict between Silas and "young Wilson" over how to build a load of hay, saying, "Yes, I took care to keep well out of earshot," he also agrees that "I know, that's Silas' one accomplishment" and goes on to describe it at some length. Although Warren cannot share the extremity of her solicitude he recognizes its force and sincerity; the wryly gentle mockeries of his interpolations qualify her passionate concern but don't dispose of it.

Mary sums up this concern with a wistfully negative picture of the hired man's life:

> 'Poor Silas, so concerned for other folk,
> And nothing to look backward to with pride,
> And nothing to look forward to with hope,
> So now and never any different.'

The verse balances past and future, places Silas' present condition at the center of focus and brings out the secret which has preoccupied Mary—her intimation of his approaching death. Once again, at a key moment, the quality of the verse changes significantly, this time through a narrative elevation:

> Part of a moon was falling down the west,
> Dragging the whole sky with it to the hills.
> Its light poured softly in her lap. She saw it
> And spread her apron to it. She put out her hand
> Among the harp-like morning-glory strings,
> Taut with the dew from garden bed to eaves,
> As if she played unheard some tenderness
> That wrought on him beside her in the night.
> "Warren," she said, "he has come home to die."

We recall the minister's vision of permanence in "The Black Cottage." Mary does not speak, but inhabits, for a wordless moment, a nature other than the way things are, beautifully responsive to her private cares and feelings—a nature in which "Light poured softly in her lap," in which flowers become a harp for her to play on. And her unheard melodies somehow work on Warren, or so it seems. Frost's own concluding remark in his preface to Robinson's *King Jasper* has its point here:

> Give us immedicable woes—woes that nothing can be done for—woes, flat and final. And then to play. The play's the thing. Play's the thing. All virtue in "as if."

The mention of woes refers to Robinson's particular sense of experience, but Frost extends the remark into a general truth about the nature of poetry. Given woes flat and final, the poet's special power is his ability to shape these woes into beautiful and satisfying forms of play. It is this sense in which Frost allows his imagined persons, like Mary, to become poets in moments of stylistic elevation—"As if she played unheard some tenderness.'

But if all virtue lies in "as if," Frost would also admit, I think, that there is virtue in knowing how far to carry play. Frequently he imagines characters so absorbed in their ways of seeing that they forget the "as if" and turn their play into life. In "West-Running Brook," for example, the woman is so convinced that the brook has spoken to her that she finally tells her husband ". . . if not to you/ It was to me—in an annunciation." And on a more disturbing level,

the girl in a later poem, "The Subverted Flower," sees her lover become a beast:

> She looked and saw the shame:
> A hand hung like a paw,
> An arm worked like a saw
> As if to be persuasive,
> An ingratiating laugh
> That cut the snout in half,
> An eye became evasive.

As with the gravedigging in "Home Burial," life becomes an image,
the ordinary world an extraordinary nightmare of a single mind. It
is of great interest that Frost, the sturdy defender of common sense,
as the account runs, should be so taken up with imagining private
moments of vision that reduce, distort, or deny quotidian nature.

In "The Death of the Hired Man" the tenderness of an "as if"
does not serve to overwhelm Warren's voice, for he remains himself
enough to mock gently some of Mary's speech. He can still un-
sentimentally define "home" as "the place where, when you have to
go there,/ They have to take you in" which takes its place next to
Mary's more accommodating "Something you somehow haven't to
deserve." In his masques, Frost pays tribute to both Reason and
Mercy, and they receive their due here as well through the com-
plementary accents of husband and wife. As Warren goes finally
to confront the subject of their conversation Mary stays behind,
saying

> 'I'll sit and see if that small sailing cloud
> Will hit or miss the moon.'
>
>   It hit the moon.
> Then there were three there, making a dim row,
> The moon, the little silver cloud, and she.
>
> Warren returned—too soon, it seemed to her,
> Slipped to her side, caught up her hand and waited.
>
> 'Warren?' she questioned.
>
>   'Dead,' was all he answered.

W. H. Auden, admiring Frost's skill in achieving "naturalistic conversation" in the dialogues, went on to add that "His characters are
people in whom 'poetic' language would be out of place, and on the
rare occasions when he introduces it, it strikes a false note. . . ."

This objection can be answered first by justifying Mary's "poetic" language in terms of the whole poem; as her earlier gesture to the moon was prelude to her announcement of Silas' impending death, so the all too short watch at the end becomes an image for the abruptness of Warren's final message. The sense of completeness in this finality is expressed by situation, image, and phrase; Frost's use of "all" in the final line needs no comment.

If we move beyond "The Death of the Hired Man" and recall the stylized nature of crucial passages in both "Home Burial" and "The Black Cottage," it becomes evident that any attempt to treat the dialogues as but faithful representations of colloquial speech will be inadequate to the poems we read. Frost's willingness to violate the decorum of "naturalistic conversation" which he himself has set up, creates, in the best of the dialogues, something close to a new poetic genre in which the dramatic intermingling of personal vision and social fact is achieved by a style flexible enough to express both demands, yet keep them distinct.

IV

Frost's use of the dialogue form after *North of Boston* became increasingly sporadic. After *Mountain Interval* (1917), the poems in dialogue seem pronouncedly more relaxed, as if to assure a reader that he can let down from the pressure and economy of the lyric. Except for the masques and one or two humorous specialties in the later books, "West-Running Brook" is effectively the last serious dialogue, and even here the great prophetic evocation of "Substance lapsing unsubstantial" and "the tribute of the current to the source" detaches itself strikingly from the low-keyed banter which precedes it. What the writing of these dramatic dialogues did for Frost, I should suppose, was to equip him with an unshakable confidence in the ability of his voice to express complex experience without the resort to shrillness or pious affectation (one thinks of Spender's unfortunate "I think continually of those who are truly great"). This is the supremely equipped voice that speaks with most assurance in the late "Directive":

> The height of the adventure is the height
> Of country where two village cultures faded
> Into each other. Both of them are lost.
> And if you're lost enough to find yourself

By now, pull in your ladder road behind you
And put a sign up CLOSED to all but me.
Then make yourself at home. . . .

One can see why a contemporary narrative poet such as Robert Lowell pays tribute to *North of Boston*. Frost's claim has been that "the possibilities for tune from the dramatic tones of meaning struck across the rigidity of a limited meter are endless." It was in *North of Boston* that these possibilities first became actual.

Poetry in an Age of Prose: Arnold and Gray

BY NEIL H. HERTZ

IN MATTHEW ARNOLD's view of English poetry, Gray occupies a unique position. He is the hero-victim of an "age of prose":

> Though they may write in verse, though they may in a certain sense be masters of the art of versification, Dryden and Pope are not classics of our poetry, they are classics of our prose.
> Gray is our poetical classic of that literature and age. . . . He is the scantiest and frailest of classics in our poetry, but he is a classic.
> (*from* "The Study of Poetry")

> Gray, a born poet, fell upon an age of prose. He fell upon an age whose task was such as to call forth in general men's powers of understanding, wit and cleverness, rather than their deepest powers of mind and soul. As regards literary production, the task of the eighteenth century in England was not the poetic interpretation of the world, its task was to create a plain, clear, straightforward, efficient prose. Poetry obeyed the bent of mind requisite for the due fulfillment of this task in the century. It was intellectual, argumentative, ingenious; not seeing things in their truth and beauty, not interpretative. Gray, with the qualities of mind and soul of a genuine poet, was isolated in his century. Maintaining and fortifying them by lofty studies, he yet could not fully educe and enjoy them; the want of a genial atmosphere, the failure of sympathy in his contemporaries, were too great.
> (*from* "Thomas Gray")

Arnold's judgment of the great Augustans is usually taken as a sign that he had inherited an essentially Romantic notion of what was and what was not "poetic." Certainly these passages recall, in the distinctions they make between "versification" and "poetry," "poetry" and "prose," the "intellectual" and the "interpretative," some of the categories with which Romantic theorists rewrote literary history. And it is likely that Arnold's commitment to those distinctions prevented him from seeing that the work of Dryden or Pope might be more than "versification," might be at once "intellectual" *and* "interpretative." But is Arnold's Romanticism also responsible for his excessively high opinion of Gray? The language of these passages suggests that it is; but in this case it does so not by recalling the vocabulary of Romantic critical theory, but by making Gray appear very much like a character in a Romantic poem. The phrases that indicate Gray's place in some larger context—"frailest of classics in our poetry," "isolated in his century"—are, of course, figures of speech, shorthand for the acts of judgment Arnold makes as a literary historian. But we are bound to take them in a more personal sense as well, as indications that Gray's life was a poignant one. However little they tell us about Gray, words like "frailest" and "isolated" tend to assimilate Arnold's sketch of him to the more familiar portrait of the Romantic solitary. Here, for comparison, are the concluding stanzas of one of Wordsworth's early poems:

> But who is He, with modest looks,
> And clad in homely russet brown?
> He murmurs near the running brooks
> A music sweeter than their own.
>
> He is retired as noon-tide dew,
> Or fountain in a noon-day grove;
> And you must love him, ere to you
> He will seem worthy of your love.
>
> The outward shows of sky and earth,
> Of hill and valley, he has viewed;
> And impulses of deeper birth
> Have come to him in solitude.
>
> In common things that round us lie
> Some random truths he can impart,—
> The harvest of a quiet eye
> That broods and sleeps on his own heart.
>
> But he is weak; both Man and Boy,
> Hath been an idler in the land;
> Contented if he might enjoy
> The things that others understand.
>
> —Come hither in thy hour of strength;
> Come, weak as is a breaking wave!
> Here stretch thy body at full length;
> Or build thy house upon this grave.
>   (*from* "A Poet's Epitaph," 37–60)

The personal qualities of the solitary suggested in Arnold's prose are here more fully elaborated in the description of the "weak," "retired" figure; and when Wordsworth contrasts his man, an "idler," with those "others" whose way of dealing with things is to "understand," he anticipates the distinction Arnold makes in more explicitly historical terms. Arnold calls the eighteenth century "an age whose task was such as to call forth in general men's powers of understanding, wit and cleverness, rather than their deepest powers of mind and soul." He never says that the "deepest powers of mind and soul" operate only in idleness, but his emphasis on the eighteenth century's "task" (the word occurs four times in the short passage quoted), like his characterization of eighteenth century prose as "efficient," helps to convey an attitude toward the busyness and achievement of the period that is related to Wordsworth's scorn for those "others."

But in at least one important respect our analogy with "A Poet's Epitaph" breaks down: the claims Arnold makes for Gray are at once more limited and less ambiguous than those of Wordsworth for his solitary hero. Gray's frail isolation is never made to seem in any way valuable, in any sense the cause of his distinction as a poet. Isolation was simply a sad necessity, given the temper of his age. "The want of a genial atmosphere, the failure of sympathy in his contemporaries," are not treated as mixed blessings, but as genuine misfortunes. Another way of putting this is to note that there is nothing in Arnold's essays that is like the remarkable last stanza of "A Poet's Epitaph" in asserting the value of solitude and weakness. Wordsworth is there insisting that the idler's weakness *is* strength, even as he acknowledges, in the beautiful simile of the breaking wave, that the claim is paradoxical. Nothing so "unreasonable" can be found in Arnold: in writing of Gray he evokes the pathos of solitude without suggesting that the solitary may enjoy certain extraordinary compensations.

However moderate his treatment of poetic solitude may seem when compared with Wordsworth's, Arnold's relation to Gray is nevertheless best understood in terms of the Romantic image of the lonely poet. Reading through Arnold's essays, one has the sense that he was much more interested in what Gray could be made to stand for than he was in Gray's achievement as a poet. In "The Study of Poetry," of all the "classics" and near classics discussed, from Homer to Burns, Gray is the only one whose work is not quoted; and even in the essay devoted to him, where Arnold speaks of his "high qualities of mind and soul," and invites the reader to "see these in the man first, then observe how they appear in his poetry," that final step is never taken. Instead, Arnold is chiefly concerned with a question he returns to several times during the essay: "In a poet of such magnitude, how shall we explain his scantiness of production?" The question would seem to demand a psychological answer, but it is not in purely psychological terms that Arnold finally "explains" Gray. Although he quotes at length from Gray's letters, using them to demonstrate traits of their author's character, and although he considers some psychological explanations proposed by others, Arnold's own answer, what he calls "the reason, the indubitable reason as I cannot but think it," is the one found in the paragraph I began by quoting. We have seen that it explains Gray less in psychological than in historical terms, but that the historical language itself has overtones of the Romantic myth of the solitary.

The essays hint that it was Gray's loneliness and his vulnerability to the "prosaic" spirit of his age, as much as his distinction as a poet, that made him an appealing figure to Arnold. But in the essays this is no more than a hint, caught in phrases like "isolated in his century." There is a text, however, that provides a valuable poetic gloss to Arnold's critical writing on Gray. In "The Scholar Gipsy" we can observe Arnold situating himself in relation to Gray, and doing so, more clearly than in the essays, in the language of Romantic solitude. For in creating his own version of a solitary, Arnold drew on the "Youth to Fortune and to Fame unknown" in the *Elegy written in a Country Church-Yard*. It is not surprising that he did so. From the time of its publication in 1751 through the end of the eighteenth century, the *Elegy* was one of the most imitated poems in English, and well into the next century Gray's melancholy "Youth" remained an attractive image of the poet. About many of these imitations there is little that can be said, beyond establishing their debt to Gray. But the connection of "The Scholar Gipsy" with the *Elegy* is a more interesting one. Arnold's echoes of Gray are not scattered at random through his stanzas, but seem to fall into a pattern that corresponds closely to the dramatic movement of the poem. At a climactic moment in the poet's monologue, one stops hearing language reminiscent of the *Elegy* and begins to hear what sounds like another, very different, sort of poetic language, that of Keats's "Ode to a Nightingale." The shift is striking enough in itself, and can tell us enough about Arnold's relation to Gray, to make it worth looking at in detail. The moment comes about half-way through the poem. Arnold, who has imagined himself following traces of the legendary scholar through the countryside, becomes convinced that he has actually seen him, then comes to himself and says:

> But what—I dream! Two hundred years are flown
>   Since first thy story ran through Oxford halls
>   And the grave Glanvil did the tale inscribe
> That thou wert wander'd from the studious walls
>   To learn strange arts, and join a Gipsy tribe:
>   And thou from earth art gone
> Long since, and in some quiet churchyard laid;
>   Some country nook, where o'er thy unknown grave
>   Tall grasses and white flowering nettles wave—
>   Under a dark red-fruited yew-tree's shade.
>
> —No, no, thou hast not felt the lapse of hours.
> For what wears out the life of mortal men?
>   'Tis that from change to change their being rolls:
>   'Tis that repeated shocks, again, again,
>   Exhaust the energy of strongest souls,
>   And numb the elastic powers.
> Till having us'd our nerves with bliss and teen,
>   And tir'd upon a thousand schemes our wit,
>   To the just-pausing Genius we remit
>   Our worn-out life, and are—what we have been.
>
> Thou hast not liv'd, why should'st thou perish, so?
>   Thou hadst *one* aim, *one* business, *one* desire:
>   Else wert thou long since number'd with the dead—
>   Else hadst thou spent, like other men, thy fire.
>   The generations of thy peers are fled,
>   And we ourselves shall go;
>   But thou possessest an immortal lot,
>   And we imagine thee exempt from age
>   And living as thou liv'st on Glanvil's page,
>   Because thou hadst—what we, alas, have not!
>   (*131–160*)

This passage is the turning point of the poem. When Arnold denies that the scholar-gipsy is dead, his tone takes on an intensity not heard before. The voice that established the gentle, melancholy mood of the first half of the poem, with its pastoral imagery and its affectionate catalogue of local place names, gives way to a less placid voice, one fond of exclamations ("O Life unlike to ours!" [166]), of urgent rhetorical questioning ("For what wears out the life of mortal men?" [142]) and urgent imperatives ("Fly hence, our contact fear!" [206]).

Critics have pointed out that the excitement that comes into Arnold's tone has a particular quality, and have located that quality in the Nightingale Ode, specifically in its last two stanzas:

> Thou wast not born for death, immortal Bird!
>   No hungry generations tread thee down;
> The voice I hear this passing night was heard
>   In ancient days by emperor and clown:
> Perhaps the self-same song that found a path
>   Through the sad heart of Ruth, when, sick for home,
>   She stood in tears amid the alien corn;
>   The same that oft-times hath
>   Charm'd magic casements, opening on the foam
>   Of perilous seas, in faery lands forlorn.
>
> Forlorn! the very word is like a bell
>   To toll me back from thee to my sole self!
> Adieu! the fancy cannot cheat so well
>   As she is fam'd to do, deceiving elf.
> Adieu! Adieu! thy plaintive anthem fades
>   Past the near meadows, over the still stream,
>   Up the hill-side; and now 'tis buried deep
>   In the next valley-glades:
>   Was it a vision, or a waking dream?
>   Fled is that music:—Do I wake or sleep?

Although Arnold's lines could not be called an "imitation" of the Ode, accumulating details give them a definitely Keatsian ring. There are echoes of single words ("generations" and "immortal," for example), and there is Arnold's "But what—I dream!" which comes to sound, in this persuasive context, like a reminiscence of the last lines of the Ode, even though Arnold is settling a question that Keats characteristically leaves up in the air. Yet even if these similarities did not exist, we would certainly still hear the resonance, in Arnold's intense "—No, no, thou hast not felt the lapse of hours," of the even greater intensity of "Thou wast not born for death, immortal Bird!"

The sudden fervor with which Arnold proclaims the scholar's immortality makes it easy to ignore the lines at the end of the preceding stanza, where his death is calmly accepted in the language of the *Elegy*. When Arnold imagines the scholar

in some quiet churchyard laid;
Some country nook, where o'er thy unknown grave
Tall grasses and white flowering nettles wave—
Under a dark red-fruited yew-tree's shade,

he seems to have had in mind both the "Country Church-Yard" of
Gray's title, and the stanza that describes where the villagers are
buried and where the "Youth" himself will someday lie:

Beneath those rugged elms, that yew-tree's shade
Where heaves the turf in many a mould'ring heap,
Each in his narrow cell for ever laid,
The rude Forefathers of the hamlet sleep.
(13-16)

Nor is it only in his death that Arnold's figure resembles Gray's:
the influence of the lonely "Youth" can be felt in the stanzas in the
first half of "The Scholar Gipsy," where the scholar is seen sometimes languidly at rest, sometimes moving against the landscape:

Maidens, who from the distant hamlets come
To dance around the Fyfield elm in May,
Oft through the darkening fields have seen thee roam,
Or cross a stile into the public way.
Oft thou hast given them store
Of flowers—the frail-leaf'd, white anemone,
Dark bluebells drench'd with dews of summer eves,
And purple orchises with spotted leaves—
But none hath words she can report of thee.

And, above Godstow Bridge, when hay-time's here
In June, and many a scythe in sunshine flames,
Men who through those wide fields of breezy grass
Where black-wing'd swallows haunt the glittering Thames,
To bathe in the abandon'd lasher pass,
Have often pass'd thee near
Sitting upon the river bank o'ergrown:
Mark'd thy outlandish garb, thy figure spare,
Thy dark vague eyes, and soft abstracted air;
But, when they came from bathing, thou wert gone.

At some lone homestead in the Cumner hills,
Where at her open door the housewife darns,
Thou hast been seen, or hanging on a gate
To watch the threshers in the mossy barns.
Children, who early range these slopes and late
For cresses from the rills,

Have known thee watching, all an April day,
  The springing pastures and the feeding kine;
And mark'd thee, when the stars come out and shine,
  Through the long dewy grass move slow away.

                                                    (82–110)

The influence that is usually pointed out in this passage is that of "To Autumn," where Keats, too, presents a figure glimpsed in various attitudes against a richly evoked pastoral background. But unlike Keats's personification, the scholar-gipsy is (up to the turning point of the poem) a recognizably human figure, closely associated with the landscape, but not to be identified with Nature. However Keatsian Arnold's images of the countryside may be, the sense he conveys of the scholar himself is closer to that embodied in the description of the "Youth" in the *Elegy*:

For thee, who mindful of th' unhonour'd Dead,
  Dost in these lines their artless tale relate;
If chance, by lonely contemplation led,
  Some kindred Spirit shall enquire thy fate,—

Haply some hoary-headed Swain may say,
  "Oft have we seen him at the peep of dawn
Brushing with hasty steps the dews away,
  To meet the sun upon the upland lawn.

"There at the foot of yonder nodding beech,
  That wreathes its old fantastic roots so high,
His listless length at noontide would he stretch,
  And pore upon the brook that babbles by.

"Hard by yon wood, now smiling as in scorn,
  Mutt'ring his wayward fancies he would rove;
Now drooping, woeful-wan, like one forlorn,
  Or craz'd with care, or cross'd in hopeless love.

"One morn I miss'd him on the custom'd hill,
  Along the heath, and near his fav'rite tree;
Another came; nor yet beside the rill,
  Nor up the lawn, nor at the wood was he:

"The next, with dirges due in sad array
  Slow through the church-way path we saw him borne:—
Approach and read (for thou can'st read) the lay
  Grav'd on the stone beneath yon aged thorn."

                                                    (93–116)

Rural solitaries inclined to languor and to apparently aimless wandering are common enough in poetry after the middle of the eighteenth century: what suggests a more specific connection between Arnold's figure and Gray's is that each exists in a relation of shy familiarity with the other inhabitants of the region. The maidens or the bathers in Arnold's Oxfordshire are imagined as coming to accept the "outlandish" scholar as a common, even a welcome, sight; just as Gray's "hoary-headed Swain," though he doesn't understand what the youth was doing, can accept his oddness and still speak of him with a certain amount of affection. Both poets keep their lonely figures in touch, however tenuously, with society. Both offer images of what the eighteenth century called "solitude," rather than of that more extreme version of solitude, Romantic "isolation."

When Arnold denies, in Keatsian language, that the scholar is dead, he is, in effect, turning away from the poetry of eighteenth century solitude. From that point on, it is hard to find anything in "The Scholar Gipsy" that recalls the *Elegy*. Certainly the abruptness with which Arnold changes his tone is far from the steady composure of Gray's speaker, whose voice can range over a variety of tones without ever losing its underlying elegiac note. Yet apparently Arnold found Gray's range too narrow. The attitudes which could be expressed in accents of gentle, detached melancholy, and embodied in pastoral images of rural society and a qualified rural solitude, no longer seemed appropriate when he turned to consider what he calls "this strange disease of modern life" (203).

We can see clearly what some of those attitudes were by looking more closely at the *Elegy*, particularly at the lines where Gray, like Arnold, is attempting to bring a solitary figure into some relation with images of contemporary society. The speaker of the *Elegy* had begun by meditating on the villagers buried in the churchyard, and had gone on to compare their lives with those of the "Proud," the figures of the great world who are buried in more elaborate surroundings. Here he returns to the villagers:

> Far from the madding crowd's ignoble strife,
>   Their sober wishes never learn'd to stray;
> Along the cool sequester'd vale of life
>   They kept the noiseless tenor of their way.
>
> Yet ev'n these bones from insult to protect
>   Some frail memorial still erected nigh,
> With uncouth rhimes and shapeless sculpture deck'd,
> 80 Implores the passing tribute of a sigh.

Their name, their years, spelt by th' unletter'd muse
    The place of fame and elegy supply:
And many a holy text around she strews,
    That teach the rustic moralist to die.

For who, to dumb Forgetfulness a prey,
    This pleasing anxious being e'er resign'd,
Left the warm precincts of the chearful day,
    Nor cast one longing ling'ring look behind?

On some fond breast the parting soul relies,
90   Some pious drops the closing eye requires;
E'en from the tomb the voice of Nature cries,
    E'en in our Ashes live their wonted Fires.

For thee, who mindful of th' unhonour'd Dead,
    Dost in these lines their artless tale relate;
If chance, by lonely contemplation led,
    Some kindred spirit shall enquire thy fate,—

Haply some hoary-headed Swain may say,
    "Oft have we seen him at the peep of dawn
Brushing with hasty steps the dews away,
100   To meet the sun upon the upland lawn.

"There at the foot of yonder nodding beech. . . ."
                   (73–101)

As one's attention shifts from the speaker's thoughtful evaluation of society to the landscape that is the setting for the youth's solitude, the easy, deliberate pace of Gray's stanzas tends to smooth over a transition that is as remarkable, if not so violent, as Arnold's "—No, no, thou hast not felt the lapse of hours." For the lonely youth who is about to be described is identified as the person who, "mindful of th' unhonour'd Dead,/ Dost in these lines their artless tale relate" (93–94)—that is, he is the urbane speaker of the *Elegy* himself. The connection is a surprising one. For ninety lines we have heard someone talking with an Augustan assurance of tone about large moral issues. His voice was more or less anonymous, deriving its authority from conventional wisdom (as in "The paths of glory lead but to the grave" [36]), rather than from any personal fineness of moral perception. Now the owner of that voice is heard not only meditating on his individuality, but yielding, with what seems like very un-Augustan self-indulgence, to an impulse to cast himself in a melodramatic role, imagining his own untimely death and composing his own epitaph.

Yet what is most remarkable about the last half of the *Elegy* is not that it reveals Gray's Romanticism, but that it displays certain lingering Augustan habits of expression. The stanzas just quoted maintain a careful balance between one's sense of the speaker's gloomy self-concern and feelings of more generalized pathos. So careful is this balance, in fact, that one cannot be sure what direction the speaker's thoughts are taking. They seem to be drifting toward the images of himself as a misunderstood, doomed eccentric. For example, his use of the first-person pronoun in "E'en in our Ashes live their wonted Fires" (92) enables him to move gracefully from considering mortality in general (in terms of the "the parting soul" or "the closing eye") to thinking about his own singular "fate," as he goes on to do in the next stanza. Yet the line also marks the moment when the speaker's awareness of his own difference seems most submerged; for the first time in the poem, he is explicitly acknowledging that he shares something with the people whose lives he has been distantly contemplating.

The controlling sense of decorum operating in these transitional stanzas gives a wider relevance to the speaker's brooding thoughts on death, and keeps the *Elegy* from flying apart into two very different poems, one about society, the other about solitude. We may still find it hard to recognize the speaker of the earlier lines in the melancholy youth, but Gray does not seem to have been aware of this difficulty. And that, I think, says more about his Augustanism than does any rhetorical device in the *Elegy*. Details of the portrait of the youth—the poses he strikes, his self-consciousness, his early death—show how close Gray came to creating a full-fledged Romantic solitary. But he was not prepared, as Wordsworth would be, fifty years later, to see in solitude a state that was valuable in itself; he could only measure its value in relation to society. In connecting the portrait of the youth with the grave moral observations of the earlier stanzas, Gray intends to justify solitude by making it seem the condition of being able to reflect on society. The youth's eccentricity, the poem suggests, does not disqualify him for the role of Augustan poet-moralist; rather it enables him to view, in distant perspective, both the "madding crowd's ignoble strife" and the more sober but limited lives of the villagers. And, although the youth's observations are made in melancholy solitude, he is able to imagine an audience, the unknown "kindred spirit." In fact, it is his confidence in the existence of such "kindred spirits" that gives the speaker of the *Elegy* the assured tone we hear early in the poem.

At the beginning of "The Scholar Gipsy," when Arnold places himself "in this high field's dark corner" (12), he seems, like Gray's speaker, to be trying to find in solitude a point of view, a perspective on society. But with whom could this perspective be shared? The "Shepherd" addressed in the opening lines may be more immediately present than Gray's hypothetical "kindred spirit," but he is there only to be sent away:

> Go, for they call you, Shepherd, from the hill;
>   Go, Shepherd, and untie the wattled cotes:
>   No longer leave thy wistful flock unfed,
>   Nor let thy bawling fellows rack their throats,
>   Nor the cropp'd herbage shoot another head.
>   But when the fields are still,
>   And the tired men and dogs all gone to rest,
>   And only the white sheep are sometimes seen
>   Cross and recross the strips of moon-blanch'd green,
>   Come, Shepherd, and again renew the quest!
>   (1–10)

Although he is invited to come again at night and "renew the quest," the nature of the "quest" is left vague, and the Shepherd's participation in it is never spoken of again. Indeed his presence makes so little difference in Arnold's tone that it is impossible to tell just when he moves out of earshot. He is still being addressed in line 22, but in the lines immediately following, the sound of a bemused voice contemplating a slightly enchanted Nature obliterates whatever sense we may have had that Arnold was talking to anyone in particular:

> Screen'd is this nook o'er the high, half-reap'd field,
>   And here till sun-down, Shepherd, will I be.
>   Through the thick corn the scarlet poppies peep,
>   And round green roots and yellowing stalks I see
>   Pale blue convolvulus in tendrils creep:
>   And air-swept lindens yield
>   Their scent, and rustle down their perfum'd showers
>   Of bloom on the bent grass where I am laid,
>   And bower me from the August sun with shade;
>   And the eye travels down to Oxford's towers.
>   (21–30)

There is nothing like this in the *Elegy*: the highly charged pastoral background, the paradoxical sense of activity in repose, set the scene for an imaginative excursion that has little to do with the meditations of Gray's poet-moralist. His thoughts turned by "Glanvil's book" (31) to the suggestively "poetic" scholar, Arnold begins his "dream." At first he is simply musing on an attractive legend, but soon his voice betrays an involvement with the legend which, though expressed in calm, elegiac rhythms, is nonetheless intense:

> And I myself seem half to know thy looks,
>   And put the shepherds, Wanderer, on thy trace;
> And boys who in lone wheatfields scare the rooks
>   I ask if thou hast pass'd their quiet place:
>   Or in my boat I lie
> Moor'd to the cool bank in the summer heats,
>   Mid wide grass meadows which the sunshine fills,
>   And watch the warm green-muffled Cumner hills,
>   And wonder if thou haunt'st their shy retreats.
>
> For most, I know, thou lov'st retired ground.
>   Thee, at the ferry, Oxford riders blithe,
>   Returning home on summer nights, have met
>   Crossing the stripling Thames at Bab-lock-hithe,
>   Trailing in the cool stream thy fingers wet,
>   As the slow punt swings round:
>   And leaning backwards in a pensive dream,
>   And fostering in thy lap a heap of flowers
>   Pluck'd in shy fields and distant Wychwood bowers,
>   And thine eyes resting on the moonlit stream. . . .
>   (62–80)

Lying in his boat (66) or wondering (70), Arnold sees himself in attitudes and states of mind in which he also imagines the scholar: the first twelve stanzas present not one, but two "shy," "abstracted" wanderers in the landscape. But the relation that Arnold imagines between himself and the scholar can never be one of simple identification, however attractive that might be. For whatever the scholar-gipsy may be searching for when his eyes are "resting on the moonlit stream," Arnold is searching for the scholar-gipsy.

Such a "quest," characterized by a tenuous feeling of identification with the fleeting figure just around the bend—"past the near meadows . . . up the hill-side," in the language of the Nightingale Ode— is a familiar Romantic theme. But we have already noticed that the scholar-gipsy isn't quite like the nightingale: his casual contact with other rural figures in a sense domesticates him. And the natural scene Arnold described, once he moves out of his bower, is a recognizable and unmysterious one, with landmarks and place names. When Keats addresses the nightingale, he is standing in "verdurous glooms and winding mossy ways"; Arnold, when he finally imagines an encounter with the scholar, is on a particular "wooden bridge," not far from "Hinksey" and "the Cumner range" (123–127).

When Arnold turns on himself with "But what—I dream!" (131), we feel that the turn was inevitable, not because he was bound to wake up to the fact that the scholar had been dead two hundred years (a moment later, he denies this), but because it was impossible to go on dreaming in quite the same terms. Arnold's dream had been of a figure in somewhat the same relation to society as Gray's youth, for whom rural solitude, in 1750, offered a means of achieving moral perspective. However, that was no longer the case one hundred years later. Faced with "this strange disease of modern life," the wisdom of statements like "the paths of glory lead but to the grave" would not seem deeply pertinent. A meeting with the scholar "on the wooden bridge," and a conversation in which such truths might be exchanged, was unimaginable. Reminding himself that the scholar is dead, and that their meeting cannot take place, Arnold is acknowledging that it is not in terms of ordinary social intercourse that the scholar-gipsy's wisdom may be made relevant to "modern life." In the next stanza Arnold goes on dreaming, but now it is no longer of the scholar's possible connections with society, but of his complete and necessary isolation:

> —No, no, thou hast not felt the lapse of hours.
>   For what wears out the life of mortal men?
>   'Tis that from change to change their being rolls:
>   'Tis that repeated shocks, again, again,
>   Exhaust the energy of strongest souls,
>   And numb the elastic powers.
>   Till having us'd our nerves with bliss and teen,
>   And tir'd upon a thousand schemes our wit,
>   To the just-pausing Genius we remit
>   Our worn-out life, and are—what we have been.
>   (141–150)

In denying the scholar's mortality, Arnold must also deny his own sense of identification with him, and when he does, he can no longer distinguish himself from the rest of society: a sudden distance is created in these lines between the scholar and the "I" of the poem. The "mortal men" who are spoken of in the third person in lines 142–143 have become "us" by the end of the stanza. Arnold must see himself as one of the "worn-out," "baffled" sufferers of the "strange disease"; there is no longer any question of placing that condition in some comfortably distant perspective. The most he can do is, on the one hand, to repeatedly urge the scholar-gipsy to "fly hence" (206), and, on the other, to imagine the transcendence he cannot himself achieve:

> Still nursing the unconquerable hope,
>   Still clutching the inviolable shade,
>   With a free onward impulse brushing through,
>   By night, the silver'd branches of the glade—
>   Far on the forest skirts, where none pursue,
>   On some wild pastoral slope
>   Emerge, and resting on the moonlit pales,
>   Freshen thy flowers, as in former years,
>   With dew, or listen with enchanted ears,
>   From the dark dingles, to the nightingales.
>   (211–220)

This rendezvous, in moonlight, "on some wild pastoral slope," sounds very much like the opportunity to "renew the quest" that Arnold promised his shepherd friend at the beginning of the poem. But if then it seemed unlikely that the shepherd would be back, it is even clearer now that Arnold himself is excluded from this sort of communion.

The stanza does more, however, than describe a moment of Keatsian communion: to get to the "moonlit pales" where he can "listen with enchanted ears," the scholar-gipsy is imagined in purposeful and vigorous motion—"with a free onward impulse brushing through." Elsewhere in the later stanzas, too, when he is compared with "mortal men," he is seen in satisfying activity:

> For early didst thou leave the world, with powers
>   Fresh, undiverted to the world without,
>   Firm to their mark, not spent on other things;
>   Free from the sick fatigue, the languid doubt,
>   Which much to have tried, in much been baffled, brings.
>   O Life unlike to ours!
>   Who fluctuate idly without term or scope. . . .
>   (161–167)

It is hard for the reader to reconcile this new sense of the scholar's activity with the memorable images of him "leaning backwards in a pensive dream" (77) or "sitting upon the river bank o'ergrown" (97) or "watching, all an April day" (107), in the stanzas where Arnold could imagine him as some sort of "kindred spirit," at ease in the Oxford countryside. In fact, only after Arnold has given up any hope of identifying himself with the scholar, only when it is clear that no relation, however fleeting, can exist between the scholar and the world of "mortal men," can Arnold imagine him as an active figure. And this is simply another way of saying that Arnold could find no satisfying images of activity in the world of "mortal men." Victorian society could only supply him with instances of "sick fatigue" (164) or "sick hurry" (204), and there was little to choose between them.

Whether or not these images say all that can be said about England in the 1850's, they tell us a good deal about Arnold's vision of society in this poem, by suggesting the source of that vision. When he insists on the absolute separation of his own world from that "inviolable shade" (212) where he imagines the scholar, or when he warns the scholar away from "our feverish contact" (221), for fear that his "glad perennial youth would fade,/ Fade, and grow old at last, and die like ours" (229–230), he is again echoing the Nightingale Ode, where Keats confronts

> The weariness, the fever, and the fret
>   Here, where men sit and hear each other groan;
> Where palsy shakes a few, sad, last grey hairs,
>   Where youth grows pale, and spectre-thin, and dies;
>   Where but to think is to be full of sorrow
>   And leaden-eyed despairs . . .

But just as the most Augustan qualities of Gray's *Elegy* were unavailable to Arnold, so were the most Romantic qualities of the "Ode to a Nightingale." Like Keats, Arnold is anxious to transcend his situation by some act of the imagination. But Keats limits himself in his Ode to dramatizing the dilemma of imaginative transcendence without resolving it: his "Do I wake or sleep?" doesn't demand an answer because it has no audience, yet the poem is not felt to be incomplete. Arnold could not be content with this sort of ambiguity, for he writes here, as always, with the consciousness of a body of readers who have no trouble at all in distinguishing dreams from facts. His "But what—I dream!" is an assertion, not a question, and the poem doesn't end there. It goes on, as we have seen, to suggest both the quality of the "dream"—as it is embodied in the scholar-gipsy—and its absolute distinction from waking life.

Shortly before the end of the poem, Arnold is firmly established back in the world where any satisfying activity is inconceivable, and convinced that, if imaginative acts transcending that world can take place at all, they take place "on some mild pastoral slope" beyond his reach. The situation is an intolerable one, and his sense of just how intolerable it is seems to have caused Arnold to shift his ground once more, and produce the startling simile with which the poem concludes:

> Then fly our greetings, fly our speech and smiles!
> —As some grave Tyrian trader, from the sea,
>   Descried at sunrise an emerging prow
> Lifting the cool-hair'd creepers stealthily,
>   The fringes of a southward-facing brow
>   Among the Aegean isles;
> And saw the merry Grecian coaster come,
>   Freighted with amber grapes, and Chian wine,
>   Green bursting figs, and tunnies steep'd in brine;
> And knew the intruders on his ancient home,
>
> The young light-hearted Masters of the waves;
>   And snatch'd his rudder, and shook out more sail,
>   And day and night held on indignantly
> O'er the blue Midland waters with the gale,
>   Betwixt the Syrtes and soft Sicily,
>   To where the Atlantic raves
> Outside the Western Straits, and unbent sails
>   There, where down cloudy cliffs, through sheets of foam,
>   Shy traffickers, the dark Iberians come;
> And on the beach undid his corded bales.
>   (231–250)

The effect of these stanzas is to bring back together the worlds whose complete separation seemed so certain, and so unbearable, just a few lines before. The "grave Tyrian trader" is, like the scholar-gipsy, imagined in flight, but his flight will not take him entirely beyond the limits of society: it will bring him into contact not with the nightingales of line 220, but with "mortal men," the "dark Iberians." Here would seem to be the image of purposeful activity that Arnold was apparently unable to introduce elsewhere in the poem.

Even more striking than this shift is the new sense of the conditions from which figures like the scholar, or the Tyrian trader, should flee. The world of "sick fatigue" and "sick hurry" has been transformed into that of the "merry Grecian coaster" with its marvelously attractive cargo. Even before the formal simile began, Arnold was already shifting the terms in which he described the symptoms of "infection" in Victorian society. When he contrasted the scholar's immortal vigor with "our worn-out life" (150), he seemed to be

speaking of (and for) that fraction of society who are conscious
sufferers—the irresolute and overthoughtful. And it is still with these
that Arnold associates himself in the twenty-third stanza:

> But fly our paths, our feverish contact fly!
> For strong the infection of our mental strife . . .
>   (221–222)

But in line 231 the scholar is being warned away from "our greet-
ings, . . . our speech and smiles": Arnold is imagining himself sharing the gestures of the hearty Philistines he will later satirize in his
prose. The reference to the "merry Grecian coaster" picks up this
hint, and the rest of the simile offers a vision of something suspici-
ously like Victorian commercial activity. It seems to picture a single,
happier world, where sensitive, "grave" figures can be in touch with
other men, yet where acts of lonely and heroic self-reliance are still
possible. But although the "grave Tyrian" is courageously steering
westward "to where the Atlantic raves," his mission is simply trade,
and his "indignant" response to the "merry Grecian coaster" could
almost be that of a salesman forced out of his territory by a vigorous
competitor. I doubt that Arnold intended this irony. More likely, he
meant to conclude his poem with an image which would both suggest
the value of solitude and maintain its relevance to Victorian life. But
the simile does neither very successfully. Instead it demonstrates once
more how hard it was for Arnold either to find such an image or to
stop looking for one.

Long before eighteenth century poets turned, with renewed interest, to images of rural solitude, that state had so often been contrasted with overt action in society that it had become not just the
conventional setting for contemplation, but a powerfully suggestive
metaphor for the inner life itself. "The Scholar Gipsy" is given shape
by its use of that metaphor, first in the manner of Gray, then in that
of Keats; but it is at those moments when the metaphor will no
longer work that Arnold's own presence in the poem is most strongly
felt. The pressure that drove him to abandon the pastoral language
of the Elegy and of the "Ode to a Nightingale," and to try to create
his own version of heroic solitude, was the need to imagine the inner
life as an activity with clear consequences in the outer world. Arnold
never found the poetic language that would allow him to do that,
however, and when he turned from poetry to prose, in the 1860's, it

was to produce not metaphors of the inner life engaging itself in society, but examples of that activity.

By 1880, when he wrote "The Study of Poetry" and "Thomas Gray," Arnold was entitled to think of his own poetical career as having been shaped and finally overwhelmed by an "age of prose." Perhaps in his sketch of Gray he recognized his own features as a poet. Or perhaps Gray's strongest appeal lay in his fitness as a model for the kind of "portrait of the artist" Arnold had in mind. In either case, it is appropriate that Arnold should have written of him not as the poet of the *Elegy*, who had created a rural solitary and placed him in a pertinent relation to contemporary society, but as the unproductive poet, the solitary for whom "the failure of sympathy in his contemporaries" had been "too great."

The Authority of the Narrative Voice in *Paradise Lost*

BY ANNE DAVIDSON FERRY

THE "World/ Of woe and sorrow," [1] the world of storms and shadows, of pain and loss, of variety and abundance to which Adam and Eve are banished at the end of Milton's epic, is the world in which the narrator and the reader of *Paradise Lost* now live. This fallen world is separated from the world of prehistory in which the action of the poem takes place by a gulf of time and change as impassable for mortal men as the "Illimitable Ocean" of Chaos. Without some kind of miraculous aid we would therefore be unable to envision the world of the poem, unable to conceive the figures who live in it or to understand their words and acts. The interpreter who endows us with the power to penetrate the world of the poem is its narrator, who is present without exception in every scene. His special nature and his special gifts enable him to interpret the unknown by contrasting it for us with our own familiar existence. His tone is controlled by his personal experience of this mortal world and his inspired vision of its contrast with the golden world of Eden before the Fall and of the Paradise to come. Our response to that tone is controlled by our awareness that we can *only* share the poet's vision by contrasting the world that is lost with the one world we have ever known, the world that is gained by Adam and Eve through the paradox of the fortunate Fall.

The narrator's authority to contrast the fallen world with his vision of a world which transcends our limited mortal understanding is established by Milton in his adaptation of the conventional epic invocation. These invocations to Books I, III, VII, and IX are essential to the pattern of the epic as introductions to the unknown places of the world of prehistory and as transitions from one phase of the nar-

---

[1] P.L., VIII, 332-3. All quotations from *Paradise Lost* are taken from *The Student's Milton*, ed. F. A. Patterson (New York, F. S. Crofts & Co., 1947).

rative to the other, but above all as a means of identifying the speaker
in the poem and characterizing his special powers of vision and song.
The opening of Book VII is a beautiful example:

> Descend from Heav'n *Urania*, by that name
> If rightly thou art call'd, whose Voice divine
> Following, above th' *Olympian* Hill I soare,
> Above the flight of *Pegasean* wing.
> The meaning, not the Name I call: for thou
> Nor of the Muses nine, nor on the top
> Of old *Olympus* dwell'st, but Heav'nlie borne,
> Before the Hills appeerd, or Fountain flow'd,
> Thou with Eternal wisdom didst converse,
> Wisdom thy Sister, and with her didst play
> In presence of th' Almightie Father, pleas'd
> With thy Celestial Song. Up led by thee
> Into the Heav'n of Heav'ns I have presum'd,
> An Earthlie Guest, and drawn Empyreal Aire,
> Thy tempring; with like safetie guided down
> Return me to my Native Element:
> Least from this flying Steed unrein'd, (as once
> *Bellerophon*, though from a lower Clime)
> Dismounted, on th' *Aleian* Field I fall
> Erroneous, there to wander and forlorne.
> Half yet remaines unsung, but narrower bound
> Within the visible Diurnal Spheare;
> Standing on Earth, not rapt above the Pole,
> More safe I Sing with mortal voice, unchang'd
> To hoarce or mute, though fall'n on evil dayes,
> On evil dayes though fall'n, and evil tongues;
> In darkness, and with dangers compast round,
> And solitude; yet not alone, while thou
> Visit'st my slumbers Nightly, or when Morn
> Purples the East . . .
>
> (*VII*, 1–30)

This passage occurs precisely in the middle of the poem, when "Half
yet remaines unsung." It is spoken by the narrator who is located here
in the middle of the universe, "Standing on Earth," a metaphor
for his role in the poem as mediator between contrasting worlds. Yet
although the narrator's point of view is always at the center of the
epic, it does not always proceed from this middle region, nor is it
simply bound by "Earthlie" limits. This speaker is identified here
(and in the other epic introductions) by two metaphors, each endow-
ing him with a double nature. He is pictured first as a bird, and as a
bird he is a limited creature, an "Earthlie Guest" whose flight must

be guided by the supernatural power of the Muse lest he fall to earth, "Erroneous, there to wander and forlorne," like fallen Adam and Eve in the world of their banishment. Yet as a bird whose flight is guided by the supernatural power of the Muse, he can "soare" above his creaturely limits, mounting to a vision of the "Heav'n of Heav'ns" and breathing the pure "Empyreal Aire." In the second and parallel metaphor the narrator is pictured as a blind bard who sings "with mortal voice," and here "mortal" implies not only that he is human but also that he is familiar with the deepest sufferings of men. He dwells in "darkness," "dangers," and "solitude" like Adam after the Fall, and his blindness is a metaphor for the limits of fallen vision, its inescapable pain and loss. But as inspired poet he is comforted by the Muse whose visitations penetrate his solitary world, purging his darkness with rays of celestial light. As bird or as blind bard the narrator can therefore sing to fallen men with sympathy born of his knowledge of what men suffer and with authority granted by a vision which transcends the world of change and death.

The narrator, pictured as either bird or blind poet or as both, is present at every moment in the poem. Sometimes he directly addresses the Muse, or the characters, or the reader considered as the whole of mankind. Sometimes he narrates, describes, or explains without directly identifying us. In other scenes he is himself the immediate audience or witness, endowed by his "Celestial Patroness" (IX, 21) with a vision of Hell or Heaven or Eden, of events which occurred before the creation of the world and time, or of happenings to come when the world and time shall be no more. The invocation to Urania, for example, is fittingly placed at the beginning of Book VII because by occurring just at the middle of the epic it defines the structure of the poem and of the universe and locates the narrator at the center of both. And the invocation also reminds us that although the previous episode of Books V and VI and the story of the Creation to follow in Book VII are told directly to Adam by Raphael, they are indirectly reported to us by the narrator, who repeats the angelic words which our mortal ears unaided could not hear. Nothing takes place in the poem which is not first spoken, or heard and retold by the narrative voice. Mood and meaning are consequently controlled by his tone, and unless the reader remains aware of the distinctive role of the narrative voice he is liable to misinterpret mood and meaning from the position in the fallen world to which he, unlike the narrator, is confined.

The role of the narrator as interpreter to the fallen reader of the unfallen world, the world "invisible to mortal sight" (III, 55), determines the distinctive style of *Paradise Lost*. Truths which, according to Milton's earlier outline for a play about the Fall of Man, were to be bodied forth in the allegorical "shapes" or "mask" of *Adam unparadiz'd*, are presented in the epic poem by the narrator's elaborately sustained pattern of contrasts between the "invisible" world and our own. The bird's song, the blind bard's vision reveal these contrasts, and the style created for the narrative voice is designed to express them. The bird spirals above the earth in his flight, and the blind poet turns inward for heavenly illumination, while the reader remains in the mortal world, which is always the ground from which he looks back at the world which he lost in Adam's Fall. We know that we are continually meant to view the events of the poem from this lower world of chance and change because from the first lines the narrator reminds us of our experience in this world at the same time that he reminds us of its absolute contrasts with the world envisioned in his poem. These reminders are made explicitly, in direct comments by the narrative voice, and implicitly, in many and varied devices which characterize Milton's style in *Paradise Lost*.

The most simple of these devices is the narrator's practice of explicitly distinguishing his own situation in space and time from that of the characters in his poem or of its readers. This device is particularly useful in the introduction of a new scene, which is almost inevitably an entrance into another world. The action of the epic begins in Hell, which existed before the creation of the world or time or men, and which in the theology of the poem provided the reason for the creation of that world and of man. The narrative voice must therefore interpret his vision of Hell to us, who know only our own world, and it is essential to Milton's design that we recognize the speaker's role. The description of Hell begins then with a reminder:

> Nine times the Space that measures Day and Night
> To mortal men, he with his horrid crew
> Lay vanquisht, rowling in the fiery Gulfe
> Confounded though immortal . . .
>
> (I, 50–53)

From the opening invocation of the epic we, its audience, have been prepared to include ourselves among "men." We therefore recognize this elaborate way of phrasing "a long time" or "as long as nine whole days" to be more than a means of giving epic dignity to the style. It is a reminder that we, the readers, have lost the unfallen ways of

knowing, that we are condemned to understand only in the dimension of time what the blind bard can conceive by other categories, by
"Space" or some nontemporal scheme analogous to the unity of
divine vision which encompasses all things simultaneously. Our identification not only as "men" but as "mortal" further reminds us that
we are both limited and fallen, corrupted by the "mortal tast" (I, 2)
which was the consequence of Satan's Fall. The sign of our mortality
is that we must measure all experience by the passing of time, the
diurnal course which to us means change and loss. We are meant
to remember that the events of the poem have already occurred, to
us and to the narrator, and that it is because of what happens in the
poem, because we and all men were corrupted by the Fall, that we
stand in need of a guide to correct our reading of it. The narrative
voice is our guide.

When the narrator reminds us of his complex relation to us, he
usually at the same time places us in relation to his story and his
characters. The description of Satan's host, for example, begins:

> . . . For never since created man,
> Met such imbodied force . . .
> (I, 573-574)

Here it is not our "mortal" condition, but our "created" nature
which we remember. We are God's creatures, like Satan, and our
creation is as much a result of his fall as is our mortality; both are
contained by God's will. In the beginning of the catalogue of devils
we are told:

> Nor had they yet among the Sons of Eve
> Got them new Names . . .
> (I, 364-365)

We are the "Sons of Eve." We are looking back with the poet on
our own history, when we gave the devils the names of false gods,
and the narrator is interpreting for us that history before the time
which as "Sons of Eve" we cannot see. We are also looking forward
to our own history, for to be "Sons of Eve" is to be redeemed as well
as fallen, and the inspired speaker is reminding us of events which he
can foresee and which we will share with him in the fullness of time.

With equal explicitness the speaker distinguishes his situation and
therefore his vision from the situation and point of view of his characters. The first description of Hell, which contrasts the narrator's

vision with the understanding of "mortal men," also sets him apart
from Satan:

> At once as far as Angels kenn he views
> The dismal Situation waste and wilde . . .
>   (I, 59–60)

"Angels kenn" is by implication more extensive than that of unaided
"men," since without help Satan can survey Hell, but more limited
than the narrator's whose Muse is omniscient:

>   . . . for Heav'n hides nothing from thy view
> Nor the deep Tract of Hell . . .
>   (I, 27–28)

Unlike Satan, the speaker knows not only what is past but also what
will be "Long after known in *Palestine*" (I, 80), the future outcome
of the events in which Satan is involved, by which he is bound. To
give one final illustration, the narrator describes the vision of the
angels descending to banish man to the fallen world as "A glorious
Apparition, had not doubt/ And carnal fear that day dimm'd *Adams*
eye" (XI, 211–212). The contrast between the narrator's view and
Adam's asserts that the speaker was in some sense present at the
scene to see and judge for himself, that his sight and judgment are
truer than our fallen vision or Adam's and are therefore the measure
of meaning in the epic.

The voice which so often by a phrase distinguishes itself from
reader and characters at times speaks out directly, even at length, to
comment upon the action, to extend it into the past or future, or to
interpret the motives of characters. These passages of "author-com-
ment" have been isolated by critics as if they were detachable—
didactic, nondramatic, undemonstrated statements in a work which
otherwise convincingly acts out its meanings in the manner of dramatic literature. A further assumption commonly associated with
this attitude is that these comments are made personally by Milton,
at moments when his private enthusiasms moved him to speak, as
in the hymn to wedded love, or at other times when he felt the
dramatic life of his poem might of its own accord dim his intention
to justify God's ways, or threaten the rightness of his theological
propositions. These critical notions involve a number of misconceptions which must be examined if we are to see how the narrative
voice in Milton's epic controls its mood and meaning.

It has been a misleading practice in criticism of the poem to call the narrator in *Paradise Lost* "Milton." In any narrative the author must find some sort of voice in which to speak, yet this voice, however much it may echo his private manner of talking, can never be equated with his total personality. Wordsworth in *The Prelude* invents a voice which he identifies as himself and he endows that speaker with a biography and attitudes and feelings selected from his own experience; yet if we call that voice "Wordsworth," we must remind ourselves that it is a sustained invention, the poet's conscious artistic creation. To call the narrator of *Paradise Lost* "Milton" is to violate his intention even more drastically. For it is part of Wordsworth's artistry to suggest the qualities of "speech," to deny art, to be "natural" rather than literary. The opening lines of *The Prelude* echo Milton's epic in part in order to deny its "poetical" qualities, its formality, its literary conventions. Milton's intention, on the other hand, is to exploit literary tradition, to intensify formality, to remind the reader continually of the elaborateness of his artistry. His poem is not talk but "song," not autobiography but inspired "vision." His narrator is not "himself," but a bird, or a bard who shares prophetic powers with Moses and Isaiah and Tiresias, who shares blindness with Milton himself, but also with Homer, with Samson, with the man cured by Jesus in the Gospel of John. To be sure, Milton's selection of images to portray the narrative voice must have been influenced by his own experience, and just as surely his private enthusiasms are often expressed by the speaker in the epic. But those images create an objectified voice with a distinct identity, tone, and manner, and the attitudes which the voice expresses are in keeping with that identity.

The other misconceptions involved in much critical discussion of the didactic comments in the epic are that only on these occasions do we become aware of a narrator and that his intention is to check the drift of the poem's dramatic life. Yet the speaker who utters the hymn to wedded love, the sermon on riches in Hell, the lecture on hypocrisy, the criticisms of the corrupt clergy—these "preachier" passages in the epic—is the same speaker who describes Hell and Eden, who witnesses the council in Heaven, hears the love speeches of Adam and Eve, retells the fables of mortal poets. The direct addresses by this voice are not nervous attempts to correct the dramatic direction of the poem. They are reminders of the speaker's identity, that the reader may never lose his awareness of that distinctive voice in its unique situation. The explicit comments by the narrative voice

are part of the total pattern, are essential to the expression of the
speaker's vision, which directs the reader's interpretation by controlling the mood and meaning of the poem.

To illustrate, the description of Satan's entrance into Eden, again
our introduction to a new and unknown world, provides a number
of examples of how our interpretation is controlled by the speaker
through direct comments working organically with all the other devices of narration.

We see the earthly Paradise for the first time on the occasion of
Satan's entrance into it, but we do not see it as he does. The assertion
often repeated by critics that we see Eden through Satan's eyes illustrates again the dangers of ignoring Milton's special narrator. These
critics have, I believe, recognized in the tone that the observer of
Eden is fallen, but have identified that tone with the character rather
than with the speaker, whose presence they tend to discount or forget.
We are told what sights confront Satan, but those sights are described for us in the language of the narrator, not the language of the
fallen archangel, so that our interpretation of the scene we are made
to imagine is the speaker's. His interpretation depends in part upon
his knowledge that Satan did in fact enter the Garden, but he sees it
independently of Satan's point of view and describes it so that we
will feel what Satan cannot feel. For example, as Satan stands outside
the Garden looking up at the trees which encircle and guard its wall,
we are told that this wall "to our general Sire gave prospect large/
Into his neather Empire neighbouring round" (IV, 144–145). We
are therefore taken into the scene while Satan is still excluded from
it. We are included in its physical bounds and in its moral history;
Adam is the "general Sire" of reader and poet but not of Satan. The
Garden can therefore never mean to Satan what it means to us because it was never his to lose. Next the speaker places us at a geographical distance from the character and his setting by showing us
the outlines of the mountain Satan wishes to climb (IV, 172). This
is not the way the hill looks to Satan "Now" trying to ascend it but
how it is envisioned by the narrator. Then we are given an account
of the undergrowth obstructing Satan's path:

> . . . so thick entwin'd,
> As one continu'd brake, the undergrowth
> Of shrubs and tangling bushes had perplext
> All path of Man or Beast that past that way . . .
> (IV, 174–177)

This is not the baffled report of the character himself, but an explanation in the voice of one who knows the nature of the obstacle and its history, knows that already on other occasions the tangled growths "had perplext" man and animals.

These distinctions in point of view are expressed in part by complicated alternations of tense. To Satan the setting is physically present; the events of the scene are happening to him in the present time, or belong to his immediate past or future. To the reader Eden and all the events of the story are long past (our final redemption is not a part of the action of the poem but the subject of a prediction made in the past about our future). The narrator as fallen man shares our previous history, but as a bird whose flight circles the world of the poem, or as blind bard inspired with supernatural vision, he miraculously experiences the events and places of prehistory in the present and miraculously sees into the future. His manipulations of tenses therefore transcend our experiences of time, logic, grammar. Satan's entrance into Eden begins, "So on he fares" (IV, 131). We watch as he "comes" in the present "Now nearer" (IV, 133) (Milton's equivalent in English for the Latin "historical present"); but then we are immediately told of the obstacle which "deni'd" him access to the Garden (IV, 137), and the description continues in the past tense until the "now purer aire/ Meets his approach" (V, 153–154). When later in the scene Satan as cormorant descends from his perch in the Tree of Life, his actions are described first in the present. He "alights" (IV, 396), but that verb is modified by the previous word "Then." Next we are told as if it were past action how he assumed whatever disguises "servd" his ends (IV, 398), but that action is modified by repetitions of "now." In this first description of Eden and throughout the poem by such shifts in tense we are introduced as to a scene in a dramatic work without being allowed to forget the voice which interprets to us all the meanings of the scene by its contrast with our own present.

Once we are told that "th' arch-fellon" (IV, 179) has lawlessly entered the Garden (and the use of the epithet reminds us again of the epic poet's presence), we are then given two similes which elaborate the action, as the preceding pair of similes had elaborated the sense impressions created by the scene:

> As when a prowling Wolfe,
> Whom hunger drives to seek new haunt for prey,
> Watching where Shepherds pen thir Flocks at eeve
> In hurdl'd Cotes amid the field secure,

>   Leaps o're the fence with ease into the Fould:
>   Or as a Thief bent to unhoord the cash
>   Of some rich Burgher, whose substantial dores,
>   Cross-barrd and bolted fast, fear no assault,
>   In at the window climbes, or o're the tiles;
>   So clomb this first grand Thief into Gods Fould . . .
>   (*IV, 183–192*)

By his self-conscious use of the conventional rhetorical device of extended simile, the narrator seems here (and elsewhere throughout the
epic) to be calling attention to his deliberate artistry. The similes do
tell us more about Satan, or more accurately, give us ways of feeling
for Satan and his victims. He is like a wolf or a thief or a bad priest
—dangerous, malevolent, greedy, furtive; man is like an innocent
lamb or a guarded but all the more naïve and vulnerable citizen. But
the extended similes also tell us about the narrator. He is a poet
familiar with the literary conventions of epic and a man familiar
with a life infinitely remote from the vision he is presenting. He
knows the fallen world of innocence destroyed, of petty viciousness,
of corruption even in God's Church. Yet his familiarity with mortal
verse and his experience of mortal vice do not destroy his understanding of the archetypal world. He can penetrate Satan's disguise (the
ambiguity of "Sat like a Cormorant" in line 196 suggests either that
Satan has assumed the form of the bird or that the poet is describing
him by comparing him to a shape more familiar to the reader). He
knows what Satan is thinking, knows what Satan does not know (IV,
197–198). Because he can penetrate beyond our perception of surfaces, this speaker can interpret for us the moral meaning of the
action:

>   So little knows
>   Any, but God alone, to value right
>   The good before him, but perverts best things
>   To worst abuse, or to thir meanest use.
>   (*IV, 201–204*)

This is not "Milton" suddenly intervening between Satan's point of
view and the reader in order to speak out on his favorite theme, mis-
used freedom. This is the same narrator who has described the hill,
the undergrowth and Satan's actions, who has uncovered his dissem-
bling and told us his hidden schemes. It is the same narrator who
will describe to us what "To all delight of human sense" (IV, 206) —
his, our own and Adam's—is exposed but not to Satan's, who "Saw

undelighted all delight" (IV, 286). It is the same voice who will pre-
dict "Our Death" (IV, 221) in which, with that phrase, he acknowledges and laments his share.

These didactic comments remind us of the narrator's presence and
his special vision in order that we may accept his moral interpretation
of the story. They are intended to remind us that what we see and
feel differs from Satan's experience of the Garden as it will differ
from unfallen Adam's. They are not *opposed* to the action of the
poem, but part of the total pattern of that action, not checks upon
our immediate responses to drama, but a means of expressing the
speaker's double point of view—his fallen knowledge, and his inspired
vision. To detach the moral comments as the sole expressions of the
narrator's attitude is to oversimplify and flatten it, to make the
speaker an unauthorized judge who lectures us like a prig just when
we are most involved in the story.

The scene of Adam's Fall illustrates most fully the way direct moral
comment works with other stylistic devices to express the whole
response of the narrator to his argument. Adam's "mortal tast" is
accompanied by a didactic statement:

> . . . he scrupl'd not to eat
> Against his better knowledge, not deceav'd,
> But fondly overcome with Femal charm.
> (IX, 997–999)

If this were all that the narrative voice had to say about the Fall of
man, we would reject the authority of that voice. If we assume these
lines to be spoken as if by a witness silent until now, who has clearly
not shared our response to the preceding scene, they seem to us altogether insufficient for the action. Taken by themselves as the sole
response of which the speaker is capable, these lines would characterize him as unfeeling and inhumane, complacent because willfully
blind to the complexities of human experience. For the scene of
Adam's Fall has evoked our sympathy, our sorrow, our fear, and even
our admiration, not a simple condemnation. This comment upon
Adam's action is, however, only part of the speaker's total response,
an organic and harmonious part. All the speeches which have moved
us have been reported to us by the narrative voice whose description
and narration form one whole with his moralizing. He, as well as the
reader, sympathizes with man's plight, acknowledges his greatness,
shares and laments his loss. It is in fact his complexity of response
which evokes our own.

The scene of Adam's Fall begins immediately after Eve's decision
to offer Adam the fruit that she thinks may kill him. The contrast
between her knowing self-interest and his still innocent ignorance
and generosity is created by the voice of the narrator:

> *Adam* the while
> Waiting desirous her return, had wove
> Of choicest Flours a Garland to adorne
> Her Tresses, and her rural labours crown
> As Reapers oft are wont thir Harvest Queen.
> (IX, 838–842)

Here the narrative voice expresses in its tone affectionate approval of
Adam's pretty action. The diction is very simple, and the repetition
of "her," emphasized by alliteration of *er* sounds, is contrasted with
the reiterated "I" of Eve's earlier speech. The one-line simile evokes
by the simplest allusion the pastoral world to which Adam still belongs but which to Eve is lost forever and to us is known only in
fables. He has our sympathy because he is like the simple reaper, as
natural and dignified and loving as his unpretentious gift, which we
now will never again please Eve, now aspiring above her station as
"Harvest Queen," now sophisticated and artificial in her taste, now
aided by the serpent's courtly "overpraising" (IX, 615). Contrasts in
the speaker's style in the next passage sustain our feelings for Adam:

> Great joy he promis'd to his thoughts, and new
> Solace in her return, so long delay'd;
> Yet oft his heart, divine of something ill,
> Misgave him; hee the faultring measure felt;
> And forth to meet her went, the way she took
> That Morn when first they parted; by the Tree
> Of Knowledge he must pass, there he her met,
> Scarse from the Tree returning; in her hand
> A bough of fairest fruit that downie smil'd,
> New gatherd, and ambrosial smell diffus'd.
> (IX, 843–852)

Adam is here pictured as the simple pastoral man, so fully in harmony
with nature that he can feel its "faultring measure," yet vulnerable
in his innocence, and in his love a prey to the temptations of a
woman who will speak to him in the language of a more subtle,
vicious world. His actions are described in metrically regular lines
composed of monosyllables and ending with accented verbs, while
Eve's smiling deviousness is suggested by words and lines having

feminine endings, irregular in meter but mellifluous with profus
alliteration.

The voice which controls our response in this narrative passage i
the voice of the same speaker who reports to us the speeches of th
characters. We are reminded of his presence as audience and witnes
by the interpretative phrases with which he introduces the speeches
phrases which suggest that he knows already what words will b
spoken, and can penetrate their meanings. Eve's "excuse" or "Apolo
gie" is introduced by such a phrase: "Which with bland words a
will she thus addrest" (IX, 855). The adjective "bland" warns u
that Eve's former sweetness has turned to soothing suavity spoke
"at will," which suggests that the smoothness of her words is calcu
lated, that calculated speech now comes easily to her, and that it i
no longer guided by her reason. This warning, given us in advanc
by the narrator, proves to be just when we hear Eve's speech. He
words *are* bland, calculated, willful. She glosses over, she exaggerates
she even tells lies. Next, the narrator, having rightly predicted hov
her words would sound to us, describes for us how Adam respond
to them:

> On th' other side, *Adam*, soon as he heard
> The fatal Trespass don by *Eve*, amaz'd,
> Astonied stood and Blank, while horror chill
> Ran through his veins, and all his joynts relax'd;
> From his slack hand the Garland wreath'd for *Eve*
> Down drop'd, and all the faded Roses shed:
> Speechless he stood and pale, till thus at length
> First to himself he inward silence broke.
> (IX, 888–895)

No "bland words" can deceive still unfallen Adam. He recognize
her action as a "Trespass" and a "fatal" one. His response is at onc
both physical and moral, like the response of Nature herself (IX
782–784). It is as if he felt already the chill touch of death, like th
faded roses in Eve's intended crown. His dilemma is expressed i
these lines—his love, his loss, his inevitable death—and the tone o
the narrative voice controls our feeling for his dilemma. Our fea
evoked in part by the ugly diction, harsh consonants and deep
sounds of the preceding lines—("Astonied stood and Blank, whil
horror chill/ Ran through his veins, and all his joynts relax'd")—i
mixed with the pity and nostalgia we feel at the allusion to th
blossoms of the lost pastoral world. With Adam and with the speake

we feel the beauty of the love which the garland symbolizes and we
grieve for the fading of that beauty at the same time that we feel the
horror of the choice which Adam does not hesitate to make. For in
the very act of choosing Eve he is destined to lose her, because they
and we will be doomed to mortality; and Adam knows this. His
speech is moving, passionate, romantic, but it is never deceived. He
knows that Eve is like the garland "Defac't, deflourd, and now to
Death devote" (IX, 901). He knows that they are "ruind" (IX,
906), and resigns himself to that ruin. His choice is to die *with* Eve,
not *for* her, and already his passion is a kind of beautiful self-concern.
Because his fear is for his own loneliness without her, not for her
plight, the very union which he claims indissoluble is severed by his
self-concern, and "I" becomes the center of his consciousness as it
became for Eve when she had eaten the forbidden fruit (IX, 804–
833) and as it had been for Adam before the completion of himself
in Eve's creation (VIII, 267–299). In these lines he is even speaking
to himself, which no longer means speaking to Eve.

By the tone of the narrative voice in the lines addressed to the
reader between Adam's first speech to himself and his words to Eve,
we know that the speaker who is our guide is not inhumanely indifferent to Adam's tragedy:

> So having said, as one from sad dismay
> Recomforted, and after thoughts disturbd
> Submitting to what seemd remediless,
> Thus in calme mood his Words to *Eve* he turnd.
> (IX, 917–920)

These lines express sympathy rather than condemnation, but the
words "seemd remediless" suggest that more than this simple response is appropriate to Adam's speech. Most obviously, these words
mean that it seems to Adam that he must resign himself to death
because he cannot choose to live without Eve. To the reader and the
speaker, also, this seems to be his irremediable plight, for we have
been moved by the familiar accents of passion and loneliness and
fear, emotions which seem to us inescapable in human experience.
We recognize and grieve for Adam's plight, which seems without
remedy to us in still another sense, because our experience of the
mortal world he is now to enter teaches us that Adam's choice of
Eve dooms him to lose her. Yet the verb "seem" in the poem is
almost always a warning against oversimplification. The narrative
voice uses it to remind us that unlike other epics, his cannot be

interpreted by mortal imaginations alone, that contrasted with our
fallen knowledge is the inspired vision of the blind bard whose darkness is purged by the inner light. What "seems" true to the fallen
reader and narrator and to Adam as he sins may not be divine truth.
The words "remediless" and "Recomforted" can then recall the truth
that Adam chooses to ignore, that there is a Remedy and a Com-
forter for those who use their free will to follow reason, love virtue,
obey God. His willful choice to share with Eve either "bliss or woe"
(IX, 916) is really a willful choice of "woe," a word consistently
associated in the poem with Hell. By choosing to follow Eve he is
rejecting the possibility of "bliss," the state of angels in Heaven and
of unfallen man in his "blissful Paradise" (IV, 208) on earth. The
choice is not inevitable; it is his sin that he chooses to think it is.

The warning, here gently hinted by the speaker, is justified by the
speeches which he then reports. Adam's words to Eve sound less
noble than his previous speech. Like Eve after her Fall, like the
monster Sin herself, he generates sins which quickly multiply: despair (926), ambition (935–937), blasphemy (938–941), and finally
the absurd pride to think as Satan does that the fame of the Creator
should depend upon the fate of the creature (948–950). Like Satan
he has chosen the "Lot" of the damned, and with Eve he will "under-
goe like doom" (IX, 953). His final appeal to the "Bond of Nature"
(IX, 956) is at once an excuse and a mistake. He is wrong to claim
that his nature predetermines him, since we have already been shown
the act of sin as a violation of nature, and wrong to insist that Eve
cannot be "severd" from him since he himself had earlier predicted
the danger of such an unnatural separation (IX, 252). Yet because
he has ceased to reason he can no longer recognize false from true
language. His last words before the Fall reverberate with irony which
only the narrator and the reader can hear. When Adam says "to
loose thee were to loose my self" (IX, 959), he means only that he
cannot live without Eve. But to us, because we have an inspired
interpreter, the words mean also that he has in fact lost Eve, for she
will die, at the same time that he has also lost himself, as Satan is
lost, as he knew Eve to be "lost" (IX, 900), because he will die and
because he is damned.

Eve's lies in the following speech justify even more loudly the narrator's warning that to fallen minds there is a discrepancy between
what "seems" and what is. By lying, she is deliberately exploiting that
discrepancy at the same time that she is its helpless victim. The one-

ness with Adam which she seeks is lost forever. The "happie trial" (IX, 975) in which she triumphs is a mockery (and as terrible a distortion of the heavenly trial of love in Book III as was Satan's hateful sacrifice in Book II), for, although she cannot see it, both the meaning of the word "love" and the capacity to feel it have already been transformed by the Fall.

These speeches prepare us to question Eve's concept of "enobl'd" love (IX, 992). Adam's speech to himself was beautiful, with the beauty of mortal poetry which celebrates human love and loss; but the narrative voice has warned us to question that poetry, and the warning is brilliantly justified in fallen Adam's first speech when he proves himself (by Milton's echoes of Homeric passages) to be the ancestor of Paris, who threw away honor for love and whose passion was fabled to have brought mankind a "world of woe":

> For never did thy Beautie since the day
> I saw thee first and wedded thee, adorn'd
> With all perfections, so enflame my sense
> With ardor to enjoy thee, fairer now
> Then ever, bountie of this vertuous Tree.
> (IX, 1029–1033)

The metaphors of fire which are repeated here in the lines spoken by and about Adam tell us that already he shares Satan's "Lot." The same "hot Hell" (IX, 467) burns within them both. Love has become lust and Eden is Hell.

The didactic comment which the narrative voice speaks as Adam eats is not then an isolated interruption by "Milton" intended to check our unqualified sympathy for the drama of Adam's Fall. It is a part of the total pattern of the speaker's feelings as he reports and interprets the Fall to fallen men. It is spoken by the voice of the same narrator who has been moved by Adam's love speech, yet who knows and cautions against the limits of that feeling, who finds that caution justified by the cheapening of Adam's language which comes with the degeneration of his emotions. Yet even at this moment of severest condemnation the speaker does not lose all his sympathy for Adam, "fondly overcome with Femal charm" (IX, 999). The word "fondly" means not only "foolishly" but "lovingly," and the word "charm" suggests that Eve's powers do exist, that about them too he is not deceived, that her beauty and "sweet Converse and Love" (IX, 909), almost like the magical enchantments of a Circe, have overcome him. Adam therefore deserves our condemnation as a willful sinner at the same time that he retains our sympathy as a helpless victim.

The narrator's lines immediately after this comment intensify the expression of his grief and sympathy for Adam:

> Earth trembl'd from her entrails, as again
> In pangs, and Nature gave a second groan,
> Skie lowr'd, and muttering Thunder, som sad drops
> Wept at compleating of the mortal Sin
> Original . . .
>
> (IX, 1000–1004)

The speaker's response to the Fall is one with Nature's. The earth is torn by the horror of the act (as it was to be again when Christ died to redeem Adam's Fall), at the same time that the sky weeps with sorrow for man's suffering and death. Heaven itself expresses both anger and grief in the thunderbolts of wrath and the waters of mercy. This passage marks the climax of feelings evoked by the scene of Adam's Fall. These feelings are shared by the reader only because his interpretation of the scene has been controlled by the narrative voice, by the fusion of direct moral comment with the many other devices of language used to express the wholeness of the blind bard's vision, the harmony of the bird's song.

In this scene and throughout the poem didactic comment is expressed in a language of statement, in diction which largely avoids allusiveness, figurative concreteness, or the evocation of a multiplicity of conflicting feelings. This is one kind of language which characterizes the blind bard, now cut off from the changing light of nature, from the colors and surfaces of things and the varied ways of men. This is the language in which he prays for the inner light to "see and tell/ Of things invisible to mortal sight" (III, 54–55), and the very abstractness of these statements is one means of reminding us that the speaker's moral vision of his argument surpasses our fallen understanding by its steadiness, its wholeness, its purity.

Yet even in his role as moral interpreter, prophetic seer, he never ceases to admit that we share experiences and values with him. He recognizes the possibilities of error and confusion and vice which we meet daily, and at the same time trusts our rationality and virtue. He assumes that we recognize and deplore with him the corruption of the clergy, that we too condemn hypocrisy, that we are also appalled by the "bought smile/ Of Harlots, loveless, joyless, unindeard,/ Casual fruition" (IV, 765–767). He is even capable of a comment which seems to me effective in its mild amusement and sympathy— "No fear lest Dinner coole" (V, 396)—because it reminds us that he shares with us a world different in its homeliest details from the one which he is interpreting to us. The language of statement has the authority of the divine light which it reflects, but it never loses sympathy with the characters in the poem or loses faith in the capacity of the reader's mind to be illumined by the inner light, his feelings to be stirred by heavenly harmonies.

The Poet-Readers of Wallace Stevens

BY THOMAS B. WHITBREAD

WALLACE STEVENS, especially in his prolific last two decades, placed very high value on the activity of a poet. In accepting the National Book Award for his *Collected Poems*, he said,

> I think then that the first thing that a poet should do as he comes out of his cavern is to put on the strength of his particular calling as a poet, to address himself to what Rilke called the mighty burden of poetry and to have the courage to say that, in his sense of things, the significance of poetry is second to none.

And in a statement "On Poetic Truth," a year or so before his death, he remarks that the function of poetry is to give us

> the sense that we can touch and feel a solid reality which does not wholly dissolve itself into the conceptions of our own minds. It is the individual and particular that does this. And the wonder and mystery of art, as indeed of religion in the last resort, is the revelation of something "wholly other" by which the inexpressible loneliness of thinking is broken and enriched.

Poets can give readers such revelations. And in several of his later poems Stevens simultaneously considers and exhibits the process of such revelation, the act of communicating a sense of a reality other than one's own mind. The communication can take place between Stevens or any poet and his reader only when the poet speaks his sense of reality most faithfully and the reader most attentively hears the poet's words. An implicit compact between poet and reader must precede illumination. It is no accident, then, that in the central poems I shall consider, Stevens, as poet, takes on the *persona* of a reader of reality while often talking to, or about, a character who is also a reader. In these poems, Stevens explores the poetic powers of

the mind through dramatizing various imaginative ways in which
characters who are readers view summer reality. My aim in reading
these poems is to show the drama of each, map the territory Stevens
explores, and define the revelation he gives of the value of poetry.

The most motionless of Stevens' characters, and one of the most
moving, is the reader in "The House Was Quiet and the World Was
Calm":

> The house was quiet and the world was calm.
> The reader became the book; and summer night
>
> Was like the conscious being of the book.
> The house was quiet and the world was calm.
>
> The words were spoken as if there was no book,
> Except that the reader leaned above the page,
>
> Wanted to lean, wanted much most to be
> The scholar to whom his book is true, to whom
>
> The summer night is like a perfection of thought.
> The house was quiet because it had to be.
>
> The quiet was part of the meaning, part of the mind:
> The access of perfection to the page.
>
> And the world was calm. The truth in a calm world,
> In which there is no other meaning, itself
>
> Is calm, itself is summer and night, itself
> Is the reader leaning late and reading there.

In this act of reading, time, which goes on—as words follow one
another in the poem—is metaphorically, almost mystically, transcended through a partly attained, partly wished-for unity, in being
quiet and calm, among the reader, the book, and summer night. And
the reader's sense of this unity, including mastery over change
through becoming part of a repetition final in itself, is analogically
represented by Stevens through his repetitions of words and phrases
in the structure of the poem. Line four contains the same words as
line one, but says more, does more than evoke a quiet house and a
calm world, because by line four we know there are a reader in the
house and summer night in the world, and that reader and summer
night, bringing with them quiet house and calm world, are merging
in "the book." "The book" is first an actual volume, being read by
"The reader," who is so wrapped up, so rapt, in it, that one can say
he "became the book." But if "summer night/ Was like the con-

scious being of the book," perhaps the book includes the reader's surroundings, the atmosphere, which he senses as live, breathes in, in the act of reading the very book which, after all, he has "become."

"The words were spoken," by the reader who is the book, "as if there was no book." This simile, as is often the case in later Stevens, is quickly qualified:

> The words were spoken as if there was no book,
> Except that the reader leaned above the page,
>
> Wanted to lean, wanted much most to be
> The scholar to whom his book is true, to whom
>
> The summer night is like a perfection of thought.

There *was* a book, with pages, over one of which the reader "leaned," wanting to lean, wanting with utmost intensity, more than anything else, to find truth in his book, to sense the summer night as like a perfection of thought: that is, to be *able* so to sense the summer night *because* he feels a perfection of thought in himself, because to him his book is true. The reader, then, had attained such unity, *except* that he "wanted much most" to attain it—a version, in the life of the mind, of a sense of happiness dissipated or diminished by conscious striving for a sense of happiness. Or, he had reached a degree of unity, and wanted more. He wanted to be a "scholar"; he was only a "reader." Still, the essence of what Stevens is saying, with implicit approval, is that this reader has attained a certain condition of truth, a moment of full, completed being, a partnership with reality:

> The truth in a calm world,
> In which there is no other meaning, itself
>
> Is calm, itself is summer and night, itself
> Is the reader leaning late and reading there.

If the reader could go much further in this direction, enter most fully the realms of quiet and calm, and stay there, a permanent scholar, he would be, in this direction, immensely real. Completely mastering repetition, he would be a more than ordinary man, even greater and more unusual than the "man-hero" Stevens posits in *Notes Toward a Supreme Fiction*:

> Perhaps,
> The man-hero is not the exceptional monster,
> But he that of repetition is most master.

He would be a scholar-hero. To do this, he would have to transcend time. And time is substantively transcended only by death. If our individual lives, as they go on, are all we can know, are, for us, reality —a belief often asserted by Stevens in both poems and essays, as readers of "Sunday Morning" and other repeatedly anthologized poems have overemphasized—the condition of time is always with us and its limitation is final. All that people do, including writing and reading poems, takes place within time. And any reader, confronted with this limit, will, when he closes his book, lose whatever sense of unity he may have had, prepare for bed, and, perhaps, reflect on the condition of time. Such a human reader and his superhuman antithesis figure in "All the Preludes to Felicity" (*The Pure Good of Theory*, I):

> It is time that beats in the breast and it is time
> That batters against the mind, silent and proud,
> The mind that knows it is destroyed by time.
>
> Time is a horse that runs in the heart, a horse
> Without a rider on a road at night.
> The mind sits listening and hears it pass.
>
> It is someone walking rapidly in the street.
> The reader by the window has finished his book
> And tells the hour by the lateness of the sounds.
>
> Even breathing is the beating of time, in kind:
> A retardation of its battering,
> A horse grotesquely taut, a walker like
>
> A shadow in mid-earth . . . If we propose
> A large-sculptured, platonic person, free from time,
> And imagine for him the speech he cannot speak,
>
> A form, then, protected from the battering, may
> Mature: A capable being may replace
> Dark horse and walker walking rapidly.
>
> Felicity, ah! Time is the hooded enemy,
> The inimical music, the enchantered space
> In which the enchanted preludes have their place.

One might think of Eliot's "Only through time time is conquered." But Stevens isn't saying this. In his view, time is not conquered, not, finally, opposed, but simply known. Time is the limiting condition in which even the "large-sculptured, platonic person, free from time" has to be imagined, in which poems have to be written, in which both the seeming transcendence of time which reading can bring and the inevitable end of seeming and of reading—both the live imaginative experience and the informed meditations which follow it for Keats's gazer at the Grecian urn, both the flight from and the return to his "sole self" for Keats's listener to the nightingale's song —must take place. In "All the Preludes to Felicity," time is imaged in a series of similar but not identical roles, bluntly announced: the heart, thumping; the thought of death, battering against the self-conscious mind, elevated and aloof, which thinks of itself as in time; a galloping horse, first located within the heart, then riderless on a road at night, in both cases heard by the mind, which self-consciously "sits listening" in a chair, possibly by a window, above both road and heart; a rapid walker in the street, heard and read as signifying late-ness by the reader who "has finished his book"; and, in its way, breathing, which retards the battering of time by opposing its own beating, its inhale-exhale, "A horse grotesquely taut, a walker like/ A shadow in mid-earth . . ."—a horse caught in a vise, like the lungs within the rib cage, yet continually moving in place, shadow-walker in mid-body. "Dark horse and walker walking rapidly," heartbeat and breathing and the battering thought of death, *may* be replaced by "A capable being," "A form . . . protected from the battering," *if*: "If we propose/ A large-sculptured, platonic person, free from time,/ And imagine for him the speech he cannot speak. . ."

But proposing, imagining, saying "if" is easy—we can, and Stevens often does, make up such major men and give them tongues—easy, that is, compared with somehow bringing such a "capable being" into being, let alone maturity. The "large-sculptured, platonic per-son" has tremendous imaginative life as a desired ideal. But even as imagined, though free from time, and because free from time, "he cannot speak." It is no more likely that such a person will exist than that the reader in "The House Was Quiet . . ." will become the scholar he wants "much most" to be. Yet the desire for freedom from time, for the felicity of eternal life (forgetting the shadows, which try to justify death, of Tithonus and the Struldbrugs), is intensely real. Desire and doubt jostle in the ironic exclamation, "Felicity, ah!" And the irony of imagined timelessness and all "en-chanted," sung, "preludes" having their place in "the enchantered space" of time is central to the final sentence:

> Time is the hooded enemy,
> The inimical music, the enchantered space
> In which the enchanted preludes have their place.

Imaginings, poems (including this one), the "preludes" of the red robin, all of "the vast repetitions final in/ Themselves and, therefore, good" (*Notes Toward a Supreme Fiction*, "It Must Give Pleasure," IX) are subject to time the serpent, time the siren, time the ambiguous enchanter of the world in which we live, the enchanter who, master of change, gives each man more or less chance to compose enchanted preludes before he dies.

When we read the poems in which Stevens proposes various "platonic persons," attempting in imagination to transcend the limits of time and place, we should remember, and will often be reminded by the poet, that he is fully aware that all of a man, including his mind, lives in time, and that persons imagined as out of time are not, in a basic physical sense, real. What then is the poet-reader's relation to reality? The human mind, despite all its saying nay to old myths, still wants to say yes. And the poet, conceiving new metaphors, can provide the reader with new texts, not chapters of Holy Writ, but poems to which a yes, however provisional, hedged, and momentary, can be said.

> To say the solar chariot is junk
>
> Is not a variation but an end.
> Yet to speak of the whole world as metaphor
> Is still to stick to the contents of the mind
>
> And the desire to believe in a metaphor.
> It is to stick to the nicer knowledge of
> Belief, that what it believes in is not true.
>
> ("Fire-monsters in the Milky Brain")

This is a very nice, and for Stevens a very necessary, knowledge. "Poetry is the supreme fiction, madame"; *and* "The greatest poverty is not to live/ In a physical world, to feel that one's desire" for a platonic person in whom to believe "Is too difficult to tell from despair." Yet, in a physical world which, clearly seen, contains a great deal of poverty and ill, we happily do have the color and delight of poetic uses of language, of metaphorical heightenings, subtleties, variations in our descriptions of the real:

> Natives of poverty, children of malheur,
> The gaiety of language is our seigneur.

Stevens' view of the relationship between reality and the imagination is most clearly stated in a passage from remarks made in accepting

an honor at Bard College in 1948, printed in *Opus Posthumous* under
the title "Poetic Acts":

> . . . Ordinarily the poet is associated with the word, not with the
> act; and ordinarily the word collects its strength from the imagination
> or, with its aid, from reality. The poet finds that as between these two
> sources: the imagination and reality, the imagination is false, what-
> ever else may be said of it, and reality is true; and being concerned
> that poetry should be a thing of vital and virile importance, he com-
> mits himself to reality, which then becomes his inescapable and ever-
> present difficulty and inamorata. In any event, he has lost nothing;
> for the imagination, while it might have led him to purities beyond
> definition, never yet progressed except by particulars. Having gained
> the world, the imaginative remains available to him in respect to all
> the particulars of the world. Instead of having lost anything, he has
> gained a sense of direction and a certainty of understanding. He has
> strengthened himself to resist the bogus. He has become like a man
> who can see what he wants to see and touch what he wants to touch.
> In all his poems with all their enchantments for the poet himself,
> there is the final enchantment that they are true. The significance of
> the poetic act then is that it is evidence. It is instance and illustration.
> It is an illumination of a surface, the movement of a self in the rock.
> Above all it is a new engagement with life.

The poet's word is strong as expressing (1) the imagined, as if it
were real, or (2) the real, variously imagined. But since the imagination is false, reality true, the imagination, if its poems are to compel
the reader's feeling credence, is dependent on particulars of experience. The poet, therefore, must first of all gain the real world as
obstacle and beloved. He can then with confidence imaginatively
describe, represent, meditate upon all the particulars of the world,
limited only by his own predilections and affinities, his own arenas
of interest. And he will have a sense of truth giving body to both
what he senses and what he says, both his responses to the imagined
real and his poems about it. His "enchanted preludes" will be firmly
rooted in time and place, "difficulty and inamorata." Each of
Stevens' poems, to use his terms describing "the significance of the
poetic act," may be taken as giving its unique "evidence," "instance,"
"illustration," "illumination," "movement," its "new engagement
with life."

A character very like the poet who "commits himself to reality"
is the "realist" in "Phosphor Reading by His Own Light"—another
reader in a summer night, but reading the night, not a book, in an
attitude of passive receptiveness, rather than desire for any transcendence:

It is difficult to read. The page is dark.
Yet he knows what it is that he expects.

The page is blank or a frame without a glass
Or a glass that is empty when he looks.

The greenness of night lies on the page and goes
Down deeply in the empty glass . . .

Look, realist, not knowing what you expect.
The green falls on you as you look,

Falls on and makes and gives, even a speech.
And you think that that is what you expect,

That elemental parent, the green night,
Teaching a fusky alphabet.

Reading the first line directly after the title, we imagine that the speaker is Phosphor, saying how hard it is to read by his own not very bright light. The immediate revelation, implied by "he" in the second line, that the speaker is talking about Phosphor contradicts but doesn't erase this notion. As a result, when the voice turns from description to address—"Look, realist, not knowing what you expect" —we have some sense of internal monologue, of someone talking to himself, telling himself how to be, like an enlightened Phosphor. Our sense of a merger between Phosphor and the speaker is tenuous compared with our certainty that the speaker is talking about Phosphor in the first six lines, then, in the last six, talking to a "realist" who is primarily someone other than the speaker, and could be any reader of the poem who, while reading it, becomes imaginatively engaged in its particular demanded role of active audience. But, however dim, fuzzy, or phosphorescent it may be, our sense that what we have here may be one character regarding himself severally—a view encouraged by the title—complicates and softens the differences between the two halves of the poem.

These differences, characteristically presented through repeated phrases significantly altered, seem clear. Phosphor "knows what it is that he expects." As a result, he sees nothing: "The page is a blank or a frame without a glass/ Or a glass that is empty when he looks," a mirror giving no reflection, no fullness of face, no imaged substance. "The greenness of night lies on the page and goes/ Down deeply in the empty glass," now a glass whose contents may have gone down deeply into Phosphor; he is perhaps too drunk with his sureness, his knowledge and expectations to see "The greenness of night" lying "on the page," deep down "in the empty glass." For him the page is dark and blank, the glass empty. Phosphor's own light, it seems, is inadequate for reading the green night. In contrast, the realist is told to "Look, . . . not knowing what you expect," without any preconceptions about what he might see. His open receptiveness is rewarded by his being clad, made, and given speech by the "green" above and around him:

> The green falls on you as you look,
>
> Falls on and makes and gives, even a speech.
> And you think that that is what you expect,
>
> That elemental parent, the green night,
> Teaching a fusky alphabet.

The realist thinks he expects, as and after it happens, such falling-on, such embrace and teaching from the elemental reality of his situation, "the green night." This parental night gives him words about itself, "a speech." It teaches "a fusky"—"dusky" merged with the Latin *fuscus*—"alphabet." It makes him a maker. The moral is plain: this realist, as poet, has gained his moment and corner of the world, and has done so by committing himself to the care of whatever he might see. To be taught the "fusky alphabet" of the green night, one must be ready to receive its mantle; one cannot be phosphorescent, because light obscures and dissipates darkness. The dark must be read in the dark. Poor Phosphor, unlike the realist, is limited by his own light, his certainty.

So much seems clear. But the whole poem *is* titled "Phosphor Reading by His Own Light." And our initial sense of merging identities still lingers at its end, drawing our attention to a wry irony lurking in the verb "think": "And you think that that is what you expect." The speaker is gently mocking his realist, the more nicely if he's talking to himself: you *think* that you expect being given a speech by the green night, but how can this be, when you looked, and look, not knowing what you expect? The mockery becomes more than slightly sardonic when we reflect that *thinking* one is getting what one expects is a step away from not expecting anything in particular and a step toward *knowing* what one expects and, therefore, being unlikely to get it. Can the realist be in danger of becoming like Phosphor? This concealed question, typical of Stevens' wit in its implicitness and acidity, gives the title a hidden ironic point in relation to the last half of the poem in addition to its obvious relevance to the first, and strengthens our view that the poem is in essence a dramatic rendering of two ways of approaching reality—the one, by one's own lights, the other, by reality's lights or lack of them. The surface point of the poem is that the second approach is much more likely to lead to vivid experience of reality and to responsive poems. The concealed point, which may well be the more basic, is that the realist's approach easily slides into Phosphor's in any one person: the realist is very likely to turn his spontaneous experience into an expectation of the same which precludes it; to avoid seeing blankness and emptiness, he must set aside his knowledges, must tell himself over and over again to come freshly and openly to whatever is. This has to be so because things, in time, change: while the closest resemblances can be felt between this green night and that, the two are, finally, not the same. Each spontaneity is unique. And each green night, in however many ways describable as like all the others, must be approached with respect and love as itself in order to be read and learned from anew.

Is there any relation between a poet's reading reality in this way and a traditional metaphysic, or a traditional theological account of reality? The question is answered in "God Is Good. It Is a Beautiful Night":

> Look round, brown moon, brown bird, as you rise to fly,
> Look round at the head and zither
> On the ground.
>
> Look round you as you start to rise, brown moon,
> At the book and shoe, the rotted rose
> At the door.
>
> This was the place to which you came last night,
> Flew close to, flew to without rising away.
> Now, again,
>
> In your light, the head is speaking. It reads the book.
> It becomes the scholar again, seeking celestial
> Rendezvous,
>
> Picking thin music on the rustiest string,
> Squeezing the reddest fragrance from the stump
> Of summer.
>
> The venerable song falls from your fiery wings.
> The song of the great space of your age pierces
> The fresh night.

The two statements of the title, considered in sequence, could imply God as cause, through His Goodness, of the Beautiful Night. More likely, they are two ways of saying the same thing, the two halves of an equation. In fact, in the body of the poem, much more is said about the night than about God, who possibly lurks luminously, somewhat like "a large-sculptured, platonic person," within the "celestial/ Rendezvous" which "the scholar" seeks, but otherwise "He" seems out of the picture. We may think of "Less and Less Human, O Savage Spirit," where Stevens says that "If there must be a god in the house, must be," he should move "silently" as "moon-light." In "God Is Good. It Is a Beautiful Night" there is a physical house, implied by "the door," and a more important metaphysical house, floored by "the ground" and roofed by "great space." Within both houses God is equally silent in this poem, but the moon-bird has a "venerable song" which "falls" from its "fiery wings," much as the green falls on the realist in "Phosphor Reading . . ." This song, like the piper's "ditties" on Keats's urn, is audible only to the imagination; it is imaged as an arrow of light which "pierces/ The fresh night"; its burden or substance is "of the great space of" the "age" of the aliform moon, of the vast distances it has traversed in space and time, essentially of its own ancientness. Stevens is very sure (in "Less and Less Human . . .") that gods, who seem to him as alien to man's imaginings and speakings as are dead philosophies —"Plato's ghost," an insubstantial shade, or "Aristotle's skeleton," fleshless, bloodless—should be both physically and metaphysically quiet, should shut up if they have to hang around, should stick to the wall like starry wallpaper. He is equally sure that the moon, though, like a god, nonhuman, actually exists: being real, it can stimulate the imagination into seeing it as a bird, its light as song.

The speaker so sees the moon in the first line of "God Is Good. . .": "Look round, brown moon, brown bird, as you rise to fly." He directs its attention to "the head and zither" both "On the ground." The head first strikes us as disembodied, an object as separate and discrete as the zither. More likely, the head is the most important part of a person stretched out supine on the grass, perhaps a person who has played the zither and laid it down. But "the book and shoe, the rotted rose/ At the door," further objects at which the brown moon is told to look, emphasize our sense of the head as sufficient in detachment. At the same time, we gather that the person lying is at least a potential reader, perhaps barefoot, prob-ably on a lawn beside a house in which he lives, and that the season is late summer ("the rotted rose"). This person, reclining there, seems ready to take things in. Perhaps he, or, in some sense, "the place" in which he is, took the moon in the night before: "This was the place to which you came last night,/ Flew close to, flew to without rising away."

"Now, again," as the moon-bird departs, rising-flying, "In your light," the speaker tells it, "the head is speaking. It reads the book." The speech is primarily within the mind of the head, reading; and, since moonlight seems a necessary condition of the head's speaking, the book, as in "The House Was Quiet and the World Was Calm," becomes more than a volume, becomes the reader's surroundings. Also, very much as in "The House Was Quiet . . . ," the reading head "becomes the scholar again, seeking celestial/ Rendezvous." Here "the scholar" is in a situation like that of the reader who "wanted much most to be/ The scholar to whom his book is true, to whom/ The summer night is like a perfection of thought." Both readers have attained a partial elevation, a partial harmony with reality. But, as the reader in "The House Was Quiet . . ." doesn't reach the full truth and "perfection of thought" he desires, so the head-reader-scholar in "God is Good. . ." doesn't find the "celestial/ Rendezvous" he seeks. What he does find is not God, but a beautiful night; which is, after all, something, not nothing. And he finds words about the night: in a larger sense, the scholar-poet, as equivalent to the speaker, finds the words of this poem; as character within the poem, the words which are inadequate "music" played on one decaying "string" of an instrument which, if it is the earlier "zither," is now within his head. Within the impregnating light of the moon-bird, the head is speaking, reading, becoming the scholar, seeking transcendence, and

> Picking thin music on the rustiest string,
> Squeezing the reddest fragrance from the stump
> Of summer.

Summer, like the "thin music," is diminished, near its end, and at its most concentrated and distilled. In expressing his sense of summer, the head (or poet) squeezes it dry, milks it of its "reddest fragrance," its odorous essence, the last drop of its deepest blood. Soon the rotted rose will completely decay, summer will yield to autumn, the man will go indoors. But a moment has been captured: the light-song of the moon-bird has mantled the man, granted him

as its realistic reader faithful speaking of what he sees and feels, of
his late-summer moment within the dwarfing cycles of time and
space through which the moon moves. Stevens is not far from his
character, his words are very much a reading of the book, in the
speaker's final address to the ancient flier:

> The venerable song falls from your fiery wings.
> The song of the great space of your age pierces
> The fresh night.

The poet-reader transcends his reality through imagining it in the
way he does, in the metaphors of his reading, his poem. And he
transcends late-summer decay only by being fully open to it, by coming to it as realist, not as Phosphor, by accepting and embracing it as
difficulty and inamorata.

Stevens asserts the poet's power and value as imaginative reader
with climactic force in the last poem I consider, "Large Red Man
Reading":

> There were ghosts that returned to earth to hear his phrases,
> As he sat there reading, aloud, the great blue tabulae.
> They were those from the wilderness of stars that had expected
> more.
>
> There were those that returned to hear him read from the poem
> of life,
> Of the pans above the stove, the pots on the table, the tulips
> among them.
> They were those that would have wept to step barefoot into
> reality,
>
> That would have wept and been happy, have shivered in the frost
> And cried out to feel it again, have run fingers over leaves
> And against the most coiled thorn, have seized on what was ugly
>
> And laughed, as he sat there reading, from out of the purple
> tabulae,
> The outlines of being and its expressings, the syllables of
> its law:
> Poesis, poesis, the literal characters, the vatic lines,
>
> Which in those ears and in those thin, those spended hearts,
> Took on color, took on shape and the size of things as they are
> And spoke the feeling for them, which was what they had lacked.

The "Large Red Man" is the Essential Poet, and his book is nothing less than everything that is: "the poem of life," "the outlines

of being and its expressings," the subject of the poem and the poem itself. His all-inclusive poem-subject naturally embraces both the real, the actual—"the literal characters"—and the imaginative, the oracular—"the vatic lines." Most important, his phrases express *feeling*: they imbue the "ears" and the "thin," the "spended hearts" of his ghostly listeners not only with "color," with "shape and the size of things as they are," but with "the feeling for them," for things as they are and for the listeners, which was what his listeners "had lacked." Nowhere does Stevens "compound the imagination's Latin with/ The lingua franca et jocundissima" more successfully and more movingly than in this poem, which both describes and itself represents such speaking, such compounding.

The "Large Red Man Reading" is, then, Stevens' ideal poet. He is a complete man-hero, in fuller mastery of repetitions than the momentarily elevated, momentarily speech-given poet-readers we have met earlier: the reader of "The House Was Quiet . . . ," the realist of "Phosphor Reading . . . ," the scholar of "God Is Good. . . ." He is Stevens' most admirable and most major kind of major man. And he is most admirable precisely in giving feeling to people who have need of it. Through his expressings of being, his faithful imaginings of reality, he communicates the life of feeling to

> . . . those that would have wept to step barefoot into reality,
>
> That would have wept and been happy, have shivered in the frost
> And cried out to feel it again, have run fingers over leaves
> And against the most coiled thorn, have seized on what was ugly
>
> And laughed. . . .

He is the poet as minister to the indifferent, doctor to the deprived. He gives value to their existence. In doing so he is large, red, supremely vital. A dry irony colors this notion when we observe that he has a very receptive audience of listeners who would have resorted to masochisms, to shivering jubilations, probably naked, in frost, to delighted fingering of thorns, in order to feel. But, we further reflect, they don't have to go that far: the reader sits between them and such extremes, Virgil to their Dantes. And the particular images in the poem of what he reads—"Of the pans above the stove, the pots on the table, the tulips among them"—are everyday, homey, the utensils of cooking side by side with flowers which give color to the kitchen. They are familiar and familial. Here and often, the familiar and the familial, home and kin, the near in feeling, spoken by one or another poet-reader, are the stays which in Stevens' view stand between desiring, time-bound men and the extremes of thorns.

As Stevens says in an address titled "Honors and Acts" (included in *Opus Posthumous*):

> In one direction [the genius of poetry] moves toward the ultimate things of pure poetry; in the other it speaks to great numbers of people of themselves, making extraordinary texts and memorable music out of what they feel and know. In both cases it makes itself manifest in a kind of speech that comes from secrecy. Its position is always an inner position, never certain, never fixed. It is to be found beneath the poet's word and deep within the reader's eye in those chambers in which the genius of poetry sits alone with her candle in a moving solitude.

In this statement of faith in its high value, Stevens sees one kind of poetry, the kind he most often wrote, as communication to others, in "extraordinary texts and memorable music," of what one person feels and knows. In both kinds, the "speech," the communication, comes from an uncertain and unfixed, complex and changing, secret source, a chamber "beneath the poet's word"; it enters into a chamber "deep within the reader's eye," in another person's mind and feelings. "The genius of poetry" resides in both places, "alone with her candle," in a "solitude" (like that in "The House Was Quiet and the World Was Calm") which is "moving" in two senses: it changes its position, and it moves both poet and reader. Yet, in each separate person, it is in a solitude. Poet and reader are alone, with the genius of poetry sitting alone in each. But she is in each. And the poem, the "speech," does go from one person's solitude into the other's. Thus understanding is possible. And thus poetry is a major—for Stevens the major—sanction of life. Man as poet has a power over life which dominates life by saying his feelings and knowings, or his felt and known imaginings of the realities he feels and knows, in conscientious and high-trying text and music. For the familiar to him may seem revelation to another. "And the wonder and mystery of art, as indeed of religion in the last resort, is the revelation of something 'wholly other' by which the inexpressible loneliness of thinking is broken and enriched."

The poet, as seen in Stevens' theory and practice, and in his poems of poets reading, tries to bake "the bread of faithful speech" which, sold and bought, said and heard, written and read, bridges the gap otherwise separating the moving solitudes. He can sometimes succeed in bridging this gap because the moving solitudes, in being residences of the genius of poetry, are similar. The breaking of the bread of faithful speech, together, between poet and reader, between two humans as poet-readers, is communication, is communion, is experience shared, which, as a kind of love, kindly as love, makes life, for the sake of such speech, "prodigiously worth living."

New Uses of Adversity:
Tragic Experience in *The Tempest*

BY STEPHEN KITAY ORGEL

The Tempest, Hemminge and Condell tell us, is a comedy. And yet, if it is read with more concern for Shakespeare's chronology than for his editors' notions of *genre*—read, that is, as a work that develops out of the great tragedies—it will be apparent how much the tragic view of life is present in the play. Even the earliest and lightest Shakespearean comedies—*The Two Gentlemen of Verona, The Comedy of Errors*—have their tragic elements, their potential disasters. This same quality becomes a very serious threat to the worlds of *The Merchant of Venice* and *Much Ado About Nothing*, and largely controls the tone of *Measure for Measure* and *All's Well that Ends Well*, plays which are, in form at least, still clearly comedies.

Similarly, behind the great tragedies lies not simply the progression of plays from *Titus Andronicus* through *Richard III* and *Richard II* to *Romeo and Juliet* and *Julius Caesar*, but also, and just as significantly, the whole range of Shakespearean comedy. The plays suffer greatly by being cut off from each other, placed in those neat piles of comedies, histories, tragedies that are the folio editors' contribution to our sense of Shakespeare. The rich world of *The Merchant of Venice*, which Shakespeare so often and so deliberately moves close to disaster; or the feasting and frustration of *Twelfth Night*, which concludes with a sense that the party is very much over and a song that is to reappear in *Lear*, turn easily enough into the worlds of *Measure for Measure* and *Troilus and Cressida*—worlds of greed, lust, disease. That the next step was, logically, into the great tragedies seems an obvious enough perception. Still, let us recall that the logical step after *Richard II* was into tragedy also; but it was a step Shakespeare evidently felt unprepared to take. In a perfectly literal way, then, comedy served Shakespeare as the training ground for tragedy. In the same way the late comedies, *Pericles, The Win-*

ter's Tale, and *The Tempest,* are filled with a sense of life learned through the tragedies; however qualified the suffering, however happy the resolution, each of them deals richly and seriously with experience which is essentially tragic. It is from this aspect that I wish to consider *The Tempest.*

Simply on the level of action, *The Tempest* has a great deal to connect it with tragedy: the shipwreck, the uninhabited island, the potential murders. Indeed, to most of the victims of the wreck, the play seems very much like a tragedy. Certainly for Alonso there is nothing till the very end to mitigate the strongest sense of loss and desolation the play presents. And yet the viewpoint of Prospero continuously qualifies that tragic sense, and reminds us that the drama cannot turn fully into tragedy. This sort of double viewpoint is nothing new in Shakespeare's comedy; Portia in *The Merchant of Venice* and the Duke in *Measure for Measure* provide something analogous; and, as with Prospero, in both cases it is their greater awareness, their heightened perceptiveness, which manages to subvert the tragedy. Portia is simply shrewder than anyone else; and the Duke has a better, fuller understanding of human nature, as well as something of the same control over the action that Prospero has. In both their plays the claims of reason and humanity are asserted over disorder, passion, violence—mercy over revenge, however justified; forgiveness and reconciliation over retribution, however merited. But there is a significant distinction to be drawn between these two examples and *The Tempest.* In *The Merchant of Venice* and *Measure for Measure* the tragedy is averted through intelligence and sympathy, perfectly ordinary qualities, perhaps somewhat heightened, which we may be expected to find in ourselves. But Prospero's claims are explicitly, unabashedly extraordinary; they are the claims of fantasy taken—as we cannot take it—literally. But the play does take it very literally; Prospero's power is the power of imagination, and it is something no other character possesses. The powerful imagination, a concept we tend to treat as an easy metaphor, is translated here into terms of action. We are continuously aware of the extent to which this world is controlled by Prospero and is even at times indistinguishable from him. The elements obey him; natural forces are an extension of his will, an external manifestation of his mind, and have, consequently, explicitly human qualities like pity and gratitude. The shipwreck, the attempted murders, the loss and desolation, are qualified here by the ubiquitous presence of the magician of the island, who has banished the wicked witch, who can command the winds and the sea, and who has as his servants the spirits of nature, all the creatures of the imagination. For Prospero, indeed, idea and action, metaphor and drama merge; the distinction between thinking a thing and doing it has essentially disappeared.

Obviously an actualized metaphor represents a different kind of action, a different notion of what it is to *act*, from the kind we ordinarily find presented in drama. But the magician and his metaphors are only a part of the play; and there is another part interwoven with it which we might call, for most of its length, at least, *The Tragedy of the Tempest*. We may tend to slight the seriousness of this aspect of the drama, overshadowed as it is by the omnipotent figure of Prospero. Nevertheless, the play opens with it; plunges us into the midst of an image of disordered nature, *the tempest*, which had served King Lear as an image for the chaos of his state and of his mind. And the opening scene on the ship, brief as it is, refers us back to *Lear* in a number of ways. The boatswain's charge to the courtiers that "you do assist the storm," his taunting "What cares these roarers for the name of King?" and "use your authority," should all remind us that Lear's tone to the elements, in a play precisely about royal authority, was one of command: "Blow, winds, and crack your cheeks!" Now, "the name of King" in its immediate context may also, if we are thinking about *Lear*, work in exactly the opposite direction; it may recall to us that throughout Lear's tempest, the king has nothing but "the name of King"; that once stripped of authority and sent into the storm, he becomes "unaccommodated man." This is a serious foreboding of what we may expect to happen to the king in *this* tempest—Alonso, wrecked on an island and threatened by both the violence of nature and the human passions of selfishness, greed and jealousy which are so evident among his followers on the ship.

Nevertheless, the boatswain's question, "What cares these roarers for the name of King?" is in the larger context ironic; for the storm *is* under the control of Prospero. As we pass from the chaos and helplessness of the ship to the authority which the winds actually obey, we are presented with a contrasting scene of order, compassion, and an almost intolerable innocence. Miranda's description of the storm we have just experienced shows us that nature, both human and elemental, has other aspects. The passage is worth pausing over because it announces a number of themes which are to be of importance throughout the play:

> If by your Art, my dearest father, you have
> Put the wild waters in this roar, allay them.
> The sky, it seems, would pour down stinking pitch,
> But that the sea, mounting to th'welkin's cheek,
> Dashes the fire out. O, I have suffered
> With those that I saw suffer! A brave vessel,
> (Who had, no doubt, some noble creature in her,)
> Dash'd all to pieces. O, the cry did knock
> Against my very heart! Poor souls, they perish'd!
> Had I been any god of power, I would
> Have sunk the sea within the earth, or ere
> It should the good ship so have swallow'd, and
> The fraughting souls within her.[1]
>
> (I, ii, 1–13)

The storm to Miranda presents an image of the whole universe in conflict, but her concern is not a metaphysical one. She fastens her attention on the destruction of the ship, as we have just done, and in contrast to the selfishness and insensitivity we have observed in the first scene, her sympathy and compassion are immediate and unqualified. "O, I have suffered/ With those that I saw suffer," she says, and that characteristic immediacy in her responses, that reciprocal suffering, is an analogue on the human level of the reciprocal violence she has perceived in the tempest. Similarly, her image of the wreck is at once translated into an image of her feelings about it: the "vessel . . . dash'd all to pieces" emits for her a cry which "did knock against my very heart." Miranda's suffering is apparent the first moment we see her; it is very real and quite uncomplicated, and it is only the first instance of many in a play which is full of suffering. Yet her compassion, real as it is, also has a certain element of shallowness, or at least of inexperience about it. She assumes "some noble creature" must be in the ship—whereas we, who have just come through the first scene, may tend to doubt it. In her innocence she idealizes whatever she experiences, and every statement she makes, all her observations and attitudes, are continually modified for us by the play's context. Here, the apparent futility of her last remark ("Had I been any god of power . . .") is qualified by the fact that Prospero *is* the "god of power" that his daughter wishes to be. As soon as we are on the island, the assertion of human control over the tempest, so ironic in the context of the first scene, is

---

[1] Quotations are from the Arden edition of *The Tempest*, ed. Frank Kermode, 6th ed. (Cambridge, Harvard University Press, 1958).

intended perfectly literally. But it is a special kind of power Miranda invokes from her father, and her word for it is *art*.

Our awareness of Prospero's power, however, is conveyed here not through his magical apparatus, the wand and the cloak he is to remove with the words "Lie there, my art," but simply through the tone of his reply:

> Be collected:
> No more amazement: tell your piteous heart
> There's no harm done.
> *Mir.*   O, woe the day!
> *Pros.*   No harm.
> (I, *ii*, 13–15)

He speaks as one speaks to a child, simply, gently and firmly; more important, he speaks with a sureness and succinctness which, in tragedy, are possible only at the very end. His tone is that of a character with a full comprehension of the experience of the drama; and the sense it gives us is of a mind achieving full control of itself, so that when Prospero proceeds to explain the background of the play in the subsequent recitation of his sufferings, we feel that we can with understanding participate in the end of a long and complex action. We have been dramatically prepared, that is, for the recitation simply by Prospero's tone.

Prospero's magic power is directly related to his control over his past suffering, and we see him working out the last traces of bitterness and vindictiveness in the sharp expostulations that punctuate that speech to his daughter—"Dost thou attend me?" "I pray thee mark me." "Dost thou hear?" (These are not to be taken as evidence that Miranda's attention is wandering, though they are usually, ludicrously, treated as such in productions of the play; Miranda's reply to "Dost thou hear?"—"Your tale, sir, would cure deafness" —betrays humor as well as sympathy.) What we see as Prospero describes the loss of his dukedom is his retrospective suffering being played out before our eyes. But the controlling of the experience is evident too, as the tone of Prospero's monologue moves from violence against his enemies to a wry and familiar but most untypical playfulness with his daughter ("Well demanded, wench . . ."), and finally to the tone of "Now I arise" and "I am ready now"; to that tone of authority and sureness which we observed in his first lines and which are characteristic of him throughout the play.

Prospero's suffering, then, is essentially behind him. By contrast, the play presents a variety of characters in varying degrees of grief or passion. The first of these, and, after Miranda, probably the least complicated, is Ferdinand. We see him shipwrecked and desolate after the storm; but what we hear is Ariel singing:

> Come unto these yellow sands,
>   And then take hands:
> Courtsied when you have and kiss'd
>   The wild waves whist:
> Foot it featly here and there,
>   And sweet sprites bear
> The burthen.
>
> (I, ii, 377–383)

The usual editorial interpretation of "the wild waves whist" as an absolute construction is syntactically unnecessary and renders the song meaningless. The song is about relationships in nature between the spirits and the elements, about kissing the waves into silence, quieting the tempest with love. Ferdinand comments:

> Where should this music be? i'th'air or th'earth?
> It sounds no more: and, sure, it waits upon
> Some god o'th'island. Sitting upon a bank,
> Weeping again the King my father's wrack,
> This music crept by me upon the waters,
> Allaying both their fury and my passion
> With its sweet air: thence I have follow'd it,
> Or it hath drawn me rather.
>
> (I, ii, 390–397)

Ferdinand is overcome with grief, but the first thing we sense about him is a continual tone of wonder, like Miranda's, an almost passive receptiveness to experience of all kinds. His nature is very close to the elemental nature that surrounds him; the fury of the waves and his own passion are scarcely to be distinguished, and Ariel's music has the same effect on both. (Ferdinand shows himself, incidentally, more perceptive than most editors: "allaying . . . their fury" is simply a paraphrase of Ariel's "kiss'd/ The wild waves whist.") The "sweet air" is both the musical strain and the element, the atmosphere. The double sense of "air" is only one example of an ambiguity that functions throughout this play, where all the elements may serve as metaphors for something else. (So, for example, earlier in the scene [l. 316] Prospero addresses Caliban as "earth.") Finally the whole experience becomes ambiguous to Ferdinand; he becomes uncertain whether he has been active or passive, whether he has followed the music or been drawn by it. But his sense of the experience is perfectly correct; he perceives that the music "waits upon/ Some god o' th' island," and he is fully aware of its effect.

We keep being reminded that there is something special about nature on the island. Ariel sings again:

> Full fadom five thy father lies;
>   Of his bones are coral made;
> Those are pearls that were his eyes:
>   Nothing of him that doth fade,
> But doth suffer a sea-change
> Into something rich and strange.
>   (*I, ii, 399–404*)

Now that nature has been calmed, Ariel proceeds to deepen this mysterious experience. His song is about nature becoming art; and in it, disaster and death involve not decay and loss, but a transformation into something wonderful, something almost directly opposite to loss, tremendous richness. And the word for that transformation is *suffer*. We may recall Miranda's analogous use of "art" to describe a quality defined in the first scene as "command" and "authority." In Ariel's song we begin to be aware that the whole concept of *suffering* is now undergoing a sea-change. It is not being diminished at all, but we are seeing it from a different viewpoint, whereby the endurance of violence and destruction leaves us infinitely richer. That richness has been taken perfectly literally by the song; the drowned man has become a work of art, and the transformation has been effected by the art of the figure who has suffered most, and whose very name conveys the richness he embodies: Prospero.

Ferdinand, insofar as he can, understands all this perfectly: "The ditty does remember my drown'd father./ This is no mortal business, nor no sound/ That the earth owes" (I, ii, 408–410). He again paraphrases the song; the wonder is still there, but so is the awareness: to the limits of his information, he knows exactly what is going on. And his sense of things again is accurate. "This is no mortal business" means a number of things, but one thing it certainly means is "this is nothing to do with death." We are watching the beginning of a transformation of Ferdinand's grief into something else. It is precisely the awareness and receptiveness we have observed that make him the right man for Miranda; and especially, it is his sense of wonder that makes him immediately aware of the wonder that *is* Miranda, whose very name means "something to be wondered at."

Ferdinand's suffering is, as we have seen, relatively uncomplicated, though it is not so simple as Miranda's. Ferdinand is not merely experiencing sympathetic feelings; he has undergone a real and great loss. His father's case, however, is a different matter. Alonso suffers more deeply in the play than any other character, and though the play is certainly not primarily about Alonso, his experience has a dramatic significance which in the total picture is second only to Prospero's.

The first scene of Act II returns us to a good deal of the tone and personnel of the opening of the play. Squabbling, selfishness, and insensitivity provide the setting for Alonso's grief. For over a hundred lines he says nothing but "Prithee, peace," until at last, goaded by Antonio's and Sebastian's talk of his daughter's wedding (from which they were returning when the tempest occurred), he passionately replies:

> You cram these words into mine ears against
> The stomach of my sense. Would I had never
> Married my daughter there! for, coming thence,
> My son is lost and, in my rate, she too,
> Who is so far from Italy removed
> I ne'er again shall see her. O thou mine heir
> Of Naples and of Milan, what strange fish
> Hath made his meal on thee?
>
> (II, i, 102–109)

Even without recalling the sensitivity and perceptiveness that went with Ferdinand's simple grief, we must be aware that this is a rather crude way to talk about the death of a son. Admittedly Alonso is with a crude group, and the main intention of his words is simply to get Sebastian and Antonio to be quiet and leave him alone. Still, we are given an immediate contrast of tone in Francisco's reply:

> Sir, he may live:
> I saw him beat the surges under him,
> And ride upon their backs; he trod the water,
> Whose enmity he flung aside, and breasted
> The surge most swoln that met him; his bold head
> 'Bove the contentious waves he kept, and oared

Himself with his good arms in lusty stroke
To th' shore, that o'er his wave-worn basis bowed,
As stooping to relieve him: I not doubt
He came alive to land.

(II, i, 109–118)

The tone is one of nobility and respect; Francisco speaks with the
sort of heroic rhetoric we recall from *Julius Caesar* and *Antony and
Cleopatra*. This is the way kings *should* talk. By contrast, our first
sense of Alonso is of insensitivity, coarseness, and a general tasteless-
ness in the quality of his suffering. We feel a good deal more kindly
toward him by the end of the play, but aversion must necessarily be
our first response, and is inevitably strengthened by what we already
know about Alonso from Prospero's narrative.

The response, though, begins at once to be qualified. To Sebastian's incredibly tasteless accusation "The fault's your own"
(l. 131), Alonso replies sharply and immediately, "So is the dear'st
o' th' loss," and we feel the rightness of the reply as well as its sincerity. Notice, too, how it picks up and transforms the metaphor
Ariel had used singing to Ferdinand of Alonso's own death. That
loss became a new richness; this is just the opposite, and "dearest"
provides Shakespeare with another functional ambiguity. The sense
of the line is of a richness lost with no metaphor to qualify the
desolation.

Nevertheless, "The fault's your own" is of course precisely right;
Alonso's suffering is involved with his guilt. This is what gives his
tone a bitterness alien to his son's grieving. In a later scene, when
Ariel confronts Alonso as he has confronted Ferdinand, the king's
guilt is seen as a central issue in the drama, a motivation for the
whole action:

> *Ariel.* You are three men of sin, whom Destiny—
>   That hath to instrument this lower world
>   And what is in't,—the never-surfeited sea
>   Hath caus'd to belch up you. . . .
>   I and my fellows
>   Are ministers of Fate. . . .
>   But remember—
>   For that's my business to you,—that you three
>   From Milan did supplant good Prospero:
>   Expos'd unto the sea, which hath requit it,
>   Him and his innocent child: for which foul deed
>   The powers, delaying, not forgetting, have
>   Incens'd the seas and shores, yea, all the creatures,

Against your peace. Thee of thy son, Alonso,
They have bereft; and do pronounce by me
Ling'ring perdition—worse than any death
Can be at once—shall step by step attend
You and your ways; whose wraths to guard you from,—
Which here, in this most desolate isle, else falls
Upon your heads,—is nothing but heart-sorrow
And a clear life ensuing.

(III, iii, 53–82)

Ariel declares himself an agent of *Fate,* and the first thing we should remark is that this is not true; it is only something like the truth, which has been related in a way that these three men of sin and rather limited sensibility can understand—and only Alonso understands it. (No such explanation, we recall, was necessary for Ferdinand.) From then on, the speech is not only complex and majestic verse but very straight talk indeed: Ariel has to remind Alonso of what he has done, and why he merits punishment. "Ling'ring perdition—worse than any death/ Can be at once" is to be his fate. The spirit explicitly points the way toward not redemption, not reconciliation, but simply toward some mitigation of the punishment and of the guilt. The way is precisely one it has never occurred to Alonso to take; it involves an awareness of his crime and a sense of his responsibility.

This speech has been tailored to fit the requirements of Alonso's sensibility; that is, it presents the truth, or a version of it, in the only terms he can understand. It works; and the way we know it works is that something new happens in the verse he speaks. "O, it is monstrous, monstrous!" he cries, as Ariel's words make him aware for the first time of his crime, or of the punishment, or simply of the fact that he lives, after all, in a world where something like retribution actually exists. His sense of horror and surprise rushes in on him all at once, bringing with it a revelation. All at once, Alonso speaks a different language; the crudeness of that earlier perception of Ferdinand's death is now replaced by a new tone and an altered sensibility:

O, it is monstrous, monstrous!
Methought the billows spoke, and told me of it;
The winds did sing it to me; and the thunder,
That deep and dreadful organ-pipe, pronounc'd
The name of Prosper: it did bass my trespass.
Therefor my son i' th' ooze is bedded; and

> I'll seek him deeper than e'er plummet sounded,
> And with him there lie mudded.
>
> (III, iii, 95–102)

The language of this is obviously, suddenly, rich and complex; Alonso suddenly perceives a whole new range of experience. He has, in fact, *suffered* that sea-change before our eyes. We may recall Ferdinand's pun on "sweet air," and see that for the first time Alonso is perceiving the elements in terms of music, and not of destruction. It is now possible for him to repent, to ask Prospero's pardon when the time comes, and ultimately to be reconciled with him and reunited with his son. The sense he has of all this, however, may still strike us as a little oversimplified: the cause-and-effect relationship he finds between his crime and this retribution does not actually exist, although it may be as close as he can come to a real understanding of the action. On the other hand, nobody in the play has a better sense of it except Prospero, and he, of course, is directly responsible for the action. Let us, then, look back now, and consider what it is that Prospero does in *The Tempest*.

I have remarked earlier that Prospero's kind of action is significantly different from that of the other characters in the play; that is, Prospero alone is not limited to ordinary dramatic action; his awareness, his intelligence, and particularly his imaginative power have all been translated into terms of physical action: his metaphors have been actualized, or taken literally. Therefore our sense of his "art," his magic power, is that it is really a kind of heightened awareness and intelligence. Certainly he is aware of everything that happens in the play; and since, as we have seen, all his action is mental action, for Prospero to be *aware* of something is to be in control of it.

The magic, then, is something like Bacon's idea of science; not spells and witchcraft, but a complete understanding of nature. We may recall, too, that for Bacon the purpose of scientific inquiry was precisely to be able to control nature as Prospero does. But *nature* has larger meanings in the play, as it has in *Lear*. It means weather —*The Tempest*—and by extension an unseen and constantly active universe which is personified in the spirits whom Prospero has at his command. This is "elemental nature," and the *elements* keep reappearing in the play's imagery—the elements of wind and rain, and the four basic elements that compose the world: earth, water, fire, and air. Significantly, too, the most volatile of these, Ariel, the spirit of air, is Prospero's servant. The magician has released Ariel from

the tree where "the damn'd witch Sycorax . . . in her most un-
mitigable rage" had imprisoned him; nature suffered under the passionate, unnatural sorceress, and Prospero has relieved that suffering.
An act of kindness has moved Ariel: elemental nature, even the
volatile air, can feel gratitude. In contrast, the play presents the
other sort of nature—human nature—and we may remember, along
with the most agonizing scenes from *Lear*, a song from comedy:

> Blow, blow thou winter wind,
> Thou art not so unkind
> As man's ingratitude.

Constantly throughout the play, elemental nature is invested with
human qualities, while human nature is seen as base and vicious.
The antithesis is made very clear when, right after we have witnessed the violence of the storm in the opening scene, Prospero
describes how he and Miranda had been set adrift:

> there they hoist us,
> To cry to th' sea that roar'd to us; to sigh
> To th' winds, whose pity, sighing back again,
> Did us but loving wrong.
> (I, ii, 148–151)

We find here that same immediacy of reciprocal response between
elemental nature and human feeling that we noticed the first time
we saw Miranda. Her nature, in its innocence, is the closest in the
play to the nature of the elements. She is perfectly safe on the island
because—with one significant exception, which we shall consider
presently—the elements are all she has to deal with. But Prospero
is about to return to society, to a world of *human* nature, and
Miranda's innocence, therefore, must yield to education. "I pray
thee, mark me," says Prospero, "that a brother should/ Be so per-
fidious!" (ll. 67–68). She must be taught, like Hamlet, "that one
may smile and smile and be a villain."

In the world of *The Tempest*, Miranda is one extreme of human
nature. The opposite extreme is the figure Prospero calls "the beast
Caliban." He is usually treated by commentators as a foil to Ariel—
the airy spirit versus the earthy monster—but this seems to me
only part of the truth. For one thing, it implies an evaluation of
elemental nature—air is good, earth is bad—that is really only in-
cidental in the play. Such value judgments are, on the whole, re-

served for human nature, for characters with motives. Furthermore, to contrast Caliban with Ariel may lead us to ignore a contrast that the play clearly does set up between Caliban and Miranda. Both were raised on the island, both equally inexperienced, both the objects of Prospero's loving care; but Miranda's nature turns toward order, obedience, compassion, and reason; and Caliban's toward violence, destruction, the indulgence of appetites, sensual passion, and particularly lust. The situation is presented almost as a scientific experiment: if two children brought up under the same conditions behave differently, we may argue that they are different *by nature*. Miranda has been carefully educated; Caliban is incapable of learning. The two are contrasted throughout the play. For example, they have precisely the same response to the first strangers they have ever seen; both idealize them. Miranda says of Ferdinand, "I might call him/ A thing divine"; Caliban says of Stephano, "that's a brave god." And by the end of the play they have both learned a good deal about human nature. Caliban is quite disenchanted, Miranda is wide-eyed with wonder; but he has instinctively—that is, *naturally* —made the wrong choice, and she has made the right one.

Prospero is very hard on Caliban; perhaps, we may feel, too hard. Certainly in this case our sympathies are engaged in a most unexpected way. Prospero's attitude, and our response to it, play a large part in determining the total effect of the play, and it is worth pausing to consider them in general terms. We may begin by noting that whatever harshness Prospero expresses the play justifies at once when Caliban, reminded that he had repaid all his master's kindness by trying to rape Miranda, is both unrepentant and retrospectively lecherous. Furthermore, Caliban is the only figure in this world for whom a direct relationship between crime and retribution (such as Ariel has described to Alonso) has always actually existed; to Caliban that is, Ariel and the spirits of nature, creatures of Prospero's imagination, really are "ministers of Fate." Caliban suffers horribly at Prospero's hands, but unlike people a little higher on the scale of human nature, his suffering does not change him. He learns nothing from it—not even how to avoid it. Prospero finds him unregenerate and inhuman.

Nevertheless, the problem of our sympathy remains. To say this is not to be sentimental about Caliban; the point is that *our* sense of this figure is different from Prospero's—that is, this is the one place in the play where what Prospero says and what we perceive

do not coincide. We shall consider why presently. Here it is sufficient
to note that Prospero's description accounts only for the invective,
the violence, the *bad nature* of Caliban; it accounts for remarks like,
"You taught me language, and my profit on't/ Is, I know how to
curse." We hear more than cursing in Caliban's language. If we
stop to consider how we know what the island is like, where our
sense of its lushness and particularity comes from, we shall realize
that it comes almost entirely from Caliban—from verse like this:

> I prithee, let me bring thee where crabs grow;
> And I with my long nails will dig thee pig-nuts;
> Show thee a jay's nest, and instruct thee how
> To snare the nimble marmoset; I'll bring thee
> To clustering filberts, and sometimes I'll get thee
> Young scamels from the rock.
> (II, *ii*, 167–172)

It is the specificity that is important here; such catalogues of a full
and wild nature communicate considerable vitality, and tell us something about the island that is not conveyed by Ariel's singing. Even
Caliban's invective has an unexpected richness. We should look too
at his description of how Prospero's spirits torture him:

> Sometime like apes, that mow and chatter at me,
> And after bite me; then like hedgehogs, which
> Lie tumbling in my barefoot way, and mount
> Their pricks at my footfall; sometime am I
> All wound with adders, who with cloven tongues
> Do hiss me into madness.
> (II, *ii*, 9–14)

Here we perceive that he too is fully aware of a continuously active—
for him, horribly active—universe. Nor is his awareness limited only
to ugly things, and he produces one of the great set pieces of the
play:

> Be not afeard; the isle is full of noises,
> Sounds and sweet airs, that give delight, and hurt not.
> Sometimes a thousand twangling instruments
> Will hum about mine ears; and sometime voices,
> That, if I then had wak'd after long sleep,
> Will make me sleep again: and then, in dreaming,
> The clouds methought would open, and show riches

Ready to drop upon me; that, when I wak'd
I cried to dream again.

(III, ii, 133–141)

Of course, the fact that this is addressed to Stephano (whose only response is, "I shall have my music for nothing") will keep us from too uncritical an admiration for Caliban's sensibility. It is also true that the wonderful quality of the island becomes here an image of frustration for Caliban—frustration both in the dream and out of it, because even if the riches did descend, what value would they have on the island? Nevertheless, the primary effect of the passage is of a marvelous and rich fantasy, a dream world which, at rare moments, may merge with the real world to give even the most unregenerate sufferer a respite.

Our sense of Caliban, then, is of violence, cunning, but also of something else we cannot dismiss as Prospero does: a sensuous and fantastic perception of certain kinds of experience. Caliban is the mind that cannot learn, that will not impose controls on its passion; he is the creature for whom *passio*—suffering—has no meaning. In a very different way from Prospero, he does not distinguish between the world of his fantasies and the real world, and in an important sense the island is as much the realm of Caliban's imagination as of Prospero's. But Caliban's creativity, from the lowest level of his lust to the highest of his fantasy, is chaotic and unreasoning, whereas Prospero's is controlled; his power is "art."

It is precisely what Caliban represents, passion unmitigated by any moral sense, will unmoved by any ties of love or faith, that has been the chief danger to Prospero's life. These are the qualities we observed on the ship in the opening scene of the play; and certainly both Prospero's account of his past, and the ease with which Caliban makes gods of Stephano and Trinculo, imply that there is a place for Calibans in the world of Milan and Naples. Prospero's twelve years of suffering have in part been educating him to an awareness of what that world is really like. But on the island, at least, for Prospero to be aware is to control; and his control of "nature" is a control not only of the elements but of his own base nature as well, of the Caliban in himself. What cannot, like Alonso, be educated, can at least, like Stephano and Trinculo, be kept in abeyance or foiled. So nothing Caliban represents is attractive to Prospero any more—not even the sensuous richness of the fantasy, because it is unreasoning and uncontrolled. And this must be a measure of how far Prospero is beyond us, too, with our sympathy for unregenerate nature. We too are being instructed.

Prospero leads the play, then, through suffering to reconciliation and a new life. He moves the action first toward the revelation which is Alonso's salvation, and second toward the wedding masque (IV, i), with its vision of an ordered nature and bountiful fruition. This is Prospero's creation, the most palpable example we are shown of his art.

The masque is first of all an interruption of the dramatic action, a point at which we lose our sense of the progress of time. It is important to remark this, because both the chronology of the action and the length of time it occupies are worked out with considerable care and ingenuity in the play. In fact this and *The Comedy of Errors* are the only Shakespeare plays in which the amount of time represented and the time actually consumed in performance substantially coincide. Therefore it is especially significant that the masque has a very different sort of time scheme from the play.

Time is an essential element of what we ordinarily mean by drama. People act on each other, things happen in time. In comedy, it is not only the medium but also the agent that solves all problems. In tragedy, time has a different aspect: for Hamlet, "the *time* is out of joint"—both the age and the sequence of events, but not the court or the world or particular people—and time begins to look more like an enemy, like that archetype Elizabethan villain Mutability, involving the action in change, decay, and death. The action of *The Tempest*, as we have seen, partakes of both these senses of time, the comic and the tragic. But the masque requires a pause in that action, and partakes, as we shall see, of neither.

The plot of *The Tempest*, then, loses nothing if the masque is omitted, as it usually is in modern productions. Indeed, Prospero himself contributes to our initial sense of its unimportance by referring to it as "some vanity of mine art." Nevertheless, this attitude has been thoroughly qualified for us by the masque itself when Ferdinand interrupts it to pronounce it "a most majestic vision, and/ Harmonious charmingly." Majesty, the qualities of the ruler generally, has been one of the chief concerns of the play; and harmony, or music, has provided much of its metaphor, its poetic structure. Ferdinand, then, perceives an integral connection between the vision and his experience (and ours) on the island. We may perceive that

the connection is dramatically integral as well. At the beginning of
Act IV, when Prospero releases Ferdinand and offers him Miranda's
hand in marriage, a new formality and ceremoniousness of tone
set the scene in which vows are to be pronounced and the lovers'
plot resolved. "Here, afore Heaven," says Prospero, "I ratify this my
rich gift," and thereby prepares us for the solemn celebration represented by the masque. But something remarkable happens to the
dramatic verse as well:

> Then, as my gift, and thine own acquisition
> Worthily purchas'd, take my daughter: but
> If thou dost break her virgin-knot before
> All sanctimonious ceremonies may
> With full and holy rite be minister'd,
> No sweet aspersion shall the heavens let fall
> To make this contract grow; but barren hate,
> Sour-ey'd disdain, and discord shall bestrew
> The union of your bed with weeds so loathly
> That you shall hate it both: therefore take heed,
> As Hymen's lamps shall light you.
>   (IV, i, 13-23)

As the play looks forward to "sanctimonious ceremonies"—as the action moves toward the masque—the verse begins to use personifications instead of metaphors. "Barren hate, sour-ey'd disdain and discord," and Hymen are figures out of an allegory, and a masque is
precisely an allegory put onto a stage. The dialogue, the movement
of the poetry, correspondingly becomes more formal. Ferdinand's
elaborate reply might almost be a prescribed one, and Prospero
with his "fairly spoke" gives the sense that his prospective son-in-
law has indeed given the right answer.

The threatening figures Prospero has invoked in the passage just
cited, hate, disdain, discord, have been sowing weeds on the marriage
bed, which should be fruitful. In contrast, the masque itself opens
with an invocation of Ceres, a grain goddess and the deity who pre-
sides over the harvest. We find, logically enough, images of growth
and fruition in the masque. But the fertility implied here is of quite
a different sort from what we have found on the island. Caliban is
a hunter and fisherman; the islanders live on wild things. But the
masque is about agriculture, and refers us to a highly civilized society—Ceres even remarks on "this short-grass'd green" (l. 83): this
action takes place on a well-kept lawn. The season adduced is "spongy
April," the very beginning of the agricultural year. Crops have not

quite begun to sprout yet, and similarly the nymphs are "cold" and "chaste," the bachelor with spring fever is "lass-lorn" (ll. 65–68). But as the masque continues, the season changes. After a scant fifty lines we find "Vines with clust'ring bunches growing;/ Plants with goodly burthen bowing" (ll. 112–113). And shortly before Prospero stops the performance, Iris invokes the "sunburn'd sicklemen, of August weary" (l. 134): it is now harvesttime. A whole season of growth, fruition, and harvest has been encompassed in about seventy-five lines.

It is clear enough what the masque is doing. The play is at this point moving away from the island and back to civilization. The natural bounty of the island has up to this point been presented entirely in Caliban's terms. Now the masque gives us Prospero's terms; not "dams for fish," "clust'ring filberts and young scamels," whatever they are, but an ordered and orderly agriculture. This is a world with a different sense of time and another kind of nature. We ought also to be aware that something is missing from the natural world the masque depicts. There is, in this cycle of seasons, no winter. Indeed, Ceres is explicit about it: "Spring come to you at the farthest/ In the very end of harvest" (ll. 114–115)—after autumn, that is, spring will return at once. And something else is missing from this world. It is the whole sense of darkness, the undertone of tragedy that fills the play. We may remark how lightly the one tragic allusion is treated:

> *Ceres.*   Tell me, heavenly bow,
>   If Venus or her son, as thou dost know,
>   Do now attend the queen? Since they did plot
>   The means that dusky Dis my daughter got,
>   Her and her blind boy's scandal'd company
>   I have forsworn.
>   (IV, i, 86–91)

Ceres, speaking of the rape of her daughter Proserpina, uses not a tone of tragic bereavement, but one of social outrage. This is all the more to the point since it is precisely that abduction which is directly responsible for the very fact that winter exists at all in nature.

There is, then, in this cycle of the seasons of birth, fruition, and harvest, no winter—no death. So, when Prospero interrupts, it is to stress that what is missing from the masque is nevertheless very real. The vision of permanence is in danger of blinding us to the necessities of the moment, for it is precisely death in the persons of

Stephano, Trinculo, and Caliban that is threatening now. Throughout this short play, Prospero's special quality has been, above all, an awareness of *time*, of the right moment, the exact instant when action must be taken:

> By accident most strange, bountiful Fortune,
> (Now my dear lady) hath mine enemies
> Brought to this shore; and by my prescience
> I find my zenith doth depend upon
> A most auspicious star, whose influence
> If now I court not, but omit, my fortunes
> Will ever after droop;
>
> (I, *ii*, 178–184)

and the repeated "*now*" looms large throughout the drama. We have observed that the chronology of the action is worked out with remarkable precision, and the play makes a point of letting us know how close the correspondence is between the duration of the performance and the length of time it represents. Both Alonso and the boatswain remark in the last scene that the wreck occurred less than three hours before; and one sense we ought to have is of how quickly the whole action has happened—a sense that Prospero has indeed seized the decisive moment. His safety and the success of his designs depend on his awareness of time as dramatic, as a series of crises. But the masque is presenting a world which is an eternal and unchanging cycle, a world without drama, without crises, without immediacy, and in a very real sense there is in the action of the play—in the prosecution of Prospero's designs—no *time* for the masque.

So Prospero's "majestic vision" has a double aspect. It is finally the only place in the play where Caliban's sense of the richness of the island, which is necessarily our sense as well, is qualified; where we see, as we must see, that there is a better kind of natural bounty, an ordered nature in which man lives not as a predator but as a part. It shows us, in fact, Prospero's sense of nature, one ideal of the world of Prospero's imagination. But the masque-vision is also, paradoxically, a threat to that ideal, which depends so utterly on the magician's complete awareness of all parts of his world. We must, then, take Prospero's comment on his masque very seriously:

> Our revels now are ended. These our actors,
> As I foretold you, were all spirits, and
> Are melted into air, into thin air:

And, like the baseless fabric of this vision,
The cloud-capp'd towers, the gorgeous palaces,
The solemn temples, the great globe itself,
Yea, all which it inherit, shall dissolve
And, like this insubstantial pageant faded,
Leave not a rack behind. We are such stuff
As dreams are made on; and our little life
Is rounded with a sleep.

(*IV, i, 148–158*)

"Our revels now are ended": *revels* is a technical theatrical term for a masque, and has its modern sense in addition. The serious business of the play, then, the tragic world of Alonso, the treachery of Sebastian and Antonio, the conspiracy of Stephano, Trinculo, and Caliban, all are now at hand. The speech follows that most crucial moment in the play when Prospero's awareness of a world of fancy has made him forgetful for the first time of the real world, has almost deprived him of his control over the action and thereby almost turned the drama to tragedy. The dangers of an uncontrolled imagination such as Caliban's are now brought dramatically and immediately home to us in the very person of Prospero. For the magician, returned to the hard facts of the play's continuing action, the world of imagination is rapidly vanishing. But the realities of Prospero's world are also the play's metaphors; the spirits have, literally, "melted into air," and they now provide a poetic analogue of the larger reality of life outside the drama:

. . . the great globe itself,
Yea, all which it inherit, shall dissolve
And, like this insubstantial pageant faded,
Leave not a rack behind.

This does more than move us beyond the world of the play. "Pageant" is another technical term, meaning both a stage and the setting on it, and "the great globe" was also, of course, literally the scene of the action. The theatrical terminology, the striking ambiguity, are ultimately to be taken up and justified in Prospero's epilogue, where his awareness extends not only beyond the fictive world but beyond the limits of his theater as well; where, acknowledging himself an actor on a stage, he takes on both the audience's understanding and the dramatist's control. Similar conclusions offered by Puck and Feste are in their plays perfectly conventional; but the epilogue to *The Tempest* has a power and point that derive from its organic relation to a movement within the drama; and it is the revels speech that makes this possible. The ability to think metaphorically, which only Prospero possesses, is in the revels speech directly related to the strongest and fullest sense of reality in the play. Nowhere else except in his epilogue is the extent of Prospero's awareness larger or clearer, and the world he summons up, the kinds of relationships he establishes, are ones of which Miranda and Ferdinand cannot even conceive. Ferdinand had thought the masque a happy ending to his adventures, but Prospero's play has only just reached its climax.

In a sense, it is the implications of the masque that have brought the play to this climax; and Prospero's interruption is full of a consciousness of the dangers not only of the conspiracy he has forgotten but also of the imaginative world that has tempted him to forget it. Ferdinand's comment during the masque had led him to plead, "Let me live here ever;/ So rare a wonder'd father and a wise/ Makes this place Paradise"; but Prospero at the end of the masque is implicitly criticizing both that "Paradise" and his son-in-law's callowness as he urges Ferdinand, "be cheerful, sir./ Our revels now are ended." The conclusion of the revels, the vision of the masque as an "insubstantial pageant," and all that that vision implies for Prospero, provide a vital transition in the play to the renunciation of extraordinary powers and the return to the ordinary world.

That the transition is a painful one for Prospero to make is apparent enough from its violence. Ferdinand remarks, "Your father's in some passion/ That works him strongly"; Miranda observes, "Never till this day/ Saw I him touch'd with anger, so distemper'd" (ll. 143–145). Both perceive how uncharacteristic his behavior is, though Miranda might have recalled the several outbursts that punctuated her father's earlier tale of his sufferings. Prospero's momentary return to passion, striking in the first act and even more evident in the fourth, takes on still greater significance as the play moves to its conclusion, returning its figures to society, and linking the magician at last more with the world of humanity than with the elements.

The opening of the fifth act, then, finds Prospero asserting not his magical power over his victims, but his human sympathy with them, and renouncing not the world of Milan and Naples, but the island and his art. Ariel has been moved by the plight of the king and his followers; Prospero, who comprehends both Ariel and Alonso, both nature and man, comments:

> Hast thou, which are but air, a touch, a feeling
> Of their afflictions, and shall not myself,
> One of their kind, that relish all as sharply
> Passion as they, be kindlier mov'd than thou art?
> Though with their high wrongs I am struck to th' quick,
> Yet with my nobler reason 'gainst my fury
> Do I take part: the rarer action is
> In virtue than in vengeance: they being penitent,
> The sole drift of my purpose doth extend
> Not a frown further.
>
> (V, i, 21–30)

It is *natural* to forgive, to be guided by reason, but—and this is what is striking about the speech—both passion and the desire for revenge are here seen to be natural as well. Vengeance is properly the Lord's, and Prospero is coming to seem less and less like God. If repentance is demanded of Alonso, mercy is equally demanded of Prospero. Here we may recall Miranda's use of "art" and Ariel's of "suffer," and remark that Prospero's word for the alternative to "vengeance" is not mercy, but something much larger: "virtue." This is the quality which is to replace Prospero's magic, and by this point in the play it includes everything that magic had represented: for Prospero the man, reason and understanding, for Prospero the restored Duke, power and justice. So this one action toward which the drama has been moving, Prospero's pardon of his enemies, is the culmination of his "art" and implies a whole way of life for the good ruler he will become.

This is followed by the great monologue "Ye elves of hills, brooks, standing lakes, and groves," in which Prospero anatomizes the world he has controlled and is leaving, the world of nature and its spirits, and even of the dead:

> graves at my command
> Have wak'd their sleepers, op'd, and let 'em forth
> By my so potent Art. But this rough magic
> I here abjure;
>
> (V, i, 48–51)

and in the space of a single line the renunciation takes place; we see the "potent Art" become "rough magic" before our eyes.

Where, then, at the end, are we left? The play ends happily, certainly; the potential violence, the incipient disaster have been averted. The tragedy, that is, *has* been qualified. But unlike *Measure for Measure* or *All's Well that Ends Well*, it has been qualified in a way that does not diminish or dismiss any of the play's tragic implications. There is no sense at the end of *The Tempest* that everything is all right now. Alonso's repentance and the restoration of Prospero's dukedom solve two old problems; but they are by no means the only problems the play has presented. When Miranda sees all the shipwreck victims finally assembled, she marvels "how beauteous mankind is! O brave new world,/ That has such people in't!" But two of the people in it are Sebastian and Antonio; and Prospero's brief answer, " 'Tis new to thee," implies that there are old problems Miranda cannot even conceive of, as well as a good deal of unfinished business. Prospero's "art" still enables him to promise "auspicious gales" for the voyage home—the voyage away from elemental nature and back to society, a world full of people. But we know what *human* nature can be like; and Prospero, leaving the island, is beyond magic and has only his virtue to protect him.

King Lear and the Theory of the "Sight Pattern"

BY PAUL J. ALPERS

MODERN critics characteristically treat metaphors, rather than characters and actions, as primary data in Shakespeare's plays; interpretations are developed through tracing sequences of metaphors and their relation to larger symbolic aspects of the plays. In this essay I want to examine one of the most widely accepted interpretations of this sort—the so-called "sight pattern" in King Lear. The following composite quotation gives the main features of the argument:

> In King Lear an unusual amount of imagery drawn from vision and the eyes prompts us to apprehend a symbolism of sight and blindness having its culmination in Gloucester's tragedy.] . . . The blinding of Gloucester might well be gratuitous melodrama but for its being imbedded in a field of meanings centered in the concept of seeing. This sight pattern relentlessly brings into play the problem of seeing and what is always implied is that the problem is one of insight. . . . It is commonly recognized that just as Lear finds "reason in madness" so Gloucester learns to "see" in his blindness. . . . The whole play is built on this double paradox.[1]

But when we return to the play itself, we discover that the data of the sight pattern simply are not there: in the numerous references to the eyes there is no dominating metaphor of "sight for insight." When we ask what is there, we find we must reinterpret not only the references to the eyes but also the blinding of Gloucester and the relationship between the two plots. For the sight pattern, as usually conceived, raises issues that go beyond the interpretation of specific

[1] J. I. M. Stewart, Character and Motive in Shakespeare (New York, Longman's, Green & Co., 1949), pp. 20–21; R. B. Heilman, This Great Stage (Baton Rouge, Louisiana State University Press, 1948), p. 25; L. C. Knights, Some Shakespearean Themes (London, Chatto & Windus, 1959), p. 107; K. Muir, ed., King Lear (Cambridge, Harvard University Press, Arden edition, 1952), lx.

lines and passages. It codifies two widely held and misleading attitudes toward *Lear*—that insight, the perception of abstractly formulated moral truths, is the crucial issue in the play, and that these moral truths are as readily perceived as are objects in the external world. If we treat events and feelings in *Lear* as paths to or equivalents of insight, we necessarily dilute the intensity and human reality of all the suffering, malice, and love that we find in the play. And if we assume that moral truths are as clear as day, we find ourselves in the insufferable position of patronizing Lear for his moral confusions. Undoubtedly we are aware, as he for a while is not, that Cordelia is good and Goneril and Regan wicked. But the play in no way encourages us to feel that we know what is good for Lear and that the whole point of his suffering is that he should share in our knowledge.

I want first to discuss the main feelings and ideas associated with the eyes in the first half of the play—that is, until the blinding of Gloucester, where imagery supports action and the two plots come together. The idea that there is a dominating metaphor of sight for insight in *Lear* probably begins with a misunderstanding of Kent's words in the first scene:

> See better, Lear, and let me still remain
> The true blank of thine eye.[2]
>   (I, i, 158–159)

"See better" has been taken to mean "Judge the worth of your daughters correctly"; Kent is urging Lear to see things "as they are." It is assumed that seeing is essentially passive—the viewer's reception of sense impressions from the world outside him. This Lockean notion of sight underlies the sight pattern's equation of physical sight and moral insight. Nothing could be further from Kent's idea of the way a king sees. Kent is replying to Lear's "Out of my sight!" Lear's words, though they may express a desire to remove an offending object from the field of vision, are the command of a king: "Out of my sight" is tantamount to the banishment that is soon pronounced on Kent. The phrase assumes that the king's sight is an active emanation that sheds grace and favor; to be out of it is, in effect, not to exist. Hence Kent expands "See better" by saying, "And let me still remain/ The true blank of thine eye." The blank

---

[2] Quotations from *King Lear* are from the text edited by Alfred Harbage (Baltimore, Md., Penguin Books, 1958).

is the center of a target; in recalling Lear's earlier threat, "the bow is bent and drawn; make from the shaft," Kent's metaphor affirms Lear's characterization of himself as a titanic force, awesome even when it is beneficent. Lear's eyes do not passively view the dramatic action, but directly participate in it.

The emanation of force or "influence" from Lear's eyes is a special case. Only a king can claim:

> Ay, every inch a king.
> When I do stare, see how the subject quakes.
> (IV, vi, 106–107)

But the eyes of ordinary mortals also participate in, rather than observe, dramatic action. In the first half of the play, the eyes are characteristically represented as the organs through which feeling toward other people is expressed. Cordelia speaks scornfully of "a still-soliciting eye" (I, i); Goneril tells Oswald to "let his knights have colder looks among you" (I, iii); Lear says to Oswald, "Do you bandy looks with me, you rascal?" (I, iv), and his first greeting to Goneril is, "How now, daughter? What makes that frontlet on? You are too much of late i' th' frown" (I, iv). These references to the eyes reach a climax in Lear's appeal to Regan after he has fled Goneril's house. Lear says that Goneril "looked black upon me," and calls upon the lightning to "dart your blinding flames/ Into her scornful eyes!" When Regan objects that he will sometime curse her too, Lear replies:

> No, Regan, thou shalt never have my curse.
> Thy tender-hefted nature shall not give
> Thee o'er to harshness. Her eyes are fierce, but thine
> Do comfort, and not burn.
> (II, iv, 165–168)

All these passages emphasize the dramatic relationships and feelings that exist between individuals. They thus support a major theme that is stated when Cordelia says, "I love your Majesty/ According to my bond" (I, i). "Bond" here means both "obligation" and "relationship." The two meanings are linked throughout *Lear*, but it is the second meaning that the references to the eyes support. They constantly draw our attention not to the perception of moral obligations, but to the actual human relationships that give rise to moral obligations.

The misconceptions of the sight pattern come from reducing every mention of the eyes to a lowest common denominator of "sight equals insight." This falsifies even the passages that do refer to the eyes as the organs of vision. The most important of these in the first two acts are the Fool's speeches:

> *Fool.* Shalt see thy other daughter will use thee kindly; for
>   though she's as like this as a crab's like an apple [i.e., in
> appearance], yet I can tell what I can tell.
> *Lear.* What canst tell, boy?
> *Fool.* She will taste as like this as a crab does to a crab.
>   Thou canst tell why one's nose stands i' th' middle on's face?
> *Lear.* No.
> *Fool.* Why, to keep one's eyes of either side 's nose, that
>   what a man cannot smell out he may spy into.
>
> (I, v, 12–20)

Later the Fool says to Kent:

> All that follow their noses are led by their eyes but blind men,
> and there's not a nose among twenty but can smell him that's
> stinking.
>
> (II, iv, 66–68)

If sight here is identical with the kind of insight Lear lacks, then the meaning of the Fool's remarks is a moral generalization that comprehends all the action and themes of the play. But what immediately strikes us in these speeches, and what comes from the Fool's association of sight with smell and taste, is that "eyes" are instruments of physical closeness and immediacy. It is this distinct and individual quality that gives the speeches their meaning. When the eye imagery becomes central to the play, in the blinding of Gloucester, the fool's representation of sight as a gross sense will be joined to the dominant idea of the eyes as the organs that express human feeling.

Every reader is shocked by the dreadful scene in which Cornwall puts out Gloucester's eyes (III, vii), and the aesthetic justification of the scene has been considered one of the distinct successes of the modern critical approach to Shakespeare. The justification depends on the assumption that this scene, since its action is simpler (or cruder) than that of other scenes in the play, is the literal projection of a metaphor. Transformed in this way into a gigantic symbol, the blinding of Gloucester is then placed at the center of the sight pattern. But this interpretation is based on a virtual re-writing of the scene. The following account of the blinding of Glou-cester, by one of the best recent critics of Shakespeare, is an instruc-tive example:

> The spectacle of the suffering thus inflicted is almost intolerable, and only in relation to the vast conception of the whole tragedy, in which it forms a turning point, can its inclusion be justified. For it is no accident that the moment in which Gloucester loses his sight, the victim of what appears to be, and is, a gratuitous act of evil, is also that in which the birth of his spiritual understanding is con-firmed. . . . This new development is, indeed, the exteriorization of a central paradox, implied in Shakespeare's use of the image of sight. Those who "see," who pride themselves on their clear-sighted appraisal of the world and its ways, find themselves betrayed by their sight, are in fact, in a very real and tragic sense, blind; while those who have lost their eyes may, in the very moment of losing them, receive a flash of moral illumination, in fact, "see." The achievement by Gloucester of this kind of "sight" at the moment of his blinding can only be compared with the growth into moral insight that accompanies Lear's collapse into madness.
>
> (D. A. Traversi, *An Approach to Shakespeare*)

But just what is the "flash of moral illumination" achieved "in the very moment" of the blinding?

> *Gloucester.* Edmund, enkindle all the sparks of nature
>   To quit this horrid act.
> *Regan.*   Out, treacherous villain;
>   Thou call'st on him that hates thee. It was he
>   That made the overture of thy treasons to us;
>   Who is too good to pity thee.
> *Gloucester.* O my follies! Then Edgar was abused.
>   Kind gods, forgive me that, and prosper him.
>   (III, vii, 86–92)

Gloucester's new "spiritual understanding" is nothing more than a recognition of the fact that Edgar was not a treacherous son. It is due, moreover, to no internal illumination, but to Regan's final ges-ture of malice. We are turning things topsy-turvy if we call this "moral insight" and deny that name to the speech in which Glouces-ter, just before his eyes are put out, rebukes Regan for her treat-ment of Lear. We must take the scene at face value and ask why it moves not toward general moral insights, but toward Gloucester's particular recognitions about his sons.

We can first of all unburden ourselves of the assumption that the scene is simply a metaphor—a simplified restatement of what happens to Lear. It presents aspects of human experience that are different from those emphasized in Lear's half of the play. Instead of a psychological view of individual man, Shakespeare at this point gives us an ethical and social view of the world of men. The shift is marked by the way in which the scene reenacts moments from Lear's insane trial of his daughters in the preceding scene (III, vi). Just before Gloucester is brought in, Cornwall says:

> Though well we may not pass upon his life
> Without the form of justice, yet our power
> Shall do a court'sy to our wrath, which men
> May blame, but not control.
>   (III, vii, 23–26)

Cornwall dignifies his frankness by speaking of himself with something of Lear's royal manner. The mock (that is, hallucinatory) justice of the old king is succeeded by the mock justice, in the usual sense, of the new. As the scene progresses, there are repeated transformations of earlier details. When Gloucester is brought in, Regan greets him with a venomous "ingrateful fox": the kind of epithet Lear bestowed on her under the pressure of extreme suffering is for Regan a gesture of anger in ordinary discourse. Gloucester is then tied to a chair, and Regan plucks his beard. She makes an action out of Lear's helplessly violent accusation of Goneril: "I here take my oath before this honorable assembly, she kicked the poor King her father." The chaos of Lear's trial expresses his psychological state; the contrasting purposefulness with which Cornwall and Regan question Gloucester expresses an attitude toward their victim. At the climax of their assault Gloucester says, "I am tied to th' stake, and I must stand the course." The "course" is the dogs' attack in bearbaiting. Gloucester's experience makes literal Lear's hallucination: "The little dogs and all,/ Tray, Blanch, and Sweetheart—see, they bark at me." As we move from Lear to Gloucester, the horror of psychological suffering is transformed to the moral horror of what one person can do to another. The action of the scene seems simple and crude not because it is the physical embodiment of a metaphor, but because it is an intensified rendering of man's actual dealings with other men.

Together with the simplified character of the action, we find a new and distinctive manner in Gloucester's speeches. When he rebukes Regan for plucking his beard, he displays a richness of language and a rhythmic assurance that are unlike anything we have heard from him:

> Naughty lady,
> These hairs which thou dost ravish from my chin
> Will quicken and accuse thee. I am your host.
> With robber's hands my hospitable favors
> You should not ruffle thus.
> (III, *vii*, 36–40)

With their verbal and moral amplitude, these lines are in the characteristic vein of Lear's speeches to his daughters. Gloucester, who has been entirely unaware that Edmund is gleefully abusing him, now resembles Lear in his consciousness of injury and the scope with which he interprets it. But he displays none of Lear's excessiveness. His speech is not an outburst, and his indignation is neither shocking to us nor painful to himself. The result is that for the first time since the opening scene the response to an offense seems entirely just and adequate.

Gloucester's new mode prevails in the most important speech of the scene, just before his eyes are put out:

> *Regan.* Wherefore to Dover?
> *Gloucester.* Because I would not see thy cruel nails
> Pluck out his poor old eyes; nor thy fierce sister
> In his anointed flesh stick boarish fangs.
> The sea, with such a storm as his bare head
> In hell-black night endured, would have buoyed up
> And quenched the stellèd fires.
> Yet, poor old heart, he holp the heavens to rain.
> If wolves had at thy gate howled that stern time,
> Thou shouldst have said, 'Good porter, turn the key.'
> All cruels else subscribe. But I shall see
> The wingèd vengeance overtake such children.
> (III, *vii*, 55–66)

In this, as in the earlier speech, Lear's metaphors for and majestic dealing with offenses against him are divested of all that is both personal and kingly and are, so to speak, put in the mouth of Everyman. Gloucester's closing lines restate, on the grounds of common and natural human feeling, the final, insane version of Lear's numerous appeals to the avenging powers of heaven—"To have a thousand

with red burning spits/ Come hizzing in upon 'em" (III, vi).
Gloucester's words barely suggest the dramatic presence of a particular person: they are not a threat, as they would be with Lear, and
yet they are not controlled by Gloucester's usual cracker-barrel style.
With its résumé of so much preceding imagery, the speech has the
effect of a choric commentary on the action. But it also has a special
and essential dramatic effect. There is a remarkable disproportion between Regan's provocation ("Wherefore to Dover?") and the scope
of Gloucester's reply, just as there is between the sisters' reduction of
Lear's retinue and the magnitude of his response. But where Lear's
responses are to be referred to Lear himself (both to his role as king
and father and to his irascible and authoritarian temperament),
Gloucester's speech seems a just characterization of the way in which
Cornwall and Regan have borne down on him in their questioning.
Similarly, Regan's plucking of Gloucester's beard is exposed as despicable by the dignity and justness of Gloucester's response. We feel
very forcibly the brutality of Regan's acts in this scene, and this is
entirely due to the way Shakespeare makes us see them. The sisters'
final cruelty to Lear—their turning him out in the storm—is worse,
as a "real" human act, than anything so far done to Gloucester in
this scene. But we so strongly feel that Lear has produced the storm
from his own feelings—has gone out into it under his own impetus—
that we hardly separate shutting him out in a real storm as a distinct
human act.

We can now ask what justifies the blinding of Gloucester: why is
it poetically inevitable and not a gratuitous exploitation of our feelings? It is patently not true that physical action is simply the vehicle
of a metaphor here: the eye images by no means control our imagination, and Shakespeare draws our attention to Regan's cruelties as real
acts. Considered solely in its general character, as physical brutality,
the blinding is justified by the fact that the scene is about human
cruelty. The imagery of the eyes provides the poetic rationale, not
for physical outrage itself, but for the blinding as the representation
of physical outrage. The scene, in other words, is not produced by
the imagery; the imagery is picked up and intensified at a crucial
point in the scene.

The relevant metaphor occurs in Gloucester's reply to Regan, a
dozen lines before his eyes are put out:

> Because I would not see thy cruel nails
> Pluck out his poor old eyes.

This image obviously has nothing to do with sight, and we must ask what force it has as a metaphor for cruelty. In point of violence and physical grossness, it is less horrible than several other images—for example, Gloucester's next metaphor, "nor thy fierce sister/ In his anointed flesh stick boarish fangs." The peculiar horror suggested by plucking out the eyes comes from a feeling that the eyes are exceptionally delicate and vulnerable and yet extremely important and valuable. Gloucester's metaphor draws on Lear's most important speech about the eyes—his refusal to weep at Goneril's treatment of him—where the physical and moral qualities of the eyes are closely associated:

> Life and death, I am ashamed
> That thou hast power to shake my manhood thus!
> That these hot tears, which break from me perforce,
> Should make thee worth them. Blasts and fogs upon thee!
> Th' untented woundings of a father's curse
> Pierce every sense about thee! Old fond [i.e., foolish] eyes,
> Beweep this cause again I'll pluck ye out
> And cast you, with the waters that you loose,
> To temper clay.
>
> (I, iv, 287–295)

The notion that the eyes express feelings toward other human beings is here endowed with a sense of physical urgency and immediacy ("these hot tears") and is expanded to suggest that the eyes' actions establish bonds between human beings ("should make thee worth them"). Lear confirms the special value of the eyes by the shift of tone in "Old fond eyes" and the sense of majestic sadness it produces. The eyes are small and worthless—they can be plucked out and cast away, they are old and foolish—but at the same time they are potent and important. By expressing feelings about Goneril, Lear's eyes threaten to destroy him, so that they must be cast away and their tears are given the fine amplitude of "waters that you loose." Lear's words expand the biblical injunction, "If thine eye offend thee, pluck it out, and cast it from thee" (Matthew 18, 9), and this allusion focuses the double feeling about the eyes—they are mere flesh and yet it is morally important to be rid of them. In the final phrase, this double feeling becomes an identification of the eyes' moral and physical properties. "Temper clay" (literally to prepare clay for use by mixing it with water) is a metaphor for the mollifying of human feeling that Lear rejects. There is no separating physical vehicle from moral tenor in the metaphor, because the tears that express mollified feeling are themselves real water, and "clay" has the force of a synonym for flesh.

The usual defense of the blinding of Gloucester—that metaphor by its very presence mitigates physical horror—is particularly inappropriate. For Lear's speech and Gloucester's metaphor for cruelty associate the moral value with the physical properties of the eyes, and support the identification, in the blinding itself, of moral and physical outrage. The shock of the act is registered when Cornwall takes Gloucester's moral rebuke as an actual threat:

> *Gloucester.*   But I shall see
>   The wingèd vengeance overtake such children.
> *Cornwall.* See't shalt thou never. Fellows, hold the chair.
>   Upon these eyes of thine I'll set my foot.
>   (III, *vii*, 65–68)

Appallingly, Cornwall takes Gloucester at his word—as if vengeance depended on Gloucester's presence as witness. Cornwall's rage suddenly calls up, in a brutal and primitive form, the idea of the eyes as expressive and influential organs, and Regan, with sophisticated brutality, repeats it: "One side will mock another. Th' other too!" After his servant attempts to intervene and is slain by Regan, Cornwall's rage is concentrated on the eyes as physical organs:

> *Servant.*   My lord, you have one eye left
>   To see some mischief on him. O!
> *Cornwall.* Lest it see more, prevent it. Out, vile jelly.
>   Where is thy lustre now?
>   (III, *vii*, 81–84)

Cornwall's primitive brutality again gets a sophisticated restatement by Regan:

> Go thrust him out at gates, and let him smell
> His way to Dover.
>   (III, *vii*, 93–94)

In these despicable words, the idea of the eyes as expressive organs is joined to the fool's representation of sight as, like smell, one of the grosser senses. Cornwall's and Regan's contempt for moral feeling is now seen as a loathing of flesh itself.

Through the imagery of the eyes, we see the blinding of Gloucester as a dreadful abuse of "what human eyes are." The true horror of the scene lies in what this awareness suggests. An act of physical violation is not an isolated barbarity but the climax of the previous ruptures of affection and obligation that we metaphorically call "violations" of human bonds. To this horror is added another—the awareness that Gloucester's eyes *are* mere jelly and that all the moral values we feel to be violated by Cornwall reside in the luster that is so readily extinguished. Our identification of moral value and fleshly frailty is in direct proportion to and inseparable from our moral dismay: to the extent that we are shocked by Regan's "Let him smell his way to Dover" we feel how appallingly it characterizes the state to which Gloucester has been reduced. Horror in this scene takes on a ghastly pathos, because the value of the eyes is directly identified with their vulnerability.

We can now answer the question with which we began: Why does the scene move from the general moral insights that Gloucester shares with all men to a particular recognition ("Then Edgar was abused") that is not magnified or elaborated by any of Lear's sort of poetry? The significance of "what Gloucester learns" is of a kind directly opposite to that proposed by the sight pattern, which takes truly perceived realities to be something like Platonic ideas—both more abstract and more real than the mere phenomena of life. Thus, Heilman, the leading theorist of the sight pattern, expounds Cornwall's "Out, vile jelly": "What Cornwall does not know is that Gloucester now sees better than he has ever seen; perhaps the final guarantee of his insight is his loss of outward sight. The vile jelly, the material seeing, had but caught reflections from the outer surface of life." This commentary seems to me clumsy, not to say cold-hearted, but it is the kind of thing the sight pattern forces on us. If recognizing that "Edgar was abused" is general moral insight, then Edgar must somehow be a reality that transcends "the outer surface of life." But the point and force of the scene lie in the reality attributed to the actual relations between men, and in the awesome sense we have that a bond of love depends on physical wholeness, presence, and contact. Gloucester's moral recognition must involve a recognition about Edgar as Edgar—a real person and a real son, not merely the embodiment of a virtue or an abstract truth.

Gloucester himself makes these points in the next scene:

> I have no way, and therefore want no eyes;
> I stumbled when I saw. Full oft 'tis seen
> Our means secure us, and our mere defects
> Prove our commodities. O dear son Edgar,

The food of thy abusèd father's wrath,
Might I but live to see thee in my touch
I'ld say I had eyes again!
(IV, i, 18-24)

For the sight pattern, Gloucester's self-awareness in "I stumbled when I saw" must be treated as an insight. But the kind of aphoristic moral paradox that the sight pattern seeks is rather to be found in the next lines—"Our means secure us, and our mere defects/ Prove our commodities." As its impersonal tone ("Full oft 'tis seen") indicates, this is a gnomic statement—one that purports to cover many cases without any particular reference to the speaker. If such general insights were sufficient to human experience, the speech—and indeed Gloucester's experience—could end at this point. But "I stumbled when I saw" is intensely personal and dramatic, rather than gnomic. The paradox applies only to Gloucester himself, and the directness and simplicity of the line differ sharply from the rather formal language and structure of the next two lines. Gloucester is not summarizing his experience in a moral reflection; he is, first of all, answering the old man's "You cannot see your way," and he is attempting to deal with his feelings of remorse, misery, and suffering. The eye imagery not only supports the personal and dramatic elements in the line, but also endows them with physical qualities. The Fool's speeches and Regan's dreadful variant, "Let him smell his way to Dover," enforce the suggestions of grossness and clumsiness in "stumbled." As in the blinding of Gloucester, the poetry supports the physical reality of the action—Gloucester groping around the stage with his eyes bleeding. The absurdity of congratulating Gloucester for his insights in this speech is exposed by the final use of eye imagery—"Might I but live to see thee in my touch/ I'ld say I had eyes again!" What is important to Gloucester is not insight, but a relationship for which the only possible metaphor is physical contact.

The symbolism of the eyes enforces the human reality of the bonds that have been violated in the play and the physical reality of metaphors for mental and emotional suffering. As a version of Lear's story, the Gloucester subplot is so down to earth and literal that initially it borders on farce. In the blinding of Gloucester, the two plots are brought together, and the literalizations of the subplot emerge as pressing realities that are crucial to the meaning of the play. To see this we must examine the relationship between the two plots.

Just as the blinding of Gloucester is not a simplified restatement of Lear's experience, so the whole subplot is not to be dismissed as a

mere parallel to the main plot. Its relation to the main plot can best
be understood by considering how differently Lear and Gloucester
stand for Everyman. Gloucester is Everyman in the sense that he
is ordinary—indistinguishable from other men in temperament and
intelligence. Lear's role as Everyman is indicated by the anonymous
gentleman's characterization of him in the storm:

> Strives in his little world of man to outscorn
> The to-and-fro-conflicting wind and rain.
> (*III, i*, 10–11)

Renaissance thought conceived of the individual as a microcosm, or
"little world"—a miniature copy of the created universe. Lear not
only feels nature's storms within himself; he also pits his little world
against the world outside him. His audacity and grandeur remind us
that his role as microcosm, containing within himself all nature and
human nature, is inseparable from his role as king—the human individual who most fully makes man's claim to be sovereign over the
earth and God's chief creature. Lear is Everyman because he is the
individual human being who most eloquently stands for all men.

Interpretations of *Lear* tend to treat the play solely from the stand-
point of the individual as king and microcosm. Either they treat all
the significant action as emanating from and occurring within Lear,
or they put Shakespeare and the reader in a godlike relation to the
play. In either case they share Lear's kingly assumption that the human personality is autonomous: an individual can comprehend and
deal with all that the play presents of nature and human nature.
Surely this is a strange assumption for dealing with a play that
notoriously overwhelms and exhausts us. The play carries over to us
Lear's command to himself: "Expose thyself to feel what wretches
feel" (III, iv). One cannot obey this injunction and still remain
totally in command of one's experience, and this, it seems to me, is
the point of the Gloucester plot. It restates Lear's experience as king
and microcosm in terms of common human experience. Individual
experience is ordinary, physical, down to earth, and does not answer
to Lear's cosmic valuations; other men are dramatically encountered
as other men and not as reflections of one's own personality. The
Gloucester plot presents Everyman as suffering, not initiating his
experience; it shows a condition in which "out of control" is not an
emotional or moral state (which could be corrected), but a fact of
the human condition. So long as we measure Lear by an ideal image
of the autonomous personality, his tragedy is merely personal.

Through the perspective of the subplot, we see Lear's tragedy as a tragedy of Everyman—the inevitable destruction of the individual who attempts to be a microcosm in a macrocosm that has no order of its own.

By its emphasis on insight, the sight pattern commits itself to a belief that the individual is autonomous, for it is assumed that when moral truths are perceived they automatically determine (or govern) personality. But when Lear and Gloucester meet on the heath, a flurry of sight imagery completely undermines the notion that moral insight is morally adequate:

> Gloucester. Dost thou know me?
> Lear. I remember thine eyes well enough. Dost thou squiny at me?
>   No, do thy worst, blind Cupid; I'll not love. Read thou
>   this challenge; mark but the penning of it.
> Gloucester. Were all thy letters suns, I could not see.
> Edgar. [aside] I would not take this from report—it is,
>   And my heart breaks at it.
> Lear. Read.
> Gloucester. What, with the case of eyes?
> Lear. O, ho, are you there with me? No eyes in your head,
>   nor no money in your purse? Your eyes are in a heavy case,
>   your purse in a light; yet you see how this world goes.
> Gloucester. I see it feelingly.
> Lear. What, art mad? A man may see how this world goes with
>   no eyes. Look with thine ears. See how yond justice
>   rails upon yond simple thief. . .
>
>   (IV, vi, 134–150)

Lear's use of Gloucester's blindness as the metaphoric basis for his moral insights is a dreadful cruelty to Gloucester. Emotional suffering, which a moment before was associated with the "painful" insights of Lear's diatribe against women, is now associated with the literal pain of Gloucester's blindness. The fusion of physical and emotional suffering, first registered by Edgar's aside, emerges in Gloucester's "I see it feelingly." This description of the way a blind man finds his way around is also a decisive echo of Gloucester's condemnation of the man "who will not see/ Because he does not feel" (IV, i); it records his pained response to Lear's behavior—as if to say, "Nothing makes me see how the world goes more than the way you are treating me now." We now feel Lear's suffering through Gloucester's, and Lear's mental condition becomes closely identified with Gloucester's blindness. His wild hallucinations are indistinguishable from his cruelties, and both operate as a screen to keep him from seeing—not moral realities, but the man in front of him.

Lear's profoundly moving recognition of Gloucester at the end of their encounter is achieved by a switch on the most grotesque use of sight imagery in the scene:

> Get thee glass eyes
> And, like a scurvy politician, seem
> To see the things thou dost not.
> (*IV, vi*, 167–169)

The moral force of the satiric insight is in direct proportion to its cruelty as a recommendation to Gloucester. But after a burst of lunacy, Lear suddenly breaks the mold of the sight metaphor:

> If thou wilt weep my fortunes, take my eyes.
> I know thee well enough; thy name is Gloucester.
> (*IV, vi*, 173–174)

The ability to see, the recognition of Gloucester, comes when Lear offers him his own eyes and identifies weeping as their function. The tenderness and generosity of these lines are held in poise with a feeling that "If thou wilt weep my fortunes" is the condition of a gift and that, through the majesty of Lear's gesture, "take my eyes" has literal force. Lear's earlier threat to pluck out his eyes in order to prevent their weeping is now a gesture of love.

Up to this point in the play, the connection that the eye imagery establishes between the plots is indicated by two almost identical phrases. The doctor tells Cordelia that there are "many simples operative, whose power/ Will close the eye of anguish" (IV, iv). Sixty lines later, the doctor's metaphor is made literal when Edgar says to his father, "Why, then, your other senses grow imperfect/ By your eyes' anguish" (IV, vi). The eye imagery of the subplot gives an unremitting physical force to the bodily metaphors of the main plot. Lear's "I am not ague-proof" (IV, vi), an insight for which he is often commended, gets its decisively tragic implications from the reality of Gloucester's wound and the fact that it was inflicted by hostile forces he was helpless to oppose. Now, in the encounter between the two protagonists, Lear's experience is assimilated to Gloucester's. Because Lear's cruelties make him blind to Gloucester's presence and are felt through Gloucester's physical suffering, the

complex of meanings established when Gloucester's eyes are put out
is brought to bear on Lear. The result is a virtual identification of
eyes with the expressive powers that establish bonds between human
beings.

In recognizing Gloucester, Lear absorbs Gloucester's physical suffering and all it signifies into his own experience. His majestic hint
of self-mutilation when he offers Gloucester his eyes has tragic implications that are developed a dozen lines later. A gentleman sent by
Cordelia comes to rescue Lear:

> Gentleman. O, here he is! Lay hand upon him.—Sir,
>   Your most dear daughter—
> Lear. No rescue? What, a prisoner? I am even
>   The natural fool of fortune. Use me well;
>   You shall have ransom. Let me have surgeons;
>   I am cut to th' brains.
> Gentleman.   You shall have anything.
> Lear. No seconds? All myself?
>   Why, this would make a man a man of salt,
>   To use his eyes for garden waterpots,
>   Ay, and laying autumn's dust.
>   (IV, vi, 185–194)

Lear's sense of his experience here is very close to Gloucester's. He
calls himself "the natural fool of fortune" and in the next breath
equates his suffering with intense physical pain. His second speech
is a reprise of his address to his "Old fond eyes." What was formerly
a magisterial refusal to yield to the feelings stirred by Goneril's actions now renders a feeling of emotional release: the lines are, in
fact, the weeping of his fortunes that Lear asked of Gloucester. But
"becoming like Gloucester" does not suggest the moral development
that most critics find in Lear. One feels Lear's grotesqueness very
strongly in this brief episode. The suggestions of "natural fool of
fortune" are developed in the second speech through Lear's own
feeling of absurdity: it is first indicated by the tone of surprise and
helplessness in "Why, this would make a man a man of salt" and is
capped by the physical grotesqueness of the image of the eyes as
waterpots. The feeling of grotesqueness clearly comes from the continuing presence of Lear's kingly instincts. Just as his first speech is
a characteristic bit of cosmic self-dramatization, so in the second he
is trying to master his feelings in the very moment of yielding to
them: he instinctively feels his identity is being destroyed.

The question is how we are to evaluate the fact that Lear's absurdity comes from his attempt to deal with Gloucester's experience in a kingly manner. The sight pattern assumes that it is possible and natural to be master of one's experience. In the present context this means mastering the insight that one cannot control one's experience. If Lear's kingly instincts are keeping this insight from functioning properly, then they are simply an unfortunate character trait—the last traces of his old, bad self. It seems to me, on the other hand, that the figure Lear presents, despite its absurdity, has general force and authority for the play. Lear is torn apart by his tenacious hold on his identity and on all his experiences—both all he has been through ("suffered" in its broadest sense) and the experiences of each moment—dramatic encounters with other men and impulses from within. Lear's grotesqueness in this scene comes precisely from his attempt to behave again as an autonomous personality.

The test of the play's attitude toward the autonomy of individual personality is Lear's reconciliation with Cordelia. In this scene, as in the reunion of Lear and Gloucester, the crucial issue is not insight, but recognition. When Lear awakens, his first words to Cordelia are:

> You do me wrong to take me out o' th' grave.
> Thou art a soul in bliss; but I am bound
> Upon a wheel of fire, that mine own tears
> Do scald like molten lead.
> (IV, vii, 45–48)

These lines are so potent that critics have often taken them as a sign of Lear's rebirth into a new personality. But as Cordelia herself says, Lear is "Still, still, far wide!" A very different kind of poetry leads Lear to the recognition that the "soul in bliss" is "my child Cordelia":

> *Lear.* Where have I been? Where am I? Fair daylight?
> I am mightily abused. I should e'en die with pity
> To see another thus. I know not what to say.
> I will not swear these are my hands. Let's see—
> I feel this pin prick. Would I were assured
> Of my condition.
> *Cordelia.*   O look upon me, sir,
> And hold your hand in benediction o'er me.
> You must not kneel.
> *Lear.*   Pray, do not mock me.
> I am a very foolish fond old man,
> Fourscore and upward, not an hour more nor less;
> And, to deal plainly,

I fear I am not in my perfect mind.
Methinks I should know you, and know this man;
Yet I am doubtful, for I am mainly ignorant
What place this is; and all the skill I have
Remembers not these garments; nor I know not
Where I did lodge last night. Do not laugh at me;
For, as I am a man, I think this lady
To be my child Cordelia.
Cordelia.   And so I am! I am!
Lear. Be your tears wet? Yes, faith. I pray weep not.
If you have poison for me, I will drink it.
I know you do not love me; for your sisters
Have, as I do remember, done me wrong.
You have some cause, they have not.
Cordelia.   No cause, no cause.
Lear. Am I in France?
Kent.   In your own kingdom, sir.
Lear. Do not abuse me.

                                     (IV, *vii*, 52–77)

The richness and fullness of Lear's first speech change to colloquial
rambling and, when rhythmic assurance is regained after the recognition of Cordelia, to an unbelievable plainness. Lear is fully assimilated to Gloucester's experience here. Having forsaken his kingship,
he is a "very foolish fond old man," and in his constant fear of
abuse is precisely in the role of Gloucester, who passively suffers all
his ills. Lear's sense perceptions are blurred, yet as they become
certain, simple touch and sight ("I feel this pin prick," "Be your
tears wet?") are sufficient to reestablish and sufficiently express the
bond of love. Similarly, Cordelia's exclamations of love ("And so I
am! I am!" and "No cause, no cause") are almost speechless gestures
—the verbal equivalents of simple physical contact. And inseparable
from these aspects of the scene is our awareness of the physical
destruction Lear has undergone—the enfeeblement that somehow
enables him to experience renewed contact with Cordelia.

Lear is like Gloucester in the simplicity of his feelings, of his self-
awareness, and of his responses to Cordelia. For most critics these
are the signs of a new personal identity in Lear. But Lear is also like
Gloucester in his humiliation, and everything in the play and in the
scene makes us aware that this humiliation is the consequence of
suffering and an experience of suffering—not merely a moral virtue,
humility, apprehended by Lear. Traversi calls the following lines a
"confession of guilt":

> I know you do not love me; for your sisters
> Have, as I do remember, done me wrong.
> You have some cause, they have not.
>
> (IV, vii, 73-75)

A confession of guilt is a decisive moral act—not at all what is suggested by the childlike "I know you do not love me" and the weakness and vagueness of "as I do remember." These elements in the speech bring out the pathos of Lear's expressing tenderness and love in terms of justice, the theme on which he raved as the mad king in the scene with Gloucester. The clinging to both his experience and his identity as king points not to the creation of a new personality, but to the destruction that has been wrought in the old. Lear's pained recoil from Kent's "In your own kingdom, sir" fuses the two elements of his humiliation that are inextricably bound up with his recognition of Cordelia—his suffering and his uncertainty about his own identity. All this is to say that the extraordinary sense of love in this scene is inseparable from its immense sadness. The mystery is not that Cordelia *does* "cure this great breach in his abusèd nature" (IV, vii), but that love exists despite the fact that she cannot.

Lear's reconciliation with Cordelia is the promised land for many readers of the play, but can it really sustain the kind of statements made about it? "Lear wins his purgatorial reward in finding that which is most real to him, his love for Cordelia. For the first time he compasses his own reality, and its signs are humility and love" (G. Wilson Knight, *The Wheel of Fire*). Another critic shifts the focus from Lear himself to the author and reader, and claims that the play as a whole is a "complete endorsement of a particular quality of being." This quality is love—"the condition of intellectual clarity, the energizing centre from which personality may grow unhampered by the need for self-assertion or evasive subterfuge" (L. C. Knights, *Some Shakespearean Themes*). Both these views assume that love in *King Lear* is a phenomenon of the autonomous personality and is thus, as an experience, a quality of being or a mode of understanding. But love in this scene and everywhere in the play is a dramatic relation between human beings; the experience of love always involves the dramatic pressures of feeling and the dramatic presence or absence of the beloved. Ecstatic interpretations of the reunion with Cordelia depend on three interconnected fallacies that are neatly recorded in G. Wilson Knight's description of the scene: "Now the healing balm of uttermost humility and love. He humbles himself, not to Cordelia, but to the love now royally enthroned in his heart erstwhile usurped." The primary mistake of equating Lear's being humbled with the virtue of humility is compounded by the use of royal metaphors for Lear's psychological condition. These two errors cooperate with and depend on making the scene an action that occurs within Lear. But all the feeling that Knight's rhetoric attempts to convey would be destroyed if the scene were not a dramatic encounter. Cordelia is Cordelia. Surely there is no need to identify her with the abstraction Love in order to say that she is extraordinarily loving.

If we treat Lear's recognition of Cordelia as a moral awareness that gives him a new personal identity, we must claim that his suffering is a good. It seems to me we must say that Lear's suffering is shocking and heartbreaking and also (not "and yet") it enables him to say "Thou art a soul in bliss" and then to recognize his daughter. Furthermore, "good" and "bad" elements are not separable entities, but are throughout the play fused in direct dramatic experience. For it is experience, not understanding, that is tested in *King Lear*. All man's capacities for moral awareness reside in Lear's attempt to be king and microcosm in a world of man and nature that has no order of its own. We cannot separate Lear's terrible energies and moral demands from those that confer value on Cordelia and enable him to love her; nor can we propose a definition of "human" that includes Cordelia and excludes her sisters. The tragedy lies in the inevitability with which human experience will destroy anyone who tries to comprehend it all. And the tragedy is so stark and vast because it fully honors Lear's mode of experience. No image of individual man is available to us by which we can say it could or should be otherwise.

Henry VIII: The Conscience of the King

BY PAUL BERTRAM

SIR HENRY WOTTON, who saw one of the first performances of *Henry VIII* in 1613, remarked on the "many extraordinary circumstances of Pomp and Majesty" he had seen in the play, "sufficient in truth within a while to make greatness very familiar, if not ridiculous." The touch of aristocratic disdain in that comment suggests that Wotton was startled less by the pageantry and spectacle of the play than by its uncommonly realistic close-ups of the lives of the great. To the original audiences the play must also have seemed a remarkably daring re-creation of recent history; but the sense of historical immediacy and intimacy which the play achieves is a dramatic effect, and later audiences have experienced it too. It is one of the strongest first impressions made by the play.

Other strong impressions have been made by certain of the prominent characters—Wolsey and Katherine in particular. Of Katherine's death scene, for example, Dr. Johnson wrote:

> This scene is, above any other part of *Shakespeare's* tragedies, and perhaps above any scene of any other poet, tender and pathetick, without gods, or furies, or poisons, or precipices, without the help of romantick circumstances, without improbable sallies of poetical lamentation, and without any throes of tumultuous misery.

And other critics have written almost as impressively of their responses both to Wolsey and to Katherine. Fewer critics, however, have responded so favorably to the play as a whole. And of its central character many critics have preferred to say nothing at all.

Criticism of the play traditionally includes comment on its pomp and pageantry, occasional notice of its special brand of historical realism, and a good deal of attention to the broken fortunes of

Wolsey and Katherine. Apart from these interests, however, the play seems to have elicited a wider range of disagreement throughout its critical history than almost any other play of the canon. Several points in this critical record deserve notice, and a review of them will furnish a convenient introduction to the main business of this essay—an examination of the design of the play with particular attention to the role of the King.

Since the action of the play deals with the public and private life of the King from the time he is still influenced by Wolsey until the time Elizabeth is born, the ways in which critics have regarded the character of the King have naturally affected their sense of the dramatic action. Not all critics have distinguished, however, between the King as defined by the play and the historical Henry VIII. Hazlitt, for example, failed to make any distinction whatever between the two, and although he admired the play, he praised Shakespeare for the "great truth" with which he had "represented in all the bloated deformity of mind and person" this "disgusting" man; Hazlitt even expressed surprise that Henry—with "his vulgarity, his arrogance, his sensuality, his cruelty"—was not "hooted from the English stage." This representation was, of course, the popular nineteenth century view of the historical Henry—the Holbein portrait (painted in the King's last years) seen through the eyes of historians Shakespeare never knew. The King we encounter in the play (to speak merely of his physical image for the moment) is youthful and vigorous; even before we first set eyes on him we hear reports that his chivalric accomplishments at the Field of the Cloth of Gold caused all beholders to marvel. The method by which the popular image of Henry obscured the dramatic image is interestingly suggested in a comment by the once influential German critic Ulrici (1839), whose reading was at least a little more careful than Hazlitt's:

> Shakespeare has not spared Henry's character: he appears everywhere as the obstinate, capricious, selfish and heartless man that he was—a slave to his favourites and to his passions. That Shakespeare has not *expressly* described him as such, that he has rather characterized him tacitly through his own actions, and no doubt sedulously pushed his good points into the foreground, could not—without injustice—have been expected otherwise from a national poet who wrote in the reign of Henry's daughter.

Critics who were possessed of the truth about the historical King Henry—and there was apparently only one main truth about him to

most nineteenth century minds—would naturally want Shakespeare
to share in their perception.

Commentators who saw the King in this light were naturally dis-
turbed (as was Ulrici) by the outcome of the play. James Spedding,
in his famous essay of 1850, undertook to describe and expound the
interpretative difficulty. "Our sympathy," he wrote, "is for the grief
and goodness of Queen Katharine," but "the course of the action"
after Henry's divorce from Katherine "requires us to entertain as a
theme of joy and compensatory satisfaction the coronation of Anne
Bullen and the birth of her daughter; which are in fact a part of
Katharine's injury, and amount to little less than the ultimate
triumph of wrong." *Henry VIII* is the only one of Shakespeare's histories, according to Spedding, in which we are "allowed to exult in
the success of the wrongdoer" and "to forget the penalties which
are due to guilt." Apart from the failure of the play to provide an
edifying moral conclusion, Spedding added, it was incoherent on
purely dramatic grounds; "the greater part of the fifth act" he declared to be "utterly irrelevant to the business of the play," and he
cited the quarrel between Gardiner and Cranmer as a specific instance of an episode unconnected with what precedes and what follows: "nothing in the play is explained by it, nothing depends upon
it." It is true that, if one were to regard either the story of Wolsey
or the story of Katherine as the center of the dramatic action, the
fifth act would appear to be as irrelevant to the rest of the play as it
seemed to Spedding.

The novel solution invented by Spedding to resolve the difficulties
raised by his interpretation was, as everyone knows, that nearly two-
thirds of the play had not been written by Shakespeare at all. Spedding divided the play by applying a metrical test of his own invention; according to his division, every scene in which "redundant
syllables" (feminine endings) occurred in more than half of the
lines had been written, and badly written, by John Fletcher. The
theory of this literary Lord Kelvin was that Shakespeare had written
several scenes of a projected drama on Henry VIII "and the final
separation of the English from the Romish Church" (a subject
which would have allowed him to show "such reason and religion
as there were in Henry's scruples"), that he had for some reason
been unable to complete it, and that Fletcher subsequently and independently made use of these scenes in fashioning the final play—
which Shakespeare's fellows nevertheless later published in the First
Folio.

Most recent editors of *Henry VIII*—Peter Alexander, Hardin Craig, R. A. Foakes, G. B. Harrison, C. J. Sisson—have dismissed the Spedding theory, and it has been mentioned here only because throughout all its long tenure—from the time it was popularized by the New Shakspere Society and later Victorian editors until it came under attack in the 1930's—it seems to have been largely responsible for the general neglect of the play by many critics and for the strange misrepresentations of it by others. When in 1919 T. S. Eliot was persuaded that parts of *Hamlet* were not by Shakespeare, he observed that *Hamlet* "will appear to us very differently if, instead of treating the whole action of the play as due to Shakespeare's design, we perceive his *Hamlet* to be superposed upon much cruder material which persists even in the final form." It will indeed; men are seldom able to look beyond their own horizon of expectations. To critics who saw divided authorship in *Henry VIII* it appeared that the play (as the Yale editors put it in 1925) "is not a drama at all" but rather a mere collection of scenes which were "hastily thrown together" and which "have little relation, even chronological, between them." And while several more constructive discussions of the play have been published in recent years (of which Wilson Knight's long essay in *The Crown of Life* is probably the best known and Muriel St. Clare Byrne's essay in the 1950 *Shakespeare Survey* one of the finest), objections of the following sort are still to be encountered, and still require an answer:

> Among Shakespeare's history plays *Henry VIII* is conspicuous for its disunity. As the crowd of notable historical personages parades before us, our attention is drawn first to Buckingham, then to Queen Katherine and Wolsey, and finally to Cranmer. No theme unites their successive stories except that most general of tragic themes: how are the mighty fallen! And even this unifying principle does not apply to Cranmer, who narrowly escapes the dismal fate of the other three and ends the play with the triumphant prophecy of the Elizabethan glories to come.

This succinct expression of a traditional complaint was offered by Eugene Waith in 1952, and the formulation is itself instructive; the critic abstracts a "unifying principle"—the process is neither simple nor passive—and then proceeds to damn the play for failing to live up to it. But if the hostile critics had not usually ignored or misrepresented the hero of the play as they reasoned about its structure, they might have been able to construct a more satisfactory unifying principle. For the play itself, more carefully considered, is as political in

its concerns as any of Shakespeare's English histories, and the importance of each major character depends (as usual in the histories) on
the relation between that character and the King.[1]

The King in Act I is a monarch whose reign is marked both by
the opulence of his court and by the dissatisfaction of his subjects.
The opening dialogues describe the state visit to France whose hoped-
for outcome had been enduring peace and a prosperous England.
Norfolk had been present at the Field of the Cloth of Gold, and he
describes to Buckingham the almost too splendid pageantry that had
been contrived as entertainment:

> you lost
> The view of earthly glory: men might say
> Till this time pomp was single, but now married
> To one above itself. Each following day   . .
> Became the next day's master, till the last
> Made former wonders, its. To-day the French,
> All clinquant all in gold, like heathen gods
> Shone down the English; and to-morrow they
> Made Britain India: every man that stood
> Show'd like a mine.
>
> (I, i, 13–22)

Buckingham asks who it was who "set the body and the limbs/ Of
this great sport together," and when he learns that Wolsey had
arranged it all, the "earthly glory" suddenly seems to him nothing
but "fierce vanities," and he is astonished that Wolsey, "such a
keech" (lump of congealed fat), "can with his very bulk/ Take up
the rays o'th'beneficial sun,/ And keep it from the earth." Norfolk
agrees that Wolsey is an upstart, "not propp'd by ancestry," who has
arrogantly pushed himself into a "place next to the king." Since
Wolsey was responsible for burdening the nobility with the extravagance of the French meeting, he is to blame for many of them having

> so sicken'd their estates that never
> They shall abound as formerly
> (I, i, 82–83)

and for others having sold their lands, "broke their backs with laying
manors on 'em," and beggared their children.

---

[1] The text of *Henry VIII* cited in the commentary which follows is that of
the New Arden edition by R. A. Foakes (1957). Readers interested in the play
will probably find the annotations in this edition more helpful than those in any
other to date.

Wolsey is first portrayed, then, as a solemn lord of misrule, fat on the body politic, an uncomic Falstaff come to power. His taste for opulence is later to be given as much a personal as a political emphasis—as in I, iv, where he plays the generous host and entertainer —but our initial view of him stresses his relation to the land, his bulky interposition between sun and earth or King and subject. The alliance he has arranged with the "heathen" French ("their clothes are after such a pagan cut," the Lord Chamberlain is to comment in I, iii) is a particular sore point with the nobility; the conference in the vale of Andren had been nothing but waste and "vanity," since the French are not going to keep faith; even before the meeting had been concluded, there had been a great storm which those assembled had taken as "a general prophecy":

> this tempest
> Dashing the garment of this peace, aboded
> The sudden breach on't.
>   (I, i, 92–94)

And much of the following scene develops Wolsey's effect on the social fabric at home, dramatized in the taxation issue:

> upon these taxations,
> The clothiers all not able to maintain
> The many to them longing, have put off
> The spinsters, carders, fullers, weavers, who
> Unfit for other life, compell'd by hunger
> And lack of other means, in desperate manner
> Daring th'event to th'teeth, are all in uproar . . .
>   (I, ii, 30–36)

The desperation of the nobility is matched by the suffering of the lesser classes, and the blame is again placed on Wolsey. The conflicts have been clearly embodied for the audience in a series of striking theatrical climaxes: Wolsey's strange procession across the stage (directed at I, i, 114), highlighting the clash between Wolsey and Buckingham around which most of the dialogue in the first scene is built; the destruction of Buckingham with his arrest near the end of the scene, confirming the view of the nobles that Wolsey is at the highest point of his power; and the confrontation in the next scene between Wolsey and Katherine—his proud arrogance opposed to her proud righteousness—with the King as yet a mere arbiter, not deeply interested in the taxation issue, not yet deeply involved in his responsibilities.

Wolsey's role is too wide in its range of implications to be defined wholly by its political aspect. Abergavenny tells us that the Cardinal's pride is from hell, or,

> If not from hell the devil is a niggard,
> Or has given all before, and he begins
> A new hell in himself.
>
> (I, i, 70–72)

Abergavenny and his friends see Wolsey as a satanic torturer; their language draws explicitly from the conception of England as Jerusalem that pervades every scene of this play, it looks forward to Wolsey's own later comparisons of himself to Lucifer in III, ii, and the last phrase in the passage cited hints at the pathos in Wolsey's personal drama which is to become apparent even before Wolsey expresses it directly in his final soliloquy or his address to Cromwell.

Our first encounter with the King and our first direct experience of his relation to Wolsey come in the second scene. He makes his appearance "leaning on the Cardinal's shoulder" and thanking him for apprehending Buckingham's treason, but at once Norfolk and Katherine mount their attack on Wolsey's commissions and the King challenges Wolsey to defend himself; in the Cardinal's slow reply we hear the accomplished confidence of a still powerful old man, his injured voice starched with dignity and rising (at "we") to a deliberate regality never assumed by the King, and never again to be attempted by Wolsey himself:

> if I am
> Traduc'd by ignorant tongues, which neither know
> My faculties nor person, yet will be
> The chronicles of my doing, let me say
> 'Tis but the fate of place, and the rough brake
> That virtue must go through: we must not stint
> Our necessary actions in the fear
> To cope malicious censurers, which ever
> As rav'nous fishes, do a vessel follow
> That is new trimm'd, but benefit no further
> Than vainly longing. . . .
>
> If we shall stand still,
> In fear our motion will be mock'd or carp'd at,
> We should take root here, where we sit;
> Or sit state-statues only.
>
> (I, ii, 71–81, 85–88)

It is not so much the King's revocation of Wolsey's tax as it is the
curtly instructive tone of his response that suggests his dependence
upon the Cardinal has been exaggerated by commentators:

> Things done well
> And with a care exempt themselves from fear;
> Things done without example, in their issue
> Are to be fear'd. Have you a precedent
> Of this commission? I believe, not any. . . .
>> (I, ii, 88–92)

A moment later the King is speaking to Katherine:

> The gentleman is learn'd, and a most rare speaker,
> To nature none more bound . . .
>
> This man so complete,
> Who was enroll'd 'mongst wonders (and when we,
> Almost with ravish'd list'ning, could not find
> His hour of speech a minute) he, my lady,
> Hath into monstrous habits put the graces
> That once were his, and is become as black
> As if besmear'd in hell. . . .
>> (I, ii, 111–112, 118–124)

These lines follow Katherine's "I am sorry that the Duke of Buck-
ingham/ Is run in your displeasure," and of course they sum up the
King's attitudes toward Buckingham. But Katherine's two lines
would not blot out most of the action and dialogue which precede
them, and the audience, which at this point knows more than the
King, would probably note the ironic appropriateness of the speech
to the relation between the King and Wolsey. The opening lines of
the scene had already made clear that Buckingham's condemnation
was a foregone conclusion, and the whole focus of the scene—even,
indeed especially, during the interrogation of Buckingham's Surveyor
—is on the King himself. As Miss Byrne has pointed out, "the pretended threat both to his own life and to the Tudor succession is
what brings him into the arena to deal with his own affairs." The
question of Buckingham's innocence or guilt is, in the eyes not of the
King but of the audience, left ambiguous—a point which sometimes
troubled critics preoccupied with "character":

Buckingham . . . is a contradiction. . . . Was he innocent or
guilty? It cannot be told from anything in the drama, yet this

must be the central point in his character. There is left only the uncertain inference that Wolsey bribed his servants to commit perjury.

There is left *also* the "uncertain inference" that Buckingham might seize the throne "if the king/ Should without issue die" (lines 133–134). This "contradiction" (the comment is by Denton Snider) is dramatically useful: Buckingham is made to appear sufficiently the innocent victim for Wolsey to appear his cruel tormentor, while he is made to appear sufficiently guilty to keep the audience from blaming the King, or even from regarding him simply as Wolsey's dupe. The actual trial of Buckingham is reduced to a mere offstage report by the walking Gentlemen in II, i, and even in his moving speech of farewell Buckingham himself (at II, i, 88–94) is made to identify the health of the land with the success of the King. The older critics tended to view each character and episode in isolation, since they were usually more concerned with the moral growth of the individual, the "central point" in his character, than with his place in the pattern of developing relationships. The action of the play shows us a King who reigns becoming a King who rules, and the principal episodes are made to serve this development.

The portraits of Wolsey and Katherine which have so dominated the imagination of most commentators are brought into surprisingly close association throughout the play. Both Katherine and Wolsey are older than the King, and before Act II is concluded the fortunes of each have become associated with the past. Since responsibility for bringing about the divorce is at first attached almost entirely to Wolsey, and since his later opposition to the divorce is one of the principal causes of his downfall, he and Katherine become instruments, so to speak, of each other's destruction. And it is during Katherine's final scene that (by still another of Shakespeare's many drastic and purposeful rearrangements of historical chronology and event) our last view of Wolsey—Griffith's report in IV, ii—associates his death with Katherine's. The Cardinal and Queen whom Henry inherited are undoubtedly larger and more complex figures than their later counterparts Cranmer and Anne; this is due in part to the broadening of the social vision in the later acts—after the conflicts in which Wolsey and Katherine have played leading parts are resolved and both the new Queen and Archbishop are described and seen against the celebrating crowds of the coronation and christening scenes. Acts II and III dramatize the separation from Wolsey and the divorce from Katherine, and they create a new image of the King.

The divorce from Katherine, first rumored at II, i, 140, is all but settled by the end of Act II, and it is in connection with the divorce that the question of "conscience" is first raised. (Parenthetically, the word itself is used much more frequently in this than in any other of Shakespeare's plays—although its significance is hardly a function of its mere statistical frequency.) The reasons for the divorce are not at first made clear. At one point the dialogue makes explicit what may already have been a suspicion in the minds of the audience since the King met Anne at Wolsey's banquet:

> *Chamberlain.* It seems the marriage with his brother's wife
>   Has crept too near his conscience.
> *Suffolk.*   No, his conscience
>   Has crept too near another lady.
>   (II, ii, 16–18)

But throughout this scene (as in the one preceding) the major share of credit for the divorce is emphatically assigned to Wolsey:

> He dives into the king's soul, and there scatters
> Dangers, doubts, wringing of the conscience,
> Fears and despairs, and all these for his marriage. . . .
>   (II, ii, 26–28)

And the sharp contrasts drawn between Henry and Wolsey in the speeches of Norfolk and the Lord Chamberlain (for example, "Heaven will one day open/ The king's eyes . . .") are calculated to make Henry appear simply naïve when, shortly later, he welcomes Wolsey as "the quiet of my wounded conscience" (II, ii, 74). This last point is mentioned because it is reportedly still common for directors and actors (following the lead of older editors) to treat Henry's closing words to Wolsey about Katherine—

> But conscience, conscience;
> O 'tis a tender place, and I must leave her.   *Exeunt.*

—as if they must be spoken with some sort of lusty hypocritical leer. The scene as a whole implies that Henry speaks them earnestly, and the transition to the next scene again implies that Henry's failing is a lack of self-knowledge, that he may be guilty of dull-wittedness but not of conscious malice:

> O my lord,
> Would it not grieve an able man to leave
> So sweet a bedfellow? But conscience, conscience;
> O 'tis a tender place, and I must leave her.   *Exeunt.*

> *Scene III—Enter* Anne Bullen *and an* Old Lady.
> *Anne.* Not for that neither; here's the pang that pinches:
> His highness having liv'd so long with her, and she
> So good a lady . . .
>   (II, ii, 140–143; II, iii, 1–3)

Whether or not Henry throws away his last line as he and Wolsey go off, the first phrase which Anne speaks is probably to be understood by the audience—if it is to be understood at all!—as a comment on Henry's "But conscience, conscience." The moral issue of the divorce from Katherine, so rapidly developed in the first three scenes of Act II, remains ambiguous throughout these scenes while the other characters speculate on the King's motives and reasons; it is resolved in an unexpected way during the fourth scene, after Katherine's appearance at the trial in Black-Friars.

The trial is ostensibly the trial of Katherine. Yet the dialogues in the preceding scenes have fully apprised the audience of Katherine's fate (even to the accurate prediction, at II, ii, 34–36, of her final attitude toward the King), and the outcome of the trial with respect to Katherine is no longer in itself a live dramatic issue. Near the beginning of the trial, moreover, Katherine addresses herself directly to the King rather than to the court ("Sir, I desire you do me right and justice . . ."), and from the outset of the scene it is upon the trial of Henry, not of Katherine, that the attention of the audience is mainly focused. Each time Katherine and Wolsey contradict one another (II, iv, 73 ff.) they raise questions which the audience must look to the King to answer. After Katherine delivers her final challenge to Wolsey and departs, Henry's warm praise of her (lines 131–141) establishes him in the sympathy of the audience. Then follows his great "conscience" speech, the turning point of the action and (incidentally) the longest speech in the play.

Henry begins by clearing Wolsey of any responsibility for the divorce (lines 154–165). Since the "inducement" of a "scruple" about his marriage with Arthur's widow had been attributed by others to Wolsey in the earlier scenes, this exoneration of Wolsey comes as a dramatic surprise. The consequence of Henry's taking responsibility, ironically, is to reinforce the effect of Katherine's attacks on Wolsey

by diminishing his power in our eyes; we are being prepared to see
Wolsey's role reduced to that of the mere ineffectual servant he is
to play in III, i. And by removing the blame from Wolsey, Henry's
introductory lines also reduce us to a state of blank ignorance about
the causes of the divorce itself, and therefore (unless we hasten to
fetch our explanation from the irrelevant historical sources adduced
by Victorian editors) they prepare us to absorb the explanation
which Henry himself proceeds to supply.

The dramatic importance of Henry's explanation is heavily under-
scored by the first two lines:

> I will be bold with time and your attention:
> Then mark th'inducement: thus it came; give heed to't:
> My conscience first receiv'd a tenderness,
> Scruple and prick, on certain speeches utter'd
> By th'Bishop of Bayonne, then French ambassador,
> Who had been hither sent on the debating
> A marriage 'twixt the Duke of Orleans and
> Our daughter Mary: i'th'progress of this business,
> Ere a determinate resolution, he
> (I mean the Bishop) did require a respite,
> Wherein he might the king his lord advertise
> Whether our daughter were legitimate
> Respecting this our marriage with the dowager,
> Sometimes our brother's wife.
>
> (II, iv, 166–179)

As a piece of necessary exposition on the origin of the King's "prick"
of "conscience," this passage may be merely the Shakespearean
equivalent of a historical program note, but its sequel, as the King
goes on to justify the divorce, is a powerful expression of royal concern—a speech in which any distinction between private and public
feelings has become imperceptible:

> This respite shook
> The bosom of my conscience, enter'd me,
> Yea, with a spitting power, and made to tremble
> The region of my breast, which forc'd such way
> That many maz'd considerings did throng
> And press'd in with this caution. First, methought
> I stood not in the smile of heaven, who had
> Commanded nature, that my lady's womb
> If it conceiv'd a male-child by me, should
> Do no more offices of life to't than
> The grave does to th'dead: for her male issue

Or died where they were made, or shortly after
This world had air'd them. Hence I took a thought
This was a judgement on me, that my kingdom
(Well worthy the best heir o'th'world) should not
Be gladded in't by me. Then follows that
I weigh'd the danger which my realms stood in
By this my issue's fail, and that gave to me
Many a groaning throe: thus hulling in
The wild sea of my conscience, I did steer
Toward this remedy whereupon we are
Now present here together: that's to say,
I meant to rectify my conscience, which
I then did feel full sick, and yet not well,
By all the reverend fathers of the land
And doctors learn'd. . . .

(*II, iv,* 179–204)

[181 *spitting* = stabbing]

The substance of the King's defense—the stillbirths or deaths of his sons and the danger to the succession—is new; yet the language of his defense recalls much of the language and action we have been observing in the two preceding acts (language and action not explicitly concerned with the succession): the conflicts of the opening scenes had been portrayed against the external kingdom; the prophetic tempest of the opening scene had been accompanied by images of a "sicken'd" land, its inhabitants tormented or hungry or fearful of "most poor issue." Wolsey—to cite but one contrasting image—had imagined himself as a "new trimm'd . . . vessel" sailing confidently and unharmed through a sea filled with "malicious censurers" who were "rav'nous" in their lust to destroy him (I, ii, 78–81). Between the Buckingham episode and the trial in Black-Friars, however, the disorders of the state have become the distemper of the King: "the danger which my realms stood in/ By this my issue's fail" has pierced the conscience of the King, the sickness of the land has "press'd" into "the region of my breast." After "hulling" aimlessly in a "wild sea," the King—independent of Wolsey—now attempts to "steer."

Through a remarkable piece of Shakespearean sleight-of-hand, never in the play are we made aware of Henry rejecting Katherine; indeed, he usually speaks as her advocate. By the introduction of the succession issue in particular, the action of the divorce has been made dramatically indistinguishable from the separation from Wolsey and the King's movement toward full control over his own affairs. Speaking in soliloquy near the end of the trial scene, the King shows

166

PAUL BERTRAM

impatience with "the dilatory sloth and tricks of Rome," and he apostrophizes the absent Cranmer (II, iv, 236–238). This is the earliest and most notable of the many anticipatory references (nine in all!) to his "well-beloved servant Cranmer" before Cranmer finally enters as the King's faithful instrument in Act V. Already, however, the King's supremacy has been asserted. In the next act it is established—partly through a scene which provides the emotional surrogate of a final confrontation between Henry and Katherine.

The relationship between the King and Wolsey is most richly explored in the scene in which that relationship is finally dissolved. After the not very successful interview with Katherine, Wolsey arrives at court "moody" and "discontented" (III, ii, 75, 91). His political navigations have begun to "founder" (lines 38–40). He sounds edgy and erratic long before the King (at line 201) hands him the two papers revealing that his surreptitious accumulation of wealth and his intervention in the divorce case have been discovered. Wolsey had earlier been unwilling to remain a "state-statue" (I, ii, 88), and here we find him "in most strange postures" (III, ii, 118). In two strange asides he makes clear the sources of the "mutiny in's mind":

> Anne Bullen? no; I'll no Anne Bullens for him,
> There's more in't than fair visage. Bullen?
> No, we'll no Bullens. . . .
>
> I know her for
> A spleeny Lutheran, and not wholesome to
> Our cause, that she should lie i'th'bosom of
> Our hard-rul'd king. Again there is sprung up
> An heretic, an arch-one, Cranmer, one
> Hath crawl'd into the favour of the king . . .
> (III, ii, 87–89, 98–103)

"Crawl'd" recalls the use of "crept" in both moral and sexual senses in the passage at II, ii, 16–18 cited earlier—although Suffolk's banter there was hardly loaded with the contempt with which Wolsey speaks here. Wolsey's behavior throughout III, ii, is rather like that of a jealous lover, and the dialogues between Wolsey and the King, as the excerpts below may suggest, amount to a rejection scene (that is, in much the way that *Othello* III, iii, parodies a scene of sexual seduction). Wolsey is only half ignorant that the King is reproaching him in these lines:

> My father lov'd you,
> He said he did, and with his deed did crown

His word upon you. Since I had my office
I have kept you next my heart . . .

                  as my hand has open'd bounty to you,
My heart dropp'd love, my power rain'd honour, more
On you than any; so your hand and heart,
Your brain and every function of your power,
Should, nothwithstanding that your bond of duty,
As 'twere in love's particular, be more
To me your friend, than any.
                (*III, ii, 154–157, 184–190*)

Wolsey's flattering replies are similarly impressive in their warmth
and weight of feeling:

                      I do profess
That for your highness' good I ever labour'd
More than mine own: that am, have, and will be
(Though all the world should crack their duty to you
And throw it from their soul, though perils did
Abound as thick as thought could make 'em, and
Appear in forms more horrid) yet my duty,
As doth a rock against the chiding flood,
Should the approach of this wild river break,
And stand unshaken yours.
                (*III, ii, 190–199*)

To this, the ordinary courtly lover is but a kitten. When the un-
appreciative King hands Wolsey the papers, dryly wishes him good
appetite, and departs, we hear a different tone of voice, but the
imagery is still Petrarchan:

                  What should this mean?
What sudden anger's this? How have I reap'd it?
He parted frowning from me, as if ruin
Leap'd from his eyes. So looks the chafed lion
Upon the daring huntsman that has gall'd him . . .
                (*III, ii, 203–207*)

Then follows the extraordinary succession of further changes in
Wolsey: the confusion as he discovers the inventory, the new round
of nervous calculations aimed at restoring himself in favor, the shock
as he discovers his letter to the Pope, the jealous reproaches as he is
forced to surrender the great seal which the King "with his own
hand" gave him (ironically reminiscent of Katherine's reproaches at
III, i, 98 ff.)—the progression from voice to voice of this writhing,

tortured figure, by turns self-righteous, weak, hectic, worldly-wise, fatuously self-deluding, nobly forgiving, coolly sarcastic, and occasionally resigned. His final soliloquy gives us his own late image of himself—not now the "new trimm'd . . . vessel" of Act I, but a lonely figure "swimming" in a "sea of glory" who has gone "far beyond my depth" and whose "high-blown pride" has "at length broke under me" so that he is left to drown in that same "rude stream" of "rav'nous . . . censurers" he had feared from the beginning might prevent his devoted service to the King.

The choric Gentlemen who reported in Act II that the commons wished Wolsey "ten faddom deep" (II, i, 51) return in Act IV to describe the new political climate—a time of "general joy" in which "the citizens . . . have shown at full their royal minds" (IV, i, 7–8). The coronation parade—whose "rich stream" of lords and ladies is described in the most elaborate stage direction in the Folio—superficially recalls the festivities at the Field of the Cloth of Gold; Wolsey ran that show, at which "madams . . . Not us'd to toil, did almost sweat to bear/ The pride upon them" and "dwarfish pages" were artificially "all gilt" (I, i, 22–25); the new celebration contrasts with Wolsey's pageantry in its unforced naturalness—expressed in the vigorous imagery and breathless rhythms of the Gentleman's report:

> such a noise arose
> As the shrouds make at sea in a stiff tempest,
> As loud, and to as many tunes. Hats, cloaks
> (Doublets, I think) flew up, and had their faces
> Been loose, this day they had been lost. Such joy
> I never saw before. Great-bellied women,
> That had not half a week to go, like rams
> In the old time of war, would shake the press
> And make 'em reel before 'em. No man living
> Could say 'This is my wife' there, all were woven
> So strangely in one piece.
>   (IV, i, 71–81)

And if "every man show'd like a mine" at the Field of the Cloth of Gold, now that "the old time of war" is past,

> Our king has all the Indies in his arms,
> And more, and richer, when he strains that lady;
> I cannot blame his conscience.
>   (IV, i, 45–47)

The light humor of the Gentleman's comment is appropriate to the altered—less constricted—atmosphere of the coronation scene. The celebration itself may be viewed as part of a larger pattern. Juxtaposed to the tragic events of the play, as Wilson Knight has pointed out, is a sequence of countermovements clustered mainly about Anne—it can be traced in the "sexual freedom [of] . . . the lords' conversation on the way to Wolsey's feast, through that feast, its merriment and gay talk," in the dialogues with "the Old Lady and her willingness to 'venture maidenhead' for a crown," in the "seething fertility and enthusiastic crowds" of the coronation scene, in the mixture of "religious reference with a bawdy broad-talk" throughout the Porter's scene ("what a fry of fornication is at door! On my Christian conscience this one christening will beget a thousand . . ."), and it culminates, of course, in the final prophecies of national glory spoken above the newborn royal child.

The King is kept offstage throughout Act IV (a device of Shakespearean construction, used in maybe a dozen plays, enhancing the stature of the protagonist on his return), and when we encounter him again in Act V he is being drawn into the Gardiner-Cranmer dispute. Without his intervention Cranmer would presumably have been condemned for heresy. This episode—which Spedding thought "strangely out of place," which producers usually shorten and have at times cut out, which even sympathetic interpreters of the play have sometimes glossed over—comprises almost two-thirds of Act V (scenes i and ii in the Folio and in the Foakes edition, scenes i–iii in misdivided texts), and it calls for close consideration. According to the traditional view of the structure of the play—"a chronicle-history with three and a half catastrophes" (Hertzberg), "a collection of falls" (Frank Kermode)—the episode is merely an incomplete and not very purposeful parallel to the "catastrophes" of Buckingham, Katherine, and Wolsey. Miss Byrne and R. A. Foakes, however, both lay stress on the role of the King in this episode: his active participation in the dispute—first by testing Cranmer, then by good-naturedly reassuring him, finally by intervening against Gardiner—exemplifies the virtuous exercise of royal authority and dramatizes the final commitment of the King. Again, the structure of the play seems a good deal more coherent once it is allowed that *Henry VIII* is somehow mainly about Henry VIII. But of course wise audiences are not very directly interested in anything so abstract as "structure"; they are attracted, if at all, by the experience of the play, and there is much more to attract them in the Gardiner-Cranmer episode than any schematic diagram can show.

Gardiner had made one appearance before Act V. He had been nominated by Wolsey as the King's secretary, and he entered briefly at II, ii, 116, where, in his aside to Wolsey ("But to be commanded/ For ever by your grace, whose hand has rais'd me"), he was established as Wolsey's creature in the minds of the audience. The association is strengthened in Act V; his first substantial speech (V, i, 2–5) unmistakably echoes one of Wolsey's major speeches earlier in the play (III, ii, 144–149), his subsequent flattery of the King (V, ii, 148–155) resembles—in a thinned-out fashion—Wolsey's magnificent flatteries in III, ii (although it is even more peremptorily dismissed), and at one later point he is even given his little repentance bit (V, ii, 205). But if he is a miniature Wolsey, he is a peculiarly ineffectual one. Long before Henry enters the council chamber in V, ii, we had been made aware that Gardiner's actions against Cranmer would fail; the dialogues between Henry and Dr. Butts implied as much (V, ii, 19–34), and even before the end of the preceding scene—at about the same time that Anne's child was delivered—Cranmer had been comforted by the King's words and reassured by the gift of his ring (V, i, 150). Much earlier still in V, i, there had been yet another augury that Gardiner would not succeed. Lovell is a sort of dramatic weathercock who had spoken of Wolsey with awe in Act I, and when Gardiner solicits his support against Cranmer near the beginning of V, i, his reluctance to go along with the attack hints pretty strongly that Cranmer will be perfectly safe:

> Th'archbishop
> Is the king's hand and tongue, and who dare speak
> One syllable against him?
>
> (V, i, 37–39)

Of course, this reply of Lovell's is rather comic within its context, since Gardiner has just finished uttering quite a number of subversive syllables. And comedy is the point to which these solemn remarks have been leading.

There is, as we have just seen, little suspense over the outcome of the Gardiner-Cranmer episode. And while both of the scenes which embody that episode do offer a fascinating Shakespearean sketch of political maneuverings, the older critics who read these scenes as if they were seriously concerned with ideology (for example, as if they were intended to introduce a "great ecclesiastical revolution" of which Cranmer was spokesman) completely overlooked the tone of the dialogues:

> *Lovell.*   The queen's in labour,
>   They say in great extremity, and fear'd
>   She'll with the labour end.
> *Gardiner.*   The fruit she goes with
>   I pray for heartily, that it may find
>   Good time, and live: but for the stock, Sir Thomas,
>   I wish it grubb'd up now.
> *Lovell.*   Methinks I could
>   Cry the amen, and yet my conscience says
>   She's a good creature, and sweet lady, does
>   Deserve our better wishes.
> *Gardiner.*   But sir, sir,
>   Hear me Sir Thomas, y'are a gentleman
>   Of mine own way: I know you wise, religious,
>   And let me tell you, it will ne'er be well,
>   'Twill not Sir Thomas Lovell, take't of me,
>   Till Cranmer, Cromwell, her two hands, and she
>   Sleep in their graves.
> *Lovell.*   Now sir, you speak of two
>   The most remark'd i'th'kingdom: as for Cromwell,
>   Beside that of the jewel-house, is made master
>   O'th'rolls, and the king's secretary; further sir,
>   Stands in the gap and trade of moe preferments,
>   With which the time will load him. Th'archbishop
>   Is the king's hand and tongue, and who dare speak
>   One syllable against him?
> *Gardiner.*   Yes, yes, Sir Thomas,
>   There are that dare, and I myself have ventur'd
>   To speak my mind of him: and indeed this day
>   Sir (I may tell it you) I think I have
>   Incens'd the lords o'th'council that he is
>   (For so I know he is, they know he is)
>   A most arch-heretic . . .
>
>   (V, *i*, 18–45)

The irascible Gardiner combines the wisdom of Polonius with the modesty of Glendower, and the actor who plays this pint-sized Wolsey needs a tongue as thick as the character's wit: "Hear me Sir Thomas . . . Let me tell you . . . Take't of me . . . Yes, yes, Sir Thomas,/ There are that dare, and I myself . . ." The height and weight of this teller-offer can be measured against his crony Lovell, whose will to be agreeable to whomever he's with (audible also in his earlier

scenes) is bridled only by his will to be agreeable to the whole crowd
at once ("Now sir . . . two/ The most remark'd i'th'kingdom
. . ."). Gardiner pushes his village zealotry to its suicidal limit in the
next scene, where he continues to speak as diplomatically in public
as he had in private ("That's the plain truth; your painted gloss dis-
covers/ To men that understand you, words and weakness") and
where, his hands already full with Cranmer, he takes on Cromwell
too (V, ii, 104–120). Perhaps his finest moment, however, comes
when the King enters the council chamber "frowning," and this self-
proclaimed master of blunt open dealing suddenly does his city-mouse
act:

> Dread sovereign, how much are we bound to heaven
> In daily thanks, that gave us such a prince,
> Not only good and wise, but most religious:
> One that in all obedience, makes the church
> The chief aim of his honour, and to strengthen
> That holy duty out of dear respect,
> His royal self in judgement comes to hear
> The cause betwixt her and this great offender.
>   (V, *ii* 148–155)

A few moments earlier we had seen the King literally standing above
the councilors and observing them critically—playing Prospero—and
the councilors themselves, chastened by Cranmer's display of Henry's
ring, had just taken a friendlier tack toward "this great offender";
the cantankerous Gardiner is utterly powerless and cuts an almost
pitiably comic figure. For in Act V we entered a new dramatic kingdom—the first scene had even begun with a clock striking the hour
of one—in which everything is so under control that petty malice
and sinister conspiracy, however realistically they are dramatized,
have taken on the air of an Illyrian charade.

The entire last act, in the highly original economy of this play, is
a celebration of the new order—first in the political comedy at court,
then among the festive crowds for whom the christening is a people's
holiday which the Porter's Man can compare to "may-day morning,"
and finally in Cranmer's utopian "oracle of comfort." The palmy but
frustrated hopes of the earlier meeting at Andren, suddenly asserted
and as quickly withdrawn in the imagery of the opening scene of the
play, now emerge transformed and enlarged in the swelling prophecies of "a thousand thousand blessings,/ Which time shall bring to
ripeness":

> In her days every man shall eat in safety
> Under his own vine what he plants, and sing
> The merry songs of peace to all his neighbours. . . .
>
> Peace, plenty, love, truth, terror,
> That were the servants to this chosen infant,
> Shall then be his, and like a vine grow to him . . .
> (V, *iv*, 33-35, 47-49)

The "chosen infant" who will "lighten all this isle" (II, iii, 79), although she is at the center of the ceremony, is merely the occasion —not the cause—of the "Holy-day" toward which the action of the play has been moving, and the particular identities of the three royal figures in Cranmer's lines coalesce in these final images of ritual communion between King and people. "King Henry is the one king in Shakespeare in whom you cannot dissociate man from office" (Knight), and the dénouement of *Henry VIII* invests that office with a breadth and fullness of social and human meaning which transcend the private tragedies of Katherine and Wolsey. The unity of the play should manifest itself to the reader who does not allow "the crowd of notable historical personages" who inhabit it to obscure the role of the King in their midst.

Swift and the Common Reader

BY OSWALD JOHNSTON

ONE OF THE more gratifying things about neoclassical poetry is that reading it is normally a process of having one's reasonable expectations fulfilled. Granted, there is a preliminary difficulty, which all modern readers have to get over, in the formality of neoclassical poetic language. But once one realizes that its conventions—such as epithets and periphrases, the decorums of "elevated" and "low" words, the modes of heroic and pastoral, the forms of epic, epistle, and ode—are theoretically inviolable, their very predictability becomes a positive advantage. Behind all these conventions is an assumption that both poet and reader share a confidence in the values and beliefs of a regulated civilization. Style, in other words, is a medium of moral judgment. Of course, in the case of a poet like Addison, who is so completely submerged in conventionalities as to be anonymous, the values of civilization could adequately be expressed by solemn platitudes about being correct. But a poet like Pope, who does not reduce style to a conveyance for moralistic generalities and polite learning, requires that a fuller, more discriminating attention be paid to uses of formal language. The conventions are all present, and Pope's reader is certainly expected to have the same confidence in them that Addison's reader does: but he must also respond to modulations of style—often with the same quickness of understanding that enables him to respond to inflections and changes of tone in a clever conversation. Being sensitive to Pope's poetic language means imaginatively sharing the social brilliance of his wit at the same time that one accepts his profound belief in the moral values of civilization. Lacking the former qualification puts one in danger of calling *The Rape of the Lock* a dull satire on High Life; lacking the second tempts one to call it a trivial parody of heroic poetry. But such dangers are real only if the reader fails of the confidence that neoclassical poetic language extends, and on which neoclassical poetry relies for its effects.

Therefore, a reader equipped with the reassuring knowledge that Swift, in his long life, was a contemporary of both Dryden and Pope might well feel that his normal expectations will be fulfilled by Swift's poetry. His prose is notorious for its tricks and pitfalls: but neoclassical poetry is in the long run predictable—particularly when, as in "A Description of a City Shower," it is written in the early eighteenth century, and in heroic couplets. The "Description" bears a subtitle, "*In Imitation of* VIRGIL's Georg.," which, by confirming the prejudice that eighteenth century verse has something to do with the classics, seems to invite any reader to rely on his expectations. Just as Dryden, in *MacFlecknoe*, and Pope, in the *Dunciad*, use Virgil as a means of making a judgment about bad poets, so here Swift, one might suppose, is using Virgil's pastoral-descriptive style to make some point about rainstorms in the city of London. All that is needed, it appears, to place this poem in the literary-historical categories that seem natural to it is to decide what point about rainstorms Swift is making, and the job is done:

> Careful Observers may fortel the Hour
> (By sure Prognosticks) when to dread a Show'r:
> While Rain depends, the pensive Cat gives o'er
> Her Frolicks, and pursues her Tail no more.
> $(1-4)$

By attending to the elevated solemnity of these lines, with their suggestion that the coming shower will be as dreadful an event as a hurricane or a flood or even Judgment Day, and by noticing the way in which the elevated word "pensive," reinforced in its line by the Latinate "depends," collapses into the description of the tail-chasing alley cat, one might reasonably conclude that Swift, through the disparity between style and subject, is evoking a standard against which homely details of city life can be placed. There is more evidence for such a conclusion further on:

> Mean while the South rising with dabbled Wings,
> A Sable Cloud a-thwart the Welkin flings,
> That swill'd more Liquor than it could contain,
> And like a Drunkard gives it up again.
> $(13-16)$

The collapse here, from the elevated poetic language describing the sky to the ill-behaved drunkard, is even more drastic; and if it is reasonable to consider that ill-behaved drunkards are characteristic of city landscapes in the same way that alley cats are, it is likely that these lines are repeating the procedure of the earlier passage.

> Now in contiguous Drops the Flood comes down,
> Threat'ning with Deluge this *Devoted* Town.
>
> (31–32)

Here the Latinate "contiguous" gives the rain enough poetic dignity to justify the hyperbolical "Deluge"; and since "Devoted," in an older use, can mean literally "doomed" even while it is making an ironic reference to the Londoners' churchgoing habits, Swift seems to be implying that the city of London in some way deserves both the judgment and the catastrophe of Noah's Flood.

Up to now, so many preliminary expectations about the poem have been fulfilled that it would be reasonable to expect even more: for instance, a grand climax that asserts absolutely the moral standard that the style of the poem has evidently been evoking. Pope himself does no more than this in the conclusions to, say, the fourth *Moral Essay* and the *Dunciad*. Here is Swift's conclusion:

> Now from all Parts the swelling Kennels flow,
> And bear their Trophies with them as they go:
> Filth of all Hues and Odours seem to tell
> What Street they sail'd from, by their Sight and Smell.
> They, as each Torrent drives, with rapid Force
> From *Smithfield*, or St. *Pulchre*'s shape their Course,
> And in huge Confluent join at *Snow-Hill* Ridge,
> Fall from the *Conduit* prone to *Holborn-Bridge*.
> Sweepings from Butchers Stalls, Dung, Guts, and Blood, ⎫
> Drown'd Puppies, stinking Sprats, all drench'd in Mud, ⎬
> Dead Cats and Turnip-Tops come tumbling down the Flood. ⎭
>
> (53–63)

The reader's normal expectations, whose fulfillment I have apparently been demonstrating, seem undermined by this passage. Of course, it remains possible to point out that the language is still alluding to a more elevated style: the reference to the garbage as "Trophies" and the metaphorical suggestion that the colors and smells of the flooded gutters serve the same function as heraldic ensigns indicate that Swift is thinking of Virgilian, or even Homeric,

fleets. But such an explanation tells us nothing of the moral judgment that the "normal" reader, with his solemn assumption that an
elevated style must evoke a moral standard, has been expecting. The
most direct answer, that Swift is using the style of Virgilian pastoral
and heroic description in order to judge London's sewage system, is
absurd; and, considering the virtuosity that even my purposely fal-
lacious argument has managed to uncover in the poem, it would be
unsatisfactory, not to say simple-minded, to conclude that Swift
likes the country better than the city. Obviously, something that the
normal reader does not expect has been going on in the poem. It is
time to discard the pretense and find out what Swift is up to.

If, at the beginning of the poem, one does not stop short at line
4, one finds this:

> Returning Home at Night, you'll find the Sink
> Strike your offended Sense with double Stink.
>
> (5–6)

It should be evident, from the bluntly unembarrassed recognition
that cesspools "Stink" more than usual when there is moisture in the
air, that Swift is perfectly willing to give us any homely detail he
wants, without having recourse to more elevated—more poetic—uses
of language. There is a suggestion that he is not even interested in
maintaining a style of poetic decorum—either for the sake of Virgil,
whom he is supposed to be imitating, or for the moral standard such
a style might be expected to embody. Much the same point can be
demonstrated from Swift's use of the word "swilled" in the lines on
the drunkard and the "Sable Cloud:"

> Mean while the South rising with dabbled Wings,
> A Sable Cloud a-thwart the Welkin flings,
> That swill'd more Liquor than it could contain,
> And like a Drunkard gives it up again.

In its context the single coarse word deflates the elevated language of
the previous lines perfectly well by itself: the drunkard is, so to speak,
an embellishment. Evidently a good bit of the pleasure of reading
the poem comes from the outrageous ways in which Swift makes
fun of the poetic language he pretends to be using. Because we are
told that it is "swill'd," we have no choice but to take "Liquor" in
its colloquially limited sense of strong drink rather than in the elevated, general sense that the poetic "Sable Cloud" would seem to

demand. Once this is admitted—once the elevated style has collapsed so irrevocably—the logic of the statement demands that it be completed by the undignified simile—the drunkard—with which it ends. One thing at least is clear: the drunkard is in no way being judged by the elevation of the style. If anything, the reverse has taken place; and if it is too much to say that the drunkard provides a standard by which the style can be judged, it seems inescapable that Swift's point here is to play some kind of practical joke on poetic language.

The conclusion one must draw from all this is that Swift is intent upon pushing his readers into a decidedly peculiar relationship with his poem. Contrary to our normal expectations, he does not allow us to settle upon a recognizable poetic style as a means of judgment—as a fixed standard whose values we share and against which we can measure divergences. The judgments that are made are delivered in a direct, conversational style that is pointedly antipoetical; and if we make the mistake of looking for a poetic "norm" to gratify our moral requirements, the judgment is likely to turn against us—or at least the joke will be at our expense. At any rate, the normal procedures of a reader of neoclassical verse have to be followed with extreme tact and discrimination, if not discarded. The more one relies on the conventional attitude of reverence for the classics and for the moral values of poetry, the more one is likely to be made fun of.

If the procedure of "A Description of a City Shower" is characteristic, rather than merely perverse, it will appear that Swift had an equivalent attitude to all the grander, more solemn pretensions of poetry. One would not expect, for instance, anything remotely resembling the invocation to the muse in Book I of *Paradise Lost*. Such a supposition would almost be right. The exception is to be found among the elaborate and unreadable Pindaric Odes and contemplative epistles that Swift wrote as a young man in the early 1690's, before *A Tale of a Tub* or anything else that one would normally recognize as his. It is the rare kind of exception that really does "prove" the rule, because this address to the muse, which serves as the conclusion of the last of these serious poems, is actually a dismissal, not an invocation:

> There thy enchantment broke, and from this hour
> I here renounce thy visionary pow'r;
> And since thy essence on my breath depends,
> Thus with a puff the whole delusion ends.

The passage is prophetic in more ways than one. All the poems written after this are in some manner reflections of the attitudes and procedures indicated by "A Description of a City Shower:" in fact, the majority of them, measured in bulk, consist of private jokes, political libels, epigrams, and puns in a kind of pig Latin. Prophetic in a more interesting way is the disparaging implication that poetic inspiration is, literally, breath—that is, wind. From this point on, Swift was consistently rude to muses—his own or anybody else's. In a poem called "On Poetry: a Rapsody" he offers this recipe for an invocation:

> Be mindful, when Invention fails,
> To scratch your Head, and bite your Nails.
> (89–90)

And one could place beside Milton's elevation of poets to a prophetic priesthood this celebration, from the same poem, of bardic dignity:

> Not Beggar's Brat, on Bulk begot;
> Nor Bastard of a Pedlar *Scot*;
> Nor Boy brought up to cleaning Shoes,
> The Spawn of *Bridewell*, or the Stews;
> Nor Infants dropt, the spurious Pledges
> Of *Gipsies* littering under Hedges,
> Are so disqualified by Fate
> To rise in *Church*, or *Law*, or *State*,
> As he, whom *Phebus* in his Ire
> Hath *blasted* with poetick Fire.
> (33–42)

There is more involved here than the fact that Swift made irreverent fun of poets for striking self-important attitudes. Irreverence is not in itself unusual. In fact, were one to take Milton's high solemnity as a model for poetic deportment, it would be hard to avoid accusing, say, Pope of being churlish in the same way as Swift— only to a lesser degree. But it is the degree that is all-important. There is never any question but that Pope, for all his comparatively un-Miltonic irreverence, has a full confidence in the capacity of serious poetic forms—of poetic language—to express all that he needs to express. This is tautologically obvious: poets believe in poetry; otherwise they would do something else. And such confidence, it should be evident, is only another way of defining the expectations with which we, as readers of neoclassical verse, first approached "A

Description of a City Shower." As we now know, those expectations were bound to be upset. Swift has none of Pope's confidence in the language of poetry: in "A Description of a City Shower" he uses expertly many of the available resources of poetic language only in order to engineer its own collapse. Formal language, by the peculiar logic of its construction, which insists upon elevated, figurative abstractions to the exclusion of the undignified and the literal, contains the seeds of its own destruction. All Swift need do is emphasize the meanings that are normally excluded, and "Liquor" automatically refers to drunkards, and "inspiration" to windbags.

Considering his attitude toward the serious pretensions of poetry and his capacity for using, as his main weapon, the resources of poetic language against itself, it would seem quite reasonable to suppose that much of Swift's verse is simply parody. In a way, it would be accurate to call the imitations of Virgilian styles in "A Description of a City Shower" parody. But doing so would only fix a useful label to certain details of procedure. It would not supply a category for the whole poem, which we now realize cannot be dismissed by so simple a formula. It was evidently written with other objectives in mind—objectives that go beyond the capacities of parody alone. By itself, parody is too much confined within the style it is making fun of—so much so that, as the old saying goes, it pays the style a compliment. Swift always remains enough outside the style he parodies to place it in a comic perspective, to impose on it a logic of his own, and to turn it against itself.

The first stanza of "A Love Song in the Modern Taste," one of the few pure parodies that Swift wrote, runs:

> Flutt'ring spread thy purple Pinions,
>   Gentle *Cupid* o'er my Heart;
> I a Slave in thy Dominions;
>   Nature must give Way to Art.

The conventions of pastoral love poetry that Swift is making fun of are illustrated conveniently enough by these lines describing the bower of Adam and Eve in *Paradise Lost*:

> Here Love his gold'n shafts emploies, here lights
> His constant Lamp, and waves his purple wings,
> Reigns here and revels. . .
>   (IV, 763–765)

In the contrast, the scorn expressed by Swift's mock simplicity of tone is inescapable. But the last line of Swift's stanza makes a criticism of pastoral conventions that is at once more explicit and more provocative than anything parody alone can convey: "Nature must give Way to Art." Some of the importance of this criticism is suggested by another passage from the same book of *Paradise Lost*:

> But rather to tell how, if Art could tell,
> How from that Saphire Fount the crisped Brooks,
> Rowling on Orient Pearl and sands of Gold,
> With mazie error under pendant shades
> Ran Nectar, visiting each plant, and fed
> Flours worthy of Paradise, which not nice Art
> In Beds and curious Knots, but Nature boon
> Powrd forth profuse on Hill and Dale and Plaine . . .
> (236–243)

Milton is doubting the capacity of Art—a function of knowledge and civilization—to describe Nature in a state of innocence, in the Garden of Eden. Yet after the disclaimer in the first line he goes ahead with his description of Eden, uses all the pastoral imagery at his disposal, pauses again to insist that the flowers of Paradise are arranged naturally, and continues after that for fifty lines more. In spite of his moral doubts about art, Milton cannot avoid using the pastoral conventions because, as a poet, he must depend upon the resources of his art and count on the language of poetry as the one indispensable area of agreement with his readers. Swift, as we know, is determined to break down this kind of relationship between poet and reader. Besides, the "Nature" he is referring to in his stanza is not innocent nature. It is not even pastoral nature, since pastoral is art, and the point of his statement is to suggest that art and nature are not only distinguishable but also in fundamental opposition. Because art seeks to embellish nature with formalities of pastoral language, it is not telling the truth; and because poetry, with its artfulness, is supposed to be pretty, truth, or nature, is likely to be ugly. It is as though Swift were serving notice on all readers of poetry, warning them that he will systematically demolish the standards of poetic language that they normally rely on. All he will offer as a substitute for those comfortable standards will be a far less pleasant set of assertions, which he here calls nature, or truth.

The sum of all these suggestions is tantamount to a declaration

of war on readers; for that reason alone one might find them somewhat disquieting. In particular, the implication that art is only a
disguise for a natural but unpleasant truth seems to threaten a direct
assault on our politer sensibilities—and any one who has read the
fourth book of *Gulliver's Travels* will realize the lengths to which
Swift can go to fulfill a threat of that kind. Gulliver's avowal of his
debt to the Houyhnhnm master could stand as a kind of boundary
line, marking the extreme limits Swift's attitude to poetry is liable
to attain:

> I had likewise learned from his Example an utter Detestation of all
> Falsehood or Disguise; and *Truth* appeared so amiable to me, that
> I determined upon sacrificing every thing to it.

"Sacrificing everything" includes the reader; and the fact that Swift
never goes quite so far as Gulliver will not prevent us from being,
on occasion, placed in a very precarious position.

An especially precarious approach to these limits is made by a
poem called "The Progress of Beauty," which even in its opening
stanzas seems to give a clear sign of the direction it will take:

> When first Diana leaves her Bed
> Vapors and Steams her Looks disgrace,
> A frouzy dirty colour'd red
> Sits on her cloudy wrinckled Face.
>
> But by degrees when mounted high
> Her artificiall Face appears
> Down from her Window in the Sky,
> Her Spots are gone, her Visage clears.

One of the more remarkable things about the beginning of this
poem is that it is not absolutely necessary to notice that Swift is
talking about the moon until one reads the third stanza:

> 'Twixt earthly Females and the Moon
> All Parallells exactly run;
> If Celia should appear too soon
> Alas, the Nymph would be undone.

Only now is it quite certain that the cloudy and discolored com-
plexion of the first stanza is an atmospheric phenomenon, and that
the degrees and spots of the second are astronomical details. When

Swift tells us that parallels between "earthly Females and the Moon" are exact, he is giving fair warning that the poetic logic of the usual hyperbolic comparison between the pastoral mistress and the moon will be drastically redefined. Conventionally, the moon is beautiful but remote, chaste but inconstant, aloof and serene, but productive of amorous frenzy and high tides. But Swift picks on details that have a distinctly unliterary kind of appropriateness. The possibility that the first two stanzas are describing an earthly female instead of the moon is emphasized by the fourth, and becomes a definite indication of the direction in which these exact parallels will run:

> To see her from her Pillow rise
> All reeking in a cloudy Steam,
> Crackt Lips, foul Teeth, and gummy Eyes,
> Poor Strephon, how would he blaspheme!

Evidently the antipoetic logic of Swift's simile here will leave few details unexplored. For instance, one might observe in passing that, if Celia and the moon rise at the same time, and if they both, consequently, appear only at night, the traditional association of the virtue of chastity with the moon goddess has a special ironic inappropriateness. Swift remarks later on:

> Take pattern by your Sister Star,
> Delude at once and Bless our Sight,
> When you are seen, be seen from far,
> And chiefly chuse to shine by Night.
> (*Stanza* 18)

No threat of this kind is left unfulfilled, and Celia becomes a streetwalker before the poem is over. But for the time being Swift is interested in describing the artificial face that Celia, as well as the moon, must provide for herself before she can show herself in public:

> Three Colours, Black, and Red, and White,
> So gracefull in their proper Place,
> Remove them to a diff'rent Light
> They form a frightfull hideous Face,
>
> For instance; when the Lilly slipps
> Into the Precincts of the Rose,
> And takes Possession of the Lips,
> Leaving the Purple to the Nose.
> (6–7)

It is entirely appropriate to the logic of the antipastoral Swift is developing that Celia's face should imitate a catalogue of flowers; just as, further on, it is equally logical that Venus should be the heavenly power to whom Celia owes the materials used in her cosmetic transformation:

> Thus after four important Hours
> Celia's the Wonder of her Sex;
> Say, which among the Heav'nly Pow'rs
> Could cause such wonderfull Effects.
>
> Venus, indulgent to her Kind
> Gave Women all their Hearts could wish
> When first she taught them where to find
> White Lead, and Lusitanian Dish.
>   (14–15)

It might be worthwhile pausing at this point to take stock of what is going on and, in so doing, contrast another, more familiar, cosmetic triumph: Belinda in *The Rape of the Lock*. I say "contrast" because Celia and Belinda are not strictly comparable, any more than it is appropriate to conclude from the dressing-table scene in the first canto that Belinda is, so to speak, a "painted hussy." Of course Pope criticized her for being silly, and wantonly prideful, and trivial; but we are certainly expected to find her charming all the same. Disapproval of face powder, in this context, is altogether too unimportant as an attitude to come anywhere near being serious disapproval of Belinda. Similarly, the marvelously supple and varied fun that Pope has with elevated poetic styles in *The Rape of the Lock* is in no way an indication that he has lost confidence in their ability to express feelings and embody values. But Swift considers that the poetic language he is reversing in "The Progress of Beauty" is in its normal state nothing less than a deception. By the logic of his reversal, the qualities opposite to those that pastoral poetry would maintain are the ones he asserts. Calling Belinda a nymph is a charming extravagance; calling Celia a nymph is a sardonic indication that she is a whore. Similarly, since cosmetics are literally a means of applying physical beauty artificially, Celia's use of them inevitably means that she is not only not beautiful, but positively disgusting. Art, which includes cosmetics as well as the language of pastoral convention, is discarded as a false embellishment of nature; and nature is presented as corrupt, ugly, and decadent.

By now, any reader who looks to the language of the poem for some kind of moral refuge from Swift's unpleasant details should be almost forcibly disabused. On the other hand, if the reader is knowing, if he is aware of Swift's tricks, and realizes that neither the nymph nor the moon is likely to be rescued from the antipoetic simile in which Swift has placed it—that is, if he is suspicious of art and seeks a refuge in nature—there is still nothing to feel comfortable about. Nature is too distasteful. The moon wanes as well as waxes—and, in the context of Swift's simile, that means that Celia's real face is even more vulnerable to disease and corruption than her painted one:

> But, Art no longer can prevayl
> When the Materialls all are gone,
> The best Mechanick Hand must fayl
> Where Nothing's left to work upon.
>
> Matter, as wise Logicians say,
> Cannot without a Form subsist,
> And Form, say I, as well as They,
> Must fayl if Matter brings no Grist.
>
> And this is fair Diana's Case
> For, all Astrologers maintain
> Each Night a Bit drops off her Face
> When Mortals say she's in her Wain.
>
> While Partridge wisely shews the Cause
> Efficient of the Moon's Decay,
> That Cancer with his pois'nous Claws
> Attacks her in the milky Way:
>
> But Gadbury in Art profound
> From her pale Cheeks pretends to show
> That Swain Endymion is not sound,
> Or else, that Mercury's her Foe.
>
> .   .   .   .
>
> Yet as she wasts, she grows discreet,
> Till Midnight never shows her Head;
> So rotting Celia stroles the Street
> When sober Folks are all a-bed.
>
> (20–24; 26)

Swift has made our relationship with the poem a dilemma: Celia is either "poetical" or revolting. The only "honorable" way out, apparently, is to stay at a distance and try to enjoy the ruthless ingenuity with which Swift develops the perverse logic of his antipoetic simile. But it is difficult to do this. As long as one is following the development of the poem, it is hard to contain one's feelings of revulsion within Swift's tone of rational unconcern—unless one is prepared to surrender altogether, and abandon oneself to the consequences of such an argument:

> Two Balls of Glass may serve for Eyes,
> White Lead can plaister up a Cleft,
> But these alas, are poor Supplyes
> If neither Cheeks, nor Lips be left.
>   (29)

Such a conclusion is inescapable: but any amusement it gives takes the form, I suspect, of nervous laughter. We are not too far from "A Modest Proposal" here—or, for that matter, from the Yahoos.

It would, of course, be perversely naïve to base any final claim for Swift as a poet simply on the fact that he makes his readers nervous—just as it would be improper to declare that *Gulliver's Travels* owes all its effectiveness to the revulsion aroused by the Yahoos. And, although I have so far been heading in the direction of such a claim, it requires no desperate ingenuity to correct the balance of my argument. There are several poems, among them the poems addressed to Stella, in which Swift makes use of the same procedures that extend to such drastic lengths in "The Progress of Beauty," but in which he achieves a totally different effect. Simply mentioning Stella's name is enough to suggest "the other side" of Swift's personality. The "private life" of the Dean of St. Patrick's is, of course, a celebrated literary mystery, responsible for much speculation as to whether Stella was really his half-sister, or his mistress in everything but in fact, or secretly his wife. But more important than such unanswerable questions is the actual quality—the style—of Swift's personality; of this, thanks to poems in which he expresses thoughts and feelings that are direct and private, it is possible to know a great deal.

Such a poem is the first of the yearly tributes "On Stella's Birthday," dated 1718/19; although it will tell us nothing about the legal definition of Stella's relation to Swift, it will tell us what no biographical theory ever can: something about the quality of that relationship.

> Stella this Day is thirty four,
> (We won't dispute a Year or more)
> However Stella, be not troubled,

Although thy Size and Years are doubled,
Since first I saw Thee at Sixteen
The brightest Virgin of the Green,
So little is thy Form declin'd
Made up so largely in thy Mind.
Oh, would it please the Gods to split
Thy Beauty, Size, and Years, and Wit,
No Age could furnish out a Pair
Of Nymphs so gracefull, Wise and fair
With half the Lustre of Your Eyes,
With half thy Wit, thy Years and Size:
And then before it grew too late,
How should I beg of gentle Fate,
(That either Nymph might have her Swain,)
To split my Worship too in twain.

The main procedures of this poem are characteristic. Swift is evidently making fun of elegant poetic compliments. Along with the easily recognizable mock-pastoral talk about nymphs—and one is suspicious of all Swift's nymphs—one can observe inelegantly precise references to the lady's age and shape; a characteristically impolite word, "split," which is used twice; and an extended joke at the expense of poetic conceits that quite literally equates increased virtue with enlarged size and additional years. But there is something else to notice as well: something that is involved in the absolute distinction between Stella and the unspeakable Celia that the tone of easy intimacy requires the reader to make. Celia was a nymph also; but the collapse of poetic language in "The Progress of Beauty" is inseparable from all the dreadful revelations about Celia's true nature. In this poem the clumsy variations from the manner of poetic compliment that Swift pretends to assume—the size, the years, the "Form declin'd"—only serve to make the compliment more genuine. There is none of the ruthless urgency that, in "The Progress of Beauty," forces the reader into an impossible choice between false art and monstrous nature. Here art is, perhaps, no less false; and Stella, for all that one loves her, is by no means an embodiment of chivalric ideals. Nevertheless, in this poem a good bit of the irony that accompanies the collapse of the poetic language is directed back at Swift himself, speaking the poem. It is as though he were pretending to show off by turning an elegant compliment, but instead kept making awkward mistakes, dropping inadvertent insults about age and size, and using impolite words. The reader, who with his habits and prejudices is usually a primary target of Swift's irony, is almost completely ignored. The poem seems to be an actual conversation that we overhear only by chance. There is no hindrance to an address that is intimate and direct, spoken with full confidence that every inflection will be appreciated and every private joke understood. That is what I mean by saying that the poem can tell us something about the quality of their relationship: Swift is revealed as an actual participant in a moment of communication rather than as a literary lover assuming for his mistress a posture of poetic address. It is, I think, a rare thing to find a love poem that expresses so unpretentiously, so effortlessly, and so honestly an intimacy of this order.

One might add that it is an even rarer thing to find such a poem by Swift. But the discovery is less surprising if one considers what is known about his capacity for friendship, and his delight in private jokes and games with words—and if one considers also the *Journal to Stella*. That running account of Swift's political career during Queen Anne's last years, written in a special language that consists of a punning baby talk, is actually the kind of private correspondence that the poems to Stella imitate. The last entry in the *Journal* is relevant here. It was written on the inside of the cover of Swift's last letter to Stella, shortly before he sailed from Chester on his return to Ireland: ". . . when I read the Passage upon Chester walls, as I was coming into Town, & just receivd the Lettr: I sd aloud— Agreable B—tch." Fifteen years after this, and nearly ten years after the birthday poem, in a private reminiscence begun on the day of Stella's death, Swift had another occasion to remember her as "the brightest Virgin of the Green:"

> I knew her from six years old, and had some share in her education, by directing what books she should read, and perpetually instructing her in the principles of honour and virtue; from which she never swerved in any one action or moment of her life. She was sickly from her childhood until about the age of fifteen: But then grew into perfect health, and was looked upon as one of the most beautiful, graceful, and agreeable young women in London, only a little too fat.

"On the Death of Mrs. Johnson" was not published until many years after Swift's own death: it may be presumed to have been written for no readers at all. Even here the voice is recognizable as characteristic.

There is, besides, a characteristic perverseness in the fact that Swift appears to us as most congenial when he is paying least attention to us. In the Stella poems—and the *Journal* and the other private writings—the anonymous common reader is ignored, and the irony that often turns all its force against the language readers normally trust is instead contained by a familiar situation. But Swift is usually addressing readers, not friends; and he addresses them in a voice that one cannot identify as "his own," and certainly not as congenial. The congenial moments constitute a sort of parenthesis in his career. It is, of course, a most distinguished parenthesis since, besides the Stella poems, it includes "Cadenus and Vanessa" and "Verses on the Death of Dr. Swift." If the old-fashioned question, "whether Pope was a poet," were ever seriously asked about Swift, it would be to such poems that one would point to support the Johnsonian rejoinder, "If this be not poetry, where is poetry to be found?" Yet Celia is more likely to be the heroine of his poems than is Stella. And one would not dream of adapting Johnson's reply to a defense of "The Progress of Beauty:" if the interlocutor were sufficiently shocked by the poem, the answer might well come back, "Anywhere else."

But such colloquies should remain purely hypothetical. Swift simply is not interested in "being a poet." If there is any truth at all in the legend of Dryden's observation ("Cousin Swift, you will never be a poet"), it is that Swift was still writing Pindaric Odes when Dryden is supposed to have discouraged him. After that, the whole question becomes irrelevant. All the procedures that Swift follows in his poems demonstrate how little the stricter canons of neoclassical poetry apply to him. We have seen what happens to readers who are so stubborn as to try holding him to account, asking that their normal expectations be gratified. If anything, his poems demonstrate all the limits, and none of the uses, of the conventional literary categories. If at this point a category is still wanted, it had better be looked for in the prose satires. Whereas the canons of neoclassical poetry can provide only extreme contrasts, "A Modest Proposal," A Tale of a Tub, or Gulliver's Travels will suggest repeatedly that the procedures of the poems are as essential to Swift as irony itself. The same brutal rationality that dismembers Celia is employed by the projector of "A Modest Proposal"; the same confusion of logic and language that turns pastoral metaphors upside down and converts compliments into insults characterizes the courtiers of Lilliput and the academicians of Lagado; and, finally, the same alarming tendency to turn poetic language against itself is apparent in A Tale of a Tub, where all formal uses of language become self-destructive. In effect, the prose satires are expansions of procedures that are often only suggested in the poems. Thus, if one continues to be frustrated by Swift's refusal to fulfill any conventional expectations—not to mention the contempt that accompanies the refusal—one can always take a kind of Gulliverian comfort in the reflection, "If you can get used to the Yahoos, you can get used to Celia." And if one prefers to remember Stella, all the better.

Heroic Folly: Pope's Satiric Identity

BY THOMAS R. EDWARDS, JR.

"Pope is the most fascinating of satirists, because his poetry is so largely coloured by his own personality; and his satires can only be properly understood when they are exhibited with their conflicting elements of truth and injustice; of vindictiveness and pathos; of intellectual unscrupulousness and poetical art; of passion and irony; of bold invective and ambiguous evasion."

"In the character of Sporus the reader's mind is kept so busy merely taking in the baroque zigzag of beauty and nastiness that Hervey is forgotten. Words like 'Beauty that shocks you' provide too much to think about, enlarge the mind too excitingly for it to centre itself in narrow superciliousness on a weak human character."

THE FIRST of these passages, written by W. J. Courthope some eighty years ago, fairly represents a way of reading poetry that has gone out of fashion. By "personality," we uneasily note, Courthope means "the man himself," the figure revealed by the kinds of evidence upon which the biographer relies. Pope was a complicated person, and his poetry fascinatingly reveals that personal complexity —the poems themselves become materials for biography. For us this seems too simple. We doubt that the "self" projected in a poem can confidently be equated with the "self" that is the poet in his private life; indeed, we may doubt that this latter self is anything like a constant, objective fact, in poets or anyone else. We are apt to feel more at ease with the second passage, by Geoffrey Tillotson. The emphasis still falls on the "conflicting elements" Courthope noted, but for Mr. Tillotson the conflict takes place in the mind of the reader; it is not to be referred to the real object of Pope's ridicule or to Pope's personal feelings about him. The portrait of Sporus is "baroque"—we contemplate it as esthetic event rather than biographical or historical document.

The shift in critical perspective Mr. Tillotson here reflects has unquestionably been for the good; and yet I must confess that Courthope's remarks tell me something true and important about

Pope as a poet, something I am not told by critics who scrupulously avoid the issue of "personality." Courthope recognizes the complexities of tone in Pope's satires, and if he errs in relating the complexities too easily to Pope the man, he at least reminds us that in these poems we listen to a speaking voice that is, however indirectly, a *human* voice, one that reflects and gives edge to Pope's sense of the world which was his subject.

This sense of the world, in Pope's late satires, is anything but the urbane, confident one usually associated with his name. Consider this astonishing passage from the second dialogue of the *Epilogue to the Satires* (1738):

> [*Fr.*] The Priest whose Flattery be-dropt the Crown,
> How hurt he you? he only stain'd the Gown.
> And how did, pray, the Florid Youth offend,
> Whose Speech you took, and gave it to a Friend?
>   *P.* Faith it imports not much from whom it came,
> Whoever borrow'd, could not be to blame,
> Since the whole House did afterwards the same:
> Let Courtly Wits to Wits afford supply,
> As Hog to Hog in Huts of *Westphaly*;
> If one, thro' Nature's Bounty or his Lord's,
> Has what the frugal, dirty soil affords,
> From him the next receives it, thick or thin,
> As pure a Mess almost as it came in;
> The blessed Benefit, not there confin'd,
> Drops to the third who nuzzles close behind;
> From tail to mouth, they feed, and they carouse,
> The last, full fairly gives it to the *House*.
>   *Fr.* This filthy Simile, this beastly Line,
> Quite turns my Stomach—*P.* So does Flatt'ry mine;
> And all your Courtly Civet-Cats can vent,
> Perfume to you, to me is Excrement.
>
>   (164–184)

The Friend's reasonable, polite disapproval ("pray") is first countered by "Faith it imports not much"—the offhand indifference of a speaker comfortably above his subject. But this pose of superiority vanishes in the fierce obscenity that follows. The occasion scarcely justifies such fury—politicians commit worse offenses than borrowing one another's speeches. The analogy between hogs and noble statesmen would cut more insolently if it were merely suggested; Pope's almost pedantic concern for getting in every detail of the comparison, and so magnifying the petty offense out of all reasonable proportion, seems oddly remote from the gentlemanly insinuation with which the speech began. By Augustan standards of social and poetic decorum, the Friend's protest seems just. It is indeed a filthy simile, and Pope's final rejoinder sounds rather lame. He speaks with the irrational, petulant defensiveness of a child who knows he has gone too far.

Obscenity and other kinds of verbal indecorum are important in Pope's satires. They convey most immediately a general sense that cultivated discourse cannot do full justice to a reality which increasingly reveals itself as corrupt and vile; there are after all no polite names for evil. It stands as one of the great poetic achievements that Pope was able to state his revulsion with unsparing accuracy and yet contain and use it as a functioning element in more complex poetic designs. The "Hogs of Westphaly" passage is not a flaw in the *Epilogue to the Satires* but a revealing moment of collision between blunt moral speech and a more equivocal, temporizing kind of utterance—opposing forces whose conflict gives the poem its shape and direction. At the start of the first dialogue the Friend complains about Pope's infamous lack of political tact, and his own voice nicely demonstrates the "sly, polite, insinuating stile" of the "artful Manager" Horace which he recommends to the poet:

> To Vice and Folly to confine the jest,
> Sets half the World, God knows, against the rest;
> Did not the Sneer of more impartial men
> At Sense and Virtue, balance all agen.
>   (57–60)

Normal social equilibrium requires that sense and virtue be kept in their place; the metaphor of balance, which in the *Essay on Man* and the *Moral Essays* expressed positive alternatives to the apparent chaos of immediate experience, now figures as an argument *against* the poet's position. *Fr.* is not imperceptive about behavior, but it is enough for him to relish in private the amusing discrepancies between "official" and real virtue. He is virtually a caricature of the Dryden of *Religio Laici*, preferring "common quiet" to unruly public disputes over unreal issues. In him Pope gives his mature assessment of the cool, disengaged urbanity of an Addison or a Shaftesbury, which had been an ideal of his own earlier days:

> Leave dang'rous *Truths* to unsuccessful *Satyrs*,
> And *Flattery* to fulsome *Dedicators*. . . .
> 'Tis best sometimes your Censure to restrain,

And *charitably* let the Dull be *vain:*
Your Silence there is better than your *Spite,*
For who can *rail* so long as they can *write?*
(*Essay on Criticism,* 592–599)

Fr. presents himself as a realist. His theme—like the (at least pro-
fessed) theme of Pope's much maligned contemporary Bernard
Mandeville—is the inevitable and useful imperfection of things as
they are. His voice, at times indulgent and avuncular, at times ma-
liciously feline, at times shrill with shock at Pope's plain speaking,
is the familiar voice of intelligence debilitated by too much knowledge, sophistication that marks not moral subtlety but Gerontion-
like moral paralysis.

This is more than the voice of a convenient straw man. Both *Fr.*
and *P.* are versions of Pope himself, or of any man aware of the
conflict between his social identity and his secret image of himself
as autonomous moral hero. The dialogue form articulates the inner
debate between the part of us which "knows better," which like
Pope's *Fr.* stands by our indiscretions murmuring "alas" with the
sympathetic disapproval that identifies our elders and betters, and
that other part of us which, passionately committed to its own perception of truth, will brook no compromises. Pope controls both
voices, to be sure, but the *Epilogue* moves not toward reconciliation
of extremities, as do so many of Pope's earlier poems, but toward
acceptance of *P.*'s view, in all its extravagant exaggeration.

The two dialogues develop various modes of response to the politic
voice of *P.* Until late in the poem the mode of *Dialogue I* is ironic
in the textbook sense of the word: *P.* pretends to defend "the dignity
of Vice," and the terms of the defense reveal the speciousness of any
justification of things as they are. If, as *Fr.* insists, the crimes of the
well-born are not to be dwelt upon by the satirist, the job still remains of keeping distinct the separation between classes. The vulgar
are imitating the sins of their betters with intolerable cheek: Cibber's
son "swear[s] like a Lord," Ward "draw[s] Contracts with a States-
man's skill," Bond and Peter Walter "pay their Debts [and] keep
their Faith like Kings" (that is, not at all). The joke is clear enough.
It is indeed bad for the lower classes to copy the behavior of the
great, but not because of any snobbish notion that they may thus
become *better* than they should be. In this topsy-turvy society the
highest are the worst. Plebeians may have quite as much inclination
to vice, to be sure, but in their proper condition they lack "know-
how." For them to learn the *style* of accomplished evil from those

who are naturally gifted is to make general an efficient viciousness
that might otherwise be confined to the small world of aristocrats,
where one expects it and is prepared to cope with it.

But the indirections of irony fail to undermine *Fr.*'s complacence,
and toward the end of the dialogue *P.* is driven to a more open kind
of speaking. Virtue is classless, he remarks, and therefore it need not
concern the satirist: "She's still the same, belov'd, contented thing"
whether she "dwell in a Monk, or light upon a King." (We note the
barbed difference between dwelling and lighting upon.) But Vice
has more delicacy. She is "undone, if she forgets her Birth,/ And
stoops from Angels to the Dregs of Earth." The bitterness of
"Angels" marks a change of tone; conversational give-and-take fades
away in the concluding lines (145–172) of the first dialogue, the
chilling vision of the Triumph of Vice. The everyday world is revealed as an Inferno; every human activity blurs into an ugly parody
of itself as irony of the cultivated sort is abandoned and the speaking
voice trembles with shock and rage. *Fr.*'s "political" view of a reality
sustained and ordered by opposing evils has been a delusion. Society
collapses as nobles offer up their honor and commoners their families,
and established religion abdicates its function as "grave Bishops"
bless the Goddess of Vice: "hers the Gospel is, and hers the Laws."
The oxymorons of Vice—innocence is shame and villainy sacred—
are only blunter versions of the moral evasions and mystifications
which *Fr.* has more elegantly advocated.

At the end of *Dialogue I* the debate between *Fr.* and *P.*, the political man and the moral hero, has been transcended:

> Yet may this Verse (if such a Verse remain)
> Show there was one who held it in disdain.
> (171–172)

The dialogue has been a fiction, and Pope admits it—indeed, insists
on it. Behind *Fr.* and *P.* is another voice, one which closely resembles
P.'s and yet knows that *P.* is a character in a poem; and this voice
does not shrink from shattering the dramatic illusion when gripped
by such anger and disgust. Feeling takes precedence over mere con-
sistency of form, and we see Pope finally not as poetic maker but as
passionate human being. By asserting his independence of a corrupt
social reality he defines his own isolation; his lonely voice rejects the
world in order to maintain his moral integrity.

Readers of Shakespeare's *Coriolanus* will find some recognizable traits in Pope's satiric protagonist. Both Coriolanus and P. confront a disparity between the moral ego and the demands made upon it by political and social facts. Each experiences these demands impatiently, in the arrogant assurance that his personal nature affords a surer measure of truth and right than does the politic compromising of Menenius or *Fr*. And each, at the moment of crisis, turns upon the political world and banishes *it*—a moment of heroism and equally of supreme absurdity. Coriolanus, I should say, is so terribly ambivalent a figure to us precisely because he himself shows no capacity for ambivalence. He can feel only one way at a time. At his greatest moment, the scene with his mother at the gates of Rome, his language expresses not complexity of feeling, which could save him, but alternation of feelings. He never finds the middle ground where education takes place, where both the reality and the incompatibility of conflicting motives are recognized and pondered; and he dies, with a stubbornness which is at once awesome and comically childish, insisting on the very myth about himself which brought him disaster. Analogy is however not identity. Pope in the *Epilogue* dramatizes himself as heroic clown, but in a more knowing way than Coriolanus does. Pope's satirist is both Coriolanus and Shakespeare, in effect, understanding the comic possibilities of moral heroism even as he insists on being a moral hero.

The conclusion of *Dialogue I* is Pope's equivalent to Coriolanus's insistence that "there is a world elsewhere"; *Dialogue II* recalls his awful discovery that there is no such thing. Again Pope begins in the mode of ironic indirection, as if to make one last try at preserving his balance. The satirist would be a hunter of vice, but in the face of *Fr.*'s knowledgeable explanation of the game laws the dignified possibilities of this role evaporate, and P. is left as a kind of poacher, ruefully asking if there isn't *some* prey he may legally take. As in *Dialogue I*, however, such irony is inadequate to the gravity of the problem, and P.'s voice again begins to take on the inflections of the serio-comic moral hero:

> I follow *Virtue*, where she shines, I praise,
> Point she to Priest or Elder, Whig or Tory,
> Or round a Quaker's Beaver cast a Glory.
> (95–97)

The absurd possibilities of the last image are not to be minimized. By urbane, "cultivated" standards this involuntary morality is amus-

ingly close to madness, and Pope knows it. But to express such intense conviction one can only shrug off laughter and keep on talking:

> Enough for half the Greatest of these days
> To 'scape my Censure, not expect my Praise:
> Are they not rich? what more can they pretend?
> Dare they to hope a Poet for their Friend?
>   (112–115)

Such insistent arrogance signifies much more than personal ego-
tism. The "I" of the poem is not simply the man but the man as
poet, with the poet's traditional claim to dignity and virtue that are
qualities of his craft and not just of his personality. But there is
anxiety as well as pride in this voice. Coriolanus at least inhabited a
world of substance; his heroism is founded on physical action, and
his language characteristically centers upon images of such action—
of himself or some natural surrogate for himself breaking or overwhelming something. By comparison, poetry is a pretty unsubstantial
weapon and vice a Protean object, and the exaggerated emphasis
with which Pope defines the satirist's role hints at uncertainty. His
arrogance seems in some part a defensive mannerism, an effort to
exorcise the spirit of Vice by a willful affirmation of faith in Virtue:

> Ask you what Provocation I have had?
> The strong Antipathy of Good to Bad.
> When Truth or Virtue an Affront endures,
> Th' Affront is mine, my Friend, and should be yours.
> Mine, as a Foe profess'd to false Pretence,
> Who think a Coxcomb's Honour like his Sense;
> Mine, as a Friend to ev'ry worthy mind;
> And mine as Man, who feel for all mankind.
>   (197–204)

P. here stubbornly rejects complication and moral subtlety. There
is Good and there is Bad, and their antipathy is as natural and inevitable as magnetism. Moral categories demand large letters—the
Augustan habit of capitalizing abstract nouns to lend them solidity
never did more effective service. But "antipathy" is "feeling against,"
a negative, defensive emotion, and P.'s image of himself as some
almost Promethean figure feeling for all mankind shows how far he
has been driven from the confident, ironic modesty that is the
Horatian satirist's normal air:

> *Fr.* You're strangely proud.
>   *P.* So proud, I am no Slave:

So impudent, I own myself no Knave:
So odd, my Country's Ruin makes me grave.
Yes, I am proud; I must be proud to see
Men not afraid of God, afraid of me:
Safe from the Bar, the Pulpit, and the Throne,
Yet touch'd and sham'd by *Ridicule* alone.

(205–211)

This is impressively lofty—like Coriolanus he seems "a thing/ Made
by some other deity than Nature,/ That shapes man better." Yet
again the assertion is significantly qualified. To have even the slight-
est distaste for servility is to be "strangely proud" by the standards
of this world, and the tone is rueful in its arrogance.

Still, the positive aspects of the satirist's pride are forcefully stated.
If he has to some extent been driven into this ultimate position, this
is only to say that the ground he now occupies is the center of his
case, which no longer need be qualified and compromised. Satire is
a "sacred Weapon," the "sole Dread of Folly, Vice, and Insolence"
in a world whose institutions are too feeble or corrupt to enforce
significant order. The satirist, no longer able to speak simply as a
man among men, now assumes the role of God's deputy, trying not
by persuasion but by sheer intensity of will to make an impious
society right the imbalance between its values and divine ones. His
instrument is "to all but Heav'n-directed hands deny'd," and his
target is the falsity of official distinctions, "All that makes Saints of
Queens, and Gods of Kings." And his heroic intensity affords him a
vision of the triumph of Virtue to counteract the vision of Vice in
Dialogue I:

> . . . diadem'd with Rays divine,
> Touch'd with the Flame that breaks from Virtue's Shrine,
> Her Priestless Muse forbids the Good to dye,
> And ope's the Temple of Eternity.

(232–235)

The permanence of art is eloquently asserted. Immortality rewards
artistic virtue, and while it is figurative immortality—fame—rather
than literal, still the petty achievements of the worldly cannot earn
it. The true moral scale transcends time and death, to which even
the socially mighty are subject, and the poet speaks for a power that
is ideal and eternal:

> Let Envy howl while Heav'n's whole Chorus sings,
> And bark at Honour not confer'd by Kings;

> Let Flatt'ry sickening see the Incense rise,
> Sweet to the World, and grateful to the Skies:
> Truth guards the Poet, sanctifies the line,
> And makes Immortal, Verse as mean as mine.
>
> (242–247)

But Pope recognizes, quite as clearly as Shakespeare does, the ironies that adhere to the heroic identification of self with natural virtue. The grand assurance of tone cannot disguise the fact that this assertion of the artist's unique moral dignity represents a virtual confession of defeat. Artists, Pope would be the first to insist, have their significance in a community, in relation to an audience. But the heroic stature P. claims for himself is clearly, like Coriolanus's, a function of alienation. Coriolanus himself grows more awesome and mysterious as his loyalties to other people and their causes drop away, and he is most himself—most unlike *us*—at the moment of his death, when he has managed to detach himself from every external limit to his freedom. (His death is in effect a metaphor for the moral suicide his attempts to *preserve* his moral identity have caused.) Pope's satirist would not need to glorify his role so insistently if every other kind of virtue had not disappeared from his world. He simply has no one to talk to. The select, understanding interlocutors to whom the *Moral Essays* and the *Imitations of Horace* were largely addressed have been replaced by the anonymous and hopelessly cynical "Friend," who in the ways that count is no friend at all. The dialogue has become an oration, in fact a harangue, addressed to anyone who will listen, and this provides a final twist of bitter comedy:

> Yes, the last Pen for Freedom let me draw,
> When Truth stands trembling on the edge of Law:
> Here, last of *Britons!* let your Names be read;
> Are none, none living? let me praise the Dead,
> And for that Cause which made your Fathers shine,
> Fall, by the Votes of their degen'rate Line!
>   *Fr.* Alas! alas! pray end what you began,
> And write next winter more *Essays on Man.*
>
> (248–255)

The grand tone has grown almost too grand. ("Pens" and "Votes" in this context are perilously close to the kind of anticlimax Pope ridiculed in *Peri Bathous,* his ironic treatise "On the Art of Sinking in Poetry.") And the discovery that the good men are all dead—that the celebration of virtue must be an elegy—produces a faltering of the voice that is close to the classic double-take of farce. Yet even this approach to absurdity can't stop the last furious assertion of integrity.

The Friend's concluding rebuke fixes the problem for interpretation. Like him, we recognize that P. has gone too far; such extravagance is probably not only uncivilized but futile—to reject politics is to reject the possibility of human adjustment on any but an authoritarian basis, and poets scarcely command that kind of authority. But unlike Fr. we feel, for all our "liberal" reservations, that what has happened in these dialogues is worth any number of cautious, generalized essays in moral definition. It is true (and fortunate) that Pope's handling of the Epilogue recognizes and explores the comic aspects of the Coriolanus-like moral hero, the man who will not compromise his vision of experience even though the world leaves him no positive alternative to his bitter frustration. Yet finally, I think, we respond to P. with a warm approval that Shakespeare forbids us to feel in any simple way about Coriolanus. While we recognize that heroism may be as absurd as it is venerable, and as dangerous, the recognition tellingly reveals the price of perfect virtue. The price is painfully high; to pay it one may have to abandon the defenses of urbane, ironic civility and expose oneself to ridicule. But while it is one thing to be a fool because you are one, in all innocence, it is quite another to decide that seeming a fool is preferable to the moral evasions into which urbanity can lead. (We may think of Lord Chesterfield.) Readers of Blake and the "mad" poems of Yeats should have no trouble recognizing Pope's satiric identity in the Epilogue, nor in understanding that, for all its eccentric exaggeration, it expresses a moral intelligence that is uncompromisingly complex and mature.

I have been talking about the character called "P." in this discussion of "satiric identity." The question remains as to who P. is, what relation he bears to Pope the author. My earlier suggestion that both P. and Fr. are versions of the poet may seem to be an endorsement of the now rather common idea that Pope creates in his verse a persona, a mask of rhetoric which is not to be identified with the "real" personality of the writer. In this view the comic aspects of P.'s performance would indicate that Pope projects not himself but an exaggerated figure of "the satirist" for which he does not take full responsibility, a fiction which exists to convey certain general moral attitudes to the reader but which may then be dismissed. Thus the

poet is to be seen as a kind of ventriloquist, the Joycean artist who
has refined himself out of existence—but not, apparently, for the
Joycean purpose of rendering life clearly, without the interference of
personal bias or cultural accidents. Rather, Pope's use of "masks" is
treated as a rhetorical device for efficiently manipulating his materials and his readers.

But manipulation (by any name) suggests evasiveness or even dis-
honesty. Or, as so often with Swift, it suggests a troubled uncertainty
about where one really is. As a critical metaphor, the "mask" emphasizes concealment and subterfuge quite as much as it suggests
the creation of imaginative roles for the artist himself, and the
metaphor seems ill-suited to the Pope of the late satires, who so
insistently presents his subject in terms of moral conviction and
urgency. Rhetoric is, or ought to be, more than a way of disguising
the true grounds of an appeal so as to implant in an audience attitudes that have not been reasonably contemplated by all parties.
In a great speech or poem rhetoric is an agent of responsibility, a
means of clarifying and qualifying the issues at stake. To the poet,
as to the orator, serious readers or listeners might say: "If you want
to move us, be moved yourself, and let your rhetoric *reveal* your
feelings as hesitant, tangled ordinary speech so seldom can."

It thus becomes a matter not of whether the voice in the poem
is really Pope's, as Courthope would say, or really a dramatic fiction, as we so often hear nowadays, but of our tact in defining the
relation of rhetoric to personal feeling and thought. Perhaps we may
imagine that we read the poem in stages. (What we actually do
when we read it is of course too mysterious to be perfectly expressed
by this or any other scheme.) First we listen to the voices of P. and
Fr., as we listen to real conversation, innocently supposing that one
of them is Pope's and the other some unnamed real friend's; we attend to tone, emphasis, idiom, syntax, just as we do when we try
to assess a human speaker. Next we remind ourselves that the voices
are *not* "real," that we are overhearing not conversation but a
planned imitation of it in which, for our benefit, a single intelligence
controls and directs both voices. But having taken this critically all-
important second step, we should go further—which here, as it so
often does, means going back. The "mask" is not a false face, but
an identity quite as "real" as any of the poet's other identities, including his private self (or, more likely, selves); it is fashioned not
so that critics may admire its workmanship but so that readers may
come away with a heightened sense of the motives which made the

poem necessary to write. "*P.*" is Pope—Pope provisionally freed from
the irksome restraints of social and political moderation so that his
deepest commitments may get something close to pure expression.
Fr. is Pope too, but in him are combined and punished just those
elements of civilized personality which necessarily yet tragically
thwart the full realization of one's best impulses. Pope the man
could never quite live up to the passionate moral conviction of *P.*
—his biography is full of the troubles he got into by trying—but in
the figure of *P.* he shows both his understanding and his defiance
of the truth which R. P. Blackmur has tersely restated: "We are
never equal, so far as we have one, to our view of life. Our lives are
but a parody of our best selves."

To limit interpretation of Pope's satires to the configurations of
his mask, without asking what is revealed *through* it about the human presence within, is to defeat the purpose of poetry, if I am
right in thinking that this purpose is to tell the truth about the
world as the poet sees it, with the fullest possible fidelity to the
peculiar angle from which he looks. This angle will be peculiar,
it should be insisted, even for a poet as conscious as Pope was of
the conventions within which he works. We have heard a lot—maybe
too much—about the formality of his style and the limitations of his
subject matter. The "conventional wisdom" (to appropriate a phrase
of J. K. Galbraith's) about Pope's neoclassicism should not prevent
us from seeing that in the *Epilogue to the Satires,* as in most of the
poems of his later career, he dramatizes a fundamental clash between
classical modes of thought and expression and an increasing sense
that life cannot adequately be described within the classical manner
as his age understood it. The clash is neatly epitomized by the beginning of the "Sporus" passage in the *Epistle to Dr. Arbuthnot:*

> A Lash like mine no honest man shall dread,
> But all such babling blockheads in his stead.
>   Let *Sporus* tremble—"What? that Thing of silk,
> "*Sporus,* that mere white Curd of Ass's milk?
> "Satire or Sense alas! can *Sporus* feel?
> "Who breaks a Butterfly upon a Wheel?"
> Yet let me flap this Bug with gilded wings,
> This painted Child of Dirt that stinks and stings. . . .
>   (303–310)

The lofty assertion of the satirist's respect for honesty begins to break
up in the angry alliteration of "babling blockheads" and the ominous

rise of the voice in the next line. Arbuthnot's interruption tries to forestall the explosion—his cool contempt for Sporus indicates a classical confidence in standards of judgment and an aristocratic sureness of superiority to those who do not measure up. But the "Pope" of this poem, like the P. of the *Epilogue*, will not be restrained. Sporus may be immune to satire or sense, but Pope must flap him anyway. No real good can come of it, but the inner pressure of moral outrage defies containment, and the passage proceeds with its astonishing display of vituperative invention.

What, then, does this struggle between classical restraint and personal intensity express? I should say that it informs us of the difficulty of believing in the positive power of satire, the "operative irony" which, in a famous definition of Henry James's, "implies and projects the possible other case, the case rich and edifying where the actuality is pretentious and vain." Positive satire, like pastoral, declares man's "natural" innocence and virtue; behind our appalling misconduct stands an Eden which remains at least ethically redeemable. It invokes an agreed-upon scale of natural value. When we misbehave we are acting like animals, whereas we are not animals but men, and more is expected of us. The satirist exposes our errors by appealing to or stylistically demonstrating the best human possibilities, the mode of conduct appropriate to our status in the whole scheme of things. But the "Hogs of Westphaly" passage or the portrait of Sporus, while they seem to criticize bad men on just these natural grounds, can hardly be said to encourage our belief that the satirist speaks for an intelligible moral order he understands and believes in. There is too much anger, too little suggestion of what should be. Such passages show Pope confronting a dreadful alternative to Eden, the possibility that "nature" is not fundamentally good but meaningless—which to a classically trained mind is virtually the same as evil. If so, virtue must be seen (as Hobbes saw it) to be a difficult and fragile construct which *opposes* the natural tendencies of most men. There is some complexity here. In dramatizing himself as moral hero Pope invokes an ultimate natural sanction for his integrity, just as Coriolanus does. But our sense of the comic aspects of his role marks the eccentric remoteness of the satirist's "nature" from the regular, universal, publicly knowable nature which is the neoclassic norm. The satirist seems able to show how shockingly Sporus and his beastly fellows deviate from the norm only by himself departing from it in the opposite direction. His violent voice expresses anxiety, in short; he can't comfortably sustain the tone of the confident classicist who finds "civilization," at its potential best, an embodiment of natural and divine law.

And yet for all his comic possibilities, the moral hero *is* heroic. While he cannot fully accept the classical view of the world, he resists yielding wholly to its alternative. Some of the classical breadth and impartiality of vision persists in Pope's recognition and acceptance of the ludicrous aspects of his new role, his understanding that while moral clarity is worth the sacrifices that must be made to it, the margin is at best a slim one. The satiric voice of these late poems has rejected the perceptible smugness of the *Essay on Man*. The satirist can lose his temper, and while this marks his superiority both to impervious fools like Sporus and bland "administrators" like *Fr.*, we know that he can never see in himself the gratifying mastery of reality that they see in themselves all the time. The dramatic presence is ambivalent, neurotic, recognizably human.

This is not the usual way of reading Pope, but that scarcely matters. There is no serious value in novelty per se. I have no wish to dismiss "conventional" formulations like this one of George Sherburn's, from perhaps the best general history of eighteenth century literature:

> In the larger traditionalism of Pope's generic patterns as well as in the preoccupation with public emotion eloquently expressed, Pope is the acme of "correct" neo-classical excellence. He is, perhaps permanently, our great example in English of "the poet of reason," of intellectuality in the poetic art.

Certainly the Pope I have been describing is far from this. The emotion of the later satires is preeminently private, not public; the expression may be "eloquent" but hardly in the way Mr. Sherburn means; there is little reason and less intellectuality in the passages I have cited. And yet there most certainly is a Pope who conforms to such a description; quantitatively there is much more of that Pope than of mine. It depends on the context in which you read. When you come to Pope with Dryden in mind, as history invites you to, and behind Dryden the Roman traditions of epic, satire, eclogue, elegy, and amatory verse which come into English poetry by way of the continent in the sixteenth and seventeenth centuries, you see that Pope is indeed a "neo-classical" poet. He thought of himself as such, and we cannot understand him without knowing at least generally how extensively his "sense of the past" directed his procedure in particular poems. But we resist our worlds even as we live in them—living itself is a resistance, since life never quite coincides with our ideas about it. Pope's neoclassicism is important not only because it tells us why he did things in certain ways but also because it defines the limits which as an artist he seems to have found increasingly intolerable.

More important, as T. S. Eliot observed long ago, "tradition" works both forward and backward in time; in a significant sense it does not work "in" time at all. The fact that, chronologically, we do come to Pope through Dryden and European neoclassicism should not unduly condition our response to what is on the page, nor obscure our understanding that for *readers* of literature history is a two-way street. When one has read Blake and D. H. Lawrence, to name the two most compelling moral poets since Pope himself, one can never again read Pope's satires in quite the same way. Without ceasing to be—in certain lights—"the poet of reason," Pope has an eminent place in a "simultaneous order" of poet-moralists driven by an intractable reality into a tragicomic intensity of private vision and private conviction that has only remote connections with the public ideals and possibilities they began by asserting. In his uniting of traditionally separate roles, the hero who acts and the artist who observes and suffers the complex consequences of action, he prefigures a Romantic obsession with which our literature has not yet come to terms. And he belongs among the makers or users of systems, men who would hold the world in a single imaginative whole but who, grown old and shaken by experience, must say with Yeats:

> Now that my ladder's gone,
> I must lie down where all the ladders start,
> In the foul rag-and-bone shop of the heart.

It is the acceptance of one's own vulnerability, the unbreakable ties between noble principles and the essential if often unlovely and ignoble imperfections that unite us with other men, that Pope finally comes to; and only this acceptance can keep the moralist's voice a human voice as well.

Generality in Augustan Satire

BY WILLIAM YOUNGREN

> "To Generalize is to be an Idiot. To particularize is the Alone Distinction of Merit. General Knowledges are those Knowledges that Idiots Possess." (Blake)

I

EVEN SYMPATHETIC readers of Augustan satire are often puzzled when they try to relate the poetic achievement of Dryden, Pope, and Johnson to the critical statements one usually sees quoted as representative of English neoclassicism. We value the satires for their vivid and incisive portraits—for Achitophel, Sporus, Atticus, and the rest—yet contemporary criticism, with its constant injunctions to "follow Nature," appears to have been aimed at producing mere platitudes, pious restatements of accredited sentiment. It seems the only way out is to assume that instinct conquered intellect and the Augustans simply wrote well in spite of themselves. But this is always a shaky assumption and it seems a particularly dangerous one to make about men so articulate and so purposefully cultured. In this essay I shall try to suggest some better ways out.

I think the problem centers on the notion of generality, a quality which neoclassic critics prized but toward which our feelings are ambivalent. We instinctively connect generalizations with science, and though we allow them (and even recognize them as necessary) in ordinary talk about human affairs, we balk at the idea of poetry being general. Generalizations seem always in danger of turning into mere generalities, as bland and fuzzy as those composite photographs made by superimposing the faces of Garbo and Bergman and Katharine Hepburn one on another to produce "the ideal of feminine beauty." And certainly blandness and fuzziness are the last things we want in poetry. Yet two of Dr. Johnson's most frequently quoted critical utterances explicitly demand generality in poetry, and in fact seem almost to turn poets into scientists. In *Rasselas*, speaking through Imlac, Johnson declares that the poet's business

is to examine, not the individual, but the species; to remark general
properties and large appearances; he does not number the streaks of
the tulip, or describe the different shades in the verdure of the forest.
He is to exhibit in his portraits of nature such prominent and striking
features as recall the original to every mind; and must neglect the
minuter discriminations, which one may have remarked, and another
have neglected, for those characteristics which are alike obvious to
vigilance and carelessness.

And in the *Preface to Shakespeare* he roundly asserts that "Nothing
can please many, and please long, but just representations of general
nature," then goes on to praise Shakespeare for giving us characters
who "are not modified by the customs of particular places" but instead

act and speak by the influence of those general passions and principles
by which all minds are agitated, and the whole system of life is
continued in motion. In the writings of other poets a character is
too often an individual; in those of Shakespeare it is commonly a
species.

Read as they stand, these assertions seem immensely depressing
since, as I have implied, what we ordinarily ask from poetry is precisely the individual rather than the species—Shelley's particular sky-
lark or Keats's particular nightingale rather than abstract treatises
on the *Alauda arvensis* or the *Luscinia megarhyncha*, Pope's Sporus
rather than a lecture on The Corrupt Minister. To generalize is,
most simply, to group things into sorts; but in poetry it would seem
that we are never interested in this or that sort of emotion, but
always in this or that particular precise emotion. Particularity, immediacy, vividness, sensuous concreteness—these are the qualities
that the most distinguished twentieth century critics have taught us
to group together as poetically desirable.

But rather than debating our view and Johnson's in a void, we
must give our investigation a firm basis by looking at some examples
of Augustan satire, bearing in mind the problem we have set ourselves: to determine in what sense the satire is general and to see
what, if anything, generality has to do with its value as poetry. To
get some freshness of approach, I have chosen to begin with an
Augustan poem not often discussed, Pope's "versification" of Donne's
fourth satire, titled *The Impertinent, Or, a Visit to the Court*. This
poem is also convenient because we can compare it at every point
with Donne's original, and thus sharpen our sense of what is pecul-

iarly Augustan about the way Pope works. As a start take the openings
of the two poems: [1]

> Well; I may now receive, and die; My sinne
> Indeed is great, but I have beene in
> A Purgatorie, such as fear'd hell is
> A recreation to, and scarse map of this.
> My minde, neither with prides itch, nor yet hath been
> Poyson'd with love to see, or to bee seene,
> I had no suit there, nor new suite to shew,
> Yet went to Court . . .
>
> (Donne)

> Well, if it be my time to quit the Stage,
> Adieu to all the Follies of the Age!
> I die in Charity with Fool and Knave,
> Secure of Peace at least beyond the Grave.
> I've had my *Purgatory* here betimes,
> And paid for all my Satires, all my Rhymes:
> The Poet's Hell, its Tortures, Fiends and Flames,
> To this were Trifles, Toys, and empty Names.
>   With foolish *Pride* my Heart was never fir'd,
> Nor the vain Itch *t'admire*, or *be admir'd*;
> I hop'd for no *Commission* from his Grace;
> I bought no *Benefice*, I begg'd no *Place*;
> Had no *new Verses*, or *new Suit* to show;
> Yet went to COURT!—the Dev'l wou'd have it so.
>
> (Pope)

As soon as we try to speak the lines, differences begin to emerge.
Donne's speaker is reflective and resigned, and seems to be meditating on what is ordinarily a private topic, the state of one's soul. Later,
at line 140, he is to say "Toughly and stubbornly I beare this crosse,"
which sums up beautifully the man we hear in these opening lines:
contemplating worldly things with the brave ruggedness and controlled revulsion proper to any strong-minded Christian, he is fully
aware of their evil but also has a sharp and galling sense of his
own—as we see by the way he lingers on the word "sinne" at the
end of the first line. Pope, on the other hand, immediately gives
us the brisk and ringing accents of a man consciously addressing an
audience—in fact he pointedly compares life to a stage and death

---

[1] In quoting from Pope I have followed the *Twickenham Edition* except at line
173 of the second "Moral Essay," where I have corrected the obviously mistaken
"Safe in your Secret still in Cloe's ear" by changing the first "in" to "is." The
passages from Donne, Dryden, and Johnson are taken from the volumes in the
Oxford English Texts series.

to the player's final exit. And while we are not particularly moved to associate physical stances or gestures with Donne's introspective speaker, Pope's tone and rhythms make such associations almost inevitable: his "Well" is not reflective like Donne's but exclamatory, accompanied by an impatient, well-bred toss of the head; and the sweeping "Adieu to all the Follies of the Age!" seems to demand a suitably theatrical sweep of the arm. From the start Pope's speaker really is a man on a stage, a man used to speaking in public.

The differences in general outlook and interest are equally sharp, and they are closely related to the differences in tone of voice. Donne's preoccupations are specifically religious, as we might expect from his meditative tone; for him death is really death, duly preceded by the sacrament ("I may now receive"), and a far cry from Pope's gracefully metaphorical "quitting the Stage." Also, while Donne speaks of sin and implicates himself fully, Pope speaks only of follies and attributes even those to "the Age" rather than to himself. Donne extravagantly claims that the court is a greater trial than hell itself, but hell is still "fear'd hell" and we feel its sudden ominous reality in the way the two forceful monosyllables break the meter. Behind the ironic claim lies Donne's constant, unquestioned awareness of what a real and awful thing damnation is; and his momentary extravagance is not blasphemous, but is made permissible by this awareness. Pope's hell is not the real one at all, but just a casually ticked-off collection of stage props ("Tortures, Fiends and Flames"), a not very serious version of the literary hell created by poets like Virgil and Milton. It really does sound less trying than the purgatory he has already gone through in paying for his satires and rhymes, and, since Pope speaks of himself as "Secure of Peace at least beyond the Grave," we know he does not consider genuine damnation even a remote possibility.

But perhaps the oddest thing about Pope's opening lines is the amount of detailed knowledge they assume we possess. Pope is not merely speaking in public about publicly discussable, secular matters; he is also speaking with full assurance that his audience already knows him and his world minutely. His statement of self-justification is longer and more elaborate than Donne's and, unlike Donne's, it could not apply to just any strong-minded Christian, but only to a particular poet whose satires and rhymes have aroused public controversy and for whom we have particular sympathy. He has an unusually strong sense of his own special role and later, at line 196, is to speak of himself as "the Terror of this sinful Town." Donne's oddly impersonal intimacy of tone, his meditative intensity, the frequent twistings and turnings that show an eagerness to examine and qualify his words even as he speaks them—all these indicate that he is inviting us to enter his consciousness, to feel the drama of his narrative as it unfolds before us, and at last to share a new and unique experience. But we seem to pick Pope up in the midst of a conversation, or at least in the midst of a relationship with his audience which has included many monologues like this one. He acts as though we know exactly who he is and how to feel about him, and he even manages to suggest, by a few deft strokes, a whole way of life that we are also assumed to know and share. Commissions, Benefices, Places, and his Grace are referred to with a confident nonchalance that depends on our already knowing the ins and outs of literary and ecclesiastical patronage; and the court itself is old hat to us, not, as in Donne's poem, a vague, evil immensity looming in the background. Even Pope's use of the definite article—"*the* Follies of *the* Age" as against Donne's "my sinne"—enforces our sense of the difference. Donne offers to tell us something new and deeply personal; his tone is intimate but the intimacy does not depend, as Pope's does, on our being a special sort of audience with a special body of experience, for to understand Donne we need only share his generally Christian view of the world, the flesh, and the devil. Pope offers rather to shed new light on familiar experience by bringing into contact with each other a character (himself) and a situation (the court) already known to us.

All these differences can be seen too in the first real incident of both poems, the speaker's encounter with a fatuous courtier:

> He names mee, and comes to mee; I whisper, God!
> How have I sinn'd, that thy wraths furious rod,
> This fellow chuseth me?
>
> (*Donne*, 49–51)

> He spies me out. I whisper, gracious God!
> What Sin of mine cou'd merit such a Rod?
> That all the Shot of Dulness now must be
> From this thy Blunderbuss discharg'd on me!
>
> (*Pope*, 62–65)

In Donne the irony is of course that a supercilious fool whom one can refer to contemptuously as "This fellow" can also be the punishing "furious rod" of God's wrath. But just as with the earlier irony about the court being a worse place than hell, we can feel a serious religious assertion in the background: the courtier may be a fool, but he and his world are still genuinely evil, and as such they represent part of the "Purgatorie" that fallen man has to bear—"Toughly and stubbornly"—in this world. The whole thing is a sort of deep joke that demonstrates beautifully the absurd and paradoxical state in which Adam's sin has placed us. Again Donne's tone is reflective, and the quietly intense, almost trancelike rhythm ("He names mee, and comes to mee") suggests a man wholly absorbed in his story and keeps us absorbed in it too, our attention firmly centered on the movements of the speaker's consciousness. And again Pope is abruptly and familiarly conversational ("He spies me out"); his whisper has none of the bewildered anger and hushed earnestness we hear in Donne but is an exaggerated stage whisper—we can almost see him throw up his hands in exasperation. Also, he turns Donne's bitter vision of the courtier as God's "rod" into a much more frivolous sort of joke. For readers accustomed to eighteenth century poetic diction, "rod" might just possibly be a rather strained periphrasis for gun, either offered solemnly or with tongue in cheek, as a comically inelegant parody of contemporary attempts at poetic "elegance." Pope capitalizes on this possibility by suddenly literalizing the rod into an actual gun, transforming the awesome biblical staff of punishment into a mere "Blunderbuss" (that clumsy and ineffective sort of musket the Pilgrim Fathers are always shown carrying) that randomly sprays its annoying but harmless "Shot of Dulness" at him. And the joke is clinched by a pun, since "blunderbuss" was also used in the eighteenth century as a slang term equivalent to "blockhead." Though Pope does mention sin here, the only punishment provided for it is "Dulness," which makes his God quite different from Donne's. And again, his choice of "Dulness" as the ultimate adversity suggests that Pope is not only speaking in public but is also appealing to an audience very different from Donne's, an audience whose concerns are mainly social and secular, and whose specific experience is very much like his own.

Up to now we would not seem to have got very far in our pursuit of Augustan generality. Indeed the main thing our comparison has brought out is that Pope's poem presents us at once with a world full of particular objects and judgments while Donne's seems to create its world as it develops, depending only on our having a generally Christian outlook. Pope even makes offhand references to specific people we are expected to know: he inserts the names of two famous eighteenth century collectors, Sloane and Woodward (30), where Donne merely alludes to "seaven Antiquaries studies" (21); and where Donne is content to refer generally to pedants, soldiers, mountebanks and lawyers (40–41), Pope again pointedly rejects the species and gives us the individuals—Motteux, Henley, Budgel, and Gonson (50–53). And as anyone who has struggled with the notes to the *Dunciad* knows, this use of names is one of Pope's characteristic techniques. Plainly what we need is a clearer notion of generality and of the quality we consider to be its opposite, the quality we usually call particularity.

The first step in getting to such a clearer notion of generality and particularity is to stop seeing them as necessarily opposed and mutually exclusive attributes like straightness and curvature. What if they were not even opposed in the way that heat and cold or light and dark are, as contraries which can coexist in varying proportions (unlike straightness and curvature) but which are still contraries? What if saying that a line of poetry was both general and particular did not imply that it was general only insofar as it was not particular (and vice versa), but were merely like saying that a ball is both round and red? Or to push the argument still further, what if generality and particularity could actually be conducive to each other? Once we ask such questions, we put ourselves in a better position to talk about what we actually hear in Pope's lines. First, we are able to notice that Pope's particularity is of a special sort. Though words like "Commission" and "Benefice" have a sharpness of outline that suggests they refer to clearly defined entities, the definition of these entities does not take place in the poem—or at least Pope pretends that it does not, and that is what matters here. The meanings of such terms all seem to have been fixed and agreed on at some earlier time, and now Pope simply moves the terms themselves into place, like chessmen. His intimacy of tone, as we have seen, depends on the assumption that we share enough of his experience to understand what he means if he uses words in this way. Furthermore, with the specific meaning comes a specific evaluation; each important word strikes our ears with a confident solidity that seems to say "And you know what *that* means!" This is partly owing to the use of the definite article I noted above and partly to certain obvious mannerisms of informal conversation. But most importantly it is a rhythmic matter, a way of making words *sound* which suggests a way of viewing their relation to experience.

When we read "With foolish *Pride* my Heart was never fir'd," the clipped and "finished" sound of the line makes the word *"Pride"* stand out from its surroundings; it has the air of having been confidently selected from a ready stock and dropped neatly into place because it is precisely the word it is and no other would have done. The rhythm of the line helps to isolate the word for contemplation. Donne's lines do not ordinarily have this sort of surface polish; they flow, stop, change course, then flow off in another direction. When we read "My minde, neither with prides itch, nor yet hath been/ Poyson'd with love to see, or to bee seene," the suspensions of rhythm, syntax, and sense keep us pressing on, following the twists and turns of the narration over the rhymes and into the event Donne is describing. His couplets are not closed like Pope's, and his rhymes do not call attention to themselves as Pope's do; for while Pope uses rhyme-words to point and sharpen his lines, Donne makes his rhymes studiedly unobtrusive so that they will provide an artful counterpoint to the seemingly artless flow of narrative and reflection. Thus "prides itch" and "love to see, or to bee seene" are heard primarily as part of the continuous flow of Donne's verse, not as self-sufficient counters like Pope's *"Pride"* and "the vain Itch *t'admire,* or *be admir'd,"* which seem to point directly to concrete objects outside the poem. And in Donne's version when we come to the words "went to Court," we feel that we are being told about a specific personal experience occurring at a definite moment in time. But Pope prepares us differently for the same words. The objects which terms like *"Pride"* seem to point to are certainly sharp and concrete, but they are not placed in time or committed to any single event; they seem rather to sum up and judge many similar events. Thus when we come, in Pope's version, to the phrase "went to COURT," our interest is not directed primarily to a single experience but rather to a specific and familiar *kind* of experience, "Going to Court."

The more we look at Pope's page, the more the words seem to stand apart from one another like the parts of a machine in an "exploded" diagram, each word possessing its own special weight of meaning and value. Pope manages rhythmically and tonally to suggest that we already agree with these established meanings and values, and he makes us feel, behind each important term, the accumulated weight of the particular experiences which it focuses and defines. The sharpness and clarity with which each term stands out led us to say at once that Pope is being "particular." But we can now see that he is being "general" as well. All we usually mean when we say a statement is general is that it refers to some group or class of occasions or events rather than to just one; and it is clear Pope's statements fulfill the condition. If this conclusion still seems odd, it is because when we think of general statements, we do not think of poetry but rather of sentences like "All cats eat fish" or "The force is equal to the product of the mass and the acceleration." But in going from our definition of generality to such examples, we make an odd and misleading jump. We act on the very questionable assumption that to apply to more than one occasion or event, a statement must be as neutral, toneless, and thoroughly unpoetic as the ordinary inductive and deductive generalities we loosely associate with the methods of science. Later I shall say something about where this assumption comes from; for the present it is enough merely to note it and question it. As we have seen, Pope is anything but a neutral and toneless poet; and yet it seems perfectly correct to say that he achieves a kind of generality. By giving us the sense that his words come into his poem fully formed, each bearing the character of its past and representing a definite class of experiences, he prevents us from losing ourselves in the particular incidents he is relating and keeps us aware of a larger world outside the poem, the world of established standards in which "Going to Court" is a certain type of familiar experience with certain clear implications. The point is that Pope's generality involves constant moral evaluation rather than scientific neutrality; furthermore, it is not at all opposed to the particularity we have noticed, but allied to it, for Pope can only achieve this sort of generality because his important terms are so vivid and so sharply outlined.

To look at it another way, we might say that while Donne's poem flows on and we follow its course as we read, Pope's seems almost to "stand still." While Donne relates, naturally though with tortuous effort, the events that took place at court and the thoughts and responses they provoked in him, Pope continually interrupts his story to add vivid stage directions and tonal mimicry:

> He, like to a high stretcht lute string squeakt, O Sir,
> 'Tis sweet to talke of Kings.
>
> (*Donne*, 73–74)

> At this, entranc'd, he lifts his Hands and Eyes,
> Squeaks like a high-stretch'd Lutestring, and replies:
> "Oh 'tis the sweetest of all earthly things
> "To gaze on Princes, and to talk of Kings!"
>
> (*Pope*, 98–101)

The sharp pictorial detail that distinguishes Pope's version from Donne's forces our attention outward to a social scene, a scene not continuously being recalled or relived as in Donne's poem but static, viewed from the outside. We do not watch one action or thought succeed another in Pope as in Donne; in the couplet just cited, the carefully cadenced insertion of "entranc'd," the emphatic placing of the ridiculous word "Squeaks," and the addition of the details about the courtier's hands and eyes all make it impossible for us to move naturally and easily from verb to verb ("lifts . . . Squeaks . . . replies") as we do in Donne or as we normally do when we read or listen to a story. There is obviously "movement" in Pope's lines in the sense that we read from word to word rather than taking in the poem at a single glance as we do a painting or statue. But there is no movement in the scene the lines describe—as there is in Donne, where the two movements frequently merge. Pope seems rather to direct us from one part to another of a static tableau, a picture as fixed and complete as the meanings of his individual terms. When he changes Donne's past tense to present (as in the lines just quoted), the effect is not to make the progress of the action more vivid, but to catch the way a particular act looked and so to bring out its character—here, the arch silliness of the courtier's exclamation. And even where Pope retains the past tense, he often finds ways to make us feel we are watching something already accomplished rather than something in process. Thus when the courtier is first approaching, Donne writes:

> Therefore I suffered this; Towards me did runne
> A thing more strange, then on Niles slime, the Sunne
> E'r bred; or all which into Noahs Arke came;
> A thing, which would have pos'd Adam to name . . .
> (Donne, 17–20)

Pope emends:

> Scarce was I enter'd, when behold! there came
> A Thing which *Adam* had been pos'd to name . . .
> (Pope, 24–25)

That word "behold!"—which takes the incident out of a narrative past and thrusts it under our noses—is not exceptional but characteristic. The Augustan satirists are constantly urging us to see or observe or watch or behold, in order to gain the sort of focus we see Pope gaining here, focus on a fixed external object.[2]

The peculiarly static nature of Pope's poem comes out most clearly in the climactic encounter of the beauties and the wits. Donne's version, as we might expect by this time, is leisurely, discursive, and sardonic:

> Now,
> The Ladies come; As Pirats, which doe know
> That there came weak ships fraught with Cutchannel,
> The men board them; and praise, as they thinke, well,
> Their beauties; they the mens wits; Both are bought.
> Why good wits ne'r weare scarlet gownes, I thought
> This cause, These men, mens wits for speeches buy,
> And women buy all reds which scarlets die.
> He call'd her beauty limetwigs, her haire net;
> She feares her drugs ill laid, her haire loose set.
> (Donne, 187–196)

Of course, there is a good deal of moral evaluation in these lines; we judge the wits and beauties by the tone Donne adopts toward them and by our sense of what the words he chooses ordinarily imply. But that is true of almost any use of language. The point is that Donne is not at pains to make us consciously aware of the evaluative function of his language. Unlike Pope, he makes no concentrated attempt to show us that he is anchoring each incident or detail in a known and stable system of categories and judgments; instead he stresses the temporal placing of his incidents, their position in a continuous narrative whose movement suggests novelty and change rather than the known and the stable. In Pope's version of the encounter, Donne's mixture of narration and reflection becomes pure scenic presentation:

> Painted for sight, and essenc'd for the smell,
> Like Frigates fraught with Spice and Cochine'l,
> Sail in the *Ladies*: How each Pyrate eyes

[2] Interestingly enough, lines 212–214 read this way in Pope's first version of the poem:

> And now the *British* Youth, engag'd no more
> At *Fig's* at *White's*, with *Felons*, or a *Whore*,
> Pay their last Duty to the *Court* . . .

But two years later he altered the first two words to make the opening line read "See! where the *British* Youth, engag'd no more." He had perhaps sensed that his poem was beginning to move like a straight narrative, and needed steadying.

So weak a Vessel, and so rich a Prize!
Top-gallant he, and she in all her Trim,
He boarding her, she striking sail to him.
"*Dear Countess!* you have Charms all Hearts to hit!"
And "*sweet Sir Fopling!* you have so much wit!"
Such Wits and Beauties are not prais'd for nought,
For both the Beauty and the Wit are *bought*.
(*Pope, 226–235*)

All the verbs that Donne uses to convey a sense of movement have
lost their vitality. The careful balances of Pope's charming first
couplet suggest a composed picture rather than an event in progress,
and they distract our attention from the verb just as the word "behold!" did in the couplet that marked the courtier's entrance. Or
to be more exact, the balances distract our attention from the tempo
and progress of the action which "Sail" indicates, and focus it on
that action's quality and appearance. The smoothness of "Sail in the
Ladies" makes it easy to slide over the verb, and Pope's sustaining
of the nautical metaphor (which Donne quickly drops) helps to
keep the vividness of the passage pictorial rather than narrative.
That is, Pope makes us see the ladies more clearly than Donne does,
but he does not make us see them in motion; Donne, by pausing
expectantly for a moment on "Now," directs our attention to the
specific moment of the entrance rather than to the way it looked.
Donne's direct and active "The men board them" is also made
static and pictorial by Pope's change to "boarding" and by his addition of the balancing phrase "striking sail"—which, incidentally,
helps to get rid of the indecorous sexual overtones of Donne's word
"board" by comically suggesting the lowering of a fan to begin conversation. Donne's digressions, reflections, and qualifications are
neatly excised, the passage rounding itself out with the mechanically
stylized conversation and the joke about "prais'd for nought." Having sketched the surrounding scene, Pope drops Sir Fopling and the
Countess into place, as examples or stock types of court silliness.

What we have learned from Pope's imitation of Donne is applicable to the question we set out to answer, since the heart of
Augustan satire is the satirical portrait used as Sir Fopling and the
Countess are used, to exemplify some general quality or problem;
thus in any major poem of Pope, Dryden, or Johnson we can see the
techniques of Pope's imitation employed to produce poetry that is
pictorial and static, and to give a sense of general implications. But
if we are to apply what we have learned, we must now move on to

more significant Augustan poems, for the creation of stock types like
Sir Fopling and the Countess is not an important enough achievement to tell us all we need to know. To see what the techniques we
have pointed out as characteristic of Augustanism can yield when
exercised on a larger scale, look first at this portrait from Pope's
Epistle to a Lady, Of the Characters of Women, better known as
the second "Moral Essay":

> "Yet Cloe sure was form'd without a spot—"
> Nature in her then err'd not, but forgot.
> "With ev'ry pleasing, ev'ry prudent part,
> "Say, what can Cloe want?"—she wants a Heart.
> She speaks, behaves, and acts just as she ought;
> But never, never, reach'd one gen'rous Thought.
> Virtue she finds too painful an endeavour,
> Content to dwell in Decencies for ever.
> So very reasonable, so unmov'd,
> As never yet to love, or to be lov'd.
> She, while her Lover pants upon her breast,
> Can mark the figures on an Indian chest;
> And when she sees her Friend in deep despair,
> Observes how much a Chintz exceeds Mohair.
> Forbid it Heav'n, a Favour or a Debt
> She e'er should cancel—but she may forget.
> Safe is your Secret still in Cloe's ear;
> But none of Cloe's shall you ever hear.
> Of all her Dears she never slander'd one,
> But cares not if a thousand are undone.
> Would Cloe know if you're alive or dead?
> She bids her Footman put it in her head.
> Cloe is prudent—would you too be wise?
> Then never break your heart when Cloe dies.
>   (157–180)

We often assume that a character in a novel or poem must be either
a stock type or a unique, living individual; yet while Cloe is obviously
not just a stock type like Sir Fopling and the Countess, we cannot
call her a living individual either, since she is so obviously being used
to exemplify a certain sort of moral failing and since Pope's poetry
makes no effort to give the illusion of life. Here as in the imitation
of Donne, Pope actively makes us aware of general implications and
prevents us from getting the sense of temporal continuity which is
usually the literary basis of that illusion. The incidents of the portrait
—or perhaps "moments" would be a better term—are sharp and
immediate, but they are not given a clear place in a definite sequence

of events. Here as at the end of the imitation of Donne, Pope is interested in arresting actions in such a way that their meaning is revealed through the way they look, rather than in giving us a sense of watching one action lead on to another. Thus he is careful not to give us a series of verbs that point clearly to consecutive acts, and he allows the vivid scene with Cloe's lover panting on her breast to last only a second before he shifts abruptly to the scene with the despairing friend. The two vignettes have no temporal relation to one another, but are put side by side mainly because they are both admirable examples of the same thing—they both show just what sort of person Cloe is.

Of course, we have never met anyone quite like Cloe before, and in that sense she is unique, an individual. But she is unique in the way that each castle we may build with a given set of blocks will be unique; her uniqueness is the sort possessed by a special composition or arrangement of familiar elements rather than the sort we attribute to a living organism. The all-embracing, common opposition of stock type to living character is not relevant to her since she has no continuous existence in time, and hence no life. Thus she is not opposed to Sir Fopling and the Countess as a living being to a dead thing, but rather as a mosaic to a single bright stone. And in a couplet like

> Virtue she finds too painful an endeavour,
> Content to dwell in Decencies for ever.

we have the same sense we had in the imitation of Donne, that the important words are indeed like stones or building blocks, self-contained units arranged in a special design. The first line of the couplet opens ringingly with "Virtue," but shrinks fastidiously into itself as the inappropriately vague and genteel "finds" (in the same sense a waiter uses when he asks us how we "found" the steak) is succeeded by "too painful" (we can almost hear Cloe sighing "simply *too* painful") and finally by the oddly active noun "endeavour," Cloe's weary word for any gesture of warmth. Then "Content," "dwell" and "for ever" help to embalm the central word "Decencies" in the lifeless and passive context suggested by the rest of Cloe's behavior, and we see that even decency can be damning if it shows itself merely in "Decencies," little rehearsals of social forms executed without "one gen'rous thought." As in the imitation of Donne, we feel, both here and in the portrait as a whole, that words with varying histories are being worked into a pattern which sums up an immense amount of moral experience.

Moving still further from our starting point, we can see that the qualities we have observed in Pope are to be found in the other Augustan satirists too. Take this famous portrait from Dryden's *Absalom and Achitophel:*

> Of these the false *Achitophel* was first:
> A Name to all succeeding Ages Curst.
> For close Designs, and crooked Counsels fit;
> Sagacious, Bold, and Turbulent of wit:
> Restless, unfixt in Principles and Place;
> In Power unpleas'd, impatient of Disgrace.
> A fiery Soul, which working out its way,
> Fretted the Pigmy Body to decay:
> And o'r inform'd the Tenement of Clay.
> A daring Pilot in extremity;
> Pleas'd with the Danger, when the Waves went high
> He sought the Storms; but for a Calm unfit,
> Would Steer too nigh the Sands, to boast his Wit.
> Great Wits are sure to Madness near ally'd;
> And thin Partitions do their Bounds divide:
> Else, why should he, with Wealth and Honour blest,
> Refuse his Age the needful hours of Rest?
> Punish a Body which he coud not please;
> Bankrupt of Life, yet Prodigal of Ease?
> And all to leave, what with his Toyl he won,
> To that unfeather'd, two Leg'd thing, a Son:
> Got, while his Soul did hudled Notions try;
> And born a shapeless Lump, like Anarchy.
> In Friendship False, Implacable in Hate:
> Resolv'd to Ruine or to Rule the State.
> To Compass this the Triple Bond he broke;
> The Pillars of the publick Safety shook:
> And fitted *Israel* for a Foreign Yoke.
> Then, seiz'd with Fear, yet still affecting Fame,
> Usurp'd a Patriott's All-attoning Name.
> So easie still it proves in Factious Times,
> With publick Zeal to cancel private Crimes:
> How safe is Treason, and how sacred ill,
> Where none can sin against the Peoples Will:
> Where Crouds can wink; and no offence be known,
> Since in anothers guilt they find their own.
>
> (150–185)

Dryden makes no more attempt than Pope to give the illusion of continuous life, and instead of providing the "story" of Absalom-Shaftesbury's career, immediately sets about summing up his character in the forceful adjectives of the opening lines. Here too we

get no sense of action leading naturally to action, for Dryden deliberately uses verbs that are abstract and do not point to acts we
can easily get hold of. "Fretted," "inform'd," "Refuse," "Punish,"
and "please" have an air of force and decision about them, but they
keep us far from any particular situation; the judgments that lie
behind the verbs are all sharp and definite, but each verb seems to
sum up many occasions rather than point to just one. The only
verbs that might permit us to visualize a single continuous sequence
of events—verbs like "went," "Steer," "broke," and "shook"—are
used in such a pointedly metaphorical way that we are kept constantly aware of some meaning or judgment beyond the particular
act and not allowed merely to follow the story. And anyway, some
of these verbs are made iterative by the auxiliary "Would." Finally,
we notice that after Dryden has piled up the evidence, he moves from
Achitophel's character to outright generalizations about "Great Wits"
and "Factious Times."

As a final example, take this portrait from Johnson's *The Vanity
of Human Wishes*:

> In full-blown dignity, see Wolsey stand,
> Law in his voice, and fortune in his hand:
> To him the church, the realm, their pow'rs consign,
> Thro' him the rays of regal bounty shine,
> Turn'd by his nod the stream of honour flows,
> His smile alone security bestows:
> Still to new heights his restless wishes tow'r,
> Claim leads to claim, and pow'r advances pow'r;
> Till conquest unresisted ceas'd to please,
> And rights submitted, left him none to seize.
> At length his sov'reign frowns—the train of state
> Mark the keen glance, and watch the sign to hate.
> Where-e'er he turns he meets a stranger's eye,
> His suppliants scorn him, and his followers fly;
> At once is lost the pride of aweful state,
> The golden canopy, the glitt'ring plate,
> The regal palace, the luxurious board,
> The liv'ried army, and the menial lord.
> With age, with cares, with maladies oppress'd,
> He seeks the refuge of monastic rest.
> Grief aids disease, remember'd folly stings,
> And his last sighs reproach the faith of kings.
>   (99–120)

Of the three, this portrait is most like a genuine narrative, but here
too time is minimized and, as in the others, everything that can be

said to "happen" seems to happen simultaneously, in a kind of generalized no-time. We notice that "the pride of aweful state" is lost "At once." Johnson's use of the present tense, like Pope's, is not at all the vivid "historical present" that a storyteller like Donne sometimes uses to make the continuous progression of his story vivid and immediate, the use we see in a line like "He names mee, and comes to mee." It is much closer to the generalizing present sense of science or philosophy, the one we use when we want to state something that is true whenever certain conditions hold. The verbs which tell the story of Wolsey's fall—"frowns," "Mark," "watch," "turns," "meets," "scorn," "fly"—are not abstract like most of Dryden's verbs, and they might well have been used to tell a smoothly flowing story; but Johnson has grouped them so thickly that the actions all seem to occur at once, and no one verb is allowed to accumulate enough atmosphere and detail to give the feel of a specific action performed as part of a continuous sequence. As in Dryden, none of the verbs ties us down to one clearly distinguishable occasion; and, like Pope in his imitation of Donne, Johnson is here only expansive and detailed when he is painting a static scene, "the pride of aweful state." Finally Wolsey in full-blown dignity merges with Wolsey reproaching the faith of kings—kings in general, we notice, not just Henry VIII—in a single consistent portrait exemplifying the vanity of human wishes.

In their different ways the three portraits are certainly sharp and vivid, yet they all project a sense of moral generality by making us see an individual life as an example of a universal truth or quality. We might almost say that instead of being shown three individual lives, we are shown three special ways of living. There will never be another Cloe or Achitophel or Wolsey—in the sense that there will be many more Countesses and Sir Foplings—yet in every line of the three portraits we feel that the satirists are being rigorously selective, inserting only what is directly relevant to the immediate purpose and never seeking to render any event in its natural fullness of detail. Thus each character emerges as a unique and yet quite analyzable—in fact a fully analyzed—combination of familiar elements rather than as a living human being. And like the opposition of living individual and stock type, the more basic opposition of generality and particularity can now be clearly seen to be irrelevant to Augustan satire. The satirists are both general and particular, and the sharp particularity of individual words or images is directly conducive to our sense that they are being used generally, to represent kinds or classes of experience.

Faced by this fact, we need not follow those critics who try to resolve the problem by invoking paradoxical entities like the "concrete universal" or by talking about a mysterious "synthesis" or "fusion" or "interpenetration" of general and particular. The truth is that there is a problem only if we view our own categories so solemnly that we radically limit the number of things language does and the number of ways it does them, only if we ignore the evidence and doggedly affirm that there is just one sort of generality and just one sort of particularity and that they are naturally and inevitably opposed. First we must distinguish between two kinds of particularity or vividness: the kind we feel in the composition of a clear static portrait, and the kind possessed by a single continuous sequence of thoughts or actions. The first is characteristic of Augustan satire, the second of Donne's poem and of ordinary narrative. Then we must distinguish between two kinds of generality: the kind in which the categories being referred to are evaluative categories, and the kind in which they are merely descriptive. We can say that the first is characteristic of Augustan satire and the second of science, if we are careful to note that in doing so we are using the words "descriptive" and "science" in too simple a way and that we should want to qualify them if we were carrying the argument further in the direction they indicate. Once we have made these distinctions, we are in a position to investigate the historical background of Augustan satiric technique.

II

What we have mainly learned so far is that generality and particularity are not opposed in Augustan satire but allied, that they are in fact merely two aspects of a single characteristic use of language. Our analyses have clearly shown that the relevant opposition is not that of generality to particularity, but that of both qualities to continuously unfolding temporal process. Initially it may surprise us that time entered the argument at all, for the relation of time to the question we started with is far from clear. Perhaps it will become clearer if we look for a moment at a famous and representative attack on generality in art, so that we may get a better idea of what we are defending if we say that poetry should be particular rather than general. This is from Bergson's famous essay on laughter:

Hence it follows that art always aims at what is *individual*. What the artist fixes on his canvas is something he has seen at a certain spot, on a certain day, at a certain hour, with a colouring that will never be seen again. What the poet sings of is a certain mood which was his, and his alone, and which will never return. What the dramatist unfolds before us is the life-history of a soul, a living tissue of feelings and events—something, in short, which has once happened and can never be repeated. We may, indeed, give general names to these feelings, but they cannot be the same thing in another soul. They are *individualised*. Thereby, and thereby only, do they belong to art; for generalities, symbols, or even types form the current coin of our daily perception.

We can see here an extreme form of the attitude toward generality in art which I initially asserted to be characteristic of modern criticism. When Bergson thinks of art he too thinks of immediacy, vividness, and particularity; and he too dismisses generality as belonging to other kinds of discourse or experience. Furthermore, behind his elevation of the individual in art we can see an important assumption about time which most of us also share, though perhaps only unconsciously. This assumption, baldly stated, is that time is the most important fact in our world, that the strongest and most basic impressions we have are impressions of continuity and flux.

Such impressions come most surely from our sense of our own inner life, our constantly evolving sensations and emotions. Any analysis of these feelings is doomed to failure, Bergson thinks, because language, the necessary instrument of analysis, inevitably distorts the reality it talks about. Therefore he is not as interested in what the poet's words actually seem to be saying (for saying involves language, and hence analysis and distortion) as in the grand rhythms of universal continuity and flux which those words may incidentally convey. The important thing about the poet's mood is not that it is more valuable than other people's moods but that it is "his, and his alone," that it is unique and somehow alive. As Bertrand Russell has said: "Life, in his [Bergson's] philosophy, is a continuous stream, in which all divisions are artificial and unreal. Separate things, beginnings and endings, are mere convenient fictions; there is only smooth, unbroken transition." But language consists precisely of "convenient fictions," names for ready-made categories into which we neatly but arbitrarily force unique sensations or events, destroying their individuality in the process. Thus language cannot, for Bergson, capture the really important world, the incommunicable and private (though somehow universal) world of ceaseless change; it can only render the objective, public, impersonal aspect of our emotions, the part that is relatively unimportant because shared with other people and not uniquely held by each of us. Moreover, Bergson feels that capturing this impersonal aspect of emotion involves losing sight of and perhaps even destroying the important and living aspect. In another essay he writes:

> The word which is sharply outlined, the brutal word, which is the receptacle of all that is stable, all that is common, and consequently impersonal, in human experience, crushes or at all events covers over the more delicate and fugitive impressions of our individual conscience.

Since time is so obviously the medium through which organisms live, Bergson believes that by artificially stopping time to extract sensations from the fluid context in which they occur, language runs the risk of killing them. By "spatializing" events or sensations (as he often puts it) language creates a logical system which is misleading because it purports to reveal everything at once, to make clear in an instant meanings which can only be rendered by a temporal progression. Bergson thinks that poets must ignore intellect or ordinary thinking and rely solely on intuition, for only intuition can enable them to break through this hard logical surface imposed by language on reality. Only artists can help to get us back past conventional categories to the original freshness and individuality of things, for only they can transmit the reality of ceaseless, unanalyzable process.

We need not pause to examine the difficulties of Bergson's attempt to talk about the artist's mysterious way of talking about (and yet not talking about) a still more mysterious reality which of course cannot be talked about. Bergson is a limiting case, and the relevant point for us is that almost all of the finest twentieth century critics— F. R. Leavis seems the one important exception—have a view of poetic language which has important affinities with Bergson's, even though their writings are generally more helpful and less mystical than his. Yeats, Pound, Eliot, and Richards have all, in their different ways, insisted on an essential difference between poetry and other uses of language, "the current coin of our daily perception." While the rest of us speak and think logically, like Bergson's deluded men, the poet fuses disparate aspects of reality in an "image" with supreme illogic or he creates an "objective correlative" for a particular emotion that cannot be pinned down by ordinary language. The poet's language is in a sense not language at all but a kind of direct substitute for material reality, and hence, these critics sometimes tell us, poems are absolutely unparaphrasable—we cannot say anything useful by speaking of a poem generally, by saying what it is "about."

Now to understand the Augustan notion of generality, we must imagine an intellectual world different from this one that we more or less share with Bergson. In this new world, if one is pressed to the wall by a philosophic questioner who demands to know the "most important fact," the answer that comes most readily is not time or process or change, but rationality or intelligibility or order. I do not in the least mean that men in the eighteenth century were somehow sublimely unconscious of the passing of time, but only that they viewed time differently from the way we do. Just as Bergson thought he glimpsed the reality of ceaseless process beneath the apparent stability yielded by language and logic, so the man of Pope's time (when and if he thought about such things) would be likely to think that he glimpsed eternal logical order or "Nature" not beneath but *in* the apparent flux of ordinary experience. If pushed hard, Pope's contemporary would even be likely to say that in spite of appearances, the passing of time produces nothing *really* new because all change, both spiritual and physical, merely involves the combination, dispersal, and recombination of the same irreducible and indestructible elements. In fact, most of the famous Augustan statements about history sound much like the passages I quoted initially from Johnson, for history, like poetry, was viewed as existing to help investigate human nature. In history too the Augustans demanded a timeless generality that clearly exhibits human nature as it is for all time, a generality which will be familiar to any reader of Gibbon, whose narrative "stands still" much the way an Augustan satire does.

The difference between our intellectual world and that of the Augustans is in no sense absolute, but is rather a difference of emphasis and priority. Yet it is a real and important difference all the same, for behind the Augustan demands for generality in history and poetry lay the firm belief that "moral knowledge is as capable of real certainty as mathematics." These words, from Locke's *Essay Concerning Human Understanding*, pull us up short: the last thing that we, as good cultural relativists, would think of comparing with morality is mathematics. And if we read further in Locke, we are still more surprised to learn that what mathematics and morality share, besides certainty, is a concern with "archetypes of the mind's own making, not intended to be the copies of anything, nor referred to the existence of anything, as to their originals." Geometry deals with perfect triangles and circles rather than with the imperfect ones we find in the world, but its theorems are true anyway; just so, Locke maintains, ideals of conduct are objectively valid even though no one has ever perfectly lived up to them. Of course, both sorts of proposition must refer to "possible" figures or actions if they are to embody real knowledge, but this hypothetical reference to reality is not what makes the two sciences of mathematics and morality universal and certain. For Locke their universality and certainty depend rather on their being "abstract," removed from the temporal conditions of ordinary reality.

In short, Locke affirms just what Bergson would deny outright and what we would at least feel nervous about claiming: that to take actions or events out of time to analyze them and generalize about them is not necessarily to distort them but is in fact the only way of getting at their real meaning. For Locke the real meaning is not private and incommunicable but public, expressed through the publicly accepted categories that our minds have created. Also, we notice that the word "abstract" does not have as many bad overtones for Locke as for us. He can use it as a term of praise for morality as well as for mathematics because he believes that the only way to make a temporal occurrence available to the mind is to abstract or draw it off from temporal conditions. But in another and very important sense, abstractions are objects of suspicion for Locke. He is at home only with particulars, and asserts repeatedly that the world contains only particular things and that all ideas are, in their nature and existence, particular. This is why he is careful to point out that general ideas do not come directly from experience but are "archetypes of the mind's own making," strictly human creations. He wants to make clear that there are no real universal entities to which general ideas correspond, entities which are *completely* abstract from experience, utterly without quality or quantity. General ideas as Locke conceives them are, then, created by our minds from the particular ideas which experience presents directly. But this is not at all to say that general ideas are in any way subjective or unreal. They and the general names which stand for them are not only objectively real; they are also absolutely necessary to human life, since communication would clearly be impossible if we had to give every particular thing a different name. Furthermore, Locke believes that all knowledge, "though founded in particular things, enlarges itself by general views." "Words," he explains, "become general by separating from them the circumstances of time and place, and any other ideas that may determine them to this or that particular existence." This act of separation is the permissible and necessary sort of abstraction, and once a particular idea is thus abstracted, it can be made "capable of representing more individuals than one." The important point is that after an idea has been made general in this way, it does not become "abstract" in the sense unacceptable to Locke—that is, it does not become completely and mysteriously divorced from particular, concrete sense experience. The general or representative significance which a particular idea takes on when it is abstracted (in the acceptable sense) and made to stand for other similar ideas is "nothing but a relation that by the mind is added" to it—nothing, that is, but a new way of looking at the idea. In becoming general, an idea therefore loses none of its particularity in the ordinary sense, none of its precision and clarity of outline, its individual force.

Thus for Locke general ideas are neither vague nor fuzzy nor disembodied, but are "precise, naked appearances in the mind," which we use "as the standards to rank real existences into sorts." And despite apparent differences, the most important philosophical opinion of the early eighteenth century was agreed on this point. Berkeley misunderstood Locke and memorably but unjustly accused him of believing that in creating general ideas, the mind tacked together "numberless inconsistencies." The result of such tacking together was what Berkeley called an "abstract general idea," a monstrosity no less repugnant to Locke than to himself, since the "abstract general idea" of triangle, to use Berkeley's example, would have to be scalene, isosceles, and equilateral all at once—plainly an impossibility. Finally Berkeley ends his polemic against "abstract general ideas" by asserting that there can be a valid general idea "which considered in itself is particular" but "becomes general by being made to represent or stand for all other particular ideas of the same sort." But as we have seen, this was just what Locke had said. Hume followed Berkeley in thinking of himself as disagreeing with Locke, but his official view of abstraction is also very close to Locke's position (though there are undeveloped hints of a quite different view in Hume's treatment). "The general idea of a line," Hume wrote, "notwithstanding all our abstractions and refinements, has in its appearance in the mind a precise degree of quantity and quality; however it be made to represent others, which have different degrees of both." Thus when all three philosophers discuss the possible and necessary sort of abstraction, they do not say that general ideas are totally "abstracted" from the form they originally take in our experience as particular ideas, but only that particular ideas are made general by being first "abstracted" from the time and place at which we experience them and then viewed as "representative" of other particular ideas like them.

Pope and the other Augustans were not philosophers, and I do not mean to suggest that there was anything like an Augustan philosophy to which they all subscribed. In fact they tended to be highly suspicious of philosophy or of any other speculative discipline cultivated at the expense of the whole man. The theory of Augustanism was precisely to be against theory as unnecessary and in bad taste— Nature, it was thought, would show herself more clearly to eyes undimmed by metaphysics. But this suspicion of philosophy did not prejudice the Augustans against Locke, Berkeley, and Hume. On the contrary, it was closely related to the philosophers' suspicion of the bad sort of abstraction. Locke was a very important figure for the Augustans precisely because he seemed the unphilosophical philosopher, the thoughtful gentleman of easy, rational piety who discussed big questions graciously, expansively, and without Hobbes's meaningless abstractions or Hobbes's vigorous bad manners. His conviction that "moral knowledge is as capable of real certainty as mathematics" was taken as axiomatic by Addison and others in the *Spectator* papers, which did so much to stabilize Augustan standards of taste and shape the image of the Augustan gentleman. And its influence can also be seen in Pope's references to the *Essay on Man* as a "System of Ethics" and in his plans for his *magnum opus*, a general "ethic work" which was to include the *Essay on Man*, the so-called "Moral Essays" and treatises on education and government. Likewise, neoclassic criticism reflects Locke's view that there is no conflict between generality and particularity; Johnson, Rymer, and the later critic Francis Jeffrey repeatedly follow what our analyses have shown to be the correct procedure in dealing with Augustan poetry. Again and again we find them linking generality and abstraction not only with precision and concreteness, but also with force, beauty, and truth. And the satirists, as we saw, use every poetic resource to abstract particulars from time and set them off so sharply that we are made to see them as "representative" and to feel the weight of experience and judgment behind them. By pointing to details like the chintz and mohair which so interest Cloe, modern critics have often tried rather apologetically to prove that Pope offers the particular as well as the general; but we can see by this time that since generality and particularity are merely different aspects of the same Augustan use of language, such critical apologies are misleading and misdirected. The very specificity of Cloe's observation underscores her cool detachment and drives home more forcibly the general point that it is wretched and inhuman to ignore another person's despair.

The fact that the Augustans more or less shared Locke's views of morality and abstraction suggests that eighteenth century literary men had an attitude toward science which was quite different from that held by most of their twentieth century counterparts. Unlike us, the Augustans did not make the jump I mentioned several pages back, from the idea of generality to the idea of unpoetic and toneless "scientific" statements, for they saw nothing necessarily toneless about science and in fact thought of their own work as scientific in an important sense. Newton had shown briefly, clearly and (as it seemed) for all time the essential structure of the natural world, and now it was up to scientists of human nature—whether writing as poets, historians or philosophers—to do the same for the human world by finding the laws that regulate our conduct. Though modern readers of literature often view science as simply a collection of toneless propositions (a view which the reader will perhaps have guessed that I find inadequate), the Augustans viewed science, by which they usually meant Newtonian mechanics, as essentially a picture or diagram. We are often told nowadays that Newton emptied the world of all color and quality, leaving it (in Whitehead's words) "a dull affair, soundless, scentless, colourless; merely the hurrying of material, endlessly, meaninglessly." That view is much commoner to the nineteenth and twentieth centuries than to the eighteenth, however. To Pope and his contemporaries it generally seemed not that Newton had devitalized the world, but that he had brought it more vividly alive by showing the order and pattern of its life. And Newton had accomplished this by providing a timeless mathematical picture that seemed to reveal the design usually obscured by natural change and process, to "catch" the meaning of Nature much as a great drawing of a face can catch, in a few perfect strokes, the essential quality of its owner's whole way of life.

Thus it is not surprising that the most common metaphors used by the Augustans to connect the task of the poet with that of the scientist were metaphors of pictorial or visual design, since both scientist and poet were to provide the true picture or view of Nature. The countless odes written in the Restoration and eighteenth century to Science and the Royal Society almost invariably give us Bacon or Newton stripping away the veil or holding up the unclouded mirror or brightening the darkness to reveal the true, hitherto hidden form of Nature to the eye of man. This emphasis on sight and shape and design is also found in literary criticism of the time, and words are frequently said to be the pictures of thoughts as thoughts are the pictures of things. The assumption is that a word, like an artist's sketch or a scientist's mathematical diagram, can contain within it the force and clarity needed to render experience timeless and intelligible. Later, in one of the distinctions that has become central to modern literary criticism, Coleridge was to contrast the "organic" form possessed by a poem with mere shape or design. The poem is a self-contained and self-developing organism, made up of parts that interpenetrate and mutually organize each other like the members of a living body, sharing a common life; but "design" denotes only a static arrangement of parts that are more like the parts of a machine than those of a living body, a pattern which can be seen in an instant and does not realize itself or "live" through time. This notion of organic form is still very much with us, and therefore it must be strongly emphasized that for the Augustans beauty and meaning in literature were almost invariably associated with just the sort of pictorial design Coleridge scorns. Pope studied painting, and his favorite word, both in his poems and his letters, for poetic or literary form is "design." We can also see the pictorial metaphor strongly present in the two Johnson passages from which we began—not only in a word like "exhibit" or in phrases like "large appearances," "portraits of nature," and "striking features," but also in the crucial term "representation," which in the eighteenth century nearly always carried the suggestion of a picture or physical image. And we can see the same metaphor behind Locke's and Hume's use of terms like "view," "sign," "appearance," and "image." Like the painter, the poet and the scientist were to seize, by an act of cultivated intuition, just those particulars which could be viewed as representative of our experience.

Once we see the correspondences between science, poetry, and painting which were so important for the Augustans we are in a better position to understand why they viewed generality and particularity as allied rather than opposed. This is precisely what most critics have failed to understand, the first major document in the misunderstanding perhaps being Blake's revealing marginal comments on Sir Joshua Reynolds' *Discourses*. Whenever Reynolds, whose views on art were similar to Johnson's, praises generality or general nature at the expense of minuteness and detail, he draws a blast like the one that stands as an epigraph to this essay; but whenever he says that painters should learn to think for themselves or should cultivate distinctness and precision of line, Blake applauds and wonders how on earth Reynolds can go on contradicting himself. Finally when Reynolds, following Locke, writes that art which truly agrees with Nature is "as true as mathematical demonstration," Blake exclaims in horror: "God forbid that Truth should be Confined to Mathematical Demonstration!" The point of course is that Reynolds is neither contradicting himself nor restricting truth to mathematics. Men like Johnson and Reynolds held that the form or outline of Nature was partly visible to us all and instantly recognizable once an artist or scientist had got rid of the accidentals and revealed the essentials, once (as Johnson wrote in his beautiful epitaph on Hogarth) the "Hand of Art" had "traced th' essential form of Grace." But neither they nor any other sensible neoclassicist believed that such revelations were ever accomplished without talent or a full exertion of mind—what Reynolds called "the real labour of thinking." To "follow Nature" was not to mouth platitudes, but to seize and render the intrinsic form and meaning—the two were not separate—of the physical or the moral world. Newton had done this in the language of mathematics, and hence mathematical certainty and mathematical ways of thought offered helpful analogies for the neoclassic critic.

Thus it is wrong to suppose—as most critics from Blake and Hazlitt down to our own day have done—that neoclassic demands for generality, as we find them in critics of major caliber, were aimed at producing cloudy abstractions or lukewarm restatements of what everyone already knew anyway. We can now answer the question with which we began by asserting that these demands were meant to produce precisely the vividness and incisiveness we admire in the best satirical portraits. The Augustans sometimes did use "general" and "abstract" with the overtones of vagueness or coldness so familiar to us, but they seem to have done so more often in informal writing than in technical criticism. In a letter to his friend Arbuthnot, Pope asserts that "General propositions are obscure, misty, and uncertain, compar'd with plain, full, and home examples." But the joker here is the word "propositions." Though, as we are often told, Pope advocated a "poetry of statement," he by no means thought poetry was composed solely or even primarily of statements or "propositions." For him, as for Locke and Berkeley and Hume, knowledge proceeded only by "general views," but meaningful generality still had to be firmly grounded in particular experience. In his letter he is talking about the sort of generality that Berkeley railed against, generality that is empty because not articulated by particular representative examples. "Examples," Pope's letter goes on, "are pictures, and strike the Senses, nay raise the Passions." By choosing "examples" as the word for the sort of concrete detail he wants in poetry, Pope implicitly advocates the other, meaningful sort of generality, for examples, after all, must be examples *of* something.

As we have seen, it is perfectly natural to feel that in the lines about the chintz and mohair Pope was making a general observation about indifference to suffering; undoubtedly he was, and undoubtedly he knew he was. But this is not at all to say that he viewed the illustrative scene with Cloe and her friend as merely decorative or thought that all the "real meaning" lay in some such maxim as: "We should not be indifferent to the sufferings of others, particularly of friends." Such a view of language would make poetry unnecessary, and we have had plenty of evidence that the Augustan or neoclassic view—which was certainly not so formulated and codified as I make it sound—made poetry very necessary indeed. The Augustan effort, undermined though it was from the first by a certain wistful and occasionally desperate skepticism, was to establish a science of human nature; and one way to do this, it seemed, was to write poetry which treated men as Newton had treated bodies, poetry which kept the reader constantly aware of standards as fixed and permanent as those of mathematics. Thus the Augustans stressed precisely, in Bergson's words, "all that is stable, all that is common, and consequently impersonal, in human experience," and they relied on just the linguistic resources which he dismissed as being unsuited to poetry: the "generalities, symbols, or even types" which "form the current coin of our daily perception." Furthermore, they sometimes found in the literature of the past the vision they sought to unfold in their own writing; it was perfectly natural for Johnson to explain the superiority of Shakespeare's characters in very Newtonian terms, by referring to "those general passions and principles by which all minds are agitated, and the whole system of life is continued in motion." Confident that the experience of all educated men had a common structure that could be shown forth if the right details were selected and set off as representative, the Augustans sought a poetic surface that presented the essential qualities of moral experience simultaneously for contemplation. Unlike Bergson, they regarded "the sharply outlined word" as precise and revealing rather than as "brutal"; and the static, pictorial surface which they thought poetry ought to have is strikingly like the hard crust which Bergson thought logic and language had imposed on life and which he declared it the artist's duty to penetrate.

The point is that though the Augustans viewed poetry as part of a general scientific endeavor, they never for a moment thought that anything else could do poetry's job. What a study of Augustan generality makes clear is, in fact, that it is perfectly possible to say what a poem is "about" (just as we say what a conversation or a news bulletin is about) without assuming or implying that poetry is replaceable. Intellectual historians have often told us that in the eighteenth century there could be no genuine aesthetics because philosophers and critics, under the influence of earlier thinkers like Locke in England and Descartes and Boileau in France, failed to see that art is an autonomous activity and that the creative imagination is an autonomous faculty, not to be confused with the reason. Misled by the achievements of seventeenth century science (so the accusation runs), they assimilated art to philosophy or even to science itself. As we have seen, the Augustans did in fact take the analogy of poetry and science very seriously. But in conclusion I want to insist that that analogy, made as they made it, reveals more about the nature of poetry than it conceals. We cannot share the Augustans' naïve confidence in the possibility of a science of human nature, but we can learn from them nevertheless. By stressing the similarities rather than the differences between poetry and science, and between poetic language and ordinary language, they saw truths that we, in our eagerness to stress the differences, are usually led to ignore. They saw that all language categorizes and generalizes and that what we want from poetry is not an end to categories but sharper and more sensitive categories, not a mysterious transcendence of generalization but finer and more concentrated generalization. And they saw as well that only the poet can furnish these things.

Jane Austen's *Emma*:

The Truths and Disguises of Human Disclosure

BY G. ARMOUR CRAIG

> "Run mad as often as you chuse; but do not faint—"
> *Love and Freindship* (1790)

IN A COMMENT on the scene in which the heroine finds that the
man she loves loves her, the narrator of *Emma* makes a pronouncement:

> Seldom, very seldom, does complete truth belong to any human
> disclosure; seldom can it happen that something is not a little dis-
> guised, or a little mistaken . . .

It is a statement capable of shocking the expectations of many
readers, for the "truth" of "human disclosure" seems to be the
object of most novel-reading if not novel-writing. How can we
experience a Confrontation of the Human Self if we are in the
hands of a novelist who believes that all communication, even at its
highest pitch, involves error and disguise? The relativism implied
here, if it is not redeemed by the certainty of some disclosure larger
than human, reduces the novelist to small dimensions: he is at best
a mere entertainer, at worst a troublesome disturber of the peace. If
we cannot learn in books how men and women truly engage with
each other, what possible use can the reading of novels be?

But no disclosure larger than human is made in *Emma*, and although this pronouncement is the most general in the whole novel,
there is no reason to think that Jane Austen had some ulterior mis-
chief in mind when she wrote it. For it fits the situation exactly.
Mr. Knightley, the most gentlemanly and sensible member of Highbury society, has made his direct though anxious declaration—"If I
loved you less, I might be able to talk about it more"—to Emma
Woodhouse, "handsome, clever, and rich," and some seventeen years
his junior. Mr. Knightley has begun the interview with the belief

that Emma's affections have been trifled with by Frank Churchill, whom, to say the least, he believes frivolous and unreliable. Emma has begun with the belief that he is about to confess his attachment to Harriet Smith, the simple girl whom she has educated and prepared for a match worthy of her benefactions, though not quite so worthy as to be the wife of Mr. Knightley. Both are mistaken, but Emma does not disclose her delusion. She conceals it with mingled feelings of relief and self-censure: she is speechless, for not only is Mr. Knightley her own but she must have been mad to believe that Harriet could be the one preferred. And so the comment is concluded: disguise or error may permeate all disclosures,

> but where, as in this case, though the conduct [her speechlessness] is mistaken, the feelings are not, it may not be very material. Mr. Knightley could not impute to Emma a more relenting heart than she possessed, or a heart more disposed to accept of his.

The solemnity of the first half of the comment is qualified by its relevance to the dramatic situation before us.

The conclusion of the comment, indeed, not only fits the particular situation but also presents the main elements of the novel as Jane Austen practiced it. The terms for these elements are not "plot," "character," and "setting," as we have been taught to think, but are much more particular and much more active. They are "conduct," "feelings," and "impute"—all verbs, or so close to verbs that we cannot expect the work they articulate ever to stand still. To Emma's present conduct—"You are silent . . . absolutely silent"— Mr. Knightley imputes feelings of sympathetic concern for himself— "But you understand me. Yes, you see, you understand my feelings, and will return them if you can." He is right about her feelings but mistaken in her conduct, for to *his* conduct Emma has just been imputing feelings of extraordinarily unsympathetic awareness of herself. His fumbling and hesitation have for her meant the prelude to a confession of love for her protégée, and her present silence is the conduct that expresses her discovery that "what she had been saying relative to Harriet had all been taken as the language of her own feelings." In short, Emma is silent because she is making an enormous revision in her interpretation of Mr. Knightley's conduct and her own. It is true that he is at this moment pretty thoroughly undisguised. But Emma is not, for she not only accepts him but also conducts her acceptance with an awareness of her delusion and of the wrong it has done to both Harriet Smith and herself. In Emma's acceptance of Mr. Knightley there is no mistake but some disguise. The acceptance itself is quickly passed over: "What did she say? Just what she ought, of course. A lady always does." This is not evasion; Jane Austen is not unequal to providing the whispered rhetoric of so tender a scene. The drama is simply elsewhere for her: it is in the imputations that Emma is now making to her own previous conduct. To put it schematically and abstractly, in *Emma* A imputes to (or infers from) the conduct of B certain feelings. But A's imputation is itself a form of conduct to which B responds by imputing certain other feelings to A; and then C comes along to impute still other feelings to both A and B, and C expresses his imputation in conduct that is subject to the imputation of D, and D in turn . . . The process, however, is not an endless displacement; this *is* an eighteenth century novel, though it probably could not have been written before 1815. Feelings, here, are expressed by conduct—and so they are in any novel. But in this novel the feelings expressed by conduct are not defined by that conduct. A does not know his own feelings; he acts on them. B is the one for whom A's feelings are an object of knowledge; and B knows them, not as A feels them, but as B infers them from A's conduct. The difference is subtle enough, and perhaps too subtle as outlined in such an algebra. But it is the subtlety that constitutes the large, strong, comic nerve of Jane Austen's imagination.

For the nerve of Jane Austen is comic, not sentimental. The fact that communication is partial and incomplete occasions no wailing to readers who hope for better things. We are a long way from the complaint made by Thackeray in *Pendennis*: "O philosophic reader, . . . a distinct universe walks about under your hat and under mine . . . you and I are but a pair of infinite isolations, with some fellow-islands a little more or less near to us." No character in *Emma*, at any rate, is an isolated island. Each participates with others in an interplay in which the mystery of the link between feeling and conduct, between motive and action, is finally not "very material." What is material, in the full sense of the word, is the action, the drama, of imputing feelings to conduct, for this is the drama in which Jane Austen distinguishes one character from another and in which the reader experiences her disclosure of truth. Even when we see a single character looking into his own feelings and conduct the relation between them is still an inference that characterizes. At the moments of her most intense self-knowledge, Emma herself imputes feelings to a suddenly recognized form of conduct, feelings that she did not know she was expressing—and her imputations do not disclose truth so much as they continue a characterization. Conduct and feeling are never one and the same, even to those who reveal them. There is always, quite literally, room for interpretation. And this is as much as to say that in the novels of Jane Austen at her best there is always room for drama. There is always play in the system by which feelings are linked to conduct: play in the sense of free movement, and play in the sense of performance—a performance to be witnessed and judged.

It is of course a commonplace that from the novels in which such interplay occurs we could not guess the existence of the French Revolution or the Napoleonic Wars (though it is not easy to find a novel published between 1811 and 1818 that meets such a test in any but the most perfunctory manner). Yet it is blindness not to see that the historical setting of *Emma* is a small community that is responding to some strange pressures from a strange outside world. It is hard, indeed, not to use the inevitable "age of transition" in reflecting on the kind of world this novel presents. Outside Highbury is a mysteriously powerful institution called "trade" from which rich men like Mr. Cole retire to a life of anxious respectability. Bath is a remote, fashionable haven for parvenus who reassure each other that tradition can be manufactured by talk—or if not by talk, then by such items of conspicuous consumption as the barouche-landau. Enscombe, the seat of the proud Churchill family, is in a northern county where feudal haughtiness still flourishes. In Weymouth and Bristol conventional social relations are queerly scrambled, and illicit flirtations have their proper habitation. London, where Emma's married sister lives and where even she can help to bring about the reunion of a pair of lovers whom Emma has officiously separated, is only sixteen miles but a much larger social distance away. Highbury may be small and serene, but like The Crown, its principal inn, it is just a little seedy. The quality of its neighborhood is declining; there are no longer enough county families even to provide a homogenous guest list for a ball. Emma's father, the first citizen, is a comic valetudinarian who rarely leaves his house and who cannot stand change. Highbury, in short, is no longer an eighteenth century county town nor is it yet a fashionable suburb like Richmond. It is precisely the place where an "imaginist," as Emma is called, can make mistakes about "rank," about the social position of any stranger who comes within her acquaintance. Miss Woodhouse of Hartfield is the heiress of thirty thousand pounds, but while this is a large certainty it is somehow an inadequate one. For Mr. Elton is mistaken about Emma's rank, and she mistakes his as well as that of others. Highbury, indeed, is a place where there can be nothing else for the imaginist—or the climber—to be mistaken about.

The first such mistake lies behind Emma's plans for Mr. Elton, the new vicar, and Harriet Smith, a parlor boarder at the local school. "Harriet Smith was the natural daughter of somebody": so she is introduced to the reader. Emma is so charmed by her unassuming manners and natural prettiness that she decides the somebody must be at least a gentleman, and she determines that "Encouragement should be given" to Harriet's unacknowledged claim to a superior rank. The most appropriate encouragement that Emma can devise is to prepare her to be the mistress of the vicarage. It is, needless to say, a scheme of which Mr. Elton remains quite ignorant, and he imputes to Emma's encouraging conduct certain feelings that she does not entertain, while to his conduct she in turn makes some equally erroneous imputations. It is true that Mr. Elton is quite right in believing Emma encourages him, and also true that she is quite right in believing he accepts her encouragement. But what neither understands is the object of the encouragement offered and accepted. The misunderstanding is hard on Harriet, it is most unpleasant for Emma, and it finally enrages Mr. Elton. But it does clarify the issue of who outranks whom. It does so, moreover, by revealing how subtle and difficult the question of rank is in the society that this novel compels us to imagine.

When she sets out to "render a service" to her young protégée and to Mr. Elton, "a young man living alone without liking it," Emma claims for herself a position superior to theirs. She not only establishes a superior rank for herself, she also asserts that Mr. Elton and Harriet are equals: their rank is the same but it is below hers. The donor is the superior of the recipient, at least when the gift is not tribute but assistance. But in accepting Emma's deliberate "encouragement," unfortunately, Mr. Elton claims a position of superiority for himself. Emma's gestures, as he sees them, reveal how very well disposed she is toward himself. The recipient is the superior of the donor, certainly when the gift is a tribute so artfully and discreetly adjusted to the sensibilities of the recipient. Mr. Elton certainly does not dream of Emma's imputation of equality between Harriet and himself, for he claims a superiority to Emma: in his version of the situation there are three ranks, Harriet's (if she may be said to have one), then Emma's, and, at the summit, his own. It all becomes an elaborate and amusing game.

Early in the game, for example, Emma proposes doing a portrait of Harriet. Elton has been praising her education of her young friend: "you have made her graceful and easy. She was a beautiful creature when she came to you; but, in my opinion, the attractions you have added are infinitely superior to what she received from nature." And upon this welcome hint—addressed, of course, not to the product but to the producer—Emma speaks her wish for a picture of her charming pupil. She is determined to provide Mr. Elton with an image of his intended that he can worship in private. "I almost long to attempt her likeness myself. You do not know it, I daresay, but two or three years ago I had a great passion for taking likenesses, and attempted several of my friends, and was thought to have a tolerable eye in general . . ." She exhibits a selection of these previous attempts, to Mr. Elton's rapturous admiration, and he ardently entreats the exercise of "so charming a talent." When the present performance, the portrait of Harriet, is completed, he outdoes everyone in his praise of it. "Oh, it is most admirable! I cannot keep my eyes from it. I never saw such a likeness." He begs to be permitted to take it to London for framing, and as he leaves, " 'What a precious deposit!' said he with a tender sigh as he received it." And Emma comments to herself: " 'This man is almost too gallant to be in love.' "

With this judgment the end of the game is in sight. For Jane Austen is not describing an escalator of endless one-upmanship, nor is she plotting a collision of rivals in a fantasy of power. Her subject is knowledge—imputation—not power, and Mr. Elton's imputations to Emma's conduct are a characterization of himself. When she comments on her portfolio of portraits, he assumes she is letting him know how thoroughly accomplished she is. That he should regard her performance as a calculated effort to win him for herself, moreover, attributes to her precisely the desire for "parade" that Emma eventually comes to see in all *his* conduct. Mr. Elton, in short, by his reading of Emma's conduct discloses himself as a vulgarian: he assumes that personal tastes and talents, not to mention friendship, are the simple instruments of social aggrandizement. And when we meet the eventual Mrs. Elton, the importunate Miss Hawkins of Bristol and Maple Grove, we find the soul mate for whom Mr. Elton has been searching, for we encounter one of the most unpleasant parvenus in English fiction. Only the pages of *Sanditon* can enlarge on the profundities of Mrs. Elton. Her husband is given to parade, but she is bound to the most ubiquitous modern superstition: she is the name dropper who merely by the incantation of the nicknames of the great is elevated to a position of familiarity with them. Mr. Elton is only a little less ambitious. He assumes that the way to Emma's heart is to praise her education of Harriet as an infinite improvement on nature. But Emma is not a magician or a monster. She certainly does not improve on Harriet's nature, or even on her own. She is only an imaginist.

Not that her mistake is less obvious than Mr. Elton's or that it too is not an exposure. If it is unthinkable that Miss Woodhouse of Hartfield should parade her talents to ensnare Mr. Elton for herself, it is equally unthinkable that a man so given to gallantry and parade should be interested in the natural daughter of no one knows who. Only in Emma's fantasy could Harriet Smith be the equal of Mr. Elton, but only in his could she be the mere sign of Emma's eager complaisance. Whatever the reader may feel about Emma's plotting —and doubtless he will feel that her separation of Harriet from her sturdy yeoman farmer is an error vulgar enough to rank her uncomfortably near Mr. Elton—and whatever delight he may take in the occasion when it all collapses after Mr. Weston's famously good wine, Jane Austen compels him to rank Emma higher than Mr. Elton; indeed, he must rank even Harriet higher than the man about whom Emma's first words are, "There is nobody in Highbury who deserves him." Emma's last words to him during their awkward carriage ride are less ambiguous: she tells him that Harriet is well rid of him, " 'not being aware, probably, any more than myself, of the very great inequality which you are so sensible of.' " This devastating remark is left to simmer in Mr. Elton's boiling rage, but Emma is incapable of ignoring Harriet, and while there have been readers of this novel who find in her management of her young friend a moral usurpation more unpleasant than Mr. Elton's inability to grant Harriet a morality to usurp, still the management is not mere parade. If the imaginist is worse than the climber, some other episode must show it.

By the end of this first episode, at any rate, the reader cannot escape the conclusion that problems of rank in this novel are not to be solved by the fantasy of any single character. Tiny as it is, the society of Highbury contains more exceptions and more recalcitrant differences than the most active imagination or the most comfortable ambition can foresee. Rank in *Emma,* as in *Pride and Prejudice,* no doubt implies a hierarchic society that has long since become antiquarian lore. The most naïve reader of Jane Austen quickly learns to respond to such terms as "gentleman," "lady," or "elegance." He may condescendingly accept Sir Thomas's abhorrence of amateur theatricals in *Mansfield Park,* Mr. Darcy's grim displeasures in *Pride and Prejudice,* or the impropriety of a secret engagement in *Emma.* But none of these novels is mere social history, and "rank" in *Emma* names a good deal more than the rungs of a mysterious ladder that reaches from the not-being of Mr. Woodhouse's coachman to the pure essence of Mrs. Churchill. It may be that Jane Austen has provided us with some very good social history in showing us how exasperatingly unreliable such a ladder could be for the late eighteenth century climber. But society in *Emma* is not a ladder. It is a web of imputations that link feelings and conduct. Rank in this society is what one character stands on when he defines the motives for the actions of another or of himself. Rank, in its fullest sense, is dramatic position. The joke is that the conduct and feelings of A are seldom, very seldom what B thinks they are, for the very good reason that they are seldom, very seldom what A tells B they are. A and B speak the same words, they use the same gestures—"encourage" and "render a service" are the most notable. But B cannot understand these words and gestures as A does unless his rank, the position from which he does his understanding, is the same as A's. The difference between the rank of Emma and that of Mr. Elton is as clear as their misunderstanding.

In common usage (and in the eighteenth century as well as the present) an imputation is more often the ascribing of a fault or crime than the attributing of a virtue, and this sense is emphasized by the subtlest ranking word in *Emma:* "suspicion." It figures most largely, and appropriately, in the response of Highbury to the relation between Frank Churchill and Jane Fairfax. He is the son of Mr. Weston's first marriage; his mother was one of the proud Churchills who, displeased by the unequal match, "threw her off with due decorum." But after her death the proud (and childless) family so far relent as to adopt the child and give him the name his mother bore so lightly. Jane Fairfax, another orphan (and like Churchill born when her father is a poor military officer), has been raised in

Highbury by her aunt and grandmother, Miss and Mrs. Bates, and she has been educated elsewhere by Colonel Campbell, her father's old commander. Frank Churchill and Jane Fairfax, we learn, have recently met at Weymouth, where she has been in residence with Colonel and Mrs. Campbell and (the since-married) Mr. and Mrs. Dixon, their daughter and son-in-law. And, we later learn, Churchill and Jane Fairfax have there entered into a secret engagement. Much is explained by this large and unconventional fact, most notably the end of Churchill's long delay in visiting Highbury to see his refurbished father and his new stepmother, Miss Taylor that was, and his somewhat erratic behavior after he arrives. The engagement must be kept secret, for it is certain to be opposed by Mrs. Churchill—of whom we know nothing except that she is ill, likely to die, and very, very proud. And yet Frank naturally wishes to be near his intended. The expedient he adopts is to pay such special attention to Emma that it will come to be a screen from behind which he may freely and unnoticed gaze tenderly at Jane. Emma herself enlarges the screen by offering him a remarkable suspicion.

Soon after his arrival in Highbury, Churchill runs off to London for the day to get his hair cut, and this frivolity is not easy to excuse. And then, the next day, a handsome piano is delivered to Jane Fairfax at the humble apartments of her aunt, and no one knows who has sent it. Emma, however, has heard that in a sailing accident at Weymouth Jane was saved from what might have been a watery grave by Mr. Dixon, and she works on this meager information with the dedication of Catherine Morland. The suspicion darts into her mind that (as in a book) Mr. Dixon, the husband of the daughter of Jane Fairfax's benefactor, is in love where he has no business to be. The piano must be the token of his melancholy and forbidden affection. And when she communicates her suspicion to Churchill, he willingly takes it up; she must be right, he says—"I can see it in no other light than as an offering of love." He boldly repeats this formula in the presence of Jane Fairfax herself: "True affection only could have prompted it." And when Emma, looking up with anxious amusement, sees upon the face of Jane not only the "deep blush of consciousness" but also "a secret smile of delight," her suspicion is shockingly confirmed. "The amiable, upright, perfect Jane Fairfax was apparently cherishing very reprehensible feelings."

The situation and its dialogue are beautifully contrived, but the contrivance, once again, gives us something more than the comic spectacle of two characters speaking different languages in the same words. It presents us with Jane Austen's characterization at its most acute. It tells us little about Jane Fairfax—she is indeed one of the curiously undeveloped characters of the novel—but it tells us a good deal about Emma and Churchill. She has awaited his visit to Highbury with another well-founded suspicion, and one that she shares with everybody of consequence, namely, that he is to be her suitor. It is a match to be expected on both sides. But while Emma is interested in Churchill and is pleased by his gallant attentions, she does not find him irresistible. He is, for example, so eager to get up a ball at The Crown that he can find no objections either to the condition of the rooms where it must be held or to the lack of a sufficient number of families suitable to be invited. His insistence on getting all the neighborhood together occasions Emma's first and most telling judgment of him: "his indifference to a confusion of rank bordered too much on inelegance of mind." It is a remark characteristic of one who has separated Harriet Smith from Robert Martin, but it also contains some relevant variants of the basic terms of this novel. He who conducts himself with indifference toward a confusion of rank exposes himself to the imputation of inelegance. For between mind and rank, just as between feeling and conduct, falls the shadow of suspicion. Frank Churchill may or may not be inelegant in mind, but his conduct certainly does involve him in a confusion of rank in the most serious sense of the word. And Emma's interpretation of his conduct involves her in a similar confusion. Churchill is so much her equal that she can confide to him one of her most interesting suspicions, an example of the penetration they must share. And much of the pleasure of this sharing is that it claims for both of them a position superior to that of poor Jane, whose accomplishments and beauty Emma has long envied. But at the same time—or at least very soon—Emma also claims for herself a position so superior to Frank Churchill's that she can reject him—or at least discourage a proposal from him. In this episode, in short, Emma does not know her own place any better than she knows Churchill's.

Emma is quite right, then, about Jane's "secret smile," though of course she does not suspect that the man at whom it is directed is sitting next to her in Miss Bates's parlor, for she is debarred from this suspicion by one more powerful—and one encouraged by Churchill's attentions to herself. And yet he in turn suspects that Emma has come close to the truth about Jane and himself. His first visit to Highbury is broken off by a summons from the Churchills, and when he calls on Emma to say good-by he tells her that he has also called in passing on Jane and her garrulous aunt. And since Miss Bates was out, he adds, he "felt it impossible" not to wait for her return. We know of course that the chaperone of his wait, old Mrs. Bates, is deaf, but Emma seems to have forgotten it—or cannot suspect the hint—and the interview continues as Frank says:

> ". . . It was better to pay my visit then—"
>   He hesitated, got up, walked to a window.
>   "In short," said he, "perhaps, Miss Woodhouse—I think you can hardly be without suspicion—"
>   He looked at her, as if wanting to read her thoughts. She hardly knew what to say. It seemed like the fore-runner of something absolutely serious, which she did not wish. Forcing herself to speak, then, in the hope of putting it by, she calmly said,
>   "You were quite in the right; it was most natural to pay your visit, then—"
>   He was silent. She believed that he was looking at her; probably reflecting on what she had said, and trying to understand the manner. She heard him sigh. It was natural for him to feel that he had *cause* to sigh. He could not believe her to be encouraging him . . .

Churchill's meaning of "suspicion" is that Emma recognizes his attachment to Jane Fairfax, and this meaning attributes to her an uncommon power of penetration. It might even imply that when she confided to him her suspicion about the donor of the piano she was signaling to him by means of a fantasy so absurd that she knew his secret and could safely be entrusted with it. Churchill's meaning of "suspicion," moreover, attributes to Emma the superiority of a shield and protector: Miss Woodhouse is so exalted a personage, in every way, that she makes the perfect blind. At the same time, however, his "suspicion" puts Emma, for all her powers of mind and rank, in a position inferior to his own: like everyone else in Highbury, she must be managed for the convenience of his secret. His *real* cause for sighing must come first. Such a view of Emma's character, again, is an exposure of his own: she is penetrating but irresponsible, imaginative but devious, observant but selfish; and to cap it all, he believes that her selfishness is with temporary solicitude put at his disposal, for there can be no interest so important as his.

But Emma's confusion is no less. When she hears the "something absolutely serious" coming at her, she starts to talk, to "put it by." According to her imputation, his reference to Jane and Miss Bates is a digression to conceal his real intentions, and she calls his bluff by going on with it—"it was most natural to pay your visit." In order to divert Frank Churchill's attention from herself, she refers, as she is later much more unhappily to do, to Jane Fairfax and to Miss Bates's "powerful, argumentative mind" as agents that might encourage him to ignore his summons from home. "Suspicion" for her means that Frank Churchill is in love with her, and although she has no impulse to return this love she cannot imagine that she should not be its object. Her refusal implies that she is his superior, yet her conduct, both during Churchill's first visit to Highbury and, especially, later, is that of an intimate and equal. She claims, in effect, a superiority so remote that the conduct in which she expresses it is in every sense irresponsible. It not only issues in flirtatious behavior, as at Box Hill; it even permits her to dream of Harriet as Churchill's equal. She cannot believe that she is not his superior, and he cannot believe that anyone so sympathetically attentive is not his inferior. Frank Churchill and Emma Woodhouse not only speak different languages in the same words, they also are not even interested in communicating with each other. As she remarks to him when he makes his last appearance in the pages of this novel, "I think there is a little likeness between us." But between people so similar—of such equal rank—there can scarcely be any real communication, especially when the only matter that can be discussed between them is the one matter to which neither is paying attention.

For all her fantasies and suspicions and for all the high comedy with which they are exposed, *Emma* is not a joke on its principal character. Certainly if it were, it would be a book most unpleasantly arch. For example, just before the evening when Mr. Elton tells Emma that she, not Harriet, is the object of his tender feelings, Emma is warned by her brother-in-law that Elton seems most attentive to her and she most encouraging to him. Emma at once dismisses the suggestion and walks on,

> amusing herself in the consideration of the blunders which often arise from a partial knowledge of the circumstances, of the mistakes which people of high pretensions to judgment are for ever falling into, and not well pleased with her brother for imagining her blind, ignorant, and in want of counsel.

The knowing reader, well aware by now what the situation is, chuckles and smiles. Hah! How apt this is! How deliciously these words prepare us for Emma's comeuppance!

But to find that such a passage comes home to roost exclusively upon Emma is to read only half the book that has been put before us. For the terms with which Emma here indicts John Knightley are not pulled out from under her when Mr. Elton grows amorous in her father's coach. They no doubt describe her conduct, but they describe Elton's as well. His knowledge of the circumstances is as partial as Emma's, his pretensions to judgment are higher, his blindness and ignorance more gross. His "comeuppance," if that is what he experiences, is so great that he must leave Highbury to recover. Emma, however, stays at home, which is as much as to say that she does not abandon the terms of her own society, but redefines them. And she does so by seeing the difference between their application to Mr. Elton's conduct and to her own. Precisely because Emma's blunder is a function of Mr. Elton's, because "blunder" and "blindness" and "ignorance" describe them both, they are the terms with which Emma restores herself, after the fiasco, to a clear sense of her position. She imputes blindness to her own conduct by understanding that of someone else.

But what of the language in which Emma defends herself to Mr. Knightley when he discovers that she has persuaded Harriet to refuse Robert Martin? Mr. Knightley is indignant when Emma argues that Harriet's beauty and good nature are such as to make her illegitimacy and her humble station as a parlor boarder no handicap at all to her prospects. "I am very much mistaken if your sex in general would not think such beauty and such temper the highest claims a woman could possess." But Mr. Knightley will have none of this storybook nonsense:

> "Upon my word, Emma, to hear you abusing the reason you have is almost enough to make me think so too. Better be without sense than misapply it as you do."

But Emma will not have done:

> ". . . I know that such a girl as Harriet is what every man delights in—what at once bewitches his senses and satisfies his judgment. Oh, Harriet may pick and choose. Were you yourself ever to marry, she is the very woman for you."

Even though this speech is brought before us as a nonchalant evasion of Mr. Knightley's censure—it is introduced by the words, " 'To be sure,' cried she playfully . . ."—is it not true that its last sentence is one that Emma later wishes she could eat? For her greatest moment of terror comes when she believes that it has come true. She is accused of raising Harriet's expectations too high; she defends herself by raising her to the highest possible expectations in Highbury. What more condign punishment than that Emma should be compelled to believe her own playful—or meddlesome—prophecy?

She certainly suffers when, many pages later, she forces herself to listen to Harriet's assurance that Mr. Knightley thinks highly of her beauty and temper, but the punishment is self-administered. It is the inverse of her confident matchmaking—and precisely as effective. It is in fact a characterizing imputation of the same kind as her fantasies about Harriet and Mr. Elton or Harriet and Frank Churchill. The small world of Highbury exists no more to frustrate than to satisfy the ego of Miss Woodhouse. She makes two simultaneous but strangely related discoveries: one, that she has been encouraging Harriet to put her maiden hopes in a "service" rendered by Mr. Knightley, not one rendered by Frank Churchill; and the other, that "Mr. Knightley must marry no one but herself!" And Emma's response to these discoveries is to take responsibility for the first but to find herself unworthy of the second. She takes solitary thought and is "ashamed of every sensation but the one revealed to her—her affection for Mr. Knightley. Every other part of her mind was disgusting." The "disgust," however, overpowers the security of her affection: Harriet is a match for Mr. Knightley, and she, Emma, is responsible. If only she had not "brought Harriet forward . . . none of this dreadful sequel would have been." And the "dreadful sequel" is described in terms of rank:

> Mr. Knightley and Harriet Smith! Such an elevation on her side! Such a debasement on his! . . . Could it be? No; it was impossible. And yet it was far, very far from impossible. Was it a new circumstance for a man of first-rate abilities, to be captivated by very inferior powers? Was it new for one, perhaps too busy to seek, to be the prize of a girl who would seek him? Was it new for anything in this world to be unequal, inconsistent, incongruous, or for chance and circumstances (as second causes) to direct human fate?

Whatever "second causes" may have to do with it, the first cause is plain: "Were this most unequal of all connections to take place, on her must rest all the reproach for having given it a beginning . . ."

Once again Emma has fallen into a confusion of rank, and by

reason of a literary, or at least a melodramatic, inelegance of mind. Not only has she not made Harriet what she is, but Harriet is not at all what she thinks she is. All that has happened is that Mr. Knightley, now, after interested observation, has concluded that he was unjust to Emma's first account of her beauty and temper, and the confidence of Harriet reposes in the fact that he now speaks to her with the same interest that Emma has always shown. The reinterpretation Emma must make, therefore, when Mr. Knightley proposes to herself is indeed immense, for the disgust that she feels toward herself is as mistaken as her pleasure in Elton's attention to Harriet's picture. She cannot at the same time be so superior to both Harriet and to Mr. Knightley as to convert her into a mate worthy of him, and also be so inferior to Harriet as to be passed over for her by Mr. Knightley. To believe, as he begins his fumbling proposal to her, that he is about to speak of Harriet is to try to take a position so impossible—and so mad—that her misunderstanding of Frank Churchill is trivial in comparison. For such a position cannot be—certainly not in the world imagined by Jane Austen.

It is true that one of the great difficulties here is Harriet herself, and this characterization seems to have given Jane Austen as much trouble as any other in the novel. Harriet is certainly not clever, and the gentle exposure of her stupidities provides some of the most comic passages of the book. But Harriet is good, and good enough to elicit the concern of Mr. Knightley that Emma so misconstrues. But while it is possible, and amusing, to change the clever for the good, as we see in the characterization of Emma, it is neither so possible nor so funny to turn the good into the clever. More cleverness in Harriet would mean more really meddlesome plotting in Emma; it would also mean that Mr. Knightley's first attitude toward her is quite proper. Harriet Smith, indeed, is precisely the character that the novelists to come in the nineteenth century would develop, though with greater attendant difficulties than Jane Austen faced here. For the good—the embodiment of eighteenth century "good nature"—who becomes the clever—the penetrating, using, managerial adventurer—is a revolutionary, but a revolutionary that no novelist for almost a hundred years quite knew how to contemplate.

But the fate of Harriet in *Emma*—a fate that so clearly depends upon some silences and difficulties in Jane Austen's treatment—may then suggest that far from being a joke on its heroine, this novel is her enormous justification. Jane Austen saw to it that the pretty little natural daughter of somebody was put in her place by Emma Woodhouse. The imaginist must win. Of course, any novel must support the values of its author, for the writing of a novel is conduct of a sort that, unlike social behavior, does for better or worse define an author's feelings and not merely express them. Here, the precariousness of Harriet's characterization implies that she is a shield for this maiden-aunt-author from the aggression of Elton, Churchill, or even Knightley. Harriet, after all, is "what every man delights in—what at once bewitches his senses and satisfies his judgment." The power of such charm must be illegitimate. Emma's management of Harriet, by such a reckoning, is a deep and dark matter indeed.

But such a reckoning must rest upon a reading of this novel that is worse than a half-reading; it is a reading that confuses *Emma* with popular fiction of the sort that even in the early nineteenth century was produced in great quantities, and fiction of a sort that Jane Austen knew well. In the autumn of the winter in which she began *Emma*, for example, she reread a novel with a surprisingly relevant title: *Self-Control*. It had been published (and had gone through three editions) in 1811 and was the first novel of Mary Brunton, the wife of an Edinburgh professor. Mrs. Brunton, as her title implies, was interested in morality at least as seriously as Jane Austen was, though her aims were somewhat more immediate. Of *Self-Control*, at any rate, she said, "I intended to show the power of the religious principle in bestowing self-command, and to bear testimony against a maxim as immoral as it is indelicate, that a reformed rake makes the best husband." It is tempting to believe that Jane Austen intended to bear testimony in favor of the hope that a reformed imaginist makes the best wife. She had tried in vain to get a copy of *Self-Control* soon after it appeared in 1811, and remarked then, "I *should* like to know what her estimate is, but am always half afraid of finding a novel *too clever*, and of finding my own story and my own people all forestalled." But anyone who looks at the first few pages of both *Emma* and *Self-Control* will find no forestalling; he will find not even the resemblance between a parody and its original. The opening of *Emma* is one long but economical sentence:

> Emma Woodhouse, handsome, clever, and rich, with a comfortable home and happy disposition, seemed to unite some of the best blessings of existence, and had lived nearly twenty-one years in the world with very little to distress or vex her.

Two more paragraphs tell us that Emma has been brought up by a mild-tempered governess and an indulgent father, and lead us to an innocuous-sounding judgment:

> The real evils, indeed, of Emma's situation were the power of having rather too much her own way, and a disposition to think a little too well of herself. These were the disadvantages which threatened alloy to her many enjoyments. The danger, however, was at present so unperceived that they did not by any means rank as misfortunes with her.

That any such "disadvantages" should ever "rank as misfortunes" is both the comedy and the strength of this novel: comedy, because such "real evils" as having one's own way and thinking too well of oneself must by their nature be "unperceived"; and strength, because the perceiving of them by her heroine is just what Jane Austen does bring about. And together they constitute irony, for Jane Austen brings about this perception without changing the terms in which Emma's conduct and feelings are linked. The "principle" that bestows "self-command" here is not "religious"; the ruling principle of every participant in Highbury society is the dramatic principle of imputing feelings to conduct, and Emma achieves self-control when she perceives the impossible position—the nonexistent rank—into which her imputations and suspicions would lead her.

The opening of *Self-Control* is not so economical, but within the first three pages we do find this general account of the heroine:

> In a solitary village, remote from her equals in age and rank, Laura necessarily lived much alone; and in solitude she acquired a grave and contemplative turn of mind. Far from the scenes of dissipation and frivolity, conversant with the grand and sublime in nature, her sentiments assumed a corresponding elevation. She had heard that there was vice in the world; she knew that there was virtue in it; and, little acquainted with other minds, deeply studious of her own, she concluded that all mankind were, like herself, engaged in a constant endeavour after excellence; that success in this struggle was at once virtue and happiness; while failure included misery as well as guilt. The habit of self-examination, early formed, and steadily maintained, made even venial trespass appear the worst of evils;—while, in the labours of duty and the pleasures of devotion, she found joys which sometimes rose to rapture.

Such is Laura Montreville. She is, of course, extremely handsome, but it will hardly do to call her clever, and she is unfortunately not rich. The "real evils" of her situation, moreover, if they exist at all, will have to be monstrous ones. For the pursuit of excellence is much more serious than the pursuit of one's own way: success in this pursuit is all good—"virtue and happiness"—and failure is all evil— "misery and guilt." Laura may be as ignorant of other minds and as attentive to her own as Emma Woodhouse would be, but it is difficult to imagine a self-examination that could produce certainties more immense than hers already has. Self-control, by powers such as these, might result in something like world-control.

Laura is at present out for "a solitary ramble," and she is overtaken by Colonel Hargrave, the man on whom she "doats"—a man who "in person was symmetry itself; his manners had all the fascination that vivacity and intelligence, joined to the highest polish, can bestow." He is "the most ardent, the most favored of lovers." But he is alas not quite what he seems: "the being on whom she doated had no resemblance to him, except in externals. It was a wild creature of her imagination, pure as her own heart, yet impassioned as the wildest dreams of fiction . . ." And Laura's imagination now receives its first shock: Colonel Hargrave at once importunes her to be his. When he mistakes her maiden shyness for practiced coyness, he clasps her "with all the vehemence of passion" and urges his suit "in language yet more unequivocal." About this disclosure there is no mistake and certainly no disguise. Laura responds in the only possible way:

> Casting on him a look of mingled horror, dismay, and anguish, she exclaimed, "Are you so base?" and, freeing herself, with convulsive struggle, sunk without sense or motion to the ground.

Each so exactly imputes the right feelings to the other's conduct that there is not only no room for error, there is no room for drama. The heroine can reinterpret nothing; she can only swoon, and the dashing villain runs in terror to a nearby stream for water to revive her.

When he returns she has got up and run home. He stops, of course, to think things over, and does so in language that sounds like one of the juvenile parodies by the author of *Emma*:

> Seduction, he perceived, would with her be a work of time and difficulty; while, could he determine to make her his wife, he was secure of her utmost gratitude and tenderness. The known honour, too, of Captain Montreville made the seduction of his daughter rather a dangerous exploit; and Colonel Hargrave knew, that, in

spite of the licence of the times, should he destroy the daughter's honour, and the father's life, he would no longer be received, even in the most fashionable circles, with the cordiality which he could at present command.

But such deadly seriousness is beyond parody. The evils—and the "fashionable world" is the chief of them—that stand opposed to Laura's self-induced certainties are as hard and unyielding as a Calvinist nightmare. The handsome Colonel cannot control himself, and there is no question of the misery and guilt in store for him. Laura, whose goodness protects her even from the seducer's base assault, not only controls herself but also ends her days rich and happy. For there are only two "ranks" in this novel: one is made up of those who succeed in pursuing the excellence that Laura knows by simple introspection, the other of those who fail in this pursuit. Laura claims superiority over Hargrave, and he claims superiority over her. No mistake is possible, and no change of imputation is possible. For Laura Montreville not only claims her superiority, she embodies it. To change or to modify, in this novel, is to destroy.

The Colonel, determined to win his prize even at the cost of marriage (which will, however, be repaid by the "gratitude and tenderness" of the inferior), soon begs Laura's forgiveness and asks her to accept his name and fortune. She promises only that if he will for two years live respectably, decently, and soberly, she will consider him once again. But the strain of the trial is too great. The authority insisted upon by Laura drives Hargrave frantic, and he is finally reduced to kidnaping and transporting her to the wilds of Canada. There she is held prisoner in a remote riverside cabin, and awaits the dread moment of his pleasure. Just before it comes, however, her guards grow a little relenting and careless. Laura takes another solitary ramble, and this time she finds an empty canoe at the riverbank. She springs into it, and the current bears her to safety. But not without one more swoon. For this river, of all things, bears her toward something like Niagara Falls (probably, in fact, the Montmorency Falls near Quebec). It takes her also to a consummation more lavish than that promised by the Colonel's frenzy, and even more impassioned than those "wildest dreams of fiction" to which his conduct was so inferior:

> With terrible speed the vessel hurried on. It was whirled round by the torrent—tossed fearfully—and hurried on again. It shot over a smoothness more dreadful than the eddying whirl. It rose upon its

prow. Laura clung to it in the convulsion of terror. A moment she trembled on the giddy verge. The next, all was darkness!

Laura awakens safe among friends and soon hears the good news that her wicked pursuer has, in his terrible guilt, done himself in. He has been totally defeated, for Laura has finally experienced, and not by any imputation, a feeling vastly superior to that which she so exactly knows is the motive for the Colonel's conduct. One of the funniest jokes in literary history is Jane Austen's comment on this episode. She may have had no more suspicion than Emma of what she was saying, but in October, 1813, she wrote:

> I am looking over "Self-Control" again, and my opinion is confirmed of its being an excellently-meant, elegantly-written work, without anything of nature or probability in it. I declare I do not know whether Laura's passage down the American river is not the most natural, possible, everyday thing she ever does.

Natural and possible, yes. But not, even for Laura Montreville, everyday.

There is in Laura's final disclosure a disguise larger than any that Jane Austen ever dreamed of, and it is not merely the disguise that D. H. Lawrence thought he could tear aside in *Lady Chatterley's Lover*. It is not just that the swoon over the waterfall is the disguise of a sexuality most horridly hidden and repressed. All this is obvious —and grotesque—enough. The real disguise, however, is that there is no "principle" in this novel that is not the outright property of its heroine. The world of *Self-Control* is a one-mind world in which the "real evils" of the heroine's situation can only perish. Laura Montreville's imputations are absolute laws, and if coyness will not enforce them then "religion"—or at least some power that puts the greatest energies of nature at her disposal—will. Not even Mrs. Elton would have presumed so much.

Emma does not justify its heroine nor does it deride her. The ranks, the positions, on which its action turns are far, very far from being the outright property of Emma Woodhouse. To find in the pages of this novel anything like a comeuppance for its heroine or vengeance for its author is to fall into a confusion of values that does indeed border on inelegance of mind. In *Emma* the presumptions of the one are inevitably confused with the presumptions of the many, and the imagination of its principal character is chastened and subdued by her perception of the complexity of the ranks that surround her. To simplify rank, to collapse distinctions, is to release destructive fantasies—Jane Austen was no doubt as conservative as Charlotte Brontë believed her. But *Emma* is a novel much more central for the nineteenth century—and after—than its penetrating, suspicious, encouraging author could have guessed. It is the masterpiece of a talent so serene, so confident, and so clear, that it could make the problem of other minds into a laughing matter. The play of mind against mind was for Jane Austen the essence of society, and she could find this essence in so unpromising a place as Highbury and in so unlikely a time as the eve of Waterloo. The truth of her disclosure was so human that it has not always been believed.

That Way Madness Lies:
Nature and Human Nature in Parkman's *La Salle*

BY WILLIAM R. TAYLOR

> "O, that way madness lies; let me shun that!"
> —*King Lear*, III, iv, 21

READING yesterday's historians can be very interesting, but it is not easy. Indeed, it is probably for this reason that it is not often done, or in any event, not done very well. Since these historians seldom any longer speak with authority about the particular past they are attempting to recover, they tend to be overlooked by those who are investigating either the age in which they lived or about which they wrote. This tendency to dismiss historical writings of another time has especially led us to neglect the narrative historians of the nineteenth century—Prescott and Parkman in America and Macaulay in England—whose diligence and literary skill are often praised but who, at least by historians, are more often patronized than read.

There is, I think, a way of approaching such writing which gives it an immediate and striking relevance and makes its usefulness to those who would understand the thinking of any historical time fully as great as the scientific writings, also in a sense outmoded, which historians of science are beginning to explore to our immense enlightenment. What the historian ultimately seeks in any age or time—what he means or, in any event, should mean by "understanding" the past—is its "feel," the impalpable yet characteristic stamp which sets it off from the life of other times and places. To reach this kind of understanding he must, like other sensitive readers, possess imagination and be willing to use it: he is finally in quest of nothing less than a sense of the past, a past, which, while cut off from his own time by all the barriers that confine us to the culture in which we live, probes questions and concerns that persist in engaging our interest.

In such a quest there are no maps, no secure guidelines; but the works of previous historians are among the best of these since they have spoken to their own times, if they have been successful, with a subtlety and assurance which can only come from their having caught within their prose, probably unconsciously, the preconceptions, expectations, and anxieties of the society in which they lived and for which they wrote. In building a past for another age they have helped to illuminate their own social and intellectual world, and, in doing so, their writings have become a valuable part of our past and of the past of every succeeding age.

The writings of great historians, then, never lose their significance, even when they may be shown to have mistaken or misjudged the society they are exploring and analyzing. This is so not simply because they reveal the values of their own time, but also because great history is always in some sense ironic. It is always, that is to say, concerned with the plight of men attempting in the light of what they know to understand the historical forces which are playing over their lives and shaping their destinies, men unknowingly caught up in the myths, expectations, and comforting illusions with which every age protectively surrounds itself. Such understanding as historical actors have, as we should be the first to know, is always partial and uncertain, like our own, and it is for this reason that historical narrative speaks to us with such immediacy. In history of this kind and in the plight of the historians who wrote it, if we are honest and alert, we can scarcely avoid seeing ourselves, since for all our advances in historical technique, our use of quantification and our tables and charts, we confront the future with great uncertainty.

Francis Parkman, more than any other historian of the nineteenth century—except possibly Henry Adams—has succeeded in retaining this kind of enduring interest, yet the reasons for his success remain obscure and unexplained, and certainly he deserves to be better known than he now is—and for different reasons. Recent attention which Parkman has received seems to owe more to personal rather than to historical achievement. A biography, his journals, and his letters are all in print but only one volume of his history. He is known principally as the author of *The Oregon Trail*, his earliest and most autobiographical book. This is less surprising than it seems, however, since in a sense Parkman made a drama out of his own life: the mysterious ailments which beset him—his partial blindness and his curious nervous debilities—and his ingenious and courageous efforts to circumvent them have made him one of the best publicized but least known figures in American intellectual life. He remains in large measure a figure of paradox, known less for what he did than for his capacity, against overwhelming odds, to do it.

Nothing about his writing, at first glance, seems to speak to us directly. He was a "stylist," yes, but it is not necessary to read very far even in his best works to find passages of ornate and mannered prose which set our teeth on edge. On the surface, at least, his histories possess most of the limitations which are said to explain the present neglect of his almost equally popular contemporaries, George Bancroft, W. H. Prescott and J. L. Motley, all of whom made great sums of money from the sale of their books. He accepted, with only minor qualification, the nineteenth century belief in Progress, especially the progress of Protestant, Anglo-Saxon civilization, which he saw as predestined to overrun the world. In other ways, too, his social views are strikingly inconsistent with the articulate liberalism of some of his most vocal admirers, like the late Bernard De Voto. He was an outspoken racist who looked upon the Indian and the Negro as inherently and irretrievably inferior, and his contempt for the Catholic nations of Europe was only barely concealed beneath the veneer of romanticism with which he provided them, and by an indomitable spirit of fair play which led him to look for virtues where he most expected to find faults. In other matters he discusses he was anything but objective and his judgments were frequently inhumane. His portrayal of the English removal of French Acadians from Nova Scotia, an event which had been sentimentalized by Longfellow's *Evangeline*, is a notorious instance of his strong pro-English bias. He felt that political democracy had debauched American society, sapped its vitality, and converted us into a nation of money-grabbers, and he was a fanatic opponent of extending suffrage to women. In all his writing, finally, and especially in what are thought to be his best books, he accepted the so-called "Great Man" theory of history which assumed that events are primarily shaped by the actions of superior individuals.

Until very recently, to be sure, he has escaped the kind of detailed criticism by other American historians which had long before condemned his colleagues to dusty shelves, but now even this kind of criticism has begun to appear: historians who have tracked him through the sources he used are beginning to make their findings public. Almost every kind of historical fallibility has been ascribed to him. His vast multivolumed work of a lifetime, *France and England in North America*, describes the conflict between French Canada and the English Colonies from the period of settlement until the Peace of Paris in 1763; yet contemporary critics have rightly pointed out that Parkman was more concerned with telling a story than with understanding the underlying reasons for the chain of events which took Montcalm and Wolfe in 1759 to the memorable battle, described by Parkman, on the Plains of Abraham below Quebec. It now appears that French Canada, torn by conflicts from within, was its own worst enemy, not England.

Parkman shows scarcely any understanding of the economy of New France and he takes the feudal terminology of its social system at face value, whereas recent studies of colonial feudalism have shown that the attempt to impose a hierarchical social system on the society of the Canadian frontier met with little more success than similar attempts elsewhere in North America. Only opportunity and the promise of social mobility proved capable of luring settlers, and modification followed modification until the end result would have been almost unrecognizable to Frenchmen familiar, say, with only the seigneurial system of metropolitan France. Students of ethnology, furthermore, have shown that Parkman, despite long and detailed descriptions of Indian life, had little knowledge of the Iroquois, their system of government or the rationale for their wars on the French and on other Indian nations, wars which he almost invariably ascribed to their natural wolfish proclivities.

Most important of all, not only did he persist in organizing many of his books around the lives of individuals, but he appears to have chosen his heroes a little at random, more for the dramatic possibilities he saw in their lives than for their historical significance. In his desire to find progressive forces at work among the French, he both exaggerated and distorted the dubious role of Count Frontenac, governor of Canada during the period of La Salle's discoveries, and he passed over explorers of much greater importance, as for example D'Iberville, the founder of Louisiana, in order to devote a key volume of his history almost entirely to La Salle who objectively accomplished comparatively little. To cap it all, he tried to obscure the fact that La Salle during the period of his explorations appears to have suffered from a grave mental infirmity and was almost paranoid by the end of his life.

If all these criticisms are true—and they appear to be—what now remains of the fabric he wove? Parkman, of course, had been bitterly criticized by a few Catholic historians in Canada from the time his books first began to appear. Now, three-quarters of a century after his death, American historians have turned upon him. What justifica-

tion remains for continuing to read him? To seize upon what appears
to be one of his most vulnerable and, at the same time, most seduc-
tive works, what can now be said for the volume devoted to La Salle,
the only integral part of his history which is now in print (Francis
Parkman, *The Discovery of the Great West: La Salle*, Rinehart,
1956)? Clearly we do—and shall—continue to read it, but why?

I suppose it is safe to assume that one can learn from another
historian only by determining what it is that *he* is investigating and
what in fact concerns *him*. It scarcely matters that his questions are
not ours, and it would be ahistorical to insist that they should be.
Obviously, we today turn to his past with different questions, but
we can discover something of importance if we can learn what drove
Parkman to write as he did, to distort, to suppress, to quote out of
context in order to make a half-crazed French explorer into a tragic
hero, a hero of the "modern world," furthermore, and, in fact, into
a kind of Founding Father. What was La Salle to him and what
significance did he attach to what he did—and failed to do? It is
Parkman's motivation which concerns us, and the motivation which
he attributes to the historical figures about whom he writes. Human
motivation is a subject we continue to approach with great caution
and uncertainty; it goes at once to the heart of all historical investigation. If an answer to the question of Parkman's own motivation is
to be found, furthermore, it must lie embedded in the book itself.
Biographical knowledge about him, if it is to prove useful, can only
come into play when certain other questions have been clarified and
defined. Everyone is struck by similarities between La Salle and Parkman, who also devoted himself fanatically to an ambitious project
and who himself struggled with nervous infirmities of one kind or
another through much of his life; but few historians, having advanced
this far, have troubled to inquire what *La Salle: The Discovery of the
Great West* is really *about*, or how it happened to get written.

A certain air of mystery and intrigue surrounded the project from
its inception. The idea of writing a biography of La Salle was one
that Parkman apparently had nursed for some fifteen years before
he set about the task in the mid-sixties, although he nowhere stated
the reason for this intense interest. He had been struck, he said, by
certain "arresting" qualities in La Salle while still an undergraduate
at Harvard, when he read about him in Bancroft's *History of the
United States*. A few years later, in 1851, the year in which he published his first historical work, *The Conspiracy of Pontiac*, he had
written to Jared Sparks, the dean of American historians and presi-

dent of Harvard College, and asked his permission to consult the large collection of materials on La Salle which Sparks had collected but which, as Parkman correctly surmised, he would never find the time to embody in a work of history. The permission was granted. Meanwhile a whole set of adverse circumstances intervened, among them the onset of partial blindness and an almost total nervous collapse: Parkman succeeded in doing very little for almost ten years. By the time he had regained the capacity to work the Civil War had begun, a number of intellectual events of singular interest to him had occurred, and the proposed volume on La Salle had fallen into place as part of the vast project to which he was to devote the next thirty years.

Finally, in May of 1867, Parkman announced his intention to devote the next volume of his history to "the discovery and occupation by the French of the valley of the Mississippi." The following summer, having made a trip to the Middle West to examine some of the principal sites which were to figure in his narrative, he set to work. Two years later he published *The Discovery of the Great West*, which became a kind of working draft for the book on La Salle that appeared in 1879. In preparing this first version of his *La Salle*, Parkman had encountered an obstacle of very considerable magnitude. The largest collection of materials relating to French discovery, and to La Salle in particular, was in the hands of an eccentric French archivist by the name of Pierre Margry, an employee in the Archives de la Marine et des Colonies in Paris. Parkman had known of Margry's collection since the fifties, when the two of them had begun to correspond, and he had spent the winter of 1868 in Paris paying court to Margry in the hope of gaining access to his materials on La Salle. For once, he failed of his purpose and was forced to go to print with only the help of the few hints he had been able to extract in conversation from this doughty historical miser. A few years later, in 1872, Parkman, through the influence of friends, was able to secure from Congress an appropriation of $10,000 to subsidize the printing of Margry's collection. Soon afterward the six volumes of the collection began to appear one by one, so that by the late seventies the early ones, which contained the information Parkman sought, were in his hands.

As soon as these documentary sources were accessible to him, Parkman was able to undertake the long-intended revision of his earlier narrative. He seems to have begun work sometime in 1878, and his revised history appeared during the following year. *The Dis-*

covery of the Great West had meanwhile gone unrevised through ten editions. The new, eleventh edition, however, contained changes of great interest. The Houghton Library at Harvard has in its collection the loose sheets of the first edition with deletions and manuscript additions that served as copy for the eleventh edition. The increased attention both dramatically and substantively given to La Salle's experiences, which now became even more the focus of the study, led Parkman to publish the new version under the title, *La Salle and the Discovery of the Great West*. In the course of making these changes, he was forced to reckon with the mounting evidence of La Salle's final madness, but he did not, significantly, make any attempt to alter the heroic mold into which he had earlier fitted him, and most of his original estimations of La Salle's character were reprinted without change or qualification. In the Margry documents, as we shall see, he had found letters by La Salle which enabled him to reconcile La Salle's mental collapse with his achievement and his heroism.

At long last, in 1879, the La Salle volume was able to take its place in the procession of studies which were making up *France and England in North America*, his "history of the American forest," as he preferred to call it. Chronologically and in order of composition it followed *Pioneers of France in the New World* (1865) and *The Jesuits in North America in the Seventeenth Century* (1867), both of which are concerned with French explorations in an earlier period. Succeeding volumes, *The Old Régime in Canada* (1874) and *Count Frontenac and New France under Louis XIV* (1877), overlap somewhat in point of time and are concerned with various problems of colonial administration in the period which included La Salle's exploits. The study of La Salle, which possesses greater dramatic unity than the others, is principally concentrated in the decade of the 1680's, although Parkman, in order to give a thread of continuity to his overall work, allows himself occasional flashbacks which permit him to pick up the themes of his earlier volumes.

The end result of this long and tedious process of research, writing, and revision is by any standards an extraordinary historical composition. The very directness with which it seems to proceed toward its climax—La Salle's discovery of the mouth of the Mississippi in April, 1682—is itself illusory since in its organization the book is almost perversely complex. This particular voyage of discovery occupies a mere twenty pages in a book of well over three hundred pages. There are three long chapters at the beginning and four in the middle, and two at the end in which La Salle himself does not appear and is scarcely discussed. The dénouement, which takes La Salle through his disastrous attempt to place a motley colony of French settlers on the lower Mississippi to his murder on the Texas prairie in 1687, is almost as long as the whole previous narrative of La Salle's activities. This revised narrative, in other words, even with the additional materials on La Salle, is far from a triumphant account of one man's successful attempt to probe the geographical unknown. Rather, it is a harrowing depiction, with many of the qualities of a recurrent nightmare, of the resistance, the obstacles, and the frustrations which attend an ambitious and visionary endeavor, and the illusory and transient nature of success itself.

Parkman had studied his Gibbon to good effect: no one, certainly not La Salle himself, escapes the pervasive irony with which he views the hopes, dreams, and simple faith of all those involved. Writing from his perspective in the Protestant post-Darwinian United States of the 1870's, Parkman reduces the factional squabbles and conspiracies of La Salle and his political enemies, Jesuit and seigneur, France and England, over possession of the rich Mississippi valley to a Lilliputian scale. It is perfectly clear from the outset that no man's hopes can be fulfilled: neither the peaceful and prosperous agricultural paradise—the "feudal domain"—envisioned by La Salle nor the "new Paraguay" with its regulated Catholic society of French peasants and pious natives which the Jesuit order aimed to establish. He never lets his readers forget that every vestige of French culture, except for a few Acadians and Creoles speaking their strange dialects, is predestined to disappear and give place to the culture and society of Parkman's contemporary America.

The narrative contains constant reminders that this is to be the case. La Salle passes by the present site of Peoria and St. Louis, and the intractable wilderness through which he forces his way is "in our own day," Parkman observes, "strangely transformed—yellow in harvest time with ripened wheat, and dotted with the roofs of a hardy and valiant yeomanry." In a footnote of several pages he also shows how, by a fascinating piece of detective work, he located the site of the Great Illinois Town near the contemporary town of Utica, Illinois. It is also perfectly clear that Parkman does not think of all of these changes as for the good. Civilization was first of all an encroachment on a virgin wilderness that still in La Salle's time retained its primal beauty. He speaks of the prairie as a "boundless pasture of the buffalo and the deer," animals doomed to disappear along with much of the other wildlife the explorers encounter. The monu-

mental "Starved Rock" which plays such a central role in the narrative is now daubed with an advertisement of a brand of pills. The
Falls of St. Anthony which Hennepin discovered is now the site of
two modern cities of questionable beauty. "Beside the falls," Parkman contemptuously interjects in a note,

> stands a city, which, by an ingenious combination of the Greek and
> Sioux languages, has received the name of Minneapolis, or City of
> the Waters, and which, in 1867, contained ten thousand inhabit-
> ants, two national banks, and an opera-house; while its rival city
> of St. Anthony, immediately opposite, boasted a gigantic water-
> cure and a State university. In short, the great natural beauty of
> the place is utterly spoiled.

Progress, though to Parkman inexorable, has not in every instance
brought improvement, and the struggle for survival—between man
and the wilderness and between Frenchman and English colonial—
which is Parkman's subject throughout his histories has brought losses
as well as gains. The losses, furthermore, are irretrievable and some
of the gains—the vigorous commercial life of the United States, for
example—he regards as of questionable value, as his slighting mention
of banks, water cures, and patent medicines suggests. At the time
Parkman was working on these early volumes, moreover, the nation
was engaged in a Civil War which Parkman regarded as strikingly
similar to the one he was busy recording, and in his *La Salle* there
are passing references to this struggle. As La Salle pushes toward his
destination down the Mississippi he passes the sites "since become
historical, of Vicksburg and Grand Gulf."

Darwin's *On the Origin of Species* had appeared in 1859, and Parkman's letters to newspapers during the Civil War and, occasionally,
his historical writing contain clear evidence that he had encountered
the new evolutionary language which then was coming into vogue.
By the time he published the first volume of his history in 1865 he
had come to see the conflict between French and English settlers in
North America as a struggle for survival between two prehistoric
beasts which assumed in his metaphors almost comical abnormalities.
New France, he wrote in his introduction to the *Pioneers*, stood for
"Feudalism, Monarchy, and Rome" and was "all head. Under king,
noble, and Jesuit, the lank, lean body would not thrive." New England, on the other hand, was "a body without a head." While neither

cut a very attractive figure in his evolutionary zoo of societies, it was apparent which would survive and why. Muscularity and materialism were destined to win out over absolutism and intellect. "Each had its strength, each its weakness, each its own modes of vigorous life: but the one was fruitful, the other barren; the one instinct with hope, the other darkening with shadows of despair." Thus it is not surprising that the most triumphant moments in La Salle's career are rendered ironically and underscore the impermanence of French imperial dominion and La Salle's personal achievement. When La Salle assembles his followers at the mouth of the Mississippi, erects a column in honor of "Louis Le Grand," and in grandiloquent language claims most of the Transallegheny West in his name Parkman conceded it was "a stupendous accession"—"on parchment," made, he quickly adds, "by virtue of a feeble human voice, inaudible at half a mile."

Throughout the narrative the human beings who move across the landscape are dwarfed by the very size of the continent and beset by forces they can neither understand nor control. At every turn Parkman emphasizes the smallness and ineffectiveness of human agency and the gigantism of nature itself. When a party of explorers in an early chapter embark on a tributary of the Wisconsin and start south, Parkman, with what become characteristic stylistic devices, renders the helplessness of their plight in the face of a personified and grandly indifferent nature:

> The river twisted among lakes and marshes choked with wild rice; and, but for their guides, they could scarcely have followed the perplexed and narrow channel. It brought them at last to the portage, where, after carrying their canoes a mile and a half over the prairie and through the marsh, they launched them on the Wisconsin, bade farewell to the waters that flowed to the St. Lawrence, and committed themselves to the current that was to bear them they knew not whither—perhaps to the Gulf of Mexico, perhaps to the South Sea or the Gulf of California. They glided calmly down the tranquil stream, by islands choked with trees and matted with entangling grape-vines; by forests, groves, and prairies, the parks and pleasure-grounds of a prodigal nature; by thickets and marshes and broad bare sand-bars; under the shadowing trees, between whose tops looked down from afar the bold brow of some woody bluff.

Many things about this passage are typical of Parkman's language whenever man encounters the wilderness, especially the idea of nature as an obstructive, constricting force. Rivers "twist" and are often compared to snakes; the underbrush is "choked" and channels or paths are "perplexed." The wilderness is an entanglement, its snares and the potential threat it offers to those who penetrate it are usually stated or implied. Exploring parties are nearly always described with passive verbs, or the activity is attributed to nature itself, as it is here. It is the river which twists and brings the party to the portage, and the explorers "commit" themselves to the Wisconsin and are borne by it "they knew not whither." The diminutive scale of the men is expressed both by the way in which nature is personified and by the perspective from which, at the end of the passage, they are viewed. The fact that the forests and prairies are described as "the parks and pleasure-grounds of a prodigal nature" implies not only the gigantism of nature but also seems to suggest that Parkman conceives of nature as a glorious spendthrift, a kind of deity-king as indifferent to his subjects as the *Roi Soleil* in whose name and for whose glory they labor. Finally, the visual imagery forces us to see the exploring party from an increasing height, as the eye is carried up from the "shadowing trees" to the "bold brow" of the bluffs which "looked down" upon them.

The vision of nature which is expressed in this and other passages is very different from that of earlier American writers like Cooper, for example, who were inclined to look upon nature as a benign and salubrious force, a source of intuitive truth or, at the very least, a recourse for those who sought out the picturesque. The pantheistic suggestion that God is immanent in the wilderness is nowhere to be found in Parkman's writing, where nature is mute—or to quote Parkman, "a voiceless solitude"—and man is solitary. There are passages, to be sure, where nature seems to smile and peace and plenty prevail, but these are almost invariably a signal for trouble, for nature when it is not indifferent and aloof is portrayed as vicissitudinous, even treacherous, like the savages who inhabit it. Nowhere does it provide reliable comfort or solace. The sunny, calm waters of Lake Huron over which La Salle makes his way are suddenly whipped by a violent storm; the gentle current of the upper Mississippi, at the moment when the Missouri enters, sends a canoe careening wildly:

> A torrent of yellow mud rushed furiously athwart the calm blue current of the Mississippi; boiling and surging, and sweeping in its course logs, branches, and uprooted trees. They had reached the mouth of the Missouri, where that savage river, descending from its mad career through a vast unknown of barbarism, poured its turbid floods into the bosom of its gentler sister.

The introduction at this early point of the ideas of savagery and madness into the personification of nature prepares the way for much that is to come: it brings to the description of nature a set of terms which are central to Parkman's portrayal of *human* nature, also regarded by him as uncontrollable, treacherous, and essentially unfathomable. Those who look to God, like the priests, in expectation that He will intervene in man's affairs, or who think of themselves as in a position to exercise some control over nature or the Indian are always viewed ironically. Parkman's language betrays his contempt for such superstitious pretensions, whether of Jesuit or Indian. During the storm on Lake Huron, for example, when La Salle's ship, the *Griffin*, seems about to capsize or be swamped, Parkman observes that those on board "clamored to the saints":

> St. Anthony of Padua was promised a chapel in his honor, if he would save them from their jeopardy; while in the same breath La Salle and the friars declared him patron of their great enterprise. The saint heard their prayers. The obedient winds were tamed. . . .

The belief held by the Jesuits that they had Christianized the Indians is handled in much the same way. When Father Allouez goes among the Foxes of Green Bay and induces them to discard their tribal deities and worship the cross, Parkman interjects: "Nay, he succeeded so well, that when he showed them his crucifix they would throw tobacco on it as an offering." When a little later Allouez tells them the story of the cross and Constantine, they go off to battle with crosses daubed on their shields and return victorious and converted.

> "Thus it is," writes Dablon, who chronicles the incident, "that our holy faith is established among these people; and we have good hope that we shall soon carry it to the famous river called the Mississippi, and perhaps even to the South Seas."

The only kind of religious faith which wins his admiration is the burning internal faith of the early Jesuit missionaries who "lived with the self-abnegation of saints and died with the devotion of martyrs," and even they seem admirable only because of what, as civilized men, they were able to endure.

The natural setting in which Parkman places his La Salle is one without any rational order and bereft of its gods, where chaotic and unpredictable forces are constantly at work. Indian nature is scarcely distinguishable from physical nature and is described in many of the same terms. Storm metaphors appear to be Parkman's favorite device for describing the onset of an Indian attack. When the Iroquois prepare for war "a storm is gathering," and their attack is compared to lightning. No reasons are assigned to the Iroquois for their assault on the Great Illinois Town; their behavior is as unaccountable and unpredictable as the weather. They are just as often compared to beasts of prey: "A hyena warfare," Parkman comments, "had been waged against the dead. . . . The threatened blow had fallen, and the wolfish hordes of the five cantons had fleshed their rabid fangs in a new victim." Having said this, Parkman, apparently feeling that his language might seem hyberbolic, gives further supporting evidence concerning the savage nature of Indian warfare in a long footnote.

All human motivation is finally caught up in the essential irrationality of a savage nature. The white man, as Parkman sees him, is not so much corrupted by the wilderness as revealed to be what he basically is. Deep unconscious cravings and brutal aggressions, long held in check, are unleashed. Men kill one another almost on a whim. Others shed the thin veneer of civilization and go native. The lure of unbridled Indian life and the easy accessibility of Indian women, Parkman implies, simply unveil human nature's essential characteristics: a brutal selfishness propelled by wild and uncontrollable passions. The terminology of savagery and civilization become interchangeable. The Iroquois are referred to as "forest Machiavels," and the attempted poisoning of La Salle in the wilderness is compared in a footnote to a contemporary incident in Paris which arose out of intrigues at court. Finally, in a touch of characteristic irony, Parkman has the civilized European pin the label of savagery on himself. After La Salle has witnessed the depredations of the Iroquois upon the Illinois, he journeys on to find the ship he had left half-built destroyed by those to whom he had entrusted its completion. Scrawled on a plank are the words *"Nous sommes tous sauvages"* followed by the Christian date. Very little plausibility is given to any man's actions, except for those few men who are "mere merchants," as Parkman calls them, and are therefore in the wilderness simply to enrich themselves or, in the case of the Jesuits, to aggrandize their order. All the rest act mostly from essentially irrational motives or at least inscrutable ones, even La Salle. "The wilderness," Parkman comments on the occasion of La Salle's murder, "is a rude touchstone, which often reveals traits that would have lain buried and unsuspected in civilized life."

The journey which La Salle is described as taking is a voyage of exploration in two senses. It is a probing of the geographical unknown in which, as Parkman puts it, "the mystery of this vast New World was more and more unveiled." It is also a journey into the human mind, an exploration of human nature: strange monstrous features turn up at each bend of the river. Horribly painted Indian idols which assure the priests that the Devil is abroad, rocks that look like the battlements of ruined châteaux, a huge catfish which perceptibly jolts a canoe and startles its occupants, an ugly spadefish, the man-devouring alligator (which the Frenchmen are astonished to learn is hatched from an egg), the mammoth desert rattlesnake and the Texas horned toad all appear successively, as do an astonishing procession of Indian tribes with their varying rituals and customs, each, it appears, a little stranger and more eccentric than the one before. In this sense Parkman was writing his own vicarious *Voyage of the Beagle*, duly recording the impression made by each novelty of American nature as it is first confronted by civilized man. But finally, and I think much more significantly, the journey for Parkman became one in which he was probing the inner recesses of human behavior, the motives which drive men to act as they do. Cannibalism and sexual perversions as practiced by the Indians, though mentioned, are too horrifying to receive detailed consideration, though the more commonplace vices of theft, lying, treachery, and murder, are discussed at length. Even vanity and plagiarism receive rather extended consideration in the long account of Father Hennepin's real and imagined journeys. While he actually did discover the Falls of St. Anthony on the upper Mississippi, in a later edition of his travels, published after La Salle's death, he fraudulently claims to have been the first to follow the river to its mouth, thus robbing La Salle of his principal claim to renown.

At this point, and at certain others, the history takes on the characteristics of a detective story as Parkman, like Poe's M. Dupin, proceeds by deduction to unravel the motives which could have led Hennepin to make such an insupportable claim and to show that the trip which he insisted he had made could not have been completed in the time which his original narrative allowed for. He then goes on to discount the apparent accuracy of Hennepin's narrative by showing with unmistakable certainty that he had lifted his description, sometimes word for word, from a journal kept by a Récollet missionary who had accompanied La Salle. In a disordered and irrational world held in check by only a few human qualities, veracity to Parkman became an almost fanatical ideal, and his indictment of Hennepin's behavior on this occasion is at least equal in its severity to his treatment of much more serious crimes. "The records of literary piracy," he concluded, "may be searched in vain for an act of depredation more recklessly impudent." The fact that Parkman employs here in reference to the pseudo-explorer Hennepin terms such as "piracy" and "depredation" which he ordinarily reserved for acts of outrage committed by the Indians only further emphasizes the thin line which in his mind divided civilized from savage behavior, and raises still again the persistent problem of what drives men in a given set of circumstances to singular acts of depravity or, in the case of La Salle and a few others, heroism.

Certainly the most serious questions posed by Parkman's documentary sources were those concerning the motive or motives which impelled La Salle to his initial success and to his ultimate ruin, which enabled him—or *compelled* him, for this proved to be the real question—to endure years of hardship in the hostile wilderness of Canada and the Mississippi Valley, to force his way again and again across frozen prairies and wind-blown lakes in the face of opposition from Canadian authorities, treacherous intervention by the Jesuits and the Iroquois and natural disasters of a kind which would have paralyzed ordinary men. Or so, at least, Parkman conceived of La Salle's situation and of his accomplishments.

An unmistakable air of uncertainty and ambiguity surrounds Parkman's discussion of La Salle's motivation from the outset of the narrative. It seems apparent that nothing about his history fascinated or troubled him more. He returns to the problem again and again, sometimes simply repeating in different words what he has said before, sometimes contradicting himself and, in several instances, obviously evading the implications of evidence which he himself cites. From time to time Parkman is forced to concede that La Salle acted out of a desire to enrich himself, out of a driving personal ambition for renown and for power, out of opportunism of the most ruthless kind and, to intimate toward the end of the narrative that he may have acted out of the compulsions of a sick and deluded mind which left him no peace and prohibited him from sparing either himself or those whom he compelled to follow him on and on and on across the wastes of southern Texas toward the "fatal river," as Parkman calls it, which La Salle was destined to trace to its mouth and in the hapless pursuit of which he finally perished. Nonetheless, despite these occasional concessions—and, in the light of the evidence he could scarcely have evaded them—his emphasis was of a different kind.

A number of things about La Salle's character are given unusual stress, often on the slenderest and least substantial kind of evidence —a feature in his history which it is not possible to dismiss lightly in view of Parkman's fanatical desire for accuracy, his tireless efforts to tie down the exact location of every physical feature, every singular rock formation, tributary, and fortified encampment which La Salle or his contemporaries encountered or inhabited. The qualities of La Salle's character upon which Parkman most insists are his gentility, his veracity, his disinterested patriotism, his self-control, and his essential modernity. A number of other qualities are implied by, or associated with, these underlying traits: will power, inexhaustible energy, and the capacity to concentrate them on the attainment of a single lofty objective. It is this last capacity which makes La Salle the outstanding exemplar of the most preeminently masculine trait in Parkman's human lexicon—"constitutional hardihood"—a subtle blend of manly fortitude, intellect, and gentility. There is no mistaking Parkman's eagerness to establish a close association between good breeding, cultivation, and courageous endurance and achievement. "The pioneer of western pioneers," Parkman comments of La Salle, "was no rude son of toil, but a man of thought, trained amid arts and letters." He then in a footnote goes on to quote a Rocky Mountain trapper who once told him that

"a gentleman of the right sort will stand hardship better than anyone else." The history of Arctic and African travel [Parkman continues], and military records of all time, are a standing evidence that a trained and developed mind is not the enemy, but the active and powerful ally, of constitutional hardihood. The culture that enervates instead of strengthening is always a false or a partial one.

Without the possession of constitutional hardihood, Parkman makes clear, La Salle's heroic achievement and endurance would have been impossible. A certain number of words and phrases which designate this quality appear and reappear like Homeric epithets throughout the narrative: "inexorable," "indomitable," "iron-hearted," "unbending," "inconquerable," "self-contained," "impenetrable," "adamant," "impregnable," "inscrutable," and many others which denote

La Salle's almost total detachment from, independence of, and imperviousness to all and everything which surrounds him.

La Salle is thus portrayed as having transcended his natural environment, as having elevated himself above the materialism, opportunism, superstitions, vices, and temptations—in other words, the sense of values—which characterize most of those who move through the forests of French Canada. While it is this quality of transcendence which gives him, as Parkman interprets his character, the "vision" necessary to achieve his purpose, the very remoteness which it implies from the feelings and needs of others is, ironically, what defeats him and leads to his "assassination," as Parkman calls it, or, really, his murder—which is what it amounts to. La Salle's heroic qualities were thus, in the end, self-defeating, and his purpose was frustrated by the great river itself—which is described with many of the same epithets—by uncomprehending followers and subordinates and by the wavering purpose of an indifferent monarch, who finally turns his attention to other matters and leaves the pitiful little settlement on Matagorda Bay to its fate. This, in brief, is the tragic portrayal of La Salle that Parkman forces upon the evidence he collected and reviewed with such painstaking care. How well does it fit, and what kind of proof is offered to demonstrate that La Salle possessed these traits which are attributed to him?

Certainly it is fair to say at the outset that these heroic qualities are supported more casually and circumstantially than any other assertions in the book. La Salle's gentility hangs by a thread. Some of his distant relatives, Parkman notes, were in the service of the crown, and his father and uncle, though merchants, lived "more like nobles than like burghers." In a footnote he goes on to add that La Salle like François Marie Arouet, known as Voltaire, took his name from his family's "estate," although he neglects to mention that this was a common practice everywhere in Europe, even among those with only small holdings. Thorstein Veblen's father, a poor Norwegian immigrant, had done the same thing. La Salle's social position is further supported by Parkman's repeated and literal application to him of such terms as "seigneur" and "feudal lord" and "domain." Parkman, moreover, considerably improved the literary qualities—and, in fact, the literacy—of La Salle's letters in the translations he made of them from French documentary sources.

The case for La Salle's modernity is scarcely stronger. He is introduced as one who "showed an inclination for the exact sciences," whatever that might have meant in Rouen of the early seventeenth century. When a large comet blazes across the sky in 1680, La Salle, Parkman observed, "coolly notes down the phenomenon, not as a portentous messenger of war and woe, but rather as an object of scientific curiosity." In doing so, he observes in a footnote, La Salle exhibited his freedom from the superstitious terror which the same comet evoked from Increase Mather in New England. He is called a "hero of modern practical enterprise" early in the book and, in the summary of his character that occurs after his murder, Parkman observes that he "belonged not to the age of the knight-errant and the saint, but to the modern world of practical study and practical action."

Questions concerning La Salle's disinterested patriotism, his sanity—and hence his self-control—and, even, his veracity are raised by a number of incidents which Parkman discusses in detail. If we are to take La Salle at his word, a more quixotic venture could scarcely have been imagined than that of landing a small party of Frenchmen at the mouth of the Mississippi, herding the intractable and feuding Indian tribes from the upper valley to the Rio Grande—a fantastic proposal in view of La Salle's extensive experience of Indian life—and capturing the Spanish silver mines in Mexico, yet this is precisely what La Salle does propose in one memorial to Louis XIV. This memorial and several other documents which Parkman cites raise both the question of La Salle's disinterestedness and that of his veracity. The case for his veracity rests mostly on the dubious evidence of a memoir written about him at the time he returned to Paris in 1678 by a person obviously bent on promoting La Salle's standing at court. Although Parkman concedes that the memoir exhibits "intensely partisan feeling," he nonetheless cites it at length on the subject of La Salle's truthfulness: "He distinguishes perfectly," Parkman quotes the memoir as saying, "between that which he knows with certainty and that which he knows with a mingling of doubt." In the case of the two memorials to the king, prepared during a second visit to Paris in 1683, there seems little question, as a recent article has shown, that La Salle was involved in a political intrigue of some kind. The passionate enemies which he had in Canada and in France are further evidence of his involvement with factional politics to a degree that Parkman, although he makes much of La Salle's many enemies, never concedes. In this instance, Parkman goes to extraordinary lengths to discount the evidence of La Salle's desire to exploit the war with Spain in the interest of advancing his own position and winning greater support for his colonizing scheme. Although he concedes that La Salle had acted somewhat disingenuously—"he thought he needed a more glittering lure to attract the eyes of Louis and Seignelay"—the explanation which he preferred was of another, quite surprising, kind.

Rather than yield to the obvious and agree that La Salle had acted opportunistically and somewhat dishonestly, Parkman quite suddenly interested himself in the charge commonly made by La Salle's enemies that he was insane, or at least suffered from a mental infirmity of some kind. All through the narrative, Parkman had turned such charges back upon La Salle's accusers with contempt and impugned their motives for making them. Now he was willing to admit that La Salle had proposed a "madcap" scheme and that "his head was turned," but this was only for the moment.

Mostly, when he considered La Salle's personality, he preferred to deal in terms which were vague and ambiguous and, finally, much more applicable to Parkman himself than to La Salle. He calls him "shy," "retiring," "reserved," and "haughty" and refers to his "shadowed nature" and his "solitary disposition." In a long chapter entitled "La Salle Painted by Himself," inserted in the 1879 edition and based on letters which Parkman discovered in the Margry documents, Parkman makes much of La Salle's brief confession of natural "timidity" that keeps him from associating freely with his men, and of his protestation that he found it difficult to write letters or to converse with men more sophisticated than himself. Since this particular letter was written not to a personal friend—to whom a shy man might be expected to reveal such things—but rather in answer to criticisms from a distrustful and disgruntled creditor, there is some suggestion that La Salle here, too, might have acted a bit disingenuously, and was certainly acting defensively. Nonetheless, Parkman rushes on to portray La Salle as he, Parkman, must have conceived of himself. He was characterized by "shyness; a morbid fear of committing himself; an incapacity to express, and much more to simulate feeling—a trait sometimes seen in those with whom feeling is most deep." This was the quality which induced him to leave France, spend his life alone in the wilderness, and propelled him to turn his attention from commerce and material pursuits, and devote himself to a principled life of honor, achievement, lofty and grandiose projects for the good of France. Despite the impression he gave to others, Parkman concluded, La Salle's was "a nature at war with itself," and the effect of this silent, internal "strife"—which Parkman concedes was an "infirmity"—was "to concentrate and intensify the force within." His final madness is allowed for, but not really acknowledged by Parkman's concession that La Salle's "lonely and shadowed nature needed the mellowing sunshine of success."

Parkman's willingness in his portrayal of La Salle to ride roughshod over his own evidence and his tortuous efforts to absolve him of any taint of opportunism or mercantile concern—to clear him, in other words, of the charge that he was what he appears to have been in fact, a Canadian *parvenu*, a man on the make—obviously calls for an explanation, especially in the case of a historian so scrupulously accurate and cautious in other matters. There is no mistaking the heroic role for which Parkman intended him. In the claims that are made for him following his death, La Salle is compared to the King of Israel, Coriolanus, paladin, crusader, and pilgrim and, in the last paragraph of the book, he is referred to as a representative specimen of "a grand type of incarnate energy and will." For Parkman this kind of assertion was clearly a matter of more than passing interest since the recovery for his own time of a concept of heroism, of masculine yet genteel fortitude, was for him, as for many of his contemporaries, an undertaking of the most pressing urgency. In other words, he was advocating the virtues of the "strenuous life" with the same kind of zeal that was soon to prompt other members of the genteel classes in the East, as for example Theodore Roosevelt, to write about masculine exploit in much the same way. This sense of urgency, which he strongly felt and to which he repeatedly gave expression in letters to the press, especially when combined with the needs put forward by his personal problems, goes a long way toward explaining why it was he found the figure of La Salle so "arresting."

It is interesting to note that Parkman's study of La Salle appears to have been commenced just after his recovery from the severe nervous collapse which followed the death of his wife in 1858. It seems clear, as several psychiatrists have recently suggested, that Parkman had suffered from some kind of neurotic ailment, at least from the time of his return from Oregon in 1848 and probably since young manhood. Recurrent attacks of nervous disability, accompanied by physical disorders of one kind or another, occurred throughout his life, but they appear to have been most severe in the period between 1848 and the close of the Civil War. The exact diagnosis of his problem—which he personified as "the Enemy"—varies a good deal from authority to authority and is scarcely to the point. The medical specialists whom Parkman himself consulted in America and

Europe were, as a matter of fact, no more successful in getting at the source of his difficulty, and one doctor told him frankly that he might expect to go mad any day. A Paris physician, Dr. Brown-Séquard, who had treated Charles Sumner after his beating in the Senate, could offer him no prospect of recovery; others prescribed hot baths, water cures, and other fashionable remedies of the day.

He himself, it would appear, was his own best diagnostician, and he seems to have sensed, at least by the early sixties, that he suffered from what we would call a compulsion neurosis that drove him mercilessly until his "health" collapsed and he was forced to remain idle for a time. In a long autobiographical letter written—for posterity—in 1864 he gave a graphic description of his symptoms. In speaking of the period in the forties when he first became conscious of having a problem, he noted, almost clinically, his progressive lack of control as he drove himself unslackingly to his historical project:

> Labor became a passion, and rest intolerable. . . . The stimulus rapidly increased. Despite of judgment and of will, his mind turned constantly towards remote objects of pursuit and strained vehemently to attain them. The condition was that of a rider whose horse runs headlong with the bit between his teeth, or of a locomotive, built of indifferent material, under a head of steam too great for its strength, hissing at a score of crevices, yet rushing on with accelerating speed to the inevitable crash.

This kind of compulsive activity was followed by an attack of "the Enemy": "a wild whirl possessed his brain, joined by a universal turmoil of the nervous system." His response to this kind of paralyzing seizure, as soon as its severities had become attenuated, was "counter-attack": work, work, all the work and activity he could force himself to perform. Thus, in a sense, he retained the illusion of control, never suspecting that compulsion was his problem and that "the Enemy," as he persisted in calling it, was what, in fact, saved him from a total collapse and, conceivably, madness. An extensive period of disability unhappily, as I have already suggested, coincided with the Civil War, and Parkman, much to his distress, was forced to sit the fighting out and content himself with writing "letters to the editor," a dismal consolation for a man who saw in struggle of all kinds, and especially in warfare, salvation for himself, for his class, and for the country as a whole.

Between the outbreak of the Civil War and 1869, the year in which he published his first edition of *The Discovery of the Great*

West, Parkman wrote something like a dozen long open letters to the Boston *Daily Advertiser* and an article for *The Nation*, all of which were concerned with the debility of the genteel classes or the weaknesses of American culture generally. Before the publication of his final version in 1879 he had taken up many of the same questions in still another article entitled "The Failure of Universal Suffrage," for the still-influential *North American Review*, which until 1876 had been edited by Henry Adams. He had also explored these matters in personal letters. What concerned him throughout this period was the apparent inability of the United States to produce a class of political and military leaders and to place men of superior talent in a position where they could employ their talents effectively for the national good. This point is emphasized in the titles he gave to some of these letters: "The Nation's Ordeal," "Where Are Our Leaders?" "Why Our Army is Not the Best in the World," "The Weak Side of Our Armies," "The Chiefs of the Nation," "Aristocrats vs. Democrats" and "Our Best Class and the National Politics."

Through the whole period of the war Parkman, in these years himself an almost totally helpless invalid, poured into these letters to the public the passionate convictions which he would have preferred to discharge in battle, and his writing exhibits the intense frustration of a man who, in a time of national emergency, was left, as he wrote to a friend in 1864, impotently "holding the pen with a hand that should have grasped the sword." A day spent at an army encampment at Readville in 1862 had left him with a bad case of the glooms, and he complained to his cousin-in-law and confidante, Mary Dwight Parkman, of the effect made upon him by seeing "the banners I was not to follow,—the men I was not to lead, the fine fellows of whom I could not be one. I thought I had known what deprivation is, but I had not. It was the lamentation of the moth, in despair, because, being burned already, he cannot fly into the candle."

These letters, coming as they do on the eve of Parkman's study of La Salle, make extraordinarily interesting reading. Even the language of his historical writing is anticipated in his talk of America's delinquencies and his call for men characterized by a sense of "honor," "traits of high and finished manhood," "chivalric courage," and the like. Political crises evoke comparison with threatening storms, and the future is "black with disaster." At the same time, it is important to note, he was opening his heart to Mary Parkman concerning his failure to win the hand of Ida Agassiz, a daughter of Louis Agassiz,

Harvard's famous zoologist and anti-Darwinian, who persisted in looking upon him as a friend rather than as a suitor—mostly, it appears, because he never revealed his true feelings to her. She soon, to Parkman's chagrin, married a wounded war hero and close friend of Parkman's, Henry Lee Higginson.

New England culture, as Parkman during these same months assessed it, was one of a civilization without effective intellectual leadership, and grown soft through its exclusive pursuit of commercial interests. The lower orders of society had become victim to the Yankee ethos. Wealth and the exclusion from positions of responsibility were meanwhile making the Brahmins into a class of effeminate dilettantes or, at best, recluses. In an irate article entitled "To the Lingerers," he called on the "worthless young imbeciles" and "wastrels" of "Beacon Street" to volunteer for service. Too much money, too much prosperity and individual opportunity, he declared, had eroded the qualities of character which had typified the Adamses, Otises, Putnams, and other Revolutionary heroes and brought a set of opportunistic demagogues to the fore—the very "scum," as he saw it, of American society—"rail-splitters" from the West and vulgar Irish ward bosses in the East. As he wrote a few months after the disastrous defeat at Bull Run:

> The individual is rare and the nation never yet seen which the smiles of fortune could not weaken or pervert. Our own unmatched prosperity has wrought its inevitable work. We are a *parvenu* nation with the faults and follies of a *parvenu*.

Parkman's fanatical commitment to the necessity of good breeding and the careful cultivation of an elite is never more apparent than in his little-known work *The Book of Roses*, a study of horticulture which he published in 1866. This book led to his only Harvard teaching appointment—in a field, ironically, far removed from history. It contains what can only be called a Brahmin theory of rose gardening, and gives still further evidence of his growing interest in evolutionary science. Much of what he has to say is highly technical and reflects the considerable interest in horticulture which he apparently formed during the long years of convalescence when he spent his days puttering around the garden of his summer house on Jamaica Pond. At certain points, however, the metaphorical tenor of his discussion of rose breeding is obvious. "Like all things living, in the world of mind or of matter," he notes, for example, the rose is beautified, enlarged, and strengthened by a course of judicious and persevering culture, continued through successive generations. The art of horticulture is no leveller. Its triumphs are achieved by rigid systems of selection and rejection, founded always on the broad basis of intrinsic worth. The good cultivator propagates no plants but the best. He carefully chooses those marked by conspicuous merit; protects them from the pollen of inferior sorts; intermarries them, perhaps, with other varieties of equal vigor and beauty; saves their seed, and raises from it another generation. From the new plants thus obtained he again chooses the best, and repeats with them the same process. Thus the rose and other plants are brought slowly to their perfect development. It is vain to look for much improvement by merely cultivating one individual. Culture alone will not make a single rose double, or a dull rose brilliant. We cultivate the parent, and look for our reward in the offspring.

Parkman, in other words, was no advocate of natural selection. One sees in this passage many of the arguments which would soon be employed in behalf of immigration restriction; but it was one thing to experiment with roses and quite another to control the evolution of society. Parkman, of course, sensed this and gave considerable attention to the vexing set of problems which social evolution presented. He came to believe that aristocracies, like individuals, were strengthened and invigorated by war which became in his thinking the grim selector of those of "martial spirit" who were most fit to rule. Only careful intermarriage and continual wars could keep such a ruling class in trim.

For a time in the early sixties Parkman appears to have believed that the Civil War was a good and beneficial thing since conflict was of the essence of vigorous national life and the North might through adversity experience the need to assume a more "martial stamp." "Already, like a keen fresh breeze," he wrote in 1861, "the war has stirred our clogged and humid atmosphere." This early optimism, however, was of short duration, and he was soon forced to recognize that, win or lose, the delinquencies of New England culture would not be remedied by this or any other war. "Our best culture," he wrote a year later, "has become, in great part, nerveless and emasculate. . . . The country has need of all its manhood." On the very day of the Union victory at Gettysburg, July 4, 1863, his pessimism reached its highest pitch. To call for a Northern aristocracy was a futile gesture, he concluded: "Who are the best? They are gone; their race is died out. . . . they have withered and dwindled away."

The trouble with Boston's "Brahmin caste," as he persisted in calling it, was the diminishing incentives which America provided for high achievement. To these men of established wealth money was scarcely an object and their social position could hardly be improved. "It lacks a career," he concluded despondently. The Brahmin caste had thus been drawn away from the active arena of political and military life and forced to find expression in the quiet but unchallenging backwaters of the professions, scholarship, and art. It had become inert, squeamish, and somewhat effeminate. The real vitality of Northern culture thus resided in those who were propelled upward by the shock waves of economic and political opportunism. Mind and muscle in the North were thus almost entirely disassociated; Northern culture had in his imagination assumed the ominous shape of the now extinct prehistoric dinosaur. "If we may be forgiven the metaphor," he wrote in 1865, "our civilization is at present a creature with a small and feeble head, a large muscular, and active body, and a tail growing at such a rate that it threatens to become unmanageable and shake the balance of the vital powers." The war itself, meanwhile, had assumed most of the characteristics he was to find in the conflict between New France and New England. The struggle which had been going on between South and North, he wrote a week or so after the victory at Gettysburg, was one between "Oligarchy and Democracy, the strong head and the strong body."

A head full of fire, a body ill-jointed, starved, attenuated, is matched against a muscular colossus, a Titan in energy and force—full of blood, full of courage, prompt for fight, and confident of victory.

The concept of heroism that found expression in Parkman's *La Salle* and throughout the historical narratives which began to make their appearance the year of Appomattox seems, then, to have sprung from a rather complex set of motives. It was, first of all, Parkman's way of coming to terms with his own illness, of reckoning with his fear of insanity and of looking into the inner recesses of his own mind. In doing so he was evidently attempting to prove to himself that great achievements of any kind—both his own and La Salle's—were an expression of healthy and vigorous manhood—of what he called "constitutional hardihood"—and an act of will, not the creation of a sick, compulsive mind or a product of what we would call neurosis. He appears to have retained some doubt about the validity of this contention, and this doubt is dramatically expressed in his evasive treatment of La Salle's motivation. His *La Salle* was also his *Voyage of the Beagle*, part of his initiation to evolutionary science, and his way of reconciling himself to a natural world in which God was not an active agent. Then, too, it was his attempt to fight in fantasy the Civil War which he had missed—a deprivation which also had a formative, and possibly decisive, influence on the careers of a number of Parkman's contemporaries and near contemporaries, among them Henry Adams and Henry James. Not least of all, it was his valiant if somewhat confused effort to help the North, and especially New England, find its head—his way of urging his own Brahmin class to assume a position of political leadership. About the fulfillment of this fond wish he seems to have entertained little hope. The century since the Peace of Paris had not altered the battleground substantially: muscle was still destined to go on triumphing over intellect, quantity over quality. "Human nature," he had written in 1863, "has not much changed since the birth of Adam."

Mark Twain, Jane Austen, and the Imagination of Society

BY RICHARD POIRIER

> To me his [Poe's] prose is unreadable—like Jane Austin's (*sic*). No, there is a difference. I could read his prose on salary, but not Jane's. Jane is entirely impossible. It seems a great pity that they allowed her to die a natural death.
>
> —MARK TWAIN, Letter to Howells, January 18, 1909

> Just that one omission alone [of Jane Austen's novels from a ship's library] would make a fairly good library out of a library that hadn't a book in it.
>
> —MARK TWAIN, *Following the Equator*

MARK TWAIN'S comments on Jane Austen represent more than an effort to bait William Dean Howells, her most distinguished American defender, or to suggest that he, Mark Twain, might add to James Fenimore Cooper's literary offenses the rumor that his first novel was an imitation of *Persuasion*. He never explains why he dislikes her, being too contemptuous to bother, but his reasons can be inferred from his writings, especially from *Huckleberry Finn*; and the more substantial criticisms of her by Emerson and Henry James express essentially what Mark Twain himself probably meant. Taken together, the reactions to Jane Austen by these three reveal a significantly American dissatisfaction with the novel of manners. The form and the social orders on which it depends offer an inhospitable context for the kinds of romantic and aspiring characters admired, with some differences, by all of them. Emerson, with his well-known distaste for what he calls "novels of costume," found Jane Austen's "vulgar in tone, sterile in invention, imprisoned in the wretched conventions of English society, without genius, wit or knowledge of the world. Never was life so pinched and narrow," he continues in his Journal for August 5, 1861, and her only subject, "marriageableness," is dismissed, with an inapplicable allusion to Byron, as the " 'nympholepsy of a fond despair,' say, rather, of an English boarding house. Suicide," he concludes, "is more respectable." About forty-five years later, Henry James, who had learned many lessons from her, complained in "The Lesson of Balzac," an address first given in Philadelphia, that her popularity ("their 'dear,' our dear, everybody's dear Jane") had been in part whipped up by "the stiff breeze of the commercial," and in part was due to

> the extraordinary grace of her facility, in fact of her unconsciousness; as if, at the most, for difficulty, for embarrassment, she sometimes, over her work basket, her tapestry flowers, in the spare, cool drawing room of other days, fell a-musing, lapsed too metaphorically, as one may say, into wool gathering, and her dropped stitches, of these pardonable, of these precious moments, were afterwards picked up as little touches of human truth, little glimpses of steady vision, little master strokes of imagination.

It is sometimes hard to know when James the critic is not overmastered by the self-aggrandizing entertainer, particularly when he shows such amused condescension to English and American writers with whom he has some literary or intellectual affinities.[1] Thus, a decade or so earlier, he had not been averse, when it came to a criticism of Emerson, to observe that the possible explanations for other vagaries of Emerson's literary taste "still leaves his indifference to Cervantes and Miss Austen unaccounted for." The reader may, for a change, have the last turn of the screw by noticing that the negative side of James's ambivalence toward Jane Austen is finally very much like Emerson's unmoderated criticism: she lacks inclusiveness. In the last important comments he was to make about her, James allows the issue to be raised by an unmistakably rhetorical question: "Why shouldn't it be argued against her," it is asked in "The New Novel," "that where her testimony complacently ends, the pressure of our appetite presumes exactly to begin?"

More than any other novelist in English, Jane Austen is supremely confident that the appetite of her audience as well as of her characters can be satisfied by society as her novels provide it. It is not surprising, therefore, that Emerson, Mark Twain, and Henry James

[1] James was never to admire even *Huckleberry Finn*, and as late as 1907 he asserts that Mark Twain would contribute "a clarionet solo only" to the composite novel, *The Whole Family*, being planned by Miss Elizabeth Jackson. (Twain declined the invitation.) On his side, Twain in 1885 would rather have been "damned to John Bunyan's heaven" than read *The Bostonians*, which ran serially in *Century* along with a section of *Huckleberry Finn*. But in a letter in 1900 he has come to the point of calling James "a master."

should find "the pressure of appetite" unsatisfied. Despite the many differences among them, they all tend to see a necessary division between a part of us that we express by accommodations to social systems, and another, more admirable, even if impractical part, that exists in the imagination only, or in a vocabulary of abstractions, or in relationships to landscape. Bad schooling that assumes the naïveté of romantic writers has made us all think at some point that Emerson is merely a booster for one human possibility and a scoffer of the other, when he is more often expressive of the tensions that, to use his term, result in an inescapable "doubleness." Huck Finn will later worry about "playing double," and if we read Emerson with such novels in mind as *Huckleberry Finn*, *The Portrait of a Lady*, or even *The Ambassadors*, where social artifice is given some positive definitions, we come upon passages that can very adequately describe the problem faced by the leading characters in these books and by their creators. The problem is that at some point, usually at the end, the heroes and heroines tend to escape definition in the social or even psychological terms on which, only to a lesser extent than in *Emma*, the novels themselves have depended. The difficulty, apparent in the structure of *Huckleberry Finn* and in many of James's novels, is thus a symptom of some larger distrust of social structures themselves. Emerson's phrasing is relevant to such works precisely because it is so general; it is if anything less general than our own language when we try to explain why Huck must "light out for the Territory" or Isabel return to Rome. Emerson complains (in "The Transcendentalist"):

> The worst feature of this double consciousness is, that the two lives, of the understanding and of the soul, which we lead, really show very little relation to each other; never meet and measure each other: one prevails now, all buzz and din; and the other prevails then, all infinitude and paradise; and, with the progress of life, the two discover no greater disposition to reconcile themselves. Yet, what is my faith? What am I? What but a thought of serenity and independence, an abode in the deep blue sky? Presently the clouds shut down again; yet we retain the belief that this pretty web we weave will at last be overshot and reticulated with veins of the blue, and that the moments will characterize the days. Patience, then, is for us, is it not? Patience, and still patience. When we pass, as we presently shall, into some new infinitude, out of this Iceland of negations, it will please us to reflect that though we had few virtues or consolations, we bore with our indigence, nor once strove to repair it with hypocrisy or false heat of any kind.

To say that one is a "thought of serenity and independence" is to claim the "freedom" imagined in *Huckleberry Finn*, in Melville, above all in James, who is obsessed with the term. But to praise "patience" with such stoical iteration and even with a kind of pathetic call for reassurance—"Patience, then, is for us, is it not? Patience and still patience."—is to recognize that there are in this life no very permanent lodgings in "the deep blue sky," at Gardencourt, or on the raft. Emerson's tough-minded romanticism is the more impressive, however, because like Henry James's it insists, as William James was also to do, not on worldly, practical alternatives to a belief, but on the ultimate practical benefits of the belief itself, even when it defies the evidence of immediate experience. "This pretty web we weave will at last," Emerson persists in hoping, "be overshot and reticulated with veins of the blue." Such a hope, and not merely the "freedom" promised by death, makes "patience" into a form of action. The illusion that society might someday, somehow be transformed by the vision and sacrifice of an Isabel Archer or the needs of a Huck Finn is necessarily among the things that their creators try to make us believe even when they themselves are skeptical. It is part of the suspense, part of the beguilement, part even of the entertainment of fiction. The humor of Huck's narrative voice, the youthful glamour of Isabel's pronouncements, the very ingenuousness of which makes us feel an amused tenderness for her—these result from styles meant to sustain us past the glowerings of our own knowledge about probable failure. Thereby, we can share in the nostalgic regret, when the failures do occur, as if for a genuine promise actually lost. There is no better description of how we should read novels of this kind than that provided by Emerson, still implicitly concerned with "doubleness," though here it is felt in the act of reading itself: "An imaginative book," he remarks in "The Poet," "renders us more service at first, by stimulating us through its tropes, than afterwards when we arrive at the precise sense of the author." The problem for a novelist like James or Mark Twain is that the tropes that stimulate us cannot represent merely "abodes in the deep blue sky." They must at some point also represent society, the enemy of "freedom," and they must acknowledge the fact that in novels a character is defined in relation to that society, even if he decides that he is really a "thought of serenity and independence." Emerson's "I" could not exist in a novel at all—he simply would not be interested in social dialogue for a sufficient length of time. As a result, even novels full of Emersonian inclinations, like *The Portrait of a Lady* or *Huckleberry Finn*, must render society in a way that endows it, however meretriciously, with the promise of "freedom," "infinitude," and "serenity," and the reader is made to feel this promise to an extent that makes him at least recognize why the hero might be deceived. Meanwhile there is a simultaneous effort, a very obvious one in *Huckleberry Finn*, to include the author and reader in a delayed action, so to speak, at once of knowledge and silence, against the innocence of the hero, and above all against the fact that he only partly recognizes society for what it is: "a conspiracy," as Emerson would have it, "against the manhood of every one of its members . . . a joint-stock company." In *Huckleberry Finn* it is a stock company of another sort, a kind of theatrical troupe; and in James it is often a conspiracy of self-interest that has all the charm of sophisticated manners.

But in their attitudes toward social artifice and manners, Mark Twain and Henry James moved, though still within a short distance, in opposite directions. One reason for James's later capacity to make a positive adjustment to social manners and deviousness is that he felt free to construct a society to meet his own requirements. By contrast, Mark Twain was emotionally committed to a particular form of society in which he had spent his youth, so that imaginary alternatives for him could never be more than gratuitous fantasy. When he does head in the direction of fantasy after *Huckleberry Finn*, with *Pudd'nhead Wilson* and *The Mysterious Stranger*, it is toward a saturnalia of repudiation. The element in *Huckleberry Finn* that makes it therefore more complicated than anything in James before *The Bostonians* is Mark Twain's affection for a character whose longings are a curious and inseparable blend of Isabel Archer's dream of "freedom" with some of Mark Twain's own nostalgic desire for community. The relatively simple dichotomy in the early James between the imagination of freedom and the facts of social life that ultimately kill it, is in *Huckleberry Finn* a struggle within a character who is not even conscious of the issues as Isabel Archer, say, would abstractly define them.

The struggle, as it must be called, is the more interesting because Mark Twain gives evidence that for him, though not for Huck, it has at least consciously already been resolved. It is made apparent, even in the first chapter of *Huckleberry Finn*, that society in any institutionalized form is merely the projection of the fantasies, generally derived from literature, both of children and adults. As a result, there is a "double consciousness" operating in the very modes of presentation: Huck's socially anxious voice never carries fully the implications of social contempt and rejection that govern the metaphorical pattern of the book. When Huck does move, after the offense and apology to Jim in Chapters XV and XVI, toward recognitions equivalent to his creator's, the dramatic organization of the novel, which depends on the social audibility of Huck's voice, first totters and then collapses. When, by contrast, the heroine of *Emma* moves toward social awarenesses equivalent to Jane Austen's, she begins to speak more directly and naturally, most like the plain-speaking and forthright Knightley, and is prepared for the "perfect happiness of the union" which is announced at the end of the novel.

In part, the objections to Jane Austen by Mark Twain and American writers of roughly similar prejudice can be explained as a blindness to society as she imagines it. Their prejudice gets between even these illustrious readers and what in fact the work of Jane Austen does express about society and artifice. They are apparently unable to see, so alien to them is her positive vision of social experience, that she is fully aware of the dangers *in* society which for them are the dangers *of* it. The capacity to imagine society as including the threat of conformity and artificiality and as offering, nevertheless, beneficial opportunities for self-discovery is never evident in Emerson, only sporadically in James, and in Twain mostly in the works before *Huckleberry Finn* and inferior to it.

The contrast to Jane Austen, so obvious in a general way, can be meaningfully particularized. In *Emma*, for example, Mrs. Elton imagines a party at Knightley's which will be held out of doors so that everything may be as "natural and simple as possible." ("I shall wear a large bonnet, and bring one of my little baskets hanging on my arm . . . a sort of gipsy party.") Knightley's reply, typically direct and restrained, affirms how much for Jane Austen, as for him, words like "simple" and "natural" can be defined very adequately by an uncomplicated observation of unfussy social habits:

> Not quite. My idea of the simple and the natural will be to have the table spread in the dining-room. The nature and simplicity of gentlemen and ladies, with their servants and furniture, I think is best observed by meals within doors. When you are tired of eating strawberries in the garden, there shall be cold meat in the house.

The dramatic issue of the novel is in a sense whether or not Emma, as she herself fears just before the episode at Box Hill, is to be considered "of Mrs. Elton's party." This, like every phrase in the episode, has an unmistakable resonance. To be "of Mrs. Elton's party" is a metaphor for submitting to social forms in which Mrs. Elton's false, affected, and pretentious ideas of the "natural" predominate, much as similar ideas fully control the society of *Huckleberry Finn*. Indeed, to be thought "natural" by society in Twain's novel means that you must have acted artificially or imitated a prescribed role. The stakes for Jane Austen and her heroine are very high indeed—to prevent society from *becoming* what it is condemned for *being* in *Huckleberry Finn*.

Mark Twain cannot imagine a society in which his hero has any choice, if he is to remain in society at all, but to be "of Tom Sawyer's party." The evidence for such a comparative limitation on the hero—and, indeed, a justification for making a comparison to the greater freedom allowed Emma—is in the similarity between the situations of the two characters at the central crisis in each book. Beside the famous picnic scene at Box Hill in *Emma*, when the heroine insults Miss Bates, we can place the corresponding scene in *Huckleberry Finn* when, in Chapter XV, Huck also insults a social inferior who is at the same time a trusting friend. The process by which each of these insults comes about is roughly the same. Emma gradually surrenders what is called her "self-command" at Box Hill to the theatrical urgings and flatteries of Frank Churchill, much as Huck often acts in imitation of the "style" of Tom Sawyer even when it ill befits his own feelings and necessities. Emma literally forgets who she is and therefore the identity of Miss Bates in relation to her, and her witty retort to one of the older lady's simplicities expresses not her true relationship to Miss Bates so much as the theatrical and self-aggrandizing role which Churchill has encouraged her to play to the whole group. Her social and psychological situation—and the literary problem thus created—is much like Huck's at the similar moment when imitation of Tom's role has led to his violation of the bond between him and Jim. The central character in each novel has violated a social contract by being artificial. Both recognize what has happened and both make amends. But at this point there appears an important and essential difference between the situations of these two, and the difference is indicative of the problem in American nineteenth century fiction of imagining personal relationships within the context of social manners. Huck's recognition cannot involve a choice, as can Emma's, against some forms of social expression in favor of others: against the Frank Churchills, Mrs. Eltons (and Tom Sawyers) of this world, and for the Mr. Knightleys. Mark Twain simply cannot provide Huck with an alternative to "games" that has any social viability or acceptance within the society of the novel. Huck's promise to do Jim "no more mean tricks" is, in effect, a rejection of the only modes of expression understood by that society. At a similar point Emma recognizes and rejects social artifice and is then in a position to accept her natural place in society as Knightley's wife.

Huck chooses at the end "to light out for the Territory ahead of the rest," while Emma, joined to Knightley in "the perfect happiness of the union," is both more firmly within the social group and yet saved from all the false kinds of undiscriminating "amiability" practiced at Box Hill. The ceremony is witnessed, significantly, not by the whole community but by a "small band of true friends." "Marriageableness," as Emerson scornfully puts it, emphatically is Jane Austen's subject. Marriage represents for her what he cannot imagine—not merely the act of choice within society but, more importantly, the union of social with natural inclinations. Naturalness and social form are fused in her work in a way that I do not think Emerson, Mark Twain of *Huckleberry Finn*, or even Henry James were able to recognize. It is no wonder that Mark Twain's difficulties begin at a comparable point where Jane Austen most brilliantly succeeds. *Huckleberry Finn* cannot dramatize the meanings accumulated at the moment of social crisis because the crisis itself reveals the inadequacy of the terms by which understandings can be expressed between the hero and the other members of his society. There is no publicly accredited vocabulary which allows Huck to reveal his inner self to others.

The comparison between Huck and Emma offers at least a tentative answer to a question of some significance, not merely for *Huckleberry Finn*, but for other American novels of the century in which there is a limited view of the inclusiveness of society and of the language by which it holds itself together. The question again is why, precisely at Box Hill, is Jane Austen able to see her way clear to a dramatic resolution of the meaning of her novel, while Mark Twain is stalled at a similar point to a degree that makes him observe, in a letter to Howells, that he liked his novel "only tolerably well, as far as I have got, & may possibly pigeonhole or burn the MS when it is done"? The threat, only partly in jest, was made in August 1876. In barely a month almost a third of the novel had been written. It was not to be finished for seven years. It had reached a point where Huck, having tricked and then apologized to Jim, decides that he can no

longer exploit his Negro friend with tricks but will instead try to
save him by tricking society. By his decision not to use the "style"
of Tom on a runaway slave (Chapter XV), Huck gives up conformist for revolutionary trickery. In Chapter XVI, at the point where
the novel came to a halt in 1876, Huck, halfway between the raft
and the shore, intends to betray his companion. Instead he saves him
from capture by inventing an elaborate lie, persuading the two men
in the skiff that the raft is occupied by the boy's contagiously sick
father. Chapter XV and XVI constitute what I shall be calling the
"reversal scenes": they bring about the dramatic crisis by which Huck
decisively reverses, for a time, the Tom Sawyerish trend in his relationship to Jim; and they also reverse his efforts to belong imaginatively to society, as most attractively represented by that "respectable"
boy Tom Sawyer. My explanation of Mark Twain's difficulty at this
point and of why, after it, his greatest novel goes to pieces will not
suggest, I trust, that *Huckleberry Finn* is inferior to *Emma*, whatever that would mean. Scene by scene, line by line, *Huckleberry Finn*
stimulates us to expectations and images of a vividness and life never
found in Jane Austen, and in saying that *Huckleberry Finn* fails in
the aggregate I am remembering Emerson's remark that often in the
arts "our best praise is given to what they aimed and promised, not
to the actual result."

For one thing, I cannot imagine how *Huckleberry Finn* could have
succeeded in resolving the issues that it creates. It makes nothing
less than an absolute disavowal, after Huck lies to protect Jim, of
any significant dramatic relationship between the hero and all the
other characters, whose habitual forms of expression define what I
mean by "society" in this novel. The failure is predictable and inescapable in view of the accomplishment, never adequately described
by commentaries on the novel, of the first sixteen chapters. These
chapters reveal an experimental mastery beyond anything that the
author's earlier work would allow us to expect. As Henry Nash Smith
points out,[2] not even Henry James had ever dared, by 1885, when
Huckleberry Finn was published as a book, to entrust the point of
view so fully to a character of such evident individuality. For reasons
that will become apparent, however, I cannot agree that Huck's point
of view is maintained with any success throughout the book. Even
in the beginning, the author uses his narrator to create, all unknown

[2] Page references to *Huckleberry Finn*, when they seem useful, will be to the
Riverside Edition (1958), Mr. Smith's introduction to which is surely the best
single essay on this novel that has so far appeared.

to Huck and through what are made to seem the most natural habits of Huck's mind—its tendency to verbal repetition—a metaphorical definition of society as no more than a fabrication of art and artifice. Thus, even while we are hearing in Huck's voice a desire for accommodation to this society, as exemplified in Tom, we are seeing in these repeated metaphors Mark Twain's own repudiation of it.

Like some of Hawthorne's better stories, *Huckleberry Finn* takes literary advantage of what Emerson, and Cooper before him, had lamented: that not only American writing but also American social life was following conventional models, especially literary ones, that too meanly limited our imagination of human potentialities. A kindred awareness in English fiction enters critically into the shaping of novelistic form only with George Eliot and later in Lawrence and Joyce. But the note is most emphatically struck in the nineteenth century in American rather than in English fiction. The element in Cooper, Hawthorne, Melville, Mark Twain, and Henry James that anticipates *Ulysses* and *Women in Love* is the recognition that society believes in a "reality" that is in fact merely its own imitations of images provided by art, especially by fiction and drama, the most social forms of literature. To accept what society calls "real" or "natural" thus became for American novelists such as these the equivalent of accepting as reality the very models and conventions of art from which they often claim to be liberating us and themselves. The problem provides the actual substance and meaning of Hawthorne's "The Maypole of Merrymount," where allegory and pastoral, in the forms of revelers and Puritans, are said to "contend for empire" and for control, by the way, of the destiny of the young lovers. Society in *Huckleberry Finn* is similarly a tissue of "bookish" assumptions and artificial forms that its members take for reality itself. Twain's initial rendering of this condition is what sets a sharp limit on any subsequent development of dramatic relationship between society and his more "natural" hero.

The profoundly creative use of language in the opening chapters allows Mark Twain, like Jane Austen, to blend immediacy and significance, pictorial entertainment and metaphoric implication in a way that imperceptibly ties the destiny of the narrator to the destiny of the culture defined by Mark Twain's images. In a style that has the easy movement of a boy's story and a compactness usually found only in poetry of considerable density, these early pages reveal a society shaped entirely by fantasy and illusion and that depends for sanction primarily on literary authority. Unlike Emma, who is offered many ways of speaking and may choose even from among competitive definitions of words, Huck's language is rigidly controlled by people who are essentially alien to him. To both adults and companions he sounds like a "numb-skull" because he takes them at their word, and finds, as the phrase goes, that he is thereby taken in. By assuming that their statements have at least some literal meaning, he unintentionally discovers the actual self-interest or self-delusion behind their language. These are rather grim suggestions, when in fact the experience of reading the opening chapters is not grim at all, and answers the objection, best phrased by Poe, that if allegory "ever established a fact, it is by dint of overturning a fiction." Poe's attack on Hawthorne includes a description of an alternative to allegorical simplicities that might be applied to the metaphoric structure I am about to examine:

> Where the suggested meaning runs through the obvious one in a *very* profound undercurrent, so as never to interfere with the upper one without our volition, so as never to show itself unless *called* to the surface, there only, for the proper uses of fictitious narrative, is it available at all.

The undercurrent has been indeed so "very profound" that it has never been clearly noticed beneath the surface of the first three chapters, which even some recent commentators have described as belonging to the tradition of *Tom Sawyer*. Such a reaction should not be impatiently dismissed, however. The narrative voice at the beginning does in fact lull our attention to implications lurking in it. The implications are Mark Twain's handiwork and are contemptuous of the tradition even while the voice is not nearly so anxious to be separated from it. As early as the second paragraph there is a metaphoric equation which effectively condemns society as embodied in Tom Sawyer; yet the condemnation is so evidently the unintentional revelation of Huck's mind that we almost prefer to ignore it as a sort of accident. The blatancy of the metaphoric comparison, if isolated from the voice that renders it, may make us want instinctively to discount it:

> The Widow Douglas she took me for her son, and allowed she would sivilize me; but it was rough living in the house all the time, considering how dismal regular and decent the widow was in all her ways; and so when I couldn't stand it no longer, I lit out. I got into my old rags, and my sugar-hogshead again, and was free and satisfied. But Tom Sawyer, he hunted me up and said he was going

to start a band of robbers, and I might join if I would go back to the widow and be respectable. So I went back.

(P. 3)

Tom Sawyer's games are intimately related, it is implied, to the "respectable" aspects of adult society. The alternative to both is "freedom," and Huck is caught between his impulse toward it and his need for company: "so I went back." The indication that, from Mark Twain's point of view, Tom Sawyer and Widow Douglas are in tacit alliance becomes an indictment of both of them in the further suggestion that to be "respectable" in her terms is the necessary condition for membership in the boy's gang. By implication, "respectable" society as represented by the Widow is equivalent to a "band of robbers." The parallel is further advanced, and with relevance to social artificiality of a specifically literary sort, by the account which immediately follows this passage of Huck's training with the Widow. Evocations of "her book," her biblical authority for believing things that are not true for Huck, anticipate the even more frequent references in the next and later chapters to Tom's "books," the romances which are also "authorities" for illusion. Before this equation is developed, however, Huck turns for the first time in the novel away from society, not by "lighting out" but by entering into a soliloquy which is in part a communion with nature and spirits. He turns, like Emerson at the opening of *Nature*, not only away from people but also away from "books," from the "study" which Emerson, in the first paragraph of his essay, rejects for the "stars":

Miss Watson she kept pecking at me, and it got tiresome and lonesome. By-and-by they fetched the niggers in and had prayers, and then everybody was off to bed. I went up to my room with a piece of candle and put it on the table. Then I set down in a chair by the window and tried to think of something cheerful, but it warn't no use. I felt so lonesome I most wished I was dead. The stars were shining, and the leaves rustled in the woods ever so mournful; and I heard an owl, away off, who-whooing about somebody that was dead, and a whippowill and a dog crying about somebody that was going to die; and the wind was trying to whisper something to me and I couldn't make out what it was, and so it made the cold shivers run over me. Then away out in the woods I heard that kind of a sound that a ghost makes when it wants to tell about something that's on its mind and can't make itself understood, and so can't rest easy in its grave and has to go about that way everynight grieving. I got so downhearted and scared I did wish I had some company.

(P. 5)

Because Huck is heard throughout as narrator of the story, it is easy to forget that with everyone, except the reader, he is a very quiet boy. He is seldom heard in conversation with anyone, and he is always inconspicuous in company, even in the "gang." His loneliness, we might say, is a want of conversation, of what, in terms of the literary problem raised by the book, can be called dramatic relationships. He listens for sounds from nature and interprets them more confidently than language, which tends to confuse or disturb him. "But I never said so," is one of his characteristic comments. The form of the book itself, an autobiography that is also a kind of interior monologue, testifies to the internalization of his feelings and reactions.

And yet, it is necessary to stress that any Emersonian detachment from society for the companionship of the "stars" would never satisfy Huck for long. His soliloquies are punctuated with the words "lonesome" and "lonely," ending in the present instance with the direct admission that "I did wish I had some company." Company is announced from below the window in the animal noises of Tom Sawyer, and the first chapter ends with tones of deep companionable satisfaction: "Then I slipped down to the ground and crawled among the trees, and, sure enough, there was Tom Sawyer waiting for me." The dramatic organization of the chapter would suggest, with some pleasure and excitement, that, by joining Tom, Huck has escaped social entrapment and achieved a degree of freedom that still involves human company. But we soon see, in Chapter II, with Tom's incessant talk about rules, gangs, and especially books and authority, a confirmation of the early hint of an essential solidarity between Tom's world and the Widow's, despite her amused assurance that Tom will not qualify for her heaven. Tom's world is dominated by games and fantasies imitated from literature, just as hers is based on illusions derived from religion and the Bible. His tricks, the first of which is an exploitation of Jim in Chapter II, are justified by the "authorities" of boys' games and, by extension, of religion and social respectability, which sanction Miss Watson's exploitation of Jim at still another level. Tom's question in Chapter II when they are discussing the conduct of a game—"Do you want to go to doing different from what's in the books, and get things all muddled up?"—implies even at this point that an argument with the "authority" of boys' games is a disruption of accredited social procedures.

The alternatives promised in Chapter II by Tom's gang and its games to the "civilized" confinements of Chapter I turn out, then, to be no essential alternatives at all. Offering confirmation of such a reading, Chapter III puts into direct juxtaposition the activities of religious, conservative, respectable society, as embodied in Widow Douglas and Miss Watson, and the activities of children, based on the authorities of romantic literature as interpreted by Tom Sawyer. We have before us the creation in words of a whole society built on games, tricks, and illusions, and the adult version is only superficially different from the children's. You play the game without asking literal-minded questions, play it as if it was "for real," or you are a "numb-skull." The purpose of showing metaphorically how the adult and childish worlds are equated in this demand is to indicate how relatively isolated is the sensibility of Huck. It prepares us, as well, to see that his treatment of Jim during the reversal scenes is a matter of playing one of Tom's tricks, and then to recognize that his apology for it violates the rules of the game both on the adults' and on children's levels. Implicit here, in the most placidly comic part of the book, is what Huck will most painfully discover later: that to give up "tricking" Jim means more than giving up Tom's games. It means, so closely are they imaginatively connected with adult forms of exploitation, that he must also believe himself damned to social ostracism and to Hell.

These significances are not declared nor are they derived merely from images. They are instead the result very often of the similarity of phrasing applied first to the Widow and Miss Watson and then to Tom. The unobtrusiveness by which a parallel is thus established results from the use of phrases having the sound merely of idiomatic repetitiousness, not uncommon in vernacular literature. For example, in the first half of Chapter III, in which Huck is advised by Miss Watson on the advantages of prayer and the Bible, there is a sequence of phrases applied to religion and its promises ("it warn't so," "spiritual gifts," "I couldn't see no advantage to it") that in slightly varied form are applied in the second half to Tom's games and the romantic books which authorize them ("but only just pretended," "done by enchantment," "I couldn't see no profit in it"). In the first half, Huck's literalness, inseparable from a concern for human profit and loss, makes Miss Watson call him a "fool," just as in the second it leads Tom Sawyer to call him a "numb-skull." The list can be extended by anyone who turns to Chapter III, and the implications are in fact summarized in the final sentence of the chapter by Huck himself: "So then I judged that all that stuff was only just one of Tom Sawyer's lies. I reckoned he believed in the A-rabs and the elephants, but as for me I think different. It had all the marks of a Sunday-school." These final remarks make the metaphoric intention of the opening chapters unmistakable. Each side of the comparison is modified by the other. Boys' games as Tom plays them are finally, so the comparisons seem to indicate, as genteel and proper as Miss Watson's religion (he always leaves payment for anything he "steals"), and the social respectability and religion which she represents are, like Tom's games, remote from the requirements of natural, literal, daily experience, from a concern for elementary human feelings that are revealed in Huck's "numb-skull" skepticism both about games and religion.

It is time to remind ourselves again, however, that as we read we are listening to a voice, not drawing metaphoric diagrams. The voice makes the reading of the metaphors and any effort to determine their weight within the total experience of these chapters extremely difficult. Even at this early point we are uncomfortably aware of a gap between Mark Twain's position, his contemptuous remoteness from society as expressed through these metaphors, and the more dramatic, socially engaged position of the hero. The gap will ultimately mean that the novel becomes simpler later on than it is here. After the reversal scenes, the drama is not allowed to offer any extenuation of the meanings imposed by what becomes a largely impersonal system of metaphors having to do with games and disguises. The sound of Huck's socially involved voice first wavers, then nearly disappears, then returns as a sickly version of what we find in these opening scenes. Here, though, it is heard distinctly enough to make the metaphors amusing and affectionate, however damaging they become if one isolates their implications.

The great difficulty for the reader in the opening chapters is that we feel no confidence in balancing the implications of the style, its tendency to repudiate what is at the same time being affectionately rendered. It is no wonder that there are many differences of opinion about the structure of the book and about whether or not it expresses an ultimate surrender to the so-called genteel tradition or a final repudiation of it, and of Hannibal, the Happy Valley of Twain's youth. Those critics who respond weakly, or not at all, to the metaphoric implications of the early chapters ignore as a consequence the extent to which Mark Twain has begun even here to isolate and dismiss the society he is also creating. They do not grant, therefore, that the condemnations are potentially so severe, even from the first page, that the continued accommodations of the hero to that society will become progressively more difficult to allow. This literary difficulty is what plagued the author in the summer of 1876, not any discovered contempt of his own, presumably released only by his trip to the Mississippi in 1882, for the scenes of his youth. His criticisms are already expressed emphatically enough in 1876, as we have just seen. On the other hand, those who do stress the evidences of repudiation in the early chapters are apt to miss the complications brought about by the freedom Mark Twain allows to the more loving and socially agreeable expressions of his hero. The latter reading is best represented by Mr. Leo Marx, whose criticisms of Mr. Eliot and Mr. Trilling for approving of the later portions of the novel seem to me decisive and justifiably admired. But I think that his own reading offers no acceptable alternative: it confuses Huck Finn with Mark Twain in the opening chapters, not letting us see how much Huck's voice modifies the social criticism, and it then confuses Mark Twain with Huck in the concluding chapters, missing, it seems to me, the degree to which we can only respond to Huck within what has become by then the author's rigidly bitter and impersonal metaphoric design.

To understand what happens to this novel is to understand what happens to Huck at the hands of his creator. The problem for the author after the crucial scenes in Chapters XV and XVI is that his book can no longer be the autobiography of Huck Finn, and must instead become a kind of documentation of why the hero cannot express in dramatic relations with any element of this society the positive values which are Mark Twain's alternative to society. Mr. Kenneth Lynn's version of the problem[3] after Chapter XVI, of which I have given some paraphrase in the preceding paragraph—that Mark Twain at this point actually discovers that he must proceed to damn the Happy Valley and was loath to do so—ignores the inferences that can be drawn from preceding chapters, but it can be modified in a way that takes us close to the primary difficulty as the author himself must have felt it. Mark Twain has written himself into a position where he can no longer sustain a double relationship to the society of his novel —of the remote contemptuous critic, on the one hand, and, on the other, of the man with illusions that some closer relationship, such as Huck himself seems to want with Tom, can be maintained. Were we to read the last sentences of Chapter III as Mr. Marx suggests— "with this statement which ends the third chapter, Huck parts company with Tom"—there would of course be no such problem as I

[3] *Mark Twain and the Southwest Tradition*, Chap. 9.

describe. Without Huck's continued longing for some kind of tie with Tom, "respectable" society at its most palatable, the novel would be a relatively unmodified criticism of society carried out by Huck himself, until the author, so Mr. Marx's argument runs, forces a surrender to society at the conclusion. As a matter of fact, Huck is cultivating an imaginative association with Tom all the way from Chapter III to Chapter XV. He consistently imitates him, and to that extent is, like the rest of this society, imitating "books" and "authorities." He repeatedly cites Tom as his own authority for tricks and adventures that are conspicuously at odds with both his feelings and self-interest. The attractions of society for Huck, his persistent wish that "I had some company," is never wholly satisfied by the companionship of Jim, which explains why, when they are separated, Huck can so easily put him out of mind. Tom is evoked, however, no matter how lengthy the separation. When he frees himself from Pap with elaborate trickery in Chapter VII, Huck "did wish Tom Sawyer was there; I knowed he would take an interest in this kind of business, and throw in the fancy touches. Nobody could spread himself like Tom Sawyer in such a thing as that." In Chapter XII, his escapade on the *Walter Scott* is justified to Jim by asking "Do you reckon Tom Sawyer would ever go by this thing?" and it could be inferred at this point that Jim, as a companion on adventures, is implicitly dismissed by the added remark that "I wish Tom Sawyer *was* here." The evocation of Walter Scott as a ruined steamboat, in the context of the metaphors already discussed, is itself an image of a romantic, conservative, and religious society in a state of wreckage. What we infer from the novel alone is confirmed and extended by Twain's excessive charge (quoted in *Mark Twain in Eruption*) that Scott was in "great measure responsible for the Civil War." It was he who made the South fall in love with "the jejune romanticism of an absurd past" and who created "a reverence for rank and cast, and pride and pleasure in them." Though expressed in 1882 after his visit to the New South, the attitudes are apparent enough in the early parts of *Huckleberry Finn*, and the term used to characterize Scott's romanticism, "jejune," has a popular meaning that was dramatized in 1876 in the adventures of boys acting out the romantic predilections of adults. Huck's imitations of Tom indicate the degree to which he must become an artificial man, an imitator of literary models, if he is to be a part of society at all or be accepted by it, like Tom, as a "real" boy.

As the novel moves to the crisis of insult and apology in Chapter

XV, "imitation" is shown, much in the manner of Box Hill, to result in the loss of "self-command" and an enslavement to alien forms of expression that distort genuine feelings. Chapter XIV, "Was Solomon Wise?" is a preparatory and comic version of Chapter XV, "Fooling Poor Old Jim." In the first, the imitative tendencies of Huck are developed to a point where, with brilliant comic significance, he has stylistically become Tom Sawyer, while transferring his own identity as a "numb-skull" to Jim ("I said these things are adventures; but he said he didn't want no more adventures"), and he tries to win the argument by citing the Widow ("the Widow told me all about it"). He thus adopts for his "authorities" the two figures who together represent aspects of the artifice which, in this novel, are equivalent to society. Huck, trying to be Tom, bases his arguments on a faith in symbolic actions, regardless of the practical consequences, while Jim, like Huck himself in earlier arguments with the real Tom, insists on them: "En what use is half a chile? I wouldn' give a dern for a million of um." To which Huck replies, much as Tom does to him, "Hang it, Jim, you've clean missed the point."

Huck's imitation and assumption of Tom's role at this point prepares us for the crucial scene about to take place. In the next chapter, after the separation in the fog, Huck continues the tricks begun by Tom in Chapter II. He tries to convince Jim that he has merely been dreaming, that what he believed were naturally stimulated feelings of loss and love were the result rather of fantasy. When Jim realizes that he is being tricked, he responds with a speech that evokes all the affectionate trust that has been evident as the unspoken reality of their relationship. It is only at this point, not at any earlier one, that Huck does separate himself from Tom:

> It was fifteen minutes before I could work myself up to go and humble myself to a nigger—but I done it, and I warn't ever sorry for it afterwards, neither. I didn't do him no more mean tricks, and I wouldn't done that one if I'd 'a knowed it would make him feel that way.

The nature of his regret here makes his later adoption of Tom's name, and his acceptance of Tom's leadership in the mock freeing of Jim, a sacrifice, as Mr. Smith points out, of the emotional growth registered in this passage. It seems to me necessary to go still further, and say that these later developments represent a nearly total collapse of Mark Twain's characterization of the hero. That the circumstances of Huck's characterization make it impossible that he ever could sustain the identity that he momentarily achieves in the reversal scenes is apparently recognized by the author in the chapter immediately following. The very title of it, "The Rattlesnake-skin Does its Work," again suggest how Huck's tricks on Jim always do have painfully real consequences. In this chapter we find Huck trapped in verbal conventions that will not allow the release of his feelings in words. The terminology he has been taught to use and that binds him in a relationship to Tom Sawyer and the others, cannot let him express the nature of his relationship to Jim. He feels the "pinch of conscience," which is to say the "pinch" of training, of system, of education. "It is merely a *thing*," according to an entry in Mark Twain's notebooks, "the creature of *training*; it is whatever one's mother and Bible and comrades and laws and systems of government and habitat and heredities have made it." In the novel itself, conscience is the product of the "games" of comrades and the "authorities" of books, including the Bible. The meanings which these impart to Huck's language are inadequate to his feelings. Having been defined most significantly for the reader in his relationship to a runaway slave, Huck is still enslaved himself to the language of Tom's world, still inescapably attached to it: "Here was this nigger, which I had as good as helped to run away, coming right out flat-footed and saying he would steal his children—children that belonged to a man I didn't even know; a man that hadn't ever done me no harm" (p. 75).

Huck's problem is the novel's problem. This last quotation, and Huck's use nearby of "right" for what Mark Twain has made us see is "wrong," of "wrong" for "right," involves a recognition by the author, as anguished as any that it anticipates in Joyce, of what happens when the hero of a novel must define his alienations from society in terms that take their meanings for *him*, as much as for anyone, from the very "authorities" he has come to reject. Joyce's theme by choice is Mark Twain's dilemma. By 1914, Joyce would be so aware of the problem as a literary and linguistic one that he would make his hero veritably an artist of words. Stephen Dedalus is a kind of Thomistic Huck Finn. He tries vainly to dissociate himself from the sources that give validation to his language—home, church, country—and he declares his freedom to "change the laws of nature" in words that reveal, by their associative connections with earlier experiences, his inescapable obligations to the past. *Huckleberry Finn* is an earlier instance of what happens to a novel when society, as the author conceives it, provides no opportunity for transforming individual sensibility into social drama. The provision is lacking because Mark Twain cannot imagine a society that offers alternatives to artificiality or that has in it, like Joyce's Dublin, evidences of an official culture that has historical dignity and value. We can understand why he was apparently unable to recognize in the novels of Jane Austen the existence of a society of alternatives. The existence of such a society in her work explains the necessary difference between *Emma* and *Huckleberry Finn* that is revealed at the point in each where the social order is disrupted by an insult. In *Emma*, the crisis results in a restoration to social intercourse of a naturalness temporarily lost through artifice; in *Huckleberry Finn* it can lead only to the hero's painful and confused recognition of what his creator has been showing all along—that what is natural for society is in fact nothing but artifice, tricks, games, and disguise. When Huck enters society again in Chapter XVII by going ashore, it is in disguise as George Jackson and among a group, the Grangerfords, who are given to extravagant forms of genteel and sentimental literary expression and to the romantic waste of a family feud. To enter society at all as it exists on the shore, to deal with it without disastrous exposure of the sort of person we know him to be, means that throughout the rest of the book Huck must move about in various disguises, tell lies, play roles even more than he has before. And he will at last become "Tom Sawyer" all over again in Chapter XXXII. Still more important, the Huck Finn shown to us at what is obviously the dramatic crisis of the book is disguised thereafter even from the reader. The style of the book after that carries his voice only sporadically and with significant moral complication only once more—for a moment in Chapter XXXI. The implications are historically important: this novel discovers that the sensibility it values most cannot reveal itself through social drama, and it is upon social drama that the existence of this or any novel depends.

There is evidence that Mark Twain himself came to this realization, that he saw his problem in the literary terms in which I am describing it, and that he recognized that his literary dilemma was a historical one. The evidence, along with his prolonged difficulties in finishing the novel, derives from what the book expresses after the reversal scenes, even though it never again substantially expresses the person whose voice there fully answers for almost the last time to the name of "Huck Finn." Thereafter, the chapters can be taken as images of justification for Mark Twain's failure to resolve the meanings accumulated at that point. Through a series of burlesque incidents, in some of which Huck plays no part at all—the Grangerfords (XVII–XVIII), the introduction of the King and the Duke (XIX–XX), the Arkansas episodes (XXI–XXIII), the Wilks sequence (XXIV–XXIX), and, finally, the staged version of the "freeing" of Jim (XXXIV–XLII)—through these only tenuously linked incidents Mark Twain pictorializes the literary and social conditions which confront the American novelist writing such a book as this. The general implication is that to be born into the world of Huckleberry Finn is to be born, as Hawthorne earlier remarked of all of us, "into a world of artificial system." "Art has become a second and stronger nature," he complains at the beginning of "New Adam and Eve"; "she is the stepmother, whose crafty tenderness has taught us to despise the bountiful and wholesome ministrations of our true parent." Between Huck and reality there is always a curtain of "style"— a term sacred to Tom Sawyer. The dominant social style, as these episodes reveal it, is imported and literary, not only from Scott, but also from *Don Quixote*, Casanova, Benvenuto Cellini, and Shakespeare, all mixed with domestic melodrama, the poetry of gift books, and, as in scenes at the Grangerfords, those "novels of costume" that Emerson said had "filled the heads of the most imitative classes" in America.

Mark Twain's arrangement of the scenes involving the Grangerfords and the King and the Duke are especially relevant to the allegorical implications of these later chapters. Having escaped the family feud, a violent expression of the sentimental romanticism that belongs to the painting and poetry of the Grangerfords, Huck is almost immediately trapped by fake royalty, whose imitations have debased Shakespeare into sentimental twaddle. But for a moment in between, we are given the beautiful idyll of Jim and Huck, so memorable that, though it runs for barely two pages, it has for some readers become equivalent to the "raft" itself and led to inaccurate schemes that too sharply separate the "raft" from the "shore," elements of which will very soon possess the raft and the life of it:

> Soon as it was night, out we shoved; when we got her out to about the middle, we let her alone, and let her float wherever the current wanted her to; then we lit the pipes, and dangled our legs in the water and talked about all kinds of things—we was always naked, day and night, whenever the mosquitoes would let us—the new clothes

Buck's folks made for me was too good to be comfortable, and besides
I didn't go much on clothes, no how.

(P. 100)

The appearance of the King and the Duke does not, as sometimes
claimed, bring a new element into the book. They are merely an
outrageous example of the artifice and theatricality so persistent from
the beginning. They appear to destroy the natural and spontaneous
life that in this brief interval of time has released its direction not
to current styles but to the current of the river, not to clothes sup-
plied by others but to personal nakedness. We are not allowed simply
to equate the "raft" with "freedom," except as it reminds us of what
was lost when the control of it falls almost at once to the powers of
fakery and theatrical enterprise. Huck and Jim are made literally the
prisoners of these things. They are in the grip of artifice, and their
nakedness will henceforth give way to traveling in costume. The
stylistic organization of the novel, as we have been observing it,
allows us to see the destiny of the "raft" in still larger terms. The
raft is like America itself, as viewed regionally here by Mark Twain
and more generally elsewhere by Cooper, Emerson, and Whitman,
all of whom at various times complained not that America was
"artless" or "bare," to recall Henry James's description, but that it
had surrendered to imitation and a dependence upon foreign models
in social conduct and in literature. It had been transformed almost
immediately from a place of "nakedness" and "freedom" into what
Whitman claimed in 1870 was a "thoroughly upholstered exterior
appearance" in excess even of the Old World.

The "Arkansas Difficulty," in Chapters XXI to XXII, contributes
to the novel's developing indictment by suggesting how even forms
of violence, that are melodramatic in their own right, effectively
touch the feelings of the community only after they have been stylized and made into a form of entertainment. When Sherburn kills
Boggs, the most conspicuous initial reaction is from the "long, lanky
man" who does an imitation for the townspeople of what has only
just occurred. As the novel describes it (p. 122), his rendition is
unmistakably theatrical, a performance for which he is paid by his
fellow citizens who "got out their bottles and treated him." Only
then do they join in the unsuccessful lynching bee, as a kind of after-
thought: "Well, by and by," the last sentence of the chapter casually
begins, "somebody said Sherburn ought to be lynched." The impli-

cation that the society of this novel can only feel things that are expressed in ways belonging not to life but to art is apparent still further in the melodrama of "tears and flapdoodle" during the episodes at the Wilks's in Chapters XXIV to XXIX. Here again, the governing "style" of the community, despite some efforts at good sense, is one of costume drama in which two of the principals are, significantly, pretending to have arrived recently from England. "'Here is my answer,'" says Mary Jane when asked to put her English "relatives" to the test: "She hove up the bag of money and put it in the king's hands, and says, 'Take this six thousand dollars, and invest it for me and my sisters any way you want to, and don't give us no receipt for it.'" We are permitted to think, in summary, that the "fine looking man," the social leader who jumps up at the performance of The Royal Nonesuch and admits that "we are sold," is substantially describing what are in effect the formative processes of society as a whole: the audience should promote the fraudulent theatricals around town, he advises, so that "Then we'll all be in the same boat" (p. 128).

During these episodes, from Chapter XVIII to XXIX, the freeing of Jim is obviously not the subject of the novel. These chapters are indicative of the fact that the book is concerned with Negro slavery only as one aspect of a more general enslavement—of feeling and intelligence within inadequate and restrictively artificial modes of expression. Dramatically, the book is victim of the conditions illustrated in these chapters, during which Huck is allowed only an attenuated relationship to what is going on. His oppositions provide no meaningful dramatic interest. He doesn't like what is happening— that about sums it up. We witness an intensification of social criticism carried out by episodic illustration and a further development of the metaphors of artifice, but there is no corresponding intensification of drama within the social life that involves Huck. He does help Mary Jane and he does not laugh at the circus performer who he thinks is endangered by the horses, again revealing his lovable seriousness about the human consequences of tricks. But such incidents are themselves flatly representative of relatively static attitudes, and catch none of the complications of response that have been developing up to the reversal scenes. Neither does the remark, by this point tiresomely indicative of a trapped mind slowing down, that "I do believe he [Jim] cared just as much for his people as white folks does for their'n. It don't seem natural, but I reckon it's so" (p. 131).

More is lost in that sentence, especially feeble in contrast to Jim's heartbreaking story about his deaf daughter, than the vivid eccentricity of voice that was an earlier indication of Huck's personal, self-critical involvement with life around him. There is a loss even of the vitality of reaction that led to the crucial insult and apology, much less the consequent knowledge of what is "natural" for Negroes. The deterioration is made even more apparent by the degree of explicitness with which Huck is allowed at a few points to condemn the activities he witnesses: "It was enough to make a body ashamed of the human race" (p. 137), is a statement with none of the rewarding complications that have been characteristic of Huck's responses to meanness and his expression of them. Even the vividness of description that results from his spontaneous feelings of relationship to sights and sounds is rarely found in the last half or more of the novel. "If I trod on a stick and broke it, it made me feel like a person had cut one of my breaths in two and I only got half, and the short half, too" (p. 35)—we need only remember such a line as this to recognize how much of Huck has disappeared from the novel when we get to the Arkansas episode, for instance, and hear what purports to be Huck's description of a town:

> On the river front some of the houses was sticking out over the bank, and they was bowed and bent, and about ready to tumble in. The people had moved out of them. The bank was caved away under one corner of some others, and that corner was hanging over. People lived in them yet, but it was dangersome, because sometimes a strip of land as wide as a house caves in at a time. Sometimes a belt of land a quarter of a mile deep will start in and cave along and cave along till it all caves into the river in one summer. Such a town as that has to be always moving back, and back, and back, because the river is always gnawing at it.
>
> (P. 119)

Huck is barely present in the language here, the virtues of which do not include the sound of the identifying narrative voice heard earlier. "People live in them yet," or "such a town as that," belong to the narrator of *Life on the Mississippi*, Mark Twain himself. It is not surprising that having put the manuscript of the novel aside in 1876, near the end of Chapter XVI, he could feel free to borrow a section of that chapter for *Life on the Mississippi* in 1882, the famous "raftsmen passage" that can be found restored to the novel in De Voto's *The Portable Twain*. And it is of course not irrelevant to my argument that the borrowing should have come from precisely the spot where Mark Twain began to feel the difficulty of maintaining Huck as the dramatic center and narrative voice of his novel.

After the reversal scenes, the novel does not again, for any considerable stretch, sound like the "autobiography" of Huckleberry Finn until "You Can't Pray a Lie," Chapter XXXI. There, the language once more expresses some of the musing, characteristically painful effort of Huck to liberate and reveal his complicated feelings. Significantly, there is also a return to some of the lyricism of description which gives evidence of his affectionate vitality of response to people and to scenery: "and I see Jim before me, all the time, in the day, and in the night-time, sometimes moonlight, sometimes storms, and we a-floating along, talking, and singing, and laughing" (p. 179). It seems as if the book is at last reassembling the hero in a style and situation that will reveal again how dangerously unique he is in this society. But it must be said that there is even here a conspicuous repetitiousness, a failure to advance the novel dramatically beyond Chapter XVI. Chapter XXXI is in many ways only a redoing of the earlier crisis, with a "pinch of conscience," a decision to do "wrong" and help Jim to freedom not more or less intense. And immediately thereafter, Huck disappears again into the artifices of society. He assumes the identity of Tom Sawyer in Chapter XXXII, "I Have a New Name." And he does so in a phrase ("I was so glad to find out who I was") that pointedly and it seems to me intentionally reminds us of how the movement of the book in its best and most autobiographical parts was committed to exactly the opposite development: of Huck's freedom from the imitative artificiality of Tom Sawyer. On the subject of "authorities" and "tricks" by which Tom would "free" the already free Jim, the narrative voice hereafter becomes sickly and accommodating, when it is not timidly pouting: "I ain't going to make no complaint. Any way that suits you suits me" (p. 224). Such a blatant, even contemptuous denial of any dramatic development for which the novel has prepared us, such an articulated destruction of the growth of the hero, seems to me an intentional and embittered demonstration to the reader of the only grounds on which Huck and his society can be brought into a dramatic relationship that will allow some degree of completion and resolution to the book. Huck's illusion—that Tom, even as he himself, has now, shockingly, become revolutionary in his use of tricks rather than conformist—does not modify for the reader the inherently distasteful "literary" quality of Tom's procedures. They would reveal a self-indulgent lack of feeling for the effect of tricks on Jim even if they were intended actually to free him.

It is necessary to repeat that this development cannot in any sense represent a surrender by Mark Twain to the genteel tradition. The implicit split in the opening chapters between Huck's narrative and the author's surreptitious metaphorical ordering of it has now become a gap between worlds. From the remoteness of a total repudiation Mark Twain witnesses with as much exasperation as we do the evidence that to remain in the society of the novel at all requires the capitulation that Huck has made to Tom. The author's judgment of Tom at the end is implied in a number of ways that belong to the impersonal metaphoric structure he has created, even while dramatically the novel can only show Huck in his acts of sulking agreement. The metaphoric pattern implies an important degree of similarity between Tom, and the King and the Duke. His tricks, like theirs, are designed to exploit human feeling, while their own is called forth only by artificial stimulation. The King and the Duke can slobber over Shakespeare and their own fabricated melodrama, knowing that their audience will do the same, and Tom can make up epitaphs for Jim ("here a captive heart busted") and be so carried away by his own versions of phrases scrawled on prison walls by such heroes as the Count of Monte Cristo that his "voice trembled, whilst he was reading them, and he most broke down" (p. 217). The three are related even more specifically, however, in their treatment of Jim. In a book so given to parallels, much is implied by the fact that at the end Tom gives Jim forty dollars for playing games with his freedom and that this is precisely the amount paid the King for selling Jim as a runaway. While the parallel is not exact, it is sufficiently indicative of the value to either party of Jim's remaining in bondage, even if in Tom's case the prolonging of his enslavement is in the interest not of economics but of games and adventures.

The style and design of any book trains us as we read to respond in some ways and not others to certain uses of language, to find some kinds of conversation artificial and others natural. It matters very little, therefore, that in some other book the author approves of certain kinds of behavior if in the one we are reading he has managed to make them ambiguously attractive or even reprehensible. *Huckleberry Finn* has so insistently educated us to feelings of exasperation about tricks, games, and theatricality that we cannot have learned our lessons and want still to be entertained by Tom's prolonged antics at the end. The uncertainty that one feels, nevertheless, about the intended effect of the concluding scenes results from the fact that the weight of prejudice urged upon us by what precedes brutally outbalances Tom's innocuous behavior, unless one places it *wholly* within the darker side of the metaphoric pattern. Mark Twain's rejection of society in this book is so contemptuous that it obliterates it as a significant dramatic opponent. The effect is apparent in his lassitude and indifference at the end when he shows Huck Finn in his dramatic relationships to the representative members of this society, young or old. Mark Twain's distaste for Tom and Aunt Polly in their final conversation is directed at their characteristically seeing even one another as embodiments of style and as acting out stereotyped roles. What Aunt Polly really wants in Tom is a literary "good-bad boy," so long as his actions are "bad" only as a "good" boy's should be:

> "Then what on earth did *you* want to set him free for, seeing he was already free?"
> "Well, that is a question, I must say; and *just* like women! Why, I wanted the *adventure* of it; and I'd 'a' waded neck-deep in blood to—goodness alive, *Aunt Polly!*"
> If she warn't standing right there, just inside the door, looking as sweet and contented as an angel half-full of pie, I wish I may never!

The cloying effect of this passage is obvious. And yet the reaction of the reader to it is strangely muffled by Huck's presentation. It is apparent that he does not respond in the way the book has prepared the reader to respond, and that he is here glaringly unlike the character we have loved and respected earlier in the book. What is most significant, however, is that Mark Twain does not seem to think it matters much that Huck be given any place in the scene at all. His unctuous "angel half-full of pie" and the effeminate exclamation "I wish I may never!" merely scan the scene in terms too abundantly provided by it already. He is merely *of* the scene, uncritically absorbed into it.

Huck is given back to us at the very end in his declaration of independence, but it is significant that he is re-created primarily in the image of flight, of "lighting out for the Territory ahead of the rest." He is a character who can exist at all only outside the society that the novel allows us to imagine, who can exist in our imagination, finally, only outside the novel itself. Huckleberry Finn became for Mark Twain a kind of obsession, appearing during the years that follow in various sketches for stories and sequels to the novel. His career in this novel asks a question that Mark Twain must have urgently wanted to answer. If he must destroy Huckleberry Finn in his insistence that society cannot accommodate anything better than Tom Sawyer, then is he not in effect destroying society as a place in which the literary imagination may operate? His dislike of Jane Austen is not only understandable but of historic importance in signaling a desire for some "Territory" where the likes of Huck Finn can live for our imagination and for his. And it is a place where "the rest" have not been. Santayana's familiar comment that American humorists "only half escape the genteel tradition" and that they cannot abandon it because "they have nothing to put in its place" recognizes the degree to which Mark Twain cannot depend, as Jane Austen can, on a society of alternatives. But this much used observation has been too uncritically applied to a novel as radical as this one and to a writer whose genius was surpassed only by his unrelenting toughness. This book does in fact abandon everything it creates or depends on. And nothing is put in their place but a vague sense that —to remember Emerson once more—"Patience, then is for us, is it not? Patience, and still patience." *Huckleberry Finn* seems to me a totally revolutionary book that should not make us surprised at the later, bitterly unmodified and not very patient view of the "mysterious stranger"—that the universe is itself only "the silly creations of an imagination that is not conscious of its freaks."

PAUL J. ALPERS has taught at Harvard and will be teaching next year at the University of California, Berkeley. He has published articles on Pope and Spenser, and is spending this year in England doing research for a book on *The Faerie Queene*.

PAUL BERTRAM is an assistant professor at Rutgers University and is at work on a study of Shakespeare's history plays.

REUBEN A. BROWER is a professor of English at Harvard University, and from 1948–1953 was Class of 1880 Professor of Greek and English at Amherst College. His publications include *The Fields of Light: An Experiment in Critical Reading; Alexander Pope, the Poetry of Allusion*, for which he received the Christian Gauss Award in 1959; *On Translation* (editor), which received the Harvard University Press Faculty Prize, Honorable Mention, in 1959; and the sections on Shaw and Yeats in *Major British Writers*. He received a Guggenheim Fellowship, 1956–1957, and is a fellow for 1961–1962 at the Center for Advanced Study in Behavorial Sciences.

G. ARMOUR CRAIG is a professor of English at Amherst College and has published articles on nineteenth and twentieth century novels. He was chairman of the English Institute in 1957–1958.

PAUL DE MAN is chairman of the Department of Comparative Literature at Cornell University. He has published articles in European and American periodicals.

THOMAS R. EDWARDS, JR. is assistant professor of English at the University of California at Riverside. He is the author of "The Colours of Fancy: An Image Cluster in Pope," in *Modern Language Notes*, 1958; "Light and Nature: A Reading of the Dunciad," in *Philological Quarterly*, 1960; and "Reconcil'd Extremes: Pope's *Epistle to Bathurst*," in *Essays in Criticism*, 1961. He has recently completed a book on Pope and is now working on a study of Blake's relation to eighteenth century poetry.

ANNE DAVIDSON FERRY, a graduate of Vassar College and Columbia University, studied at Girton College, Cambridge, and has taught at Hunter and Wellesley Colleges. She is now a lecturer in English at Harvard. She has completed a book on some seventeenth century lyric poets and a critical study of *Paradise Lost* entitled *Milton's Epic Voice*. She is the author of "The Bird, the Blind Bard, and the Fortunate Fall" in *Reason and Imagination*, Columbia University Press and Routledge & Kegan Paul (1962).

NEIL H. HERTZ is an instructor at Cornell. He is preparing a study of Wordsworth's poetry.

OSWALD JOHNSTON will be an instructor next year at Yale. He is completing a study of Byron's satire.

STEPHEN KITAY ORGEL is assistant professor of English at the University of California, Berkeley, and is working on a book on Ben Jonson and the English masque.

RICHARD POIRIER has taught at Williams College and is now assistant professor of English at Harvard University. He has written on Faulkner (in *William Faulkner: Two Decades of Criticism*), on Frost (an interview for the *Paris Review* series), and on current fiction (as editor of the *O. Henry Prize Stories*, 1961 and currently). He is the author of *The Comic Sense of Henry James* published by Chatto & Windus in England and by Oxford University Press, New York, and he is now working on a study of the relationships between American fiction and English literature, of which "Mark Twain, Jane Austen, and the Imagination of Society" is a part.

WILLIAM H. PRITCHARD is assistant professor of English at Amherst College and is writing a book on Robert Frost. An article on Frost, "Diminished Nature," has appeared in the *Massachusetts Review*.

WILLIAM R. TAYLOR has been teaching history at Harvard and has accepted an associate professorship of history at the University of Wisconsin. He is the author of *Cavalier and Yankee* (Braziller), a study of American national character before the Civil War. He is now preparing a collection of essays called *A Sense of the Past*.

THOMAS B. WHITBREAD is an assistant professor of English at the University of Texas. His poetry has appeared in many periodicals, and he was recently awarded the Aga Khan prize for fiction by the *Paris Review*.

WILLIAM YOUNGREN attended Amherst College and has received a Ph.D. from Harvard. He is now an Instructor in Humanities at Massachusetts Institute of Technology. His main interest is in tracing the relations between English criticism, aesthetic theory, and imaginative literature in the eighteenth and nineteenth centuries.